Reading Disabilities

The Interaction of Reading, Language, and Neuropsychological Deficits

This is a volume in

PERSPECTIVES IN
NEUROLINGUISTICS, NEUROPSYCHOLOGY, AND PSYCHO-
LINGUISTICS

A Series of Monographs and Treatises

A complete list of titles in this series appears at the end of this volume.

Reading Disabilities

The Interaction of Reading, Language, and Neuropsychological Deficits

DONALD G. DOEHRING

School of Human Communication Disorders
McGill University
Montreal, Quebec, Canada

RONALD L. TRITES

Neuropsychology Laboratory
Royal Ottawa Hospital
Ottawa, Ontario, Canada

P. G. PATEL

Department of Linguistics
University of Ottawa
Ottawa, Ontario, Canada

CHRISTINA A. M. FIEDOROWICZ

Department of Psychology
McGill University
Montreal, Quebec, Canada

ACADEMIC PRESS

A Subsidiary of Harcourt Brace Jovanovich, Publishers

New York   London   Toronto   Sydney   San Francisco   1981

116175

ACADEMIC PRESS, INC.
111 Fifth Avenue, New York, New York 10003

United Kingdom Edition published by
ACADEMIC PRESS, INC. (LONDON) LTD.
24/28 Oval Road, London NW1   7DX

Library of Congress Cataloging in Publication Data
Main entry under title:

Reading disabilities.
    (Perspectives in neurolinguistics, neuropsychology,
and psycholinguistics)
    Bibliography: p.
    Includes index.
    1. Reading disability. 2. Children--Language.
I. Doehring, Donald G. II. Series. [DNLM:
1. Dyslexia. WL 340.6 R287]
LB1050.5.R384   372.4   81-10932
ISBN 0-12-219180-3   AACR2

Contents

Recent Concepts of Reading Disabilities

4

The Objective Classification of Reading Disabilities

5

A Research Plan for Extending the Objective Definition of Reading Disability

6

Reading Test Results:
Three Types of Reading Skill Deficits

7

The Interaction of Reading and
Language Deficits

8

The Interaction of Reading and
Neuropsychological Deficits

9

Overall Evaluation of
Interactive Deficits

10

Training Deficient Reading Skills

11

Future Prospects

12   233

Age-Corrected Intercorrelations

Appendix A   243

Preface

During the past 20 years, there has been a great increase of interest in the theoretical and practical aspects of reading and learning to read. A number of texts have surveyed this flourishing activity and offered new insights into the perceptual, cognitive, and linguistic processes that contribute to the component skills of reading; the complex interrelationships of the reader, the text, the purposes of reading, and the sociocultural milieu in which reading takes place; and the perennial questions about why some children fail to acquire normal reading skills. This book is not simply intended to be a survey of current theories and practices related to reading disability or a retrospective attempt to distill our collective wisdom about reading disability into a new theory. We review the relevant literature and do not hesitate to offer theoretical interpretations, but the primary purpose is to describe how we have directly confronted the problem of how to make substantive progress toward understanding reading disability. We feel that this approach should be of interest to students, researchers, teachers, and professional workers in psychology, education, linguistics, and the neurosciences who are concerned with problems of reading acquisition, and also to those with more general interests in reading, language, cognition, and cerebral functioning.

Our main working hypothesis is that reading disability cannot be a unitary disorder, because reading is not a unitary skill. The many studies that have treated reading disability as a unitary disorder with a single cause have not led to an adequate explanation of this disorder. If progress is to be made, studies of reading disability must take account of the complexity of reading. This book includes a detailed consideration of the design, execution, and interpretation of unpublished research that attempts to confront the actual complexities of reading disability. We do not claim to have found the final answer to this problem, but we have arrived at some very important insights about future directions. Much work remains to be done, and a major goal of the book is to inform the reader of the issues that must be considered in further work.

When writing a book that gives actual details of research, it is difficult to avoid technicalities. The main technicality in this book is the method of statistical classification. Its basic rationale is very simple: to group subjects according to similarities in their test profiles. We have done our best to give simple, nontechnical explanations of the statistical classifications and to indicate clearly the connection between the statistical classification and the actual test performance of the individual subjects, in the hope that all readers can draw their own conclusions about our findings.

This work involved a collaborate effort. The first author, Donald G. Doehring, is an experimental psychologist who designed the reading-skill tests and the computer-assisted instructional programs, planned the testing procedures and the data analyses, and wrote the original draft of this manuscript. Ronald L. Trites, the second author, is a neuropsychologist who provided the necessary expertise in clinical neuropsychology in all aspects of the research and writing, and, in particular, designed the neuropsychological test battery, organized the testing facilities, selected the subjects, analyzed the case history information, and made a clinical interpretation of the neuropsychological results. The third author, P. G. Patel, is a linguist who provided expertise in psycholinguistics in all aspects of the research and writing. He formulated the theoretical rationale for the assessment of language skills, as well as selecting and, in some cases, constructing the language tests. The fourth author, Christina A. M. Fiedorowicz, contributed to the selection and testing of subjects, the clinical interpretation of neuropsychological results, and the design of the language test battery. She also carried out a preliminary analysis and interpretation of the neuropyschological test results as part of her master's thesis research at Carleton University.

Many others have made important contributions. Without the untiring efforts of Irene Hoshko this vast research project could not have been completed. She devoted the greatest skill and care to the administration of tests and the recording and scoring of test results, and carried out an almost unbelievable number of statistical analyses. We wish to thank Dr. Elena Boder for sending revised word lists and procedures for the Boder Reading–Spelling–Pattern test described in Chapter 10. Eric Covington and Humphrey Brown designed and constructed the computer-assisted instructional device described in Chapter 11; Juhan Leemat and George Pandi did the necessary programming in machine language and in

BASIC, respectively. Shelley Drazen helped to develop the training materials used for the computer-assisted instruction programs. Andrée Curtis, Anne Jeannotte, and Judith Stewart provided indispensable help in typing the drafts and the final manuscript. Bonnie Bryans, Daniel Ling, and Joan Backman made extremely helpful comments and suggestions about the manuscript, and Mark Aulls contributed some valuable information about reading instruction. We are most grateful to the subjects for cooperating in this research. Finally, we wish to thank the Canadian government for supporting research through grants from the Department of Health and Welfare (Project 605–1326–44) and the Medical Research Council (MA–1652).

Introduction

1

Reading is essential for educational and vocational success in our society, and the ability to read newspapers, magazines, and books adds greatly to the quality of life. Just how difficult it is to learn to read is an enigmatic question. A great many children, perhaps the majority, learn to read as effortlessly as they learn to speak, regardless of the method used to teach them; some even teach themselves. Special care may be required to teach reading to others who have sensory handicaps or whose early experience has not prepared them for the cognitive and linguistic demands of reading. A small proportion of children with no physical or social handicaps find it extremely difficult or impossible to learn to read. For these children, who are often labeled as learning disabled, reading disabled, or as having developmental dyslexia (we prefer the relatively neutral term *reading disability* and will use it throughout this book), learning to read is a formidable task, and those who wish to help the children to overcome their handicap find that task equally difficult.

Why should learning to read be so easy for most children but so difficult for a few? It is not because such children are generally deficient. They do not have the widespread difficulties in speaking, understanding speech, reasoning, and general adaptation that tend to characterize children classified as mentally retarded. Moreover, many mentally retarded individuals can master the mechanics of reading that pose such an obstacle to children with reading disability. Aside from the possibility that reading disability may somehow be the result of poor teaching, the most obvious hypothesis is that these children have a very specific impairment of abilities needed for reading, and that this deficiency may be the result of a specific deficiency of brain functioning. If this were true, it should be easy to find the cause of the reading problem and develop methods for overcoming or circumventing it. However, no simple explanation of reading disability has been found after almost a century of effort.

From the earliest work at the turn of the century to the present, numerous explanations have been offered concerning the cause of reading disability. Among the most popular are those that postulate a deficiency in a specific aspect of visual perception or language, or in the association of the two processes. Such specific disorders are often said to be the result of abnormal functioning of a specific region of the brain, usually a region within the left cerebral hemisphere. There have been persuasive proponents of each explanation, but no clear-cut confirmation of a particular theory.

The present writers approached this problem from the perspective of the cognitive, linguistic, and neurological sciences of the 1970s. Theoretical advances in these disciplines made us aware of the complexity of human abilities at all levels, from the neurological substrate through the tacit conceptualizations of thought to the overt use of language in speaking, listening, reading, and writing. The science of reading has kept pace with the other theoretical advances of the 1970s. Current reading theorists emphasize the interaction of abilities during skilled reading, and the intricately related stages that the beginning reader must go through in learning to read. These theoretical developments led us to consider the possibility that reading disability can take a number of different forms. Reading disabilities could result from the impairment of specific abilities that are associated with specific neurological dysfunctions, but there is no reason to retain the hypothesis that reading disability is a unitary disorder with a single cause. From a neuropsychological point of view, we are convinced that different types of neurological dysfunction can lead to different types of reading disabilities.

Considerable evidence has accumulated during the past decade that there are different types of reading disabilities, but further research is needed. In designing and interpreting such research, we are greatly handicapped by the lack of a theoretical framework from which experimental measures can be derived. Constructs like attention, perception, and memory are not adequately defined in relation to each other, and there is particular ambiguity concerning the distinction between language and cognition. We could not, however, wait for the ultimate theory before attempting to learn more about reading disabilities, and made the best possible use of the theoretical constructs available at the time we designed the research. Although there are some unavoidable inconsistencies, we have, for the most part, used the term *cognitive* to denote nonlinguistic nonreading abilities such as attention, perception, memory, and conceptualization; the term *neuropsychological* to denote the sensory, motor, cognitive, and linguistic measures that are used to make inferences about the integrity of brain functioning; and the term *nonreading* to differentiate cognitive and linguistic abilities from the abilities directly involved in reading.

Progress in understanding such complex disorders as reading disabilities will not be rapid. Too many factors are interacting to allow for the sudden emergence of a complete explanation. However, provisional conclusions derived from carefully designed scientific research are badly needed because children with a reading disability must, at present, be taught on the basis of the best guesses that can be derived from clinical and/or educational experience. In this book, we describe our research on reading disabilities and attempt to offer an idea of the challenging tasks that lie ahead.

The first part of the book is devoted to a selective critical review of past and present research and theory related to reading disability (Chapters 2–4), and the development of methods for objectively classifying different types of reading disabilities (Chapter 5). The second part gives the details of a large-scale investigation of the interaction of reading, language, and neuropsychological deficits in different types of reading disabilities. The methods and results are described separately for reading deficits in Chapters 6 and 7, for language deficits in Chapter 8, and for neuropsychological deficits in Chapter 9; then there is a general discussion in Chapter 10. Chapter 11 describes further research that is needed to investigate the effects of training the disabilities that were identified in this research, and the final chapter contains a reevaluation of the problems of reading disability research and a discussion of future prospects for research, theory, and practice.

Critical Analysis of the
Concept of Reading Disability

2

Progress toward understanding reading disability has been hampered by research methods that did not take account of the different factors that might be involved. However, it may be impossible to devise methods for studying complex processes without first employing research strategies that treat the processes as if they were simple. Whatever the explanation for the previous inadequacy of reading disability research, the time has come to acknowledge the difficulties that confront us in attempting to study this problem. Before reviewing previous research, we will briefly discuss some of the complications that have emerged in attempts to understand reading disability.

1. Reading seems to involve a number of component skills. All children with reading disability may not be deficient in the same skills. Although it is important to determine which skills are deficient, no one has yet been able to formulate a generally accepted theory that defines the component reading skills. Even if there were such a theory, we have not yet developed methods for accurately measuring these skills while the child is actually reading. At present, we can only make a best guess as to the identity of the component skills and then test the skills indirectly. Most studies of reading disability have tested only a single skill, usually oral word reading. In the few studies in which component reading skills were measured, the results cannot be readily compared because different component skills were tested by different types of indirect measures.

2. It will be many years before theories of brain function have evolved to the point where we fully understand the brain's role in the development of reading skills. What we know now about the maturation of the brain indicates that when there is a defect in one specific part of the brain

during early childhood, another part can take over many or all of the usual functions of the defective region. This means that only limited conclusions regarding developmental reading problems can be drawn from studies of how known brain lesions affect the previously acquired reading skills of adults. In contrast to the majority of studies of reading disability in children, studies of brain-damaged adults have often measured more than one type of reading skill, albeit indirectly, and have demonstrated that there are consistent differences in reading skill deficiencies associated with different areas of brain lesion. Recently developed methods for assessing brain activity during task performance could eventually provide similar information about children with reading disability, but the necessary techniques have not yet been applied.

3. Abilities needed for perception, memory, reasoning, and language are still developing while most children are learning to read. These abilities should be tested in children with reading disability, because reading difficulties may result from a deficiency of one or more of these types of abilities rather than directly from a brain defect. Here also we are hampered by the lack of generally accepted theories that define the component skills involved, and by the lack of direct tests of the abilities defined by existing theories as they operate during reading. Even if we were fairly confident that a particular skill had been adequately measured, a deficiency in that skill could be the result rather than the cause of deficient reading. What is needed to overcome this dilemma is a comprehensive theory that explains the interactive development of reading, language, and the cognitive abilities involved in perception, memory, and reasoning. No such theory has yet been formulated.

4. The usual definitions of developmental dyslexia do not recognize the interactive development of reading, language, and cognition. As just mentioned, reading disability could result from a deficiency in a cognitive or language ability. Almost all theories of reading disability are, in fact, based upon such a supposition. Because intelligence tests measure cognitive and linguistic abilities, it is not logical to stipulate, as do most definitions, that reading disability must involve normal intelligence. Cognitive and language abilities essential to reading could be excluded from the measures used to define normal intelligence, but we will not be entirely sure what these abilities are until there is a comprehensive theory of human ability that provides a firmer basis for defining intelligence. Even then we will have to recognize the probability that the difficulty in learning to read has, itself, impaired the development of important aspects of intelligence such as vocabulary and comprehension.

5. Another difficulty with the usual definitions of reading disability is the requirement that there be no experiential handicaps that could have

impaired reading acquisition. Unlike laboratory experiments in which we can specify all the conditions of learning, there is no way of precisely determining the relevant learning experiences of children with reading disability. Every teacher uses a somewhat different method of teaching reading, and children with reading disability have had varying amounts of additional instruction from parents and reading specialists. It is difficult to prove conclusively that the reading problem was not affected by some aspect of the previous reading experience. Likewise, it is impossible to rule out the possibility that other experiences may have interacted with reading experience to produce reading disability. We must be satisfied for the present with the indirect evidence that the disorder occurs even under what appear to be the most favorable environmental circumstances.

6. Still another difficulty with the usual definitions of reading disability is a confusion about the purpose of definition. It may be important to rigorously define "pure" reading disabilities for research purposes, but research-oriented definitions are not necessarily appropriate for the diagnosis and treatment of reading problems. Until a satisfactory definition of reading disability has finally been achieved, there may be a considerable discrepancy between scientific and practical needs with regard to the definition of reading disabilities.

Reading disability research has been handicapped by all of the complications just discussed. A typical investigation has consisted of an attempt to determine the cause of reading disability by comparing the performance of children with reading disability to that of normal readers of the same age, intelligence, and sociocultural background on a skill that might be essential to reading, such as visual pattern perception or the implicit knowledge of language rules. These studies have involved a number of questionable assumptions: (a) that disabled and normal readers can be differentiated by a single indirect measure of reading and matched according to a single index of general intelligence, with no precise control of previous learning experience; (b) that the experimental test is a valid measure of the ability in question; (c) that the ability exists as such in the structure of human abilities; (d) that a deficiency in the ability is not itself the result of a deficiency in a more basic ability; (e) that a deficiency in the ability is not the result rather than the cause of the reading problem; and (f) that poor performance of the experimental test is caused by a brain defect.

This traditional design can be improved in several ways. If a number of carefully selected cognitive and language abilities are tested, more definite conclusions can be reached about the associated deficit in nonreading abilities. If component reading skills are also tested, it may be possible to define several different types of reading problems, each related to a particular pattern of cognitive or language deficit. To determine whether the different types of reading disabilities are associated with different brain defects, a child's brain functioning can be monitored during the performance of the experimental tasks.

Even if traditional methods of studying reading disability are improved in these ways, we are still faced with the lack of a comprehensive theory, the lack of valid tests of the component skills defined by such a theory, and the lack of well-developed techniques for measuring defective brain functioning in children. Despite these limitations, the important problem of reading disability cannot be set aside. Awareness of the complexity of reading acquisition with respect to cognitive and linguistic development might suggest a complete restructuring of the concept of reading disability. However, it is worthwhile to retain the concept as a working theory, because theoretical explanation and practical training could be simpler if we could eventually relate certain kinds of reading problems to fairly specific defects of brain functioning. Investigators must, however, recognize the provisional nature of the theories upon which their experiments are based, and of the long and difficult path of experimentation that separates them from a satisfactory explanation of reading disability. It is not a simple problem.

Early Concepts of Reading Disabilities

3

The emphasis throughout this book will be on the theoretical and practical difficulties of determining the patterns of cognitive, linguistic, neurological, and reading skill deficits that are involved in reading disabilities. Past and present research and theories will be evaluated from this interactional point of view. More detailed reviews can be found elsewhere (Benton & Pearl, 1978; Critchley, 1970; Gaddis, 1980; Vellutino, 1979; Vernon, 1971).

Acquired Reading Disabilities in Brain-Damaged Adults

Disturbances of reading skill as a result of brain damage in adults were noted long before developmental reading disabilities had been recognized as such. Beginning as early as A.D. 30, a remarkable variety of reading disabilities resulting from brain damage were reported, including a man who lost only his memory for letters, another who could write but could not read what he had written, and one who was more impaired in reading his native language, German, than a second language, Latin (Benton, 1964). These disorders were called *alexias* to denote selective impairment of reading skills resulting from brain injury.

By the end of the nineteenth century, a number of cases of alexia had been carefully documented, and several systems for classifying the different types of alexias had been proposed. The alexias have been reevaluated in terms of the traditional classifications (Benson & Geschwind, 1969), and also from a more contemporary neurolinguistic point of view (Coltheart, Patterson, & Marshall, 1980; Hécaen & Kremin, 1976; Marshall & Newcombe, 1977). We will describe some of the types of alexias, defined according to the traditional classifications, to provide a historical perspective with respect to the emergence of concepts of developmental reading disabilities (this section is largely based on Fiedorowicz, 1980).

The characteristics of five different types of acquired reading disabilities are summarized in Table 3.1. The descriptions are necessarily oversimplified but do illustrate the kinds of impairment that have been found. The variety of reading problems suggested by the earliest reports is clearly evident. The first four types should probably be considered language disorders, as they all involve the hemisphere dominant for language (i.e., the left cerebral hemisphere in most individuals).

The first type of acquired reading disability is *alexia without agraphia*, and it is relatively rare and quite unique. It constitutes the "purest" type of alexia, with only word reading and color naming consistently impaired (Benson & Geschwind, 1969). Writing, spelling, and other language and nonlanguage abilities tend to be unimpaired. This pure alexia is usually the result of a particular cerebral vascular dysfunction that affects the medial region of the left occipital lobe (the most posterior brain region) and the posterior part of the corpus callosum (fibers connecting the two cerebral hemispheres). Geschwind (1962) suggested that alexia without agraphia results from an inability to transfer visually perceived language stimuli from the occipital lobe to the left-hemisphere area involved in the interpretation of visual language (the angular gyrus), and that only reading and color naming are affected because they depend on pure visual–verbal associations.

The second type of acquired reading disability, *alexia with agraphia*, involves a global reading–writing–spelling problem that extends to letters as well as to words and is accompanied by mild language impairment of the type classified as Wernicke's or fluent aphasia, as well as certain nonlanguage disorders (Benson & Geschwind, 1969). The other language disorders include difficulty in naming and "paraphasic" substitutions of words of similar meaning during speech, which is otherwise generally fluent. "Paralexic" substitutions of words of similar meaning occur during oral reading. Additional impairments include the difficulties in calculation, right–left orientation, and finger localization (finger agnosia) that—along with writing difficulty (agraphia)—are said to make up Gerstmann's syndrome as well as constructional difficulties in nonverbal copying. These more widespread deficits are associated with lesions involving the left angular gyrus, a region at the junction of the temporal, parietal, and occipital lobes that has often been implicated in developmental reading disabilities. Geschwind (1965) suggested that, because the angular gyrus plays a major role in the formation of associations between vision and audition, it may be essential to the visual–auditory associations involved in reading. The impairment of visual–auditory associations could interfere with all aspects of reading, writing, and spelling (depending, of course, on one's theory of reading).

In the next two types of acquired reading problems, the spoken language deficit predominates over the reading deficit. *Wernicke's* or *fluent aphasia with alexia and agraphia* (Benson & Geschwind, 1969) involves the same general reading deficit that occurred in alexia with agraphia but, in this syndrome, it is secondary to the predominant language deficit, which is usually characterized by severe difficulty in comprehending spoken language, repeating spoken language, and naming. Speech is generally fluent, but with paraphasic substitutions, and no striking nonlanguage deficits are noted. This pattern of deficit results from lesions of the upper posterior part of the left temporal lobe (which is located in the lower middle region of the left cerebral hemisphere), adjacent to the angular gyrus. As this is considered to be an auditory–verbal association area, lesions of this area could disrupt reading and writing (depending again on one's reading theory) by preventing auditory–verbal associations with written language, in addition to causing primary disturbances of spoken language comprehension and word retrieval.

The second type of acquired reading disorder secondary to a spoken language disorder is *Broca's* or *nonfluent aphasia with alexia and agraphia* (Benson, 1977). This is the only type of alexia in which letter-reading skills are more impaired than are word-reading skills, and the letter deficit extends to writing and to spelling. The primary impairment of spoken language is nonfluent speech that is hesitant and contains phonetic errors rather than paraphasic substitutions. There is also some difficulty in comprehending syntactic structure (agrammatism), naming, and eye movements. In this disorder, the phonetic, as opposed to the semantic, speech disturbance seems connected to a letter- as opposed to a word- reading impairment.

Two additional types of reading deficit secondary to aphasia that are not listed in Table 3.1 have been described by Benson and Geschwind (1969) and also by Whitaker (1976). *Transcortical aphasia* is a rare disorder in which both listening comprehension and speech are severely impaired, but the ability to repeat spoken language is near normal. Reading and writing are totally disrupted. Both the temporal lobe area for listening comprehension and the frontal lobe area for speech are thought to be isolated from the rest of the brain, but a connection between the two regions is preserved, permitting the patient to repeat

TABLE 3.1
Summary of the Characteristics of Five Different Types of Reading Problems That Can Result from Brain Injuries to Adults with Previously Acquired Reading Skills

Type	Reading-related skills	Other language abilities	Nonlanguage abilities	Neurological dysfunction
Alexia without agraphia or aphasia (rare)	Impaired Reading words and text Unimpaired Reading letters Writing Letter naming Oral spelling Recognizing spelled words	Sometimes impaired Color naming Calculation (no other language disorders)	Unimpaired color matching and other abilities	Left medial occipital lobe *and* splenium of corpus callosum, almost always from thrombosis involving the posterior cerebral artery
Alexia with agraphia and mild Wernicke's (fluent) aphasia	Impaired Reading letters, words, and text (paralexia) Letter naming Writing Oral spelling Recognizing spelled words	Mild impairment Naming Paraphasic substitutions Calculation	Sometimes impaired Right–left orientation Finger localization Constructional skills	Left angular gyrus from infarction, trauma, neoplasm, or anteriovenous malformation

Syndrome	Reading/Writing	Speech/Language	Other	Lesion
Wernicke's (fluent) aphasia with alexia and agraphia	Impaired (secondary to aphasia) Reading letters, words, and text Writing	Severe impairment Comprehension and repetition of spoken language Naming Paraphasic substitutions Less impaired Fluent (but paraphasic speech)	Unimpaired	Left posterior superior temporal lobe from infarct- or neoplasm
Broca's (nonfluent) aphasia with alexia and agraphia	Impaired Letter reading Letter naming Writing Oral spelling Recognizing spelled words Less Impaired Reading words and text	Severe impairment Nonfluent speech Less impaired Listening comprehension Naming	Impaired Eye movements	Broca's area of frontal lobe from neoplasms and from infarctions involving anterior branch of middle cerebral artery
Visual agnosia (controversial)	Impaired Reading letters, words, and text Writing	Unimpaired	Impaired Visual perception and production of complex forms	Right parietal lobe (?)

spoken words and phrases. In *conduction aphasia*, however, listening comprehension is unimpaired, but oral repetition is severely impaired. Parallel reading impairment occurs, with very poor oral reading but normal reading comprehension. Benson and Geschwind (1969) hypothesize that the lesion producing this disorder extends from the parietal operculum to the angular gyrus.

The final type of acquired reading disability is somewhat controversial. The majority of investigators have confined themselves to reading disorders associated with lesions of the language-dominant hemisphere, but lesions of the nondominant right hemisphere, which subserves complex visual perception and visual–motor construction, could affect the recognition and construction of the complex shapes of printed words. Such reading disorders would be considered as *agnosias* rather than as alexias, occurring as part of a generalized visual agnosia that affects both verbal and nonverbal stimuli (Hécaen & Kremin, 1976).

The acquired reading disorders illustrate the interactive complexity of the reading, language, nonlanguage, and neurological deficits that can occur in reading disabilities. If we knew as much about the interactive deficits involved in developmental reading disabilities, we would be much closer to an adequate understanding of these perplexing disorders. However, the differentiation of the acquired reading disabilities is not as unequivocal as the previous descriptions might indicate. The descriptions are based on interpretations of case history evidence derived from restricted and perhaps biased samples of patients; often-unsatisfactory neurological, neurosurgical, and autopsy evidence regarding locus of lesions; inconsistent assessment of reading and nonreading deficits; and lack of adequate information about the prior reading proficiency of many patients. Few patients manifest exactly the patterns of deficits listed in Table 3.1, some having symptoms of more than one type (Hécaen & Kremin, 1976); and as more sophisticated methods of assessment are employed, more complex patterns of language and nonlanguage impairments are found (cf. Ojemann & Mateer, 1979).

Despite these reservations, evidence regarding the different types of acquired reading disabilities supplies a direct link among reading, nonreading, and neurological deficits. The adult alexias can furnish suggestions for the construction of neuropsychological models of developmental dyslexia (Benson, 1976; Benton, 1978; Damasio, 1977; Mattis, 1978). Such models must, of course, take into consideration the difference between the mature and immature brain, as well as the difference between the proficient and the beginning reader. Although there may be only limited recovery from brain lesions in adults, the behaviors subserved by a deficient area of the immature brain may be taken over by another area; and the consequences of disrupting the previously acquired reading skills of adults may be entirely different from the consequences of impediments to reading acquisition.

Early Concepts of Developmental Reading Disabilities

Since at least one of the types of acquired alexias involves selective impairment of reading without severe impairment of other language and nonlanguage skills, it is not surprising that someone eventually made the connection between acquired alexia and selective problems of reading acquisition in children. This discovery is generally attributed to an English school doctor, W. Pringle Morgan (1896), who read a description of acquired alexia by a Scottish eye specialist, James Hinshelwood (1895), and suggested that such a disorder might also be congenital (Farnham-Diggory, 1978a). Hinshelwood's paper concerned "visual word blindness," which he considered to be an inability to recognize words resulting from damage to the visual memory center for words in the left angular gyrus. Hinshelwood himself went on to write a book entitled *Congenital Word Blindness* (1917), wherein he described cases of "otherwise sharp and intelligent" children who could not learn to read.

For present purposes, the most important aspect of the "discovery" of congenital word blindness was the assumption that there was a single type of reading disability that could occur as an isolated disorder in an otherwise completely normal child. As we shall see, the concept of a pure reading disability has been modified over the years by the postulation of a variety of underlying nonreading deficits, even though the term *specific reading disability* is often used to describe the disorder. However, the connection between visual word blindness in brain-damaged adults and pure congenital word blindness in children was probably very useful at the time it was proposed by Morgan (1896) and Hinshelwood (1917). Hinshelwood's adult cases convincingly demonstrated that very specific reading disorders could occur as a result of localized brain lesions, enabling Morgan and Hinshelwood to put forth the important practical argument that some children with reading problems were special cases because they were not deficient in other respects. Only with the advantage of hindsight might one become curious about the possible connection between the different types of acquired alexias that were known at the time and problems of reading acquisition that were not completely "pure," but were accompanied by various combinations of language and nonlanguage impairments.

The only other major theory concerning developmental reading disorders to appear before 1950 was formulated by an American neurologist and psychiatrist, Samuel T. Orton (1925). The reading disorder described by Orton was less pure and isolated than that described by Hinshelwood, but he did agree with Hinshelwood's assumption that reading involved the use of visual word images that were stored in a particular part of the brain. For Orton, however, reading disability was not the result of a deficiency within the center for visual images, but of a lag in the development of left-hemisphere dominance for language abilities. This developmental lag caused *strephosymbolia* or "twisted images," because visual images stored as mirror images in the nondominant hemisphere were not suppressed by hemispheric dominance, and interfered with the perception of normally oriented visual images in the dominant hemisphere during reading acquisition (Farnham-Diggory, 1978a; Vellutino, 1979). The developmental lag resulted not only in reading disability but also in speech and writing problems, difficulty in recognizing spoken words, stuttering, and general clumsiness.

The type of brain dysfunction postulated by Orton could affect nonreading abilities, but the consequences for reading were essentially the same as those postulated by Hinshelwood, a single type of reading disability caused by prevention of the normal functioning of the visual memory center for printed words. Neither theory was based upon direct evidence of abnormal brain structure or functioning. However, Orton's theory has been very influential in fostering the formulation of remedial reading methods (Gillingham & Stillman, 1940), further developmental lag theories, and research on cerebral dominance in reading disability and on other childhood speech and language disorders.

Later Concepts of Reading Disabilities

Renewed interest in reading disability, beginning in 1950, led to radical changes in the concepts of congenital word blindness and strephosymbolia. Research into the possible origins of the problem suggested that reading disability could be hereditary (Hallgren, 1950; Hermann & Norrie, 1958), and might also result from disorders of pregnancy and delivery (Kawi & Pasamanick, 1959). The possibility that reading disability could involve dysfunction of the left angular gyrus was still entertained, but knowledge of the plasticity of the child's developing brain argued against this form of a single focal lesion (Geschwind, 1962). A more thorough analysis of evidence regarding the role of cerebral dominance in reading disability cast some doubt on Orton's hypothesis (Zangwill, 1962). More complex explanations of the organic basis of reading disability began to emerge, such as Birch's (1962) description of how reading disability could result from developmental inadequacies during the hierarchical maturation of perceptual systems.

One inevitable consequence of more sophisticated analyses of reading disability was the abandonment of Hinshelwood's hypothesis that there was a direct causal link between pure congenital word blindness and focal dysfunction of the left angular gyrus. Instead, investigators began to search for deficiencies in nonreading skills that might have caused a reading disability, with the assumption (often implicit) that the nonreading deficits were themselves the result of the type of complex maturational disorder postulated by Birch. Bender (1957) and deHirsch (1957) thought that reading disability was caused by a disturbance in the development of visual perception, whereas Hermann (1959) said that the visual perception disorder was, itself, secondary to directional confusion. Rabinovitch, Drew, De Jong, Ingram, and Withey (1954) found Verbal IQ (VIQ) to be lower than Performance IQ (PIQ) in children with a reading disability, as have most subsequent investigators, suggesting an underlying language deficit as well as an underlying visual perception deficit. Silver and Hagin (1960) reported auditory discrimination problems as well as visual perception deficits, and Myklebust and Johnson (1962) reported difficulties in both visualizing and "auditorizing" in children with reading disability. The scope of nonreading deficit was broadened even further in a study by Doehring (1968), in which a carefully selected group of children with reading disability was found to be deficient on 31 nonreading measures, most of which involved visual or verbal abilities.

These changes in the concept of reading disability, which steadily departed from the original concept of an isolated reading disorder in otherwise normal children, were at least partially attributable to the research methods that replaced the original case history methods. More and more investigators came to apply the objective methods of experimental psychology to search for the cause of reading disability by comparison of a precisely defined experimental group of disabled readers with a carefully matched control group of normal readers on one or more nonreading ability, with statistically significant differences between groups being accepted as evidence of underlying behavioral causes of reading disability. This experimental method, which has been labeled the *single-syndrome paradigm* (Doehring, 1978), although suitable for other problems of experimental psychology, proved inappropriate for studying the host of variables involved in reading disability even when interpretations were tempered by clinical experience and practical wisdom.

As stated in Chapter 2, the simple research paradigm does not allow for the variety of factors that might be involved in reading disabilities. The research design forces the investigator to hypothesize that reading disability is a unitary disorder with a unitary cause. A single experimental group defined as poor readers by a single measure of reading achievement is matched in age, intelligence, sensory abilities, personality, and previous educational experience to a single control group of normal readers. When the experimental group is found to be significantly poorer than the control group on one or more measures of nonreading ability, the abilities in question are said to play a causal role in the reading disability. This reasearch paradigm would be entirely appropriate if Hinshelwood's theory of reading disability were correct. However, the experimenter would never find any significant deficiencies of nonreading skills, because no nonreading skills would be impaired in pure congenital word blindness. If Orton's theory were correct, the investigator might find that the experimental group was significantly deficient in speaking abilities, listening comprehension, and motor coordination. However, Orton would not interpret these deficiencies as causes of reading disabilities, but as additional consequences of the developmental lag in cerebral dominance, which actually caused a reading disability.

Research using the single-syndrome paradigm did seem to demonstrate that reading disability was not as pure as Hinshelwood had assumed, but how was one to interpret significant differences in mean scores between groups? Deficient nonreading abilities might have caused the reading disability. However, nonreading disabilities and reading disability could also have been parallel but independent consequences of a common underlying cause such as a developmental lag in cerebral dominance; or, the reading disability might have caused the nonreading deficiency. These alternative explanations cannot be resolved within the simple experimental paradigm.

The remaining problem with this research approach relates to the inability to deal with individual differences. Unless reading disability involves a uniform pattern of deficit in reading and nonreading skills, comparisons of disabled and normal readers in terms of average performance is very uninformative. The results of investigations using the single-syndrome paradigm tell us that significant proportions of disabled readers are deficient in certain nonreading skills, but we do not know how much variation there is in individual patterns of deficit. The initial scientific onslaught on the problem of reading disability seemed to destroy the idea of "otherwise sharp and intelligent" children, who Morgan and Hinshelwood had been so pleased to single out from the mass of those with reading problems associated with low intelligence, poor motivation, or inadequate educational opportunity, but did not succeed in discovering an acceptable alternative explanation of reading disability.

Different Types of Reading Disabilities

Because different types of acquired reading disabilities have been found in adults, it is reasonable to assume that there could be more than one type of developmental reading disability in children whose reading problems do not appear to be simply a function of generally low intelligence, sensory handicaps, personality problems, inadequate educational opportunity, or sociocultural factors. As early as 1960, there were reports of different types of reading disabilities by clinicians and researchers who were not constrained by the single-syndrome research paradigm. Ingram (1960) distinguished between visuospatial, auditory–linguistic, and visual–auditory association problems, on the basis of each having a different pattern of reading skill deficit. Kinsbourne and Warrington (1963) differentiated two types of reading disabilities on the basis of differences in VIQ and PIQ on the Wechsler Intelligence Scale for Children (WISC). A group of six children whose PIQ was at least 20 points higher than their VIQ had naming problems and delayed speech, whereas those whose VIQ was at least 20 points higher than their PIQ had constructional difficulty, finger agnosia, and right–left disorientation, suggestive of Gerstmann's syndrome. However, not all of the subjects with higher VIQ were severely impaired in reading, and Warrington (1967) later found that only 5% of retarded readers had VIQs 20 points higher. Johnson and Myklebust (1967) described two different types of reading disabilities, *visual dyslexia* and *auditory dyslexia*, on the basis of their clinical experience. Visual dyslexics were said to have difficulty in perceiving, remembering, and reproducing complex visual patterns and visual sequences, whereas auditory dyslexics had difficulty in analyzing spoken words into their constituents and synthesizing new words from syllables and speech sounds. Other typologies, such as that of Bannatyne (1966), were based on differences between inherited and acquired disorders rather than on differential patterns of reading and nonreading deficits.

The different types of reading disabilities could not have been derived from the restrictive research paradigm used by other investigators. The typologists had given free rein to their clinical experience in differentiating the reading disabilities. It remained for later investigators to attempt to obtain more rigorous scientific proof regarding different types of reading disabilities. Efforts to formulate broader concepts of reading disabilities were greatly aided by Wiener and Cromer's (1967) detailed logical analysis of the possible forms that reading disabilities might take. They described six possible models of reading disabilities, including the original model of a unitary disorder with a single cause (which they dismissed as unpromising), multiple causes of a unitary disorder, a unitary cause of multiple disorders, and multiple types of reading disabilities with multiple antecedent conditions. As we shall see in Chapter 4, there have been further attempts to determine the characteristics of different types of reading disabilities during the past decade. However, many investigators have continued to find the single-syndrome paradigm a useful vehicle for attempts to understand the nature of reading disability.

Recent Concepts of
Reading Disabilities

4

Until about 1970, reading disability research and theory tended to be narrowly conceived, reflecting both the simplicity of available theoretical models and the general conviction that a simple explanation could be found. The possibility that there might be more than one type of reading disability, which had been raised in the 1960s on both theoretical and empirical grounds (Ingram, 1960; Johnson & Myklebust, 1967; Kinsbourne & Warrington, 1963; Wiener & Cromer, 1967), gained further support in the 1970s. New theories of language, cognition, brain function, and reading stressed the complexity rather than the simplicity of these processes, providing additional arguments against simple explanations of reading disabilities. However, the more detailed theoretical models also supplied those interested in unitary explanations of reading disabilities with new and interesting ideas about where to look for the cause. Many investigators pursued these ideas, using some variation of the traditional single-syndrome research paradigm. Before reviewing the single-syndrome and multiple-syndrome reading disability studies of the 1970s, we will briefly describe the theoretical context in which this work was done.

Cognitive Theories

Reading is one type of cognitive activity treated by the field of cognitive psychology that was resurrected as part of a renewed interest in complex mental processes (Broadbent, 1958; Bruner, Goodnow, & Austin, 1956; Hebb, 1949; Lashley, 1951; Miller, Galanter, & Pribram,

1960). In contrast to behavioristic theories, which explained human behavior as a unitary process, cognitive theories tended to follow the lead of information theory in fractionating mental activity into component processes such as attention, brief sensory storage, perception, short-term memory, long-term memory, and reasoning (Neisser, 1967). These components are said to be hierarchically arranged on different levels (Cermak & Craik, 1978) and organized into structures designated as schemata (Kintsch, 1976; Neisser, 1976), frames (Charniak, 1977; Minsky, 1975), or scripts (Schank & Abelson, 1977). Learning is thought to involve a complex interaction among the learner's current knowledge, the type of information to be acquired, and levels of processing involved (Morris, Bransford, & Franks, 1977; Stein, 1978). *Metacognition*, the awareness of one's own cognitive activity (Brown, 1978), is said to play an important interactive role in the planning, monitoring, and evaluation of learning and problem solving. These theoretical analyses led to a consideration of new methods for facilitating learning (Bransford, 1979; Brown, in press; Glaser, Pellegrino, & Lesgold, 1978).

Theories of cognitive development have also emerged. Many are based on Piaget's theory that cognition develops through an orderly sequence of stages from simple egocentric thought to abstract inferential reasoning (Waller, 1977), but the developing processes are seen to be more complex than those envisaged by Piaget, with metacognitive abilities playing an important role (Flavell, 1979). Some cognitive abilities, such as those for associating the visual and audible components of events, are evident in early infancy and might be innate (Spelke, 1979).

The new cognitive theories have provided many suggestions about the structure of human ability, but most of the details of organization and development remain to be discovered. The trend toward more complex explanations of cognition cannot continue indefinitely, but there seems to be little chance that theorists will revert to the unitary concepts of behaviorism or the relatively simple stages of Piagetian development.

Language Theories

Reading was also a type of linguistic activity that was the focus of new theories that explained language as a much more complex activity than that described by behaviorists (cf. Skinner, 1959). These theories, like the new cognitive theories, tended to postulate different levels of interactive component processes. Theories of language production concentrated initially on the grammatical processes involved in generating sentences (Chomsky, 1957), and later became concerned with higher levels, such as the relationship between sentences in narration and conversation and the interactions with cultural and situational variables (Halliday, 1975). Theories of language perception concentrated at first on the manner in which phonological structure is abstracted from the acoustic representation of continuous speech (Liberman, Cooper, Shankweiler, & Studdert-Kennedy, 1967). They later became concerned with a more comprehensive delineation of the acoustic, phonetic, phonological, morphological, syntactic, and semantic components of language perception (Cole, 1980; Liberman, 1970; Studdert-Kennedy, 1976); and some theories describe how the component processes may interact during language perception (Marslen-Wilson, 1975). Speech perception theorists have also speculated about the relationship between perception and production (Liberman *et al.*, 1967), and some have come to postulate an auditory–articulatory space that integrates spectral and temporal cues into a single percept (Studdert-Kennedy, 1980).

The new theories of language production almost immediately gave rise to theories of the development of language production abilities. These theories were initially concerned with the acquisition of sentence grammar, and later with larger units of discourse within the framework of functional communication (Blank, Rose, & Berlin, 1978; Ervin-Tripp & Mitchell-Kernan, 1977; Lewis & Rosenbloom, 1977; Lock, 1978). Earlier theories of speech perception development postulated innate capacities for phoneme perception (Eimas, 1975), but more recent theorists have discussed possible perceptual learning mechanisms in speech perception development (Aslin & Pisoni, 1978). A number of theorists have also emphasized the role of the child's conception of language (i.e., metalinguistic awareness) in the development of higher linguistic abilities, and proposed methods for teaching metalinguistic skills (Sinclair, Jarvella, & Levelt, 1978).

The new theories of language production, perception, and development, like those of cognition, have described the complex interactions involved in the development and organization of component processes. Further research is needed to confirm and extend the theories, which, like theories of cognition, are not likely to revert to more unitary explanations.

Relationship between Language and Cognition

Few theorists make a sharp distinction between language and cognition, or between any of the processes involved in language and cognition. Verbal and nonverbal perception may be differentiated to some extent at more peripheral levels, but the distinction becomes less clear at the levels where meaning is comprehended and inferences are made. Theorists who view language and cognition as involving interactive levels of processing would find it hard to separate them at any level of mature human function. Many works on language could just as well have been called works on cognition, and vice-versa (cf. McNeill, 1979).

The interactive development of language and cognition has also been recognized. In contrast to earlier ideas about innate capacities for language (Chomsky, 1957), there has been increased speculation about how cognitive development may precede or interactively develop with language (Bloom & Lahey, 1978; Bruner, 1978; Macnamara, 1972). Both cognitive and linguistic development must, in some sense, follow a Piagetian sequence of progression from egocentric and situation-bound to independent thought and language, where metacognitive and metalinguistic awareness facilitate the continuing acquisition of higher levels of processing (Flavell, 1979).

Some simplification of theories might result from an explanation of language and cognition within a single theory. As reading is a cognitive and a linguistic process, a comprehensive cognitive–linguistic theory could simplify the task of reading theorists. However, some theorists (cf. Neisser, 1980) feel that several alternative theories are needed to explain how cognitive–linguistic adaptations actually occur, as opposed to one comprehensive theory of the human as an information-processing machine.

Theories of Brain Function

Considerable interest in theories of brain functioning was also awakened in the 1970s; particularly with respect to how the brain processes language (Heilman & Valenstein, 1979; Kinsbourne, 1978; Segalowitz & Gruber, 1977). Research on brain development led to descriptions of the plasticity of the developing brain in taking over the functioning of defective areas (cf. Dennis, 1979; Witelson, 1977), and to theories of how cognitive and linguistic development interact with brain maturation (Patel, 1977). New theories of brain–behavior relationships have kept pace with the continuing evolution of cognitive and linguistic theory (cf. Grossberg, 1980).

Reading Theories

Theories of reading changed almost immediately in response to the new cognitive and linguistic theories (Goodman, 1967; Smith, 1971), and have continued to change (Downing & Leong, 1981). Explanations of higher-level cognitive and linguistic processes in reading have been especially numerous, including theoretical formulations regarding cognitive schemata (Anderson, 1977), metacognitive awareness (Baker & Brown, 1981), memory (Daneman & Carpenter, 1980; Kintsch, 1974), comprehension (Just & Carpenter, 1980), and discourse processing (Frederiksen, 1979). Reading theories present different problems than do cognitive and linguistic theories. As Mattingly (1978) has pointed out, a philosopher of science might complain that there cannot be a psychology of reading any more than there can be a psychology of dishwashing. The processes involved in reading could, for example, differ completely from one person to another, and may even vary within the same person as a function of different purposes (Gibson, 1972). Reading involves such a confusing conglomerate of activities that some writers have despaired of formulating a single theory of reading (Gibson & Levin, 1975). However, this has not prevented theorists from attempting to explain many aspects of reading (Reber & Scarborough, 1977; Resnick & Weaver, 1979). Further advances in cognitive (Gregg & Farnham-Diggory, 1979) and linguistic theory (Shuy, 1977) have been brought to the attention of reading theorists, and recent explanations of reading make use of the concepts of interactive component processes that are intrinsic to many theories of language and cognition (Levy, 1980; Stanovich, 1980).

Theoretical comparisons of reading and speech perception are both instructive and controversial. The processes unquestionably differ at the most peripheral level, where phonetic features are extracted from speech and graphic features are extracted from print, but some theorists (cf. Conrad, 1972; Liberman & Shankweiler, 1979) postulate that print is recoded into speech at the phonological level and processed thereafter in the same manner as speech, whereas others (cf. Smith, 1971; 1973) postulate that the meaning of printed text is extracted by mechanisms that are completely independent of the speech perception system. Still other theorists (cf. Baron, 1977; LaBerge & Samuels, 1974) allow for the use of either or both paths from print to meaning as a function of the stage of reading acquisition, individual differences between readers, and different purposes for reading.

There is general recognition that reading, like other aspects of language and cognition, involves the interaction of component skills or processes. Some theorists emphasize a "bottom-up" sequence of stages from print to meaning (cf. Gough, 1972; LaBerge & Samuels, 1974), others a "top-down" control of letter and word perception by linguistic context, frames, or schemata (cf. Goodman & Goodman, 1979), and still others postulate fully interactive parallel processing during reading (cf. Rumelhart, 1977). The exact levels of processing vary according to the particular interests of the theorists. Those concerned with higher levels of discourse processing (cf. Frederiksen, 1979) might include only a stage of feature detection prior to syntactic analysis; those interested in the initial stages of processing (cf. Gough, 1972) might not include any levels beyond word recognition, and those who wish to explain how the reader deals with the lack of correspondence between speech and print might interpose phonological (Liberman & Shankweiler, 1979), syllabic (Gleitman & Rozin, 1977), morphophonemic (Mattingly, 1980), orthographic (Venezky & Massaro, 1979), or lexical (Perfetti & Lesgold, 1979) levels of processing between graphic feature extraction and semantic analysis.

Although no one has attempted to formulate a comprehensive theory of reading acquisition (Doehring & Aulls, 1979), theories of reading instruction are based on assumptions about how reading is, or should be, acquired. These theories incorporate the concepts and terminology of cognitive and linguistic theories, but the perennial disagreement persists between those who view reading as translation from printed to spoken language (the coding or phonics approach) and those who view reading as a separate, autonomous language process (the look–say or language experience approach) (Resnick, 1979a). Bottom-up theorists tend to favor the phonics approach, and top-down theorists, the language experience approach. However, some theorists incorporate both positions. LaBerge and Samuels (1974) emphasize that the lower-level processes such as letter recognition, phonological recoding, and whole-word recognition must be overlearned to the point of automaticity to facilitate control by higher-level processes; and some writers (cf. Chall, 1979; Doehring & Aulls, 1979; Sticht, 1979) describe stages of reading acquisition in which the early stages involve the acquisition of lower-level coding skills and the final stages involve higher levels of reasoning and inference.

Striking individual differences in reading acquisition can also be interpreted in terms of reading theories (Rosner, 1979), where hard-to-teach children may have to go through all the steps of learning lower-level coding skills, and easy-to-teach children may fulfill the expectancies of top-down language experience theories of instruction by learning to read without special attention to coding skills. Applications of theories of metacognitive and metalinguistic awareness to reading acquisition have varied according to the theoretical perspective of the theorists, with those favoring top-down processing (Goodman & Goodman, 1979; Smith, 1977) arguing that the beginning reader needs only the metalinguistic insights that reading is language and that written language differs from spoken language to learn to read; and those favoring bottom-up processing (cf. Liberman & Shankweiler, 1979) arguing that metalinguistic awareness of phonemic structure is essential for learning how letters correspond to speech sounds.

Application of New Theories to Concepts of Reading Disabilities

The new theories of multicomponent interactive processes in cognition, language, reading, and brain–behavior relationships offered much more scope for those who wished to search for a unitary cause of reading disability and those who entertained the possibility of multiple types of reading disabilities. The problem that confronted all investigators, whether they realized it or not, was to design studies that took adequate account of the interactive nature of reading disability. To prove that reading disability was uniquely caused by an impairment in a specific nonreading ability, deficiency in that ability by subjects with reading disability was not sufficient. It was also necessary to rule out the possibility that the nonreading impairment was not itself the result of a deficiency in either a reading or another nonreading ability. Difficulties of research design were compounded by the lack of a theoretical framework from which systematically related tests of reading and nonreading abilities could be derived. The theoretical status of important constructs such as attention and memory was completely unresolved (cf. Neisser, 1976), and no comprehensive model of reading was available (Gibson & Levin, 1975). As we review the reading disability research of the 1970s, then, the provisional nature of the findings must be kept in mind.

Single-Syndrome Reading Disability Research of the 1970s

Many investigators continued to be optimistic about the possibility of finding a single cause for a unitary form of reading disability. We can only give a brief overview of the large body of single-syndrome research. In addition to the theoretical complications mentioned earlier, differences in the populations studied and in the experimental operations for testing reading and nonreading skills make it virtually impossible to construct an explanation of reading disability by putting together the results of single-syndrome studies. Vellutino (1979) has made an effort to do this, and the reader is referred to his book for detailed descriptions of many single-syndrome studies. In the absence of a comprehensive theoretical framework, we will review single-syndrome research in several overlapping categories, beginning with visual processes.

Reading differs from speech perception at the input stage because the linguistic stimuli are sampled through active selection by eye movements. Information is extracted from print during fixations of the eyes averaging about .25 sec in duration. After each fixation, rapid eye movements of less than .10 sec, called *saccades,* change the fixation point to the next section of text to be sampled. There has been a great deal of research on eye movements in normal and poor readers (Fisher, 1979; McConkie, 1979; Pirozzolo & Rayner, 1978). Defective eye movements could impair reading acquisition, but the bulk of evidence suggests that abnormal eye movements do not constitute a unitary cause of reading disability. In fact, cases have been reported in which reading achievement was normal even when eye movements were extremely impaired as a result of neurological dysfunction (Pirozzolo, 1979). The deficient eye movements that have been found in disabled readers may, in some cases, be the result rather than the cause of the reading problem, and may, in other cases, be secondary to a defect in the spatial abilities that guide eye movements (Pirozzolo & Raynor, 1978). Even at the most peripheral level of stimulus input, then, unitary deficit hypotheses cannot be easily confirmed.

Fixated visual stimuli activate receptor cells in the retina, and there appear to be several further stages of visual processing as information is extracted from the visual input. Theorists have not arrived at any definite agreement regarding these stages and the interactions among them (Estes, 1977; Farnham-Diggory, 1978a,b; Frederiksen, 1978; Just & Carpenter, 1980; Massaro, 1975; Vellutino, 1979). The processing of information may depend to some extent on selective attention, and the information may be stored for up to .5 sec in the form of distinctive features or exact iconic representations while perceptual synthesis or some form of inital recognition occurs. Then the perceived stimuli may be held for much longer in working or short-term memory until sufficient information about the stimulus is extracted. The extraction of information involves the matching or schematization of single patterns or regularly recurring sequences of patterns that are presumably represented in long-term memory. There is no strong evidence of a deficit at any of these stages of visual processing that could function as a unitary cause of reading disability. Normal and disabled readers have not been found to differ significantly in selective attention (Pelham, 1979), sensory storage (Morrison, Giordani, & Nagy, 1977) or any of the other visual processes. Where deficient visual processes have been found in single-syndrome research, they have been interpreted as interactive language deficits rather than as visual deficits (Vellutino, 1979).

With very few exceptions, then, theorists of the 1970s abandoned hypotheses that reading disability is caused by deficiencies in visual attention, perception, or memory that interfere with the normal processing of the graphic features of letters or of the orthographic regularities of printed words. Among those who described multiple types of reading disabilities, however, a type involving visual processing was often included, as will be discussed in a later section.

LEARNING THE CORRESPONDENCE BETWEEN PRINTED AND SPOKEN LANGUAGE

Because reading disability does not seem to be the result of strictly visual deficits, single-syndrome theorists must look further along the sequence of events involved in extracting meaning from print to discover a unitary cause of reading disability. Several different paths are open to them, because reading theorists do not agree about whether phonological or speech recoding is necessary for lexical access (Foss & Hakes, 1978). Direct access theorists (Smith, 1971; 1973) hypothesize that readers can go directly from print to meaning without first coding printed language into spoken form, and that direct learning of the orthographic representation of words is more efficient than phonological recoding because the correspondence between sequences of letters and sequences of phonemes is complex and irregular. In terms of direct access theories, if visual processing deficits are ruled out and reading disability is not defined as a general language disorder, reading disability might involve a deficiency in learning to understand the relationship between printed and spoken language (i.e., a deficiency in some aspect of metalinguistic awareness). Another deficiency that could conceivably occur during direct access of meaning would be the use of inappropriate strategies of picking up information about orthographic structure (Gibson, 1977; Venezky & Massaro, 1979), but it is difficult to differentiate such deficits from grapheme–phoneme encoding problems in single-syndrome research. Direct access theorists do seem to explain all reading problems in terms of a failure to understand the personal and social functions of written language, asserting that, to acquire reading proficiency, a child must simply become aware that language conveys meaning, that written language is meaningful and has practical uses, and that there are important similarities and differences between spoken and written language (Goodman & Goodman, 1979; Smith, 1977, 1979). They do not appear to differentiate reading disabilities from other problems of reading acquisition, although they might be willing to attribute reading disabilities to the failure of instructional methods that emphasize speech recoding. A lack of the meta-linguistic awareness needed for reading acquisition could be the result of a subtle neurolinguistic deficit as well as a lack of the necessary personal and social experiences, but only a few investigators (cf. Hook & Johnson, 1978) have attempted to investigate this possibility within the single-syndrome paradigm, and further experimentation will be needed to dif-ferentiate general metalinguistic deficiencies from the specific deficien-cies of phonological awareness that will be discussed in the following sections.

VISUAL–AUDITORY ASSOCIATION

The majority of single-syndrome reading disability investigations of the 1970s were at least implicitly based on theories that all reading takes place through recoding from printed to spoken form (cf. Liberman & Shankweiler, 1979) or that reading can take place either through direct access or speech recoding (cf. Kleiman, 1975). When reading takes place through speech recoding, the visual input must be transformed into spoken language by some sort of associative process. It is this code-breaking stage that has received the most attention from those who wish to explain both the biological and the instructional causes of reading failure (Resnick, 1979a).

If reading disability were simply the result of difficulty in learning to associate written and spoken language, it would seem easy to define the exact behavioral deficit, trace it to a particular neurological dysfunction, and develop specific instructional procedures for overcoming or circum-venting it. This has not, however, turned out to be so simple. Although associative deficits have been reported in single-syndrome studies, it has not been possible to rule out alternative explanations in terms of im-pairments in attention, memory, or response strategies, or intramodal difficulty in visual, auditory, or linguistic functioning (Bryant, 1975; Vellutino, 1979). What evidence there is from single-syndrome studies seems to suggest that apparent associative deficits are not actually the result of a basic deficiency in the association of visual and auditory stimuli (Vellutino, 1979), but better experimental designs (perhaps in-volving the abandonment of the single-syndrome paradigm) are needed to provide a more adequate test of the hypotheses (Bryant, 1975).

AUDITORY PROCESSES

If visual disorders and visual–auditory association disorders are ruled out, problems involving recoding from print to speech are likely can-didates for single-syndrome investigations. Disorders that could interfere with recoding from written to spoken language include defective discrim-ination or perception of the acoustic properties of the speech signal, defective analysis or synthesis of the phonetic structure of the speech signal, and defective production of speech. Investigations of auditory abilities have tended to confound auditory and linguistic deficits (Vellutino, 1979), and there remains considerable disagreement between those who wish to explain reading disability as a language disorder (Liberman & Shankweiler, 1979; Rees, 1974) and those who feel that nonverbal auditory perception deficits may contribute to reading disability (Wepman, 1975).

The strongest evidence regarding auditory discrimination deficits in poor readers comes from a study of Tallal (1980), who found a very high correlation of .81 between nonsense-word reading and the discrimination of rapidly changing nonverbal auditory stimuli in a group of children with reading disability. In a later study of Tallal and Stark (Tallal, personal communication, 1980), the auditory rate processing deficits were found in a reading disability group with severe impairment of receptive and expressive language, but not in a reading disability group without severe language impairment. These results suggest that some reading disabilities may be the result of severe language impairment that may, itself, be the result of an auditory processing deficit. It should be noted that this distinction was revealed only when Stark and Tallal departed from the single-syndrome paradigm.

PHONOLOGICAL PROCESSES

If reading disability does not involve a general impairment of auditory processing, a more specific deficit in the linguistic processing of speech could interfere with recoding from printed to spoken form. The earliest stage of linguistic processing at which a deficit might occur is in the abstraction of linguistic features from the speech signal, and the next stage would be the synthesis of the features into phonemes. Present evidence (Brandt & Rosen, 1980) suggests that children with reading disabilities do not have particular difficulty abstracting linguistic features and perceiving strings of phonemes, but there is considerable evidence that they have great difficulty abstracting or becoming consciously aware of phonemes when they are embedded in the continuous speech signal, an ability that may be essential for recoding from print to speech.

Liberman and Shankweiler (1979) base their explanation of reading disability and other reading problems on the speech perception theory of Liberman et al. (1967), which states that reading is parasitic upon speech perception because the speech perception system was uniquely evolved for the transmission of linguistic stimuli. Because speech perception is already linked to meaning, the beginning reader simply has to learn how to translate written language into spoken language. According to this theory, there must be a transfer from a visual to a phonological representation at some stage in the reading process. A likely stage in which phonological deficits could interfere with reading acquisition is the stage at which the phonological segments corresponding to printed letters are abstracted. Phonemes are complexly encoded in the sound stream in the sense that there is no discrete separation between phonemes and that the acoustic contours of certain phonemes may change almost completely in different syllabic contexts. Because of this encoded aspect of phonemic representation, children who have little or no difficulty understanding spoken language may be unable to abstract phonemes from spoken words, a step that is probably necessary for learning to read. The ability to abstract phonemes may require a particular form of metalinguistic awareness (Mattingly, 1980).

Liberman and Shankweiler (1979) and other investigators (cf. Fox & Routh, 1975, 1980) have demonstrated that the ability to segment spoken words into phonemes develops at about the time children learn to read, is highly correlated with reading achievement in beginning readers, and is deficient in children with reading disability. The possible causal role of phonemic segmentation deficits in reading disability must be seriously considered, because of the impressive evidence that the deficit exists and the importance of phonemic segmentation for phonological decoding during the early stages of reading acquisition. However, further research is needed, as there remains some question about the exact role of phonemic segmentation in reading acquisition, particularly in studies that employ more than one measure of segmentation and blending (Backman, 1980; Hardy, Stennett, & Smythe, 1973; Leong & Haines, 1978).

After sufficient experience, many words may be read as a whole, without letter-by-letter recoding into spoken form but, even in these cases, Liberman and Shankweiler would say that speech recoding must take place for words to be processed through the speech perception system. In several studies with their colleagues they have demonstrated that phonetic perception difficulties impair the short-term memory of poor readers. Thus, the work of Liberman and Shankweiler provides several different kinds of evidence that deficient phonological perception contributes to difficulty in speech recoding in children with reading disabilities.

OTHER LANGUAGE PROCESSES

Although most attention was paid to the phonological level of linguistic processing in reading disability during the 1970s, it is possible that subtle deficits at higher linguistic levels could play a role. The causal role of such deficits would be more difficult to demonstrate, because they could easily be secondary results of a reading disability. The next stages beyond phonological processing are morphological and morphophonemic processing, in which strings of phonemes are categorized as units of meaning or morphemes, and the phonemic structure of morphemes is sometimes varied in different combinations of morphemes (e.g., the phonetic structure of the morpheme *sign* changes when it appears in the word *signature*). Children with reading disabilities appear to have difficulty at the morphological and morphophonemic levels of spoken language (Vogel, 1977). However, there is less consistent indication of deficits at the higher levels of syntactic usage (Semel & Wiig, 1975; Vogel, 1975), perhaps because appropriate measures of syntactic ability are not available.

Reading disability might also be associated with a lack of metalinguistic interest or motivation. Mattingly (1980) speculated that there may be some children who virtually abandon further language acquisition once they have developed the basic abilities for spoken language. Such children could have difficulty learning to read because of imprecise knowlege of morphophonemic representations. These subtle linguistic disorders should be kept in mind as possible sources of reading disabilities, but seem more likely to be the result of the types of environmental deprivations that are ruled out by exclusionary definitions of reading disability.

Research by Denckla and Rudel (1976) suggests that reading disability could involve difficulty in the productive as well as the receptive aspect of spoken language. Children with reading disability were found to be slower than normal readers in naming pictures, colors, letters, and numbers, but did not differ from normal readers on a somewhat comparable task that did not require a spoken response (Rudel, Denckla, & Broman, 1978). Wolf (1981) also found naming to be more impaired in children with reading disability than would be predicted from other measures of linguistic ability, with a lack of normal relationship between word frequency and naming. These findings must be interpreted with caution, as Perfetti, Finger, and Hogaboam (1978) found no difference between normal and poor readers in naming colors, pictures, and numbers, using a different criterion of poor reading. However, they might indicate that phonological processing problems in reading disability result from a faulty internal model of articulation (Studdert-Kennedy, in press) that impairs both speech perception and speech production. If so, explanations of reading disability would have to make provision for an intrinsic connection between speech perception and speech production.

MEMORY

Memory plays an important role in most reading theories (cf. Just & Carpenter, 1980; Kleiman, 1975; Levy, 1978), and there have been many studies of the memory abilities of children with reading disability.

However, no one has been able to find unequivocal evidence that memory deficits operated as causal factors in reading disability. Torgeson (1978–1979) has succinctly described the difficulties with this type of research. Memory involves a number of processes such as encoding, retention, and retrieval, and it is difficult to determine exactly which process is responsible for memory deficits. Present evidence seems to suggest that apparent memory deficits in disabled readers are actually attributable to deficiencies in the initial encoding of the information to be remembered. The recall of both visual and auditory materials may be impaired by phonological coding deficiencies in poor readers (Shankweiler, Liberman, Mark, Fowler, & Fischer, 1979), and memory deficits were not apparent to children with reading disability when phonological recoding was prevented (Cermak, Goldberg, Cermak, & Drake, 1980). Even if memory deficits were demonstrated, they might not involve the type of memory used for reading, because no one has yet found a way to assess the memory mechanisms that are actually involved in reading (Torgeson, 1978–1979). Reservations about the interpretation of memory deficits also apply to the apparent deficits in the perception of temporal order that have been found in children with reading disability (Bakker & Schroots, 1981), as temporal order measures often involve the same operations as measures of serial memory (Vellutino, 1979). Shankweiler and Liberman (1978) concluded that both temporal order deficits and memory span deficits are symptoms of difficulties in phonetic coding.

BRAIN FUNCTION

The most frequent attempts to link cerebral dysfunction to reading disability in the 1970s involved the use of the dichotic listening and visual half-field behavioral techniques to assess hemispheric specialization for language and nonlanguage abilities. The usual hypothesis was that children with reading disability would have less-than-normal lateralization of language processes in the left hemisphere, as indicated by a smaller right-ear or right visual half-field advantage. No consistent differences in lateralization have been found (Kinsbourne & Hiscock, 1978; Leong, 1980; Satz, 1976). Whether this is because of the many methodological problems with the experimental techniques, because reading disability does not involve abnormal hemispheric specialization, or because the groups studied were heterogeneous with respect to reading disability is not clear at present.

There were also a number of attempts to assess more directly the hemispheric specialization of children with reading disability by electroencephalographic (EEG) techniques. The results are just as inconclusive as those obtained by the dichotic and visual half-field behavioral studies, and there are even greater methodological problems (Conners, 1978; Denckla, 1978; Hughes. 1978). However, there is considerable optimism regarding the solution of the methodological problems and the eventual determination of reliable indices of differential brain function. This is especially true for investigations involving visual and auditory evoked responses, when EEG activity is recorded in specific brain areas during the performances of precisely defined experimental tasks. Although the methodological problems are formidable (Picton, 1976), this technique could permit investigators to go well beyond the crude indices of hemispheric specialization provided by other techniques. Some very promising results are now being obtained (cf. Bakker, Licht, Kok, & Bouma, 1980).

Even newer methods that can be used for assessing brain functioning are being developed, and some are already providing information about brain functioning in subjects with reading disability. New EEG methods include the numerical taxonomy method of John et al. (1977) and the brain electrical activity mapping (BEAM) method of Duffy, Burchfield, and Lombroso (1979), both of which involve localized EEG recording during task performance. Computerized tomography (CAT) provides information about differences in the relative sizes of corresponding areas of the left and right hemispheres (Hier, LeMay, Rosenberger, & Perlo, 1978). Measures that record changes in blood flow in different regions of the brain during task performance, including the measurement of regional cerebral blood flow (rCBF) during the inhalation of xenon (cf. Gur & Reivitch, 1980) and positron emission tomography (PET) (Ter-Pogossian, Raichle, & Sobel, 1980) may also reveal important information.

Many technological problems will have to be overcome before reliable information is obtained about reading disability by these new methods of more directly assessing localized brain functions, but all are extremely promising. Evidence obtained thus far regarding reading disability by the methods discussed shows the predicted abnormalities of left-hemisphere structure (Hier et al., 1978) and function (Duffy et al., 1979). A recent neuroanatomical study of the brain of a disabled reader also reported structural abnormalities involving the left cerebral hemisphere (Galaburda & Kemper, 1979), and an investigation of reading acquisition in children who had had one hemisphere removed in infancy suggested that the left hemisphere is more important than the right for almost all aspects of reading acquisition (Dennis, Lovett, & Weigel-Crump, 1980). Continued study of brain–behavior relationships holds much promise for the further understanding of reading disability.

DEVELOPMENTAL FACTORS

Satz and his colleagues carried out longitudinal studies of the reading and nonreading abilities of a large population of boys from kindergarten through Grade 5 (Satz, Taylor, Friel, & Fletcher, 1978). Their work was based on the theory that reading disabilities result from a lag in the maturation of the brain that differentially delays the development of perceptual skills in young children and language skills in older children. Nonreading skills measured in kindergarten were highly predictive of later success or failure in reading, and both language and nonlanguage abilities were systematically related to reading acquisition. Despite some problems in the interpretation of the exact nature of the nonreading deficits, the results of this impressive body of research provide an invaluable source of information about developmental aspects of reading disabilities.

The results of Satz *et al.* (1978) did not support the hypothesis that disabled readers will overcome their developmental lags. The majority of children with severe reading problems showed no improvements by Grade 5. This agreed with other findings that children with reading disabilities continued to have reading problems and other problems associated with deficient academic achievement in later life (Peter & Spreen, 1979; Rourke & Orr, 1977; Trites & Fiedorowicz, 1976). It is important that further research on developmental aspects of reading be studied on the basis of systematic developmental models (Fletcher, 1980; Rourke, 1976).

GENETIC FACTORS

There was renewed research interest in the 1970s in the possibility that reading disability is inherited. A number of studies were carried out using modern genetic techniques. There was considerable evidence that at least some reading disabilities are inherited, but no specific hereditary mechanisms were found, and it was generally agreed that there might be different types of reading disabilities, each involving a different mode of inheritance (Childs, Finucci, & Preston, 1978; Finucci, 1978; Foch, DeFries, McLearn, & Singer, 1977; McLearn, 1978; Owen, 1978).

Multiple-Syndrome Reading Disability
Research of the 1970s

Evidence from single-syndrome research of the 1970s suggested that at least some cases of reading disabilities might involve deficiencies in auditory discrimination, phonological coding, morphophonemic knowledge, or naming, perhaps associated with abnormal left-hemisphere function and perhaps genetically transmitted. Evidence regarding possible deficits in intermodal integration, memory, and higher language abilities was doubtful or ambiguous. Multiple-syndrome research of the 1970s tended to produce more definite evidence, not only because the reading disability groupings were less heterogeneous, but also because patterns of deficit were determined for classification purposes. This provided a more definite connection between a particular form of impairment and a particular group of disabled readers than did single-syndrome studies in which one or two measures of perception, memory, or language were obtained from a heterogeneous group of disabled readers. We will discuss nonstatistical classifications of reading disabilities by Boder, Mattis *et al.*, Denckla, Myklebust, and Pirozzolo in this chapter, as well as some related work by others, and, in Chapter 5, will discuss research in which statistical methods were used to classify reading disabilities.

BODER

Boder (1971, 1973) classified 107 children with reading disability into different types by analyzing their reading and spelling errors. The largest proportion (67%) were classified as *dysphonetic*, because their reading and spelling errors showed little or no evidence of knowledge of letter–sound correspondences. They tended to read words as wholes and to substitute semantically similar that than phonetically similar words. A much smaller proportion of children (10%) were classified as *dyseidetic*, because their reading and spelling errors showed some knowledge of letter–sound correspondences but very little ability to read words as wholes or to "revisualize" the words while spelling them. A somewhat larger proportion (23%) with the most severe reading problems were classified as mixed *dysphonetic–dyseidetic*, because they had both types of reading–spelling problems.

Boder's research is noteworthy in basing classifications on the analysis of reading and spelling errors, with direct implications for remedial training. Her classifications were in accordance with earlier reports (Johnson & Myklebust, 1967; Kinsbourne & Warrington, 1963) that separated reading disabilities into visual–perceptual and auditory–linguistic subtypes on the basis of patterns of deficit in nonreading abilities.

MATTIS, FRENCH, AND RAPIN

Mattis, French, and Rapin (1975) classified 90% of a group of 82 children into three types of reading disabilities, including 38% with a language disorder, 37% with articulation–graphomotor dyscoordination, and 16% with a visual perception disorder. *Language disorders* involved deficiencies in naming, listening comprehension, oral sentence repetition, and speech sound discrimination; *articulation–graphomotor dyscoordination* involved deficiencies in sound blending and graphomotor ability; and *visual perception disorders* involved deficiencies in a variety of visual nonverbal abilities (PIQ, Raven's Progressive Matrices, Benton Visual Retention Test). In a cross-validation study of 163 children with reading disability, 63% were classified as language disorders, 10% as articulation–graphomotor dyscoordination, 5% as visual perception disorders, and 9% as mixed disorders (Mattis, 1978). In addition, 10% were tentatively classified as having a temporal sequencing disorder of a type described by Denckla (see next section), being deficient in sentence repetition, digit span, picture arrangement, and comprehension.

The reading disability subtypes of Mattis *et al.*, like those of most other investigators, were based on nonreading deficits. They found the same visual perception disorder as had all previous investigators, with the relatively low incidence reported by Boder, but they subdivided the auditory–linguistic disorder reported by previous investigators into as many as three subtypes. The articulation–graphomotor dyscoordination subtype seems to involve a fairly specific verbal–motor deficit, but the other two auditory–linguistic subtypes are not clearly differentiated. The language disorder subtype may be more of a word retrieval problem, and the sequencing subtype may be more of a phonological coding deficit. Both subtypes could have been interpreted as a memory deficit in a single-syndrome study that included both subtypes in its sample of reading disability and tested only serial memory.

DENCKLA

Denckla (1977; 1979) reported six types of reading disabilities, including a *global–mixed language disorder* with generally poor language abilities; an *articulation–graphomotor disorder* with poor articulation, pencil use, and fine motor coordination; an *anomic–repetition disorder* with poor naming (characterized by semantic errors), digit span, and sentence repetition; a *dysphonemic sequencing disorder* with poor digit span, sentence repetition, and naming (all characterized by phonemic substitutions or reversals), plus syntactic difficulty; a *verbal learning and memorization disorder*; and a rare *correlational disorder* in which reading was normal, but below expectations relative to intelligence. Denckla's subtypes, which seem to be based on clinical observation rather than on systematic research, are comparable in some respects to those of Mattis. Where there are differences, they could reflect differences in diagnostic testing procedures, in the method of interpretation, and in the populations studied (which might explain the absence of a visual perception subtype). The variety of auditory–linguistic deficits described by Denckla suggests that further investigations might reveal more or different subtypes.

MYKLEBUST

Myklebust (1978) added several more types of reading disabilities to the auditory and visual types originally described by Johnson and Myklebust (1967). *Inner-language dyslexia* or "word calling" is a deficiency of integrative–neurosensory learning that involves normal phoneme–grapheme encoding skills but poor comprehension; *auditory dyslexia* is a deficiency of intraneurosensory learning that involves difficulty in "cognitively auditorizing," symbolizing, and coding written language that does not include an impairment of spoken language comprehension; visual dyslexics cannot cognitively visualize written language properly because of *visual–verbal agnosia* (i.e., poor visualization or symbolization rather than a deficit in visual perception or discrimination per se); *intermodal* or *cross-modal dyslexia* is an interneurosensory learning deficit in which intraneurosensory auditory and visual learning can take place, but visual processes cannot be transformed into auditory processes. Intermodal dyslexia is somewhat mysteriously subdivided into *auditory-intermodal dyslexia*, in which the deficits are "principally due to auditory involvements" and *visual-intermodal dyslexia*, in which "the principal involvements are visual."

Although Myklebust gives few details about the exact characteristics of his dyslexias, perhaps because they are not derived from specific studies, they provide an interesting contrast to other typologies. His inner-language dyslexia, or what some writers (cf. Silberberg & Silberberg, 1971) would call *hyperlexia*, seems related to the language disorders described by Mattis and Denckla, but where phoneme–grapheme encoding difficulties are specifically ruled out. This suggests the value of specifying the exact pattern of reading skill deficit that characterizes each type of reading disability. It is also interesting that Myklebust is the only writer to postulate an intermodal reading disability. Unfortunately, he gives no details about the pattern of reading and nonreading deficit in intermodal dyslexia, and no information at all is given about the auditory and visual subtypes of intermodal dyslexia.

PIROZZOLO

Pirozzolo (1979) identified two types of reading disabilities, auditory–linguistic and visual–spatial. *Auditory–linguistic disorders* involved relatively low VIQ and phonological reading difficulties, plus other language deficits. *Visual–spatial disorders*, which were only one-fourth as frequent as auditory–linguistic disorders, involved relatively low PIQ, visual discrimination errors in reading, and other visual nonverbal deficits. The two reading disability types were compared to normal readers on three very carefully controlled visual tasks. The auditory–linguistic group made normal eye movements during reading and had a normal pattern of eye movement latencies, but was relatively deficient in word recognition in the right visual half-field, presumably as a result of deficient left-hemisphere processing of verbal material. Their reading should be impaired by word recognition rather than by eye movement problems. The visual–spatial group made inaccurate eye movements when going from the end of one line to the beginning of the next, and made very slow eye movements toward the right, but had a normal pattern of right half-field superiority in word recognition. These deficiencies were interpreted by Pirozzolo, not as primary eye movement disorders, but as a secondary result of a faulty visual–spatial information-processing system, where reading was impaired by visual–spatial inefficiency rather than by deficient language processing.

Pirozzolo's research is especially interesting with regard to the precise measurement of very well defined skills, and the direct application of findings to the reading process. He also recognized the possibility that his two reading disabilities might be further subdivided. It would be interesting to see how the poor readers from the Boder, Mattis, and Denckla subtypes would perform such precise visual tasks. A study by Obrzut (1979) did, in fact, provide this type of information. Children classified as dyseidetic, dysphonetic, and mixed dyseidetic–dysphonetic according to Boder's system were compared with normal readers in their recall of competing dichotic digits presented simultaneously to the two ears and competing bisensory digits presented simultaneously to the eyes and ears. Performance of the dyseidetic group was essentially normal, and that of the dysphonetic and mixed groups was significantly impaired on both tasks. These effects were extremely consistent, occurring for both slow and fast rates of digit presentation, for both visual and auditory digits in the bisensory task, and for both Grade 2 and Grade 4 subjects. Typical of the paradoxical findings in dichotic listening experiments, the dysphonetic group—the one group that should not have had the significant right-ear advantage indicative of normal left-hemisphere dominance for language—was the only group to show a significant right-ear advantage on the dichotic task, perhaps because of ceiling effects in the normal and dyseidetic groups. If, for heuristic purposes, we equate the Pirozzolo and Obrzut groups, the visual–spatial deficits of dyseidetics did not interfere with their visual perception of digits on the bisensory task; and the right visual half-field deficit of auditory–linguistics conflicted with the strong right-ear advantage of the dysphonetics, who did, however, show overall impairment in dichotic listening and in both visual and auditory perception on the bisensory task. Interesting and theoretically salient information could be gained from research that used experimental techniques such as those of Pirozzolo and Obrzut to define more precisely different types of reading disabilities.

OTHER RELEVANT RESEARCH

The descriptions of multiple types of reading disabilities in the 1970s did not result in anything approaching perfect agreement. All writers except Denckla included a visual type, but there was no consensus regarding auditory–linguistic types, with subdivisions ranging from the single type of Boder and Pirozzolo to the six types listed by Denckla. These differences might be resolved by the use of highly integrated batteries of objective tests that are directly related to the reading process (Torgeson, 1978–1979, 1979). Because such a technological improvement is probably not close at hand, it is well to mention other research of the 1970s that might shed further light on multiple types of reading disabilities.

Although Tallal and Stark did not classify children into different types of reading disabilities, the results of their research on developmental language disabilities (cf. Stark & Tallal, 1979; Tallal & Stark, 1981) could provide important information about reading disabilities. They compared children with reading disabilities plus severe language problems to children with reading disabilities unaccompanied by severe language deficits, and also to children with articulation disorders unaccompanied by severe reading and language problems, using a large battery of tests in which task dimensions such as visual–auditory–intermodal, verbal–nonverbal, discrimination–perception–memory–conceptualization, fast–slow, and single–repetitive–sequential were systematically varied. Although their analyses are not yet complete, the results seem to indicate a generalized (verbal–nonverbal, visual–auditory–intermodal) rate processing and serial memory deficit for the reading–language disability group, accompanied by deficits in auditory discrimination, repetitive movements, and finger localization. Rate processing and serial memory deficits of the group with reading disability alone seem to be restricted to visual and cross-modal verbal stimuli, and are accompanied by deficits in auditory verbal discrimination and serial memory. The group with articulation disorders seems to have only mild deficits in nonverbal visual and cross-modal rate processing and serial memory, plus deficits in motor control and coordination (Tallal, personal communication, 1980). Because the generalized deficit in processing rapidly changing stimuli could be the result of left-hemisphere dysfunction (Schwartz & Tallal, 1980), it seems possible that there may be a particular type of reading disability in which reading acquisition at the level of grapheme–phoneme correspondence is impaired by a specific form of cerebral dysfunction, thus finally establishing the type of brain–behavior relationship envisaged by so many investigators. Further analysis of the patterns of reading and nonreading deficits in children selected as having the most severe rate processing problems might provide more direct evidence.

The work of Tallal and Stark indicates the importance of determining how multiple types of reading disabilities interact with multiple types of language disorders. For example, Myklebust's inner-language dyslexia might involve language disorders that are not included in any of the three Tallal–Stark groups. Subtypes of language disorders have been studied for a number of years (Ajuriaguerra, 1966; Aram & Nation, 1975; Arndt, Shelton, Johnson, & Furr, 1977; Ingram, 1969). A study by Wolfus, Moscovitch, and Kinsbourne (1980) described two types of developmental language impairment, an expressive group, impaired in syntax production but not in syntax comprehension, semantic ability, or digit span; and an expressive–receptive group, with milder deficits in syntax production accompanied by deficits in semantic ability, digit span, and phonological discrimination. As these groups seem to correspond roughly to the Stark–Tallal language disorder and articulation disorder groups, it would have been most interesting to know their reading status. It is noteworthy that no group with purely receptive language impairment was found. Wolfus *et al.* suggest that such disorders might not exist in isolation. If so, models of speech perception that postulate an intrinsic connection between speech perception and speech production (cf. Liberman *et al.*, 1967; Stevens, 1975; Studdert-Kennedy, 1980) may be found most appropriate for explanations of reading disabilities.

Acquired Alexia and Reading Disability

Knowledge about reading problems secondary to cerebral dysfunction in brain-damaged adults was reviewed in the 1970s by Benson (1976), Hécaen and Kremin (1976), and Marshall and Newcombe (1977). Benson speculated that the anatomical areas involved in the different forms of alexias are important for the developing child, and that structural abnormalities in these areas could interfere with reading acquisition by producing different types of reading disturbances analogous to the acquired alexias. Particular interest was paid in the 1970s to "deep" alexia, where phonemic recoding skills are lost as a result of large left-hemisphere lesions and reading appears to take place through visual access by the right hemisphere (Coltheart, Patterson, & Marshall, 1980). Although children with severe phonemic recoding problems would probably not acquire a large enough sight vocabulary to be directly comparable to deep alexics, careful study of the orthographic mechanisms used by patients with deep alexia (Saffran, 1980) and of the different patterns of oral and of silent reading errors for certain word classes (Patterson, 1979) could provide important information about patterns of reading skill deficit that might occur in reading disabilities. Jorm (1979) has argued from a single-syndrome point of view that all reading disabilities are the result of genetically- based left-hemisphere dysfunction analogous to deep alexia, whereas Holmes (1978) and Ellis (1979) suggested that some reading disabilities may be more analogous to "surface" alexias, which involve only partial failures of grapheme–phoneme conversion.

Conclusion

Only a cursory survey of the factors that have contributed to changes in the concept of reading disability in the 1970s was possible in this chapter. The reader is referred elsewhere for more detailed critical reviews (Applebee, 1971; Benton, 1975, 1978; Benton & Pearl, 1978; Valtin, 1978–1979; Vellutino, 1979); theories of reading disabilities (Cummins & Das, 1977; Levinson, 1980; Richardson, 1974; Tomatis, 1967); theories of reading (Downing & Leong, 1981; Gough & Hillinger, 1980; Just & Carpenter, 1980; Kintsch & Van Dijk, 1978; Massaro, 1975; Resnick & Weaver, 1979; Seymour, 1973); interactive models of reading (Frederiksen, 1978; Kinchla & Wolf, 1977; Levy, 1980; Rumelhart, 1977; Stanovitch, 1980), theories of brain functioning (Grossberg, 1980), and comprehensive theories of brain–behavior relationship (Bindra, 1976). In the design, analysis, and interpretation of the research described in the following chapters, we attempted to profit as best we chould from the changing knowledge of the 1970s.

The Objective Classification of
Reading Disabilities

5

Applebee (1971) and the other writers previously cited seemed to be correct in asserting that reading disabilities should not be studied as a unitary disorder with a single cause. The growing number of efforts to find multiple types of reading disabilities attests to the potential value of this approach. However, one must also be aware of the confusion that could result from different typologies, which might defy all attempts to formulate a single comprehensive explanation of reading disabilities. Some potential confusion can be reduced by basing typologies on patterns of reading skill deficits rather than on more indirect cognitive and linguistic indicators, and by using objective classification methods. The studies of multiple types of reading disabilities reported in the previous chapters classified children into subtypes by subjective appraisal of individual profiles of deficits. A study by Doehring and Hoshko (1977a) represented the first attempt to classify children's reading disabilities into different types by an objective procedure. After a failure to arrive at satisfactory classifications by the usual subjective appraisal of individual test profiles (Doehring, 1976b), a paper by Aram and Nation (1975) suggested the possible usefulness of the Q technique of factor analysis. It was found to be entirely satisfactory, as described in the following sections.

Tests of Component Reading Skills

The first step in the research was to construct a set of tests that were intended to estimate component reading skills (Doehring, 1976a). The theoretical rationale for these tests closely agreed with that of LaBerge and

Samuels (1974), who hypothesized that component skills for reading letters, syllables, and words must be overlearned to the point of rapid automatic responding, to permit the reader to concentrate on higher-level comprehension and reasoning. To this end, test items were selected to be as simple as possible to permit evaluation of the reading skills in terms of speed of accurate responding. The majority of test items were individual letters, pronounceable nonsense syllables, and one-syllable words. They were presented by four different procedures: (a) visual matching to sample—choosing which of three printed choices exactly matched a printed sample; (b) auditory–visual matching to sample—choosing which of three printed choices corresponded to a spoken sample; (c) oral reading—reading aloud a relatively long series of printed items; and (d) visual scanning—scanning horizontal rows of printed items to find and underline a target stimulus interposed among other items of the same type. The oral reading task included phrases and sentences in addition to letters, syllables, and unrelated words to assess the operation of simple comprehension skills. There was also a test of sentence comprehension in which the child had to give the missing word in a series of simple printed sentences, and tests of the oral spelling of orally presented words, the written spelling of orally presented words, and the oral naming of orally spelled words. The main statistical classifications did not include the comprehension and spelling data because of high error scores by children with reading problems.

Reading Skills of Normal Readers

To obtain normative data for later comparison with the scores of disabled readers, the reading tests were first given to 150 normal prereaders and readers in kindergarten through Grade 11 (Doehring, 1976a). On all tests there was an increase in accuracy and a decrease in latency of response with increasing grades. This was interpreted as reflecting the acquisition of rapid, automatic reading skills that approached stable limits of learning in the higher grades. There was no suggestion of a hierarchical sequence in which a basic skill had to approach a stable level of learning before the acquisition of more advanced skill could begin (Gagné, 1970). All of the skills tested, including those involved in sentence comprehension, seemed to be developing at the same time, although at different rates. These results provided the normative data needed for the evaluation of the reading skill deficits of children with reading disabilities.

Patterns of Reading Skill Deficits in Children with Reading Problems

The reading tests were next given to two samples of children with reading problems: 34 children aged 8–17 years from a summer reading program, the majority of whom met the usual criteria of reading disabilities; and 31 children aged 8–12 who also had reading problems, but whose primary diagnosis was learning difficulty (21 children), childhood aphasia (5 children), and mental retardation (5 children). Their scores on the reading tests were expressed in terms of percentiles calculated from the scores of the normal readers, thus providing profiles of reading skill deficits in which all scores were on the same scale. The reading test profiles were classified into different types of reading disabilities by the Q technique of factor analysis. Because this is the main classification procedure that has been used in our research to date, it will now be described in fairly simple terms, with further technical details given in the next chapter.

The Q Technique of Factor Analysis

The Q technique provides an easily interpreted objective method for classifying reading skill deficit. It is based on product–moment correlations between the test profiles of pairs of individual subjects (Overall & Klett, 1972). The test profiles used for the main analyses consisted of 31 reading test scores, which made it difficult to classify them precisely in terms of subjective impressions of similarity. The correlation served as an objective index of similarity. The more similar the reading test profiles of any two subjects are, the higher will be the correlation between the subjects. To determine which children had similar profiles, the profile of every child was correlated with that of every other child, resulting in a complete matrix of intercorrelations.

If there were several different types of reading disabilities, the children classified together in a given type would have highly correlated reading test profiles, as in the first two profiles shown in Figure 5.1, and there would be low correlations between their profiles and those of children with other types of reading disabilities, as in the third profile shown in Figure 5.1. Note that the correlations depend on the relative rather than the absolute difference between scores on individual tests. If a unitary form of reading disability actually did exist, all of the test profiles would show the same pattern of scores and there would be high correlations between all profiles. Or if, as some clinicians assert, every child has a

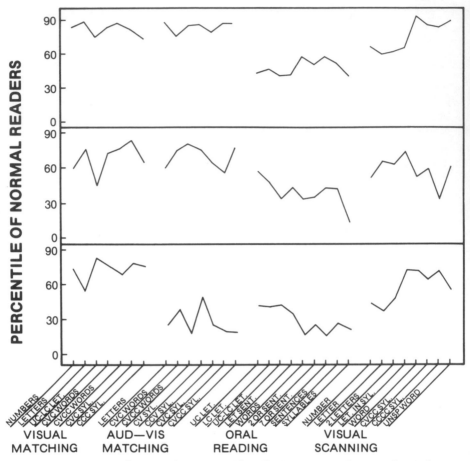

FIGURE 5.1. *Examples of reading test profiles. The first two profiles were classified into the same type of reading disability because they are highly correlated. The third profile was classified into a different type of reading disability because it is not highly correlated with the first two profiles.*

unique pattern of reading disability, each child would tend to have a different test profile, and there would be no consistent clusters of high positive correlations.

The advantage of this method of classifying reading disabilities is that it is completely objective. Once the subjects and the reading tests have been selected, the investigator's subjective biases cannot influence the outcome of the classification procedure. Any consistencies among the reading-skill profiles of children with reading problems will emerge from the correlational analysis. The characteristics of the types of reading disabilities thus identified are not abstract, and do not represent the misleading average of a set of heterogeneous reading skill profiles. The statistical classifications can be directly confirmed by examining the individual test profiles of the children classified into each type.

The only additional statistical complication is the computation of the Q factor analysis from the correlations between individual test profiles. As there are chance factors, in addition to the child's actual reading skill, that contribute to reading test scores, the correlations between test profiles will not fall into as neat and easily interpreted clusters as one would wish. Factor analysis compensates for this by enhancing the clustering of similar profiles and the separation of similar from dissimilar profiles by a statistical rotation of the matrix of correlations between individual profiles. This defines a set of factors, in which each factor can represent an "ideal" profile of scores for a given type of reading disability. The extent to which each subject's test profile can be classified into each type of reading disability is indicated by the factor loading, which reflects the correlation between the subject's reading test profile and the ideal profile for that factor, as defined by the factor analysis.

The profile of reading skill deficit that defines each type of reading disability is a factor score profile, which is an abstract representation of the common features of the profiles of children with high factor loadings on that factor. This is illustrated in Table 5.1, where hypothetical factor scores and factor loadings are given for factor analyses that might be derived from Q factor analysis. In Example 1, the Factor 1 profile defines a visual type of reading disability with low factor scores for visual skills and high factor scores for phonetic and semantic skills; and the Factor 2 profile defines a phonetic type of reading disability with low factor scores on phonetic skills and high factor scores on visual and semantic skills. The first three subjects in Example 1 have relatively high factor loadings on Factor 1 and low loadings on Factor 2, and would be classified as having a visual type of reading disability; and the last three subjects have relatively high loadings on Factor 2 and low loadings on Factor 1, and would be classified as having a phonetic type of reading disability. Example 2 shows the same factor scores as does Example 1, with the first two subjects having visual reading disability and the next two having phonetic reading disability. However, the last two subjects have relatively high factor loadings on both factors because they are deficient in both visual and phonetic skills, and would be classified as having mixed visual–phonetic reading disability. Example 3 shows what could happen if there were only a unitary form of reading disability. There would be a single factor with a single factor score profile, here characterized by phonetic deficiency, and all children with reading disability would have high loadings on that factor.

TABLE 5.1

Hypothetical Factor Score Profiles and Factor Loadings for Individual Subjects That Might Be Derived from Q Factor Analysis

Type of skill	Factor scores		Factor loadings		
	Factor 1	Factor 2	Subject	Factor 1	Factor 2
Example 1: Two independent types of reading disabilities					
Visual	Low	High	1	.67	.10
Phonetic	High	Low	2	.73	− .12
Semantic	High	High	3	.56	.01
			4	.11	.76
			5	.07	.49
			6	− .03	.63
Example 2: Two independent and one mixed type of reading disability					
Visual	Low	High	1	.65	.03
Phonetic	High	Low	2	.71	− .15
Semantic	High	High	3	− .08	.53
			4	.12	.66
			5	.45	.55
			6	.57	.48
Example 3: One unitary form of reading disability					
Visual	High		1	.86	
Phonetic	Low		2	.93	
Semantic	High		3	.78	
			4	.84	
			5	.90	
			6	.72	

Results of Statistical Classification

When the Q technique was applied to the reading test profiles of the two samples of children with reading problems, the results were interesting and interpretable (Doehring & Hoshko, 1977a). For the 34 children with primary reading problems, three different profiles of reading skill deficits were found. There were 12 children who had their highest loadings (above .50) on the first factor, 11 with their highest loadings on the second factor, and 8 with their highest loadings on the third factor, leaving only 3 without high loadings on any factor. The types of reading skill deficit defined by each factor are illustrated schematically in Table 5.2. Children with the Type O profile (oral reading problems) were poorest at oral word, phrase, and sentence reading, and near normal in

TABLE 5.2

Schematic Representation of the Types of Reading Disabilities Defined by Statistical Classification of Two Samples of Children with Reading Problems [a]

| | Type of reading disability | | | | |
| | O | A | S | V | |
Type of test	Oral reading	Intermodal association	Sequential relations	Visual perception	Unclassified
Visual matching					
Letters	Normal		Normal	Poor	
Words	Normal			Poor	
Syllables	Normal		Poor		
Auditory–visual matching					
Letters	Normal	Poor	Normal	Poor	
Words	Normal	Poor	Poor		
Syllables		Poor	Poor		
Oral reading					
Letters					
Words	Poor	Poor			
Syllables	Poor				
Visual scanning					
Letters		Normal			
Words		Normal			
Syllables					
Reading problem sample ($N = 34$)	$N = 12$	$N = 11$	$N = 8$	$N = 0$	$N = 3$
Mixed problem sample ($N = 31$)		$N = 8$ LD [b] $N = 3$ EMR	$N = 4$ LD $N = 1$ EMR $N = 3$ CA	$N = 5$ LD $N = 2$ CA	$N = 4$ LD $N = 1$ EMR

[a] Where there is no entry for a given type of test, performance was between normal and poor. The number of children classified into each type of reading disability is given for each of the two samples (from Doehring to Hoshko, 1977a).

[b] LD = Learning problem; EMR = Educable mental retardation; CA = Childhood aphasia.

the silent reading skills required by the matching-to-sample tasks; those with the Type A profile (intermodal association problems) were poorest in rapidly matching spoken and printed letters, words, and syllables; and those with the Type S profile (sequential relation problems) were notably poor in the visual and auditory–visual matching of words and syllables as compared to letters. These classifications were confirmed by independent estimates of remedial needs that were made by the teachers in the summer reading program. The Type A and Type S profiles were also found in the sample of children with mixed problems, as shown in Table 5.2, along with a Type V profile (visual perception problems) for a small number of children who were poor in rapid visual matching, with 5 children unclassified. All of the aphasic children and all but 1 of the mentally retarded children were classified into one of the three subtypes. In neither sample were there consistent differences in age, sex, or intelligence for any of the different types of reading disabilities. There was only a slight indication of mixed types of reading disabilities, with only 4 children in the two samples having factor loadings above .50 on more than one factor.

This first effort at statistical classification appeared to be successful. The types of reading disabilities that were identified were similar in some respects to those based on subjective classifications. The finding of a small number of visual perception problems agreed with almost all previous reports. Type O reading disability could be similar to the language disorders or the articulation–graphomotor disorders of Mattis *et al.* (1975), and Type S reading disability could involve the sequencing problems described by Mattis (1978). The fact that two of the four types of reading disabilities occurred in two quite different samples supported the findings of Mattis *et al.* (1975) and Mattis (1978) that the reading disabilities were not restricted to children who met the usual exclusionary criteria of dyslexia. However, the conclusions from correlational analyses must be drawn with extreme caution (Comrey, 1978). Different results might be obtained with different tests, different samples of children with reading problems, or different statistical classification procedures.

Results of Comprehension and Spelling Tests

The comprehension and the spelling tests, which were not used in the statistical classifications, also yielded interesting information. For normal readers, the speed of supplying missing words on the sentence comprehension test was more highly correlated with oral sentence reading than with oral word or with letter reading (Doehring & Hoshko, 1977b). For the children with reading problems, however, sentence comprehension was as highly correlated with oral word reading as with oral sentence reading, and examination of individual profiles revealed that sentence comprehension was almost always at the same percentile level as was oral word reading (Doehring, 1977). This suggested that the sentence comprehension of the children with reading problems was limited by their ability to read single words. It also demonstrated that the two samples did not contain the type of reading problem reported by other investigators (cf. Huttenlocher & Huttenlocher, 1973) where the basic decoding skills were relatively normal but comprehension was poor.

Because of high error rates, the·results of the spelling tests were difficult to interpret. Written spelling tended to be easiest for all children, with normal readers having the most difficulty in naming an orally spelled word and children with reading problems having the most difficulty in oral spelling (Doehring & Hoshko, 1977c).

Additional Statistical Classification

As a further check on the efficacy of the Q technique for classifying reading problems, several additional analyses were carried out (Doehring, Hoshko, & Bryans, 1979). To find out how the reading test profiles of normal readers would be statistically classified, the reading test scores of four different age groups, each of 30 normal readers, were statistically classified by the Q technique. Whereas the majority of children with reading problems had been classified into four distinct types, the normal readers were not classified into definite types. The youngest group, which one might expect to be most similar to the reading problem groups, had the most diverse classifications. When the reading test profiles of the sample of children with primary reading problems and an age-matched sample of normal readers were combined in a second analysis, the majority of the children with reading problems were classified into the same three types as before, but only a few of the normal readers were classified into one of the three previously specified types. These results demonstrated that the three types of reading disabilities were not simply exaggerations of normal individual differences in patterns of component reading skills, and that the characteristic profiles of reading skill deficits were not like those of beginning readers.

In an attempt to determine whether the same classifications would be obtained by a completely different statistical method, the reading test scores of the two samples of children with reading problems were analyzed by a set of cluster analysis techniques (Wishart, 1975). As the cluster analysis methods differ completely from the correlational method involved in factor analysis, a discovery of the same types of reading disabilities with cluster analysis would demonstrate that the original classifications were not merely artifacts of the statistical classification procedure. The same types of reading disabilities that had been defined by the Q technique were found once more when cluster analysis was used. All but five of the children from the reading problem sample and all but three of the children from the mixed problem sample were

classified into the same types as before by one of the cluster methods, Mc-
Quitty's method (Wishart, 1975). The reading disability classifications
seemed quite reliable, at least for the particular tests employed and the
samples of children tested.

Other Statistical Classification Studies

Subsequent to the first statistical classification study (Doehring &
Hoshko, 1977a), two other groups of investigators used statistical
classification techniques to classify children with reading problems on the
basis of neuropsychological test scores rather than on reading test scores.
Their studies illustrate the variety of possible approaches to statistical
classification.

Petrauskas and Rourke (1979) selected 133 children who met their
criteria for reading disabilities and 27 normal readers, all 7 and 8 years
old, from their case files. From 44 available neuropsychological measures, they selected 20 that were relatively independent of each other and
represented six different skill areas described by Reitan (1974). The 20
measures included 4 tactile, 2 sequencing, 2 motor, 4 visual–spatial, 5
auditory–verbal, and 3 abstract–conceptual tests. The total sample of
subjects was divided into two subsamples to assess the reliability of
reading disability types that might emerge from classification. The test
results for each subsample were analyzed by the Q Technique of factor
analysis, using essentially the same procedure as did Doehring and
Hoshko (1977a,b,c). Three reliable profiles of test scores were identified
in terms of factors common to the two samples; with 74 poor readers and
only 5 normal readers having high loadings on the factors. There were 40
subjects with very poor verbal fluency and sentence memory; 26 subjects
with extremely poor finger localization (finger agnosia), very poor performance on a test of immediate visual–spatial memory (Target Test),
and poor verbal fluency and sentence memory; and 13 subjects with extremely poor scores on a picture-matching concept formation test
(Matching Pictures Test), plus poor verbal fluency, sentence memory,
and immediate visual–spatial memory. All three types, then, were to
some extent deficient in verbal fluency and sentence memory, and two
types were deficient in visual–spatial memory. Two less reliable types
were also identified, one characterized by normal test performances by
normal readers, and the other containing 21 subjects with the same pattern of deficit as in Type 2 discussed earlier, but with no difficulty in
finger localization. Petrauskas and Rourke speculated that the Type 1
pattern was similar to that observed in adults with left temporal lobe le-

sions; that the Type 2 and perhaps the less reliable Type 5 deficits might reflect dysfunction of more posterior regions of the left hemisphere; and that the Type 3 deficit was similar to that of children and adults with lesions of the left frontal lobe. They also noted that VIQ was much lower than PIQ for Type 1 subjects, with much smaller VIQ deficits for the remaining types.

Fisk and Rourke (1979) analyzed the test performance of three groups of older children who were selected to be as deficient in spelling and arithmetic as in reading, including 100 children 9 and 10 years old, 100 children 11 and 12 years old, and 64 children 13 and 14 years old. From the same set of 44 measures used by Petrauskas and Rourke they selected 21 measures for Q-type factor analysis on the basis of low correlations between tests for the three groups. Unfortunately, the tests selected did not include the sentence memory, verbal fluency, and picture matching tests that helped to differentiate the types identified in the Petrauskas and Rourke study. They found two patterns of behavior deficit in all three age groups and one type common to the two older age groups. The first contained 52 children with extremely poor finger localization, the second contained 51 children with poor speech perception, and the third contained 39 children, 11–14 years old, with extremely poor finger tip writing scores. Verbal IQ was lower than PIQ in all three types, but the discrepancy was twice as great for the second type. Type 1 of Fisk and Rourke is similar to Type 2 of Petrauskas and Rourke in terms of poor finger localization; and Type 2 of Fisk and Rourke appears to be most similar to Type 1 of Petrauskas and Rourke in terms of poor verbal skills. Despite important differences in the test batteries and the selection criteria for subjects, the two studies of Rourke and his colleagues provided some consistent statistical classifications for two patterns of neuropsychological deficits associated with reading disability, one restricted to verbal skills and said to resemble the effects of adult temporal lobe lesions and the other including a difficulty in finger localization possibly indicative of more posterior left hemisphere lesions.

Satz and his colleagues used a different statistical method and selected poor readers by statistical classification. Taylor, Satz, and Friel (1979) found no difference in the pattern of reading and nonreading test performance of poor readers who met the usual criteria of reading disabilities as compared with those who did not. Therefore, Satz, Morris, and Darby (1979, as reported in Satz & Morris, 1980) used cluster analysis to select a sample of 89 poor readers from an unselected sample of 236 boys in the 10–12 age range on the basis of their reading, spelling, and arithmetic achievement scores on the Wide Range Achievement Test (WRAT). Further cluster analysis of the performance of the 89 poor readers on two

verbal measures (WISC, Similarities and Verbal Fluency) and two perceptual measures (visual–motor integration and recognition discrimination) resulted in five different clusters of test profiles whose members
were equally poor in reading achievement. The largest clusters involved
poor performance on both of the verbal measures by 27 Type 1 subjects
and poor performance on both of the perceptual measures by 23 Type 4
children. The 14 children of Type 2 had poor scores on only the Verbal
Fluency test; the 10 children of Type 3 performed poorly on all four tests;
and the 12 children of Type 5 performed well on all four tests. Types 1
and 3 were also deficient in listening vocabulary on the Peabody Picture
Vocabulary Test; and Types 1, 3, and 4 showed a higher proportion of
soft neurological signs than the remaining two types. Satz and Morris
(1980) called Type 1 a "global language impairment," Type 2, a "specific
naming disorder," Type 3, a "global language and perceptual impairment," Type 4, a "selective perceptual impairment," and Type 5, an
"unexpected learning disabled group." As in several previous studies,
more than one pattern of language deficit emerged in the Satz, Morris,
and Darby study, along with one pattern of visual perception deficit. The
emergence of a type with impairment on all four measures and another
type with no impairment on the four measures was perhaps indicative of
the need for a larger set of tests.

Besides reporting their own work, Satz and Morris (1980) made the
first detailed critique of studies that had used statistical techniques to
classify reading disabilities. After critically reviewing traditional unitary
concepts of reading disabilities and attempts to define subjectively different types of reading disabilities, Satz and Morris reviewed the Doehring and Hoshko (1977a) and the Petrauskas and Rourke (1979) studies.
They pointed out the difficulties inherent in Doehring & Hoshko's attempts to relate their subtypes to those of previous investigators, the
potential value of using more conventional statistics such as analysis of
variance to test for differences between subtypes on measures that were
not used in the statistical classifications, the lack of objective rules for
dealing with subjects who had high loadings on more than one factor, the
inability of correlational procedures such as the Q technique to classify
subjects on the basis of differences in absolute levels of scores, and problems related to the ratio of subjects to test in Q factor analysis. They
criticized Petrauskas and Rourke for preselecting subjects, for failing to
factor analyze their initial test battery, for only succeeding in classifying
half of their subjects, for failure to validate subtypes by external criteria,
and for basing inferences about brain abnormalities on preliminary un-
validated subtypes. Finally, they criticized themselves for using only a
single measure of reading achievement and too few neuropsychological

tests, for restricting their sample to children of the same age, sex, and race, with reading problems, for failure to use additional criterion measures such as teachers' observations, and for the lack of definite guidelines for applying cluster analysis to reading disability research.

Critical reviews like that of Satz and Morris are very useful at this early stage of research. Studies using either the Q technique or cluster methods can be criticized from a number of different points of view. A detailed discussion of these issues will be postponed until Chapter 12, but critical comments will be made in the intervening chapters whenever appropriate. From our point of view, one major weakness in the studies of both Rourke and Satz and their respective colleagues was the lack of a detailed assessment of patterns of reading skill deficits, as acknowledged by Satz and Morris. The use of reduced and slightly different test batteries in the two Rourke studies, apparently because of the misguided idea that the number of tests should be minimized in Q factor analysis, prevented a detailed comparison of the two studies, and the use of only four neuropsychological measures by Satz, Morris, and Darby greatly reduced their chances of finding stable, meaningful profiles of deficits. However, both sets of studies demonstrated the potential value of neuropsychological measures for statistically classifying reading disabilities. We incorporated such measures in the research plan described in the next chapter.

A Research Plan for Extending the Objective Definition of Reading Disability

6

The use of a statistical classification procedure to analyze differences in patterns of reading skill deficit provided a new scientific approach to the study of reading disability. The Q technique of factor analysis seemed appropriate for the statistical classification task, as it differentiated the reading skill profiles of disabled readers from those of normal readers, and its classifications agreed very well with those obtained by cluster analysis (Doehring, Hoshko, & Bryans, 1979). Preliminary interpretation of the four different types of reading skill deficits suggested that they involved difficulties in the formulation of the spoken equivalents of syllables and words, the intersensory association of letters and sounds, the perception of sequential relationships in pronounceable strings of letters, and the visual perception of letters, (Doehring & Hoshko, 1977a). These deficiencies of basic reading skills seemed to prevent the children from using higher-level comprehension strategies in reading, limiting them to a word-by-word reconstruction of the grammar and meaning of printed sentences (Doehring, 1977). However, achievement of objective descriptions of different types of reading disabilities by an analysis of reading performance provided little information about the origin of the disabilities.

After some reflection (see Doehring, 1976b), it became apparent that Doehring's (1968) original research strategy of evaluating a wide variety of nonreading skills should not have been completely abandoned. In the research that will be described in the following chapters, we decided to modify the research strategy once more by testing both reading and nonreading skills. Patel (1977) assembled a battery of language tests on the basis of his analyses of neurolinguistic development in children. Trites and Fiedorowicz (Trites & Fiedorowicz, 1976; Fiedorowicz, 1977; Trites, 1977, 1979) were experienced in using a clinical neuropsychological test battery to obtain information about patterns of deficits in children with a variety of problems, including reading disabilities. The use of the language tests and neuropsychology tests enabled us to evaluate nonreading abilities relevant to the patterns of reading skill deficits defined by reading tests.

In selecting the language tests, Patel was faced with the same problems that had hampered the selection of reading tests, the lack of a comprehensive theory of language development and the lack of a standard set of tests for systematically assessing developing language abilities. The tests that were selected were intended to be sensitive to the psycholinguistic processes that usually develop around the age of 7, and we hoped that the results obtained with this battery would indicate how the battery could be improved for future applications. The use of a battery of neuropsychological tests to evaluate nonreading abilities provided continuity with previous neuropsychological research on reading disability (cf. Doehring, 1968; Rourke, 1978). The neuropsychology battery, which had been developed by Trites (1977), included measures of many different language and nonlanguage abilities, as obtained from standardized tests of intelligence, perception, memory, motor skills, sensory abilities, and general cognitive functioning. The tests should be sensitive to any marked behaviorial deficiencies that could interact with different types of reading disabilities. In addition, clinical interpretation of patterns of deficits on the neuropsychological tests should provide suggestions regarding possible cerebral dysfunction associated with reading disabilities. Further details regarding the neuropsychological test battery are given in Chapter 9.

By combining a research strategy for measuring multiple nonreading skills (Doehring, 1968) with a strategy for measuring multiple reading skills (Doehring & Hoshko, 1977a), we moved even further away from the traditional research paradigm of studying one type of nonreading skill in disabled readers selected by one measure of reading ability. The new strategy did not simply consist of adding more tests, but of combining two one-dimensional approaches into a two-dimensional approach in which an attempt was made to determine how patterns of reading skill deficits interact with patterns of cognitive and linguistic deficits in different types of reading disabilities. If successful, we should be in a much better position to make inferences about the types of cerebral dysfunctions that might be involved in the reading disabilities.

A research design that involves analysis of the interaction of linguistic and neuropsychological deficits with reading skill deficits is entirely appropriate to the new theoretical analyses of reading, language, and cognition that emphasize the complex organization of these abilities. The previous research designs could only lead to the discovery of unitary forms of reading disabilities, but the new approach allows for the eventual description of the different interactions of reading and nonreading deficits that actually occur in poor readers. Some or all kinds of reading disabilities might be directly related to specific types of nonreading deficits. These deficits might in turn be directly associated with either inherited or acquired neurological deficiencies. If some types of reading disabilities were not found to be directly related to specific cognitive or language deficits and thence to neurological dysfunctions, further research might reveal the effect of a particular type of classroom or remedial teaching, or an interaction between a particular cognitive–linguistic deficit and a particular teaching method (Cronbach & Snow, 1977).

Thus, the new research approach opened the way for discovering the variety of different types of reading problems that actually exist, by providing a broader and more objective perspective than have previous approaches. Considering the provisional nature of the theories on which our tests were based, we could not expect to arrive at a final answer about the nature of reading disabilities. However, a full-scale study using this new approach should indicate the next steps to be taken.

Plan of the Research

The method used in the study to be described here was necessarily more elaborate than that used in the first statistical classification studies. A new sample of reading problems was carefully selected from referrals to a neuropsychology clinic. As the sample included a few young adults, the term subjects will be used to describe members of the sample. The same reading tests were given, and the results for the total sample and for a variety of subsamples were analyzed by the Q technique of factor analysis to ascertain the stability of the types of reading disabilities that were identified. We then analyzed the results of the language tests and neuropsychological tests by several different methods, including the Q technique of factor analysis, to determine the interaction of reading and nonreading deficits. To simplify the reader's task as much as possible, we will describe the subjects, the reading tests, and the statistical classification procedure, and then go directly into a detailed consideration of the reading test results, deferring a description of the language and neuropsychological tests until just before their results are to be discussed.

Selection of Subjects

The traditional experimental design, in which the average performance of dyslexics was compared with that of normal readers, required a careful definition of the reading disability group to ensure that differences between the poor and normal readers were not attributable to factors such as sensory disorders, low intelligence, or environmental deprivation. When using an experimental design based on the statistical classification of test profiles, it is not essential that such rigid selection criteria be used. Subjects with similar profiles of reading skill deficits must be classified together, and the resulting groupings can be examined to determine the relative severity of reading problems, the incidence of low intelligence, and so on. However, in this first study of the interaction of reading and nonreading deficits, it seemed best to select a sample that conformed to the usual criteria of reading disabilities.

With these considerations in mind, a sample was selected by Trites and Fiedorowicz from children and young adults who had been referred by pediatricians, neurologists, family physicians, or school psychologists to the Neuropsychology Clinic of the Royal Ottawa Hospital for difficulties in school. Each subject had been given a complete 6–8-hour neuropsychological battery that included a variety of tests of intellectual and language abilities, concept formation, visual perception, attention, memory, academic achievement, personality, social and behavior assessments, and sensory and motor skills. A detailed developmental, social, academic, and medical history was also obtained from interviews with parents, rating scales from teachers, hospital files, and reports from professionals. On the basis of these detailed assessments, subjects were selected for inclusion in the present study whose reading, language, and cognitive problems fell within the range of deficits suitable for purposes of statistical classification. Subjects were selected to include a representative sample of the types of reading problems that are usually referred for clinical neuropsychological evaluation. A small number of siblings of children who had been referred for reading problems were also tested, to obtain some idea about possible genetic factors.

The majority of subjects selected were delayed by at least 2 years in some aspect of standardized reading achievement and were within the normal range of intelligence. The sample did not include children with sensory or motor deficiencies, gross neurological deficits, severe emotional problems, marked environmental handicaps, or problems associated with second language learning. Children younger than 8 years were excluded, but the age range was not otherwise restricted. Any consistent age effects should be readily apparent because subjects of different ages would be classified into different subtypes. When more than one child from the same family was tested, the largest family group included 10-year-old female triplets (two identical and one fraternal) and two brothers of 11 and 14. The remaining six family groups consisted of two children each: a sister of 10 and a brother of 12, two brothers of 12 and 15, a brother of 8 and a sister of 10, two brothers of 10 and 15, a brother of 10 and a sister of 11, and two brothers of 11 and 13.

Table 6.1 shows the ages and sexes of the 88 subjects who were selected. The majority were from 8 to 14 years old, with 3 older than 20. As would be expected from all previous research, there were more males than females.

Intelligence was measured by the original or the revised version of the Wechsler Intelligence Scale for Children (WISC) (Wechsler, 1955; 1974), or the Wechsler Adult Intelligence Scale (WAIS) (Wechsler, 1949), which yield estimates of VIQ and PIQ. Although we did not restrict the variability of cognitive and linguistic skills by requiring that both VIQ and PIQ should be at least in the average range of 90 to 110, only 4 subjects had both the VIQ and PIQ below 90. The VIQ and PIQ scores of these 4 subjects were 82/77, 73/88, 78/89, and 62/82, respectively. The distributions of VIQ and PIQ for the 88 subjects are shown in Table 6.2. The majority of scores were within the range of 90–110. As in most samples of reading problems, the PIQ tended to be higher than the VIQ. There were more VIQs below 90 and more PIQs above 110. This trend is also shown by the distribution of differences between VIQ and PIQ. Verbal IQ was higher than PIQ in only 18 subjects, whereas PIQ was higher than VIQ in 68 subjects, with 41 of the subjects having a PIQ 10 or more points higher than VIQ.

TABLE 6.1
Age and Sex Distributions of the Eighty-Eight Subjects

Age	Male	Female	Total
8	5	2	7
9	9	0	9
10	8	7	15
11	9	3	12
12	7	3	10
13	14	0	14
14	9	2	11
15	3	1	4
16	2	0	2
17	1	0	1
20–27	3	0	3

TABLE 0.2
*Distributions of Verbal (VIQ) and Performance (PIQ) Intelligence Quotients,
and of Differences between VIQ and PIQ*

IQ range	Number of subjects within range		Range of VIQ–PIQ differences	Number of subjects within range	
	VIQ	PIQ		VIQ higher	PIQ higher
60–69	3		No difference	2	
70–79	8	2	1–10	14	27
80–89	12	7	11–20	2	25
90–99	29	23	21–30	2	14
100–109	29	27	31–40		2
110–119	6	18			
120–129	1	9			
130–139		2			

Conventional estimates of reading achievement were obtained from two standardized reading tests. The WRAT (Jastak & Jastak, 1965) provided an estimate of grade level for the oral reading of single words from prekindergarten to Grade 19, as well as grade-level estimates of written spelling and arithmetic achievement for the same grade range. The Durrell Analysis of Reading Difficulty (Durrell, 1955) gave a more detailed assessment of reading skills, but with norms extending only from Grades 1 through 6. The parts of the Durrell that were given included oral reading, silent reading, listening comprehension, word recognition, and word analysis. Each yields a grade-level score. The oral and silent reading scores are based on reading time and on comprehension questions for graded reading passages. The listening comprehension score is based on questions following graded passages read by the examiner. The word recognition score is the number of briefly presented words that are correctly read aloud, and the word analysis score is the number of words correctly pronounced when presented with no time limit.

For standardized reading tests, there was the usual finding (cf. Trites & Fiedorowicz, 1976) of an increasing amount of reading retardation with increasing age. On the WRAT, 62 of the subjects were 2 or more years below their expected grade level in oral word reading, 17 were 1–2 years below, and the remainder were less than 1 year below the expected level. The arithmetic grade levels tended to be about the same as the reading grade levels, but the spelling of the older subjects tended to be considerably worse than their reading. As a group, the 88 subjects were 4 years below expected grade level on the Durrell oral and silent reading tests and 3 years below on the listening comprehension, word recognition, and word analysis tests. Both oral and silent reading tended to be lower than the reading level on the WRAT even when eight subjects who scored at the sixth-grade test ceiling on one or both tests were excluded. There were 15 subjects who scored at the test ceiling on one or more of the three remaining Durrell tests. Otherwise, the grade levels for word recognition and word analysis tended to be about the same as reading levels on the WRAT, whereas listening comprehension tended to be somewhat better in younger subjects and somewhat poorer in older subjects. None of the subjects achieved the expected grade level for their age on all five of the standardized achievement reading measures on the WRAT and the Durrell.

In addition to the extensive individual neuropsychological assessment, extensive background information was obtained about birth history, developmental milestones, medical and neurological history, social and emotional development, family relations, and school performance. The family background information revealed that the majority of subjects came from middle to upper middle-class families, with about half of the parents working in blue-collar and clerical jobs and the other half in white-collar and professional positions. Among the mothers, 69 were high school graduates and 20 had postsecondary education; 61 of the fathers had high school graduation, and 22 had postsecondary education. There was a family history of reading disability in 45 cases and no reported history in 43. This probably underestimated the actual incidence of family history, as some parents seemed unwilling to admit problems in other family members.

A review of birth and developmental factors indicated that, for 28 subjects, a surprisingly high number, there was a history of pregnancy complications, including spotting, severe nausea requiring medication, exposure of the mother to measles, and so on. Sixty-seven subjects were reported as full term, with 14 premature. A relatively high rate of delivery complications were reported in 44 cases; the types of complications ranged from anoxia to the necessity for a Caesarean section. Developmental problems were reported for a number of subjects. Although only one subject was reported as delayed in walking, there was a history of delayed talking in 26, whereas for 51, the parents reported no developmental problems. Speech problems, such as articulation difficulties, were reported for 34 subjects, with the parents reporting no problems in 49 cases.

The review of the family, birth, and developmental history suggested that this group of subjects was an "at risk" population.

The Reading Tests

There were 39 tests of reading-related skills, of which 31 were intended to sample basic skills necessary for reading, and were used for the primary classification of reading disability. On these 31 tests, the subject had to match, orally read, or scan numbers, letters, syllables, and words, with some of the words being presented in the form of phrases or sentences. The other 8 tests, which involved skills directly related to the basic reading skills, involved the naming or visual scanning of nonverbal stimuli, the comprehension of sentences, and the spelling of single words. All test materials were relatively simple, to permit measurement in terms of the speed of accurate responding as much as possible. The tests were designed to obtain more specific information about the reading skills of persons with reading disability, not to be a complete survey of reading skills. With the possible exception of the spelling tests, the present set of tests proved to be adequate for statistical classification. Letter-, syllable-, and word-reading skills were assessed by more than one test within the same task, and also by more than one task. This permitted us to base conclusions about a particular skill on more than a single measure.

The 31 tests of basic reading skills included 7 visual matching-to-sample tests, 7 auditory–visual matching-to-sample tests, 9 oral reading tests, and 8 visual scanning tests. They are described in what follows. Additional details, including normative data, are given elsewhere (Doehring, 1976a).

VISUAL MATCHING–TO–SAMPLE TESTS

The visual matching-to-sample tests provided measures of silent reading skill in which transformation to speech is not essential. The stimulus material was presented in the windows of a viewing–response device. A printed number, letter, syllable, or word was displayed as the sample, along with three printed choices, one of which was identical to the sample. The subject had to press a window containing the correct choice as rapidly as possible. The speed and accuracy of the matching responses were recorded automatically. There were seven tests, each given in two sets of nine trials each. Table 6.3 shows an example of each test. The first three tests assessed skills for identifying single numbers and letters, followed by two tests for recognizing high-frequency words with regular pronunciations, one for identifying simple syllables with regular pronunciations, and one for identifying unpronounceable strings of consonants. Incorrect choices differed from correct choices by only one letter.

TABLE 6.3
Examples of Trials from Each of the Visual Matching Tests

Test		Sample	Choices		
Numbers	NU	8	8	1	6
Upper-case letters	LE	K	L	K	R
Upper and lower-case letters	UL	D	p	b	d
Familiar CVC [a] words	W3	did	lid	did	dip
Familiar CVCC words	W4	long	lost	song	long
CVC syllables	S3	sig	sig	tig	sim
CCC letter strings	CC	kzb	kzd	kzb	hzb

[a] C = consonant; V = vowel.

AUDITORY–VISUAL MATCHING-TO-SAMPLE TESTS

The auditory–visual matching-to-sample tests assessed silent reading skills for associating spoken and printed letters, syllables, and words. The task was the same as visual matching to sample, except that a tape-recorded sample was spoken through earphones rather than presented visually, and the subject had to press the window containing the printed choice that matched the spoken sample. The seven auditory–visual matching tests were given in two sets of nine trials each. Examples are shown in Table 6.4. They were constructed along the same lines as the visual matching tests, with one test of the skill for associating printed letters and spoken letter names, two for associating spoken and printed words, and four for associating spoken and printed syllables. The words and syllables were simple, with regular pronounciations, and the incorrect choices differed by only one letter from the sample.

ORAL READING TESTS

The oral reading tests assessed skills for identifying a series of printed items and formulating their spoken equivalents. On these tests, the sub-

TABLE 6.4
Examples of Trials from Each of the Auditory–Visual Matching Tests

Test		Auditory sample	Visual choices		
Letters	LE	d	D	G	L
Familiar CVC words	W3	set	met	set	sew
Familiar CVCC words	W4	find	mind	film	find
CV syllables	S2	pe	pe	pu	te
CCV syllables	CV	cla	cra	cla	pla
CVC syllables	S3	pim	bim	pif	pim
CVCC syllables	S4	sild	sild	rild	silp

ject had to read letters, words, or syllables aloud as rapidly and accurately as possible. Some of the test items involved phrases or sentences to provide an estimate of the ability to use syntactic and semantic knowledge to increase the accuracy and speed of oral reading. Table 6.5 gives examples of the nine oral reading tests. The four tests of oral letter naming were given in two sets of 26 letters each. The four tests of word reading were given in two sets containing 34 syllables each, with one test consisting of random high-frequency words, two involving meaningful phrases, and one involving meaningful sentences from children's books. The syllable test was also given in two sets of 34 syllables, and required skill in decoding common three-and four-letter spelling patterns.

VISUAL SCANNING TESTS

The visual scanning task provided another measure of simple silent reading skills, but the subject had to make a series of responses somewhat like the series of oral reading responses in contrast to the single responses required by the visual and auditory–visual matching tasks. It was a modification of an underlining test that had proven to be quite useful in previous studies of reading disabilities (Doehring, 1968; Rourke, 1975). Table 6.6 gives examples of the eight visual scanning tests, each of which was presented on a single sheet of paper with the target item printed above 18 typewritten lines containing the target items mixed with similar items. The four tests for identifying letters and numbers were followed by tests for identifying a familiar word and a simple syllable, and for identifying a string of consonants and an unspaced word.

TABLE 6.5
Examples of Stimuli from the Oral Reading Tests

Test		Example
Upper-case letters	UC	*OL ESMP ZBJY H CVAO RFDX GNS KITU*
Lower-case letters	LC	*uj gybm vopq i aslh xdns cft ekzr*
Upper and lower-case letters	UL	*SF Mzlh OndS p jXUI rEky bGt CvUA*
Letters in sentences	LS	*He must have a roof over his head*
Random words	WR	*the ago over end made for year*
Two-word phrases	2W	*Lived by the sky by the trees*
Seven-word phrases	7W	*On a rock and wiped his head to*
Sentences	WS	*For some reason it always seems to*
Nonsense syllables	SY	*saro dalt nax vio feng pob jub*

TABLE 6.6
Examples of Stimuli from Each of the Visual
Scanning Tests, with Target Items Underlined

Test		Examples
Number	NU	1 8 9 4̲ 2 7 6 4̲ 3 5
Letter	LE	v u s p f t s e s u c d
Two letters	2L	h g i̅ b t d m e̅ m t o b
Letter in syllable	LS	geyg̲ f̅inj hbjs pw̅zl vppi raie̲
Word	WD	post tops stop spot̲ sotp psot
CVCC syllable	SY	aprn apnr parn narp̲ aprn rapn
CCCC letter string	CC	sfmb bfms sbmf f̅sbm̲ fmbs
Unspaced word	UW	t o p s s t o p s p o t̲ s

Additional Tests

There were eight additional tests of reading-related skills. A color naming (CO) and picture naming (PI) test were given just prior to, and in the same manner as, the oral reading tests, in two sets of 26 stimuli each, arranged in horizontal rows, with the subject required to name the consecutive stimuli as rapidly and accurately as possible. The colors were word-sized patches of green, blue, gray, black, brown, yellow, and red; the pictures were word-sized line drawings of a car, dog, frog, turtle, duck, deer, owl, rabbit, snake, horse, pig, bat, and fish, all presented in random sequences. Two tests in which the subject had to underline a consecutive series of rectangles (RE) and a letter-sized Greek cross (FI) interpersed among other geometric figures (star, circle, crescent, etc.) were given just prior to, and in the same manner as, the visual scanning tests, with stimuli printed in horizontal rows. Further details and normative data for these four tests are given in Doehring (1976a). The sentence comprehension test (SC) described in Doehring and Hoshko (1977b) was also given, in which the subject had to say the missing word in the 16 sentences listed in Table 6.7. The three remaining tests of reading-related skills were the spelling tests described in Doehring and Hoshko (1977c), which required the subject to spell eight words (*draw, shout, circle, correct, back, train, heaven, believe*) aloud (S1), write eight words (*ball, floor, ending, scratch, feed, child, avenue, feature*) to dictation (S2), and give the spoken word (S3) for eight orally spelled words (*make, reach, result, society, will, light, advice, explain*). Both speed and accuracy were recorded for all eight of the additional tests.

TABLE 6.7
*Sentences from the Comprehension Test
in Order of Presentation, with Correct
Responses in Parentheses*

(Once) upon a time, a princess lived in a magic land.
Wash your face (and) hands before supper.
These apples are too green (to) eat.
I worked hard (all, to, every, that, one, each) day.
The (dog, cat, boy, man) chased the cat up the tree.
Mother asked me to buy a (loaf, bag) of bread at the store.
The story had a happy (ending, end).
John's pen ran out of (ink, food).
A wind (from, in, of, to) the north froze the pond.
I dropped my fork (on, onto, upon) the floor.
No, dinner's not ready (yet, now, dear).
They lived happily ever (after).
I put (salt, gravy) and pepper on my meat.
Blow out the (candles) on your birthday cake.
Our hen laid an (egg).
Look both ways before you cross the (street, road).

Administration and Scoring of the Reading Tests

The tests of reading-related skills were given in a single session of about 4 hours, with the tests of language-related skills and the standardized reading achievement tests, in the following order: WRAT, language tests, oral reading and naming tests, spelling tests, sentence comprehension test, Durrell Test, visual scanning tests, visual matching-to-sample tests, and auditory–visual matching-to-sample tests. Within each task, the tests were always given in the same order (see Doehring, 1976a; Doehring & Hoshko, 1977b,c).

The 39 tests of reading-related skills were scored in terms of both speed and accuracy to estimate the subject's relative progress in overlearning a skill to the point of rapid, automatic response (LaBerge & Samuels, 1974). Speed and accuracy were represented on a single scale for the purposes of statistical classification and the plotting of profiles. To accomplish this, subjects who were highly accurate were scored in terms of their speed of response and the less accurate subjects were scored in terms of the number of errors. The standards of accuracy, as determined by the probability of correct guessing and the actual performance of normal readers of different ages, were 6 or fewer errors on the 18 trials of the visual and auditory–visual matching tests, 7 or fewer errors on the 52 orally read letters, 14 or fewer errors on the 68 orally read words and syllables, 3 or fewer errors on the 52 color-naming and picture-naming items, 7 or fewer errors on the comprehension questions, and 3 or fewer errors on the 8 words of each spelling test. No error criterion was needed for the visual scanning tests, as accuracy was always very high. Speed of response was used as the response measure in all cases in which the accuracy standard was met. The measure of speed for the visual and auditory–visual matching, the comprehension, and the spelling tests was the median response latency over all trials for a given test, with error trials always counted as the longest latencies. For the oral reading and visual scanning tests, the measure of speed was average time per item as measures of latency were not obtained for individual items.

A single distribution of error and latency scores was made for each test, using the scores of 10 normal readers each, in Grades 1, 1.5, 2., 2.5, 3, 4, 6, 8, and 10 (Doehring, 1976a). Each distribution extended from the shortest latency to the largest number of errors. A percentile scale was then calculated for each test, with the highest percentile assigned to the most rapid response and the lowest percentile to the largest number of errors. All scores of the present sample of subjects were expressed in terms of these percentile scales. On any test, if the subject exceeded the maximum errors made by the sample of normal readers, a percentile score of 0 was assigned. This procedure enabled us to place all reading test scores on the same scale, and to score the tests in terms of grade equivalents for normal readers.

Statistical Classification Methods

We will now give further details about the statistical classification methods. As in the previous study, the primary method of statistical classification was the Q technique of factor analysis. The rationale for this technique and its advantages over other classification methods have been discussed at length by Overall and Klett (1972). All statistical classification methods use some index of similarity between test profiles. The index for one subject can be conceived of as a single point in a multi-dimensional space, with the number of dimensions corresponding to the number of tests. The points derived from subjects with similar profiles (see Figure 5.1) are grouped together in this space. The measures of similarity used in the Q technique are called vector–product indices. They are derived from the correlations between profiles. (Cluster analysis methods use different measures of similarity called distance–function indices, which are derived from differences between corresponding scores in test profiles.)

The vector–product indices are obtained through factor analysis, a statistical procedure that can be applied whenever a series of tests has been presented to a group of subjects. Factor analysis by the R technique assesses the similarity between tests, and factor analysis by the Q technique assesses the similarity between subjects. The R technique classifies tests on the basis of the correlations between tests for a particular group of subjects. The degree of similarity between tests is indicated by the relative size of their loadings on factors that are defined by the analysis. Tests with high loadings on the same factor have something in common, and the factor is given a name to denote this common characteristic. It is possible for a test to have high loadings on more than one factor, suggesting that the test measures more than one type of ability.

The Q technique of factor analysis is just the opposite of the R technique. It classifies subjects in terms of the correlations between subjects for a particular series of tests (see Table 5.1). The similarity among profiles of test scores is defined in terms of factors. The size of the factor loading indicates the degree to which a particular subject's pattern of test results resembles the factor score profile defined by the factor. In the present study, a high loading on more than one factor suggested that the subject had a mixed type of reading disability. Thus, the correlations among subjects for a particular group of tests provide the basis for factor analysis by the Q technique in the same way that the correlations among tests for a particular group of subjects provide the basis for factor analysis by the R technique.

The profiles of reading skill deficit derived from Q factor analysis provide objective definitions of different types of reading disabilities. The profiles are calculated in two different ways:

1. For each of the factors that define the reading disabilities, a factor score is calculated for each reading test. A high factor score for a given test on a given factor means that subjects with high loadings on that factor had relatively high scores on that test, and a low factor score for a given test indicates that the subjects had relatively low scores on that test. Reading disability profiles that are plotted in terms of factor scores represent a similarity index at the center of the cluster of points in multidimensional space (i.e., the most representative profile for that type of reading disability).

2. A more concrete way of representing the reading disability profiles is to plot the average grade equivalent scores of subjects with high loadings on the factors that define the types of reading disabilities. These profiles give a direct indication of both the pattern and the relative severity of the reading skill deficit for each type of reading disability. In the previous study (Doehring & Hoshko, 1977a), both methods yielded the

same general profiles of reading disabilities, and both methods were used once more in the present study.

Individual profiles of the subjects with high loadings on each factor provide the most direct representation of the reading disabilities. The similarity of the profiles objectively classified into each type of reading disability can be confirmed by direct inspection. The individual profiles will be presented in tabular form here, thus providing three different ways of characterizing the objectively defined reading disabilities.

Statistical classification is preferable for scientific purposes to subjective classification methods such as traditional clinical diagnosis, because it is completely objective and can be precisely quantified. However, the results obtained with the Q techniques and other statistical classification methods should be interpreted with caution. The reading disabilities defined by these techniques can vary as a function of the number and types of tests used and the number and types of subjects tested. For example, if a given reading skill is sampled by only one test, and other reading skills are sampled by several tests each, a deficiency of the first skill might not be revealed by statistical classification; or if only two or three subjects with a particular type of reading disability were included in a sample, that type of reading disability might not be revealed by statistical classification. These restrictions also apply, for the most part, to subjective classifications. A technical restriction mentioned by some writers (cf. Nunnally, 1967) is that the number of tests should exceed the number of subjects in Q factor analysis in the same manner that the number of subjects relative to tests must exceed the number of tests in R factor analysis. However, Overall and Klett (1972) give examples in which the Q technique was successfully used with 40 subjects and only 13 tests, and Overall (personal communication, 1977) stated that the only necessary restriction in this regard was that the number of subjects and tests be several times greater than the number of factors to be derived. We have not found any differences in factor structure as a function of sample size in the previous study or in the results to be reported in the following chapters.

We will now proceed directly to a consideration of the reading test results, postponing consideration of the language and neuropsychological tests until Chapters 8 and 9.

Reading Test Results: Three Types of Reading Skill Deficits

7

This chapter is concerned with a detailed consideration of three types of reading disabilities that were identified by statistical classification of the reading test results of the present sample of 88 subjects.

Before describing the reading disability classifications, it is of interest to examine average performance on the reading tests of the subject sample with reference to that of normal readers. Figure 7.1 shows the average performance of the sample as a whole on the 31 reading tests, expressed in terms of grade-level equivalents derived from a sample of normal readers (Doehring, 1976a). These averages are conservative estimates of the severity of reading deficit of the majority of subjects, because the sample included a number of subjects without severe reading problems and several older subjects, who were considered to be in Grade 12 for this purpose. Despite this, the trends seem to be quite clear. The sample as a whole was severely deficient in almost all reading skills. The expected grade level for the sample's average age of 12 years, 3 months was Grade 6.75 (assuming that the average age in Grade 6.0 is 11 years, 6 months). The average retardation of reading skills was almost 2 years for the visual matching-to-sample tests and for auditory–visual letter matching, and more than 2 years for visual number and letter scanning. There was a retardation of more than 3 years in auditory–visual word and syllable matching, oral letter reading, and visual scanning for words and syllables; and of more than 4 years in oral word, phrase, and sentence reading. The average level of skill for orally reading meaningless syllables barely exceeded the average for Grade 1 normal readers.

On the eight remaining tests of reading-related skills, which are not plotted in Figure 7.1, the average was at about the Grade 4 level for oral

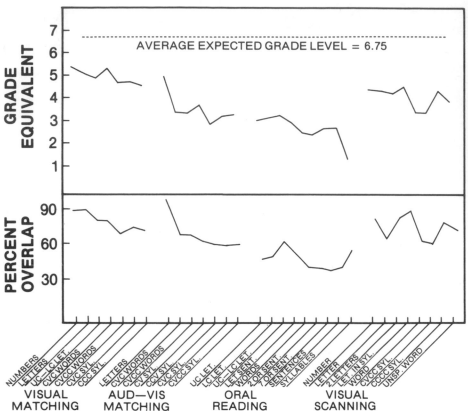

FIGURE 7.1. *The top graph shows the mean scores of the 88 subjects on the 31 reading tests, expressed as grade equivalents. The average age of the 88 subjects was 12 years, 3 months, corresponding to an expected grade level of 6.75. The bottom graph shows the percentage of subjects from the reading problem sample who scored within the same range as normal readers of their own age.*

color and picture naming and at the Grade 5 level for visual scanning for rectangles and figures. Comprehension and spelling, like oral word, phrase, and syllable reading, were between Grades 2 and 3. On the standardized achievement tests the average was at about Grade 4.5 level for WRAT reading and arithmetic and Durrell listening comprehension and word analysis, at about Grade 3.5 for WRAT spelling, and at about Grade 3 for Durrell oral reading and silent reading.

The pattern of errors on the reading tests corresponded to the trend of the average scores. Accuracy was high enough that all of the visual matching and visual scanning tests, the first four of the auditory–visual matching tests, and the oral naming and oral letter tests could be scored in terms of speed of response for over 90% of the 88 subjects. The error limits (see page 70) were exceeded by about 16% of the subjects on the remaining three auditory–visual matching tests, by about 33% on the oral word-, phrase-, and sentence-reading tests, and by 88% on the oral syllable-reading test. Even with the more lenient accuracy standards on the comprehension and spelling tests, the error limit was exceeded by 24% of the subjects on the sentence comprehension test and by about 72% on the spelling tests. Thus, the test results of the majority of subjects were scored in terms of speed of response on all tests except the oral syllable-reading test and the three spelling tests.

Weener (1981) has pointed out that it is misleading to present only average differences between learning-impaired and normal subjects of the same age, as this may imply an invariable difference between normal and learning-disabled children on the skill tested. He suggests that some index is needed of the proportion of learning-disabled subjects who score in the normal range for their ages. The overlap between the present sample and normal readers of the same ages (Doehring, 1976a) could be estimated for those 78 of the 88 subjects who were in the age range from 8 to 14. The percentage of subjects from the reading problem sample who scored within the same range as normal subjects of their own age is shown in the lower graph of Figure 7.1. This is a very crude estimate, because of the small samples of normal and reading-disabled subjects at each age level, but does demonstrate that there was not an invariable discrepancy between the normal and reading problem samples on any of the tests. The amounts of overlap tended to follow the same trends as the average scores in the upper graph. There was almost complete overlap between normal readers and subjects from the reading problem sample for auditory–visual letter matching and for visual number and letter matching; over two-thirds from the reading problem sample scored within the normal range on the remaining visual matching tests and most of the visual scanning tests, and over half on the remaining auditory–visual matching tests. Between 30 and 60% of the subjects fell within the normal range on the oral reading tests. On the remaining tests, not shown in Figure 7.1, there was an almost complete overlap for color and picture naming and for rectangle and geometric figure scanning, and 35–65% overlap for spelling. However, there was less than 20% overlap for sentence comprehension.

For the group as a whole, then, visual skills were least impaired and oral reading skills most impaired, and word and syllable skills were more impaired than letter skills on all tasks. Nonverbal skills were always better than the corresponding verbal skills, and the proficiency of sentence comprehension was once more at the same level as oral word reading, with spelling somewhat better. If all subjects displayed these median trends, we could conclude that they had a unitary form of reading disability, featured by very poor oral syllable decoding, less-impaired silent reading, and near-normal visual perception. However, there was a great deal of variability within the sample, as was clearly illustrated by the high proportion of scores within the normal range. In no case was an absolute separation between groups approached, and only on the sentence comprehension test were fewer than one-third of the reading problem sample in the normal range. The variability within the reading problem sample indicates that all subjects did not have a unitary form of reading disability, or at least that they did not all have a problem of the same severity. The most consistent deficiency was in sentence comprehension, indicating that a general lack of higher-level reading skills would have been found if these skills had been tested.

Relationships among Reading-Related Skills

After determining the average trends and the variability of the reading test performance of the 88 subjects, we examined the relationships among the reading-related skills. The correlations between tests gave some indication of the extent to which component reading skills had been tested, and provided a foundation for interpreting the patterns of individual differences in test results.

Product–moment correlations between all of the measures obtained in this study are listed in Appendix A, except for the WRAT, as its scores were not available at the time the correlations were calculated, and certain neuropsychological measures, on which not all subjects had been tested or the scores were not well enough distributed for meaningful analysis. The tests correlated include the five measures from the Durrell Achievement Test, the 39 measures of reading-related skills, the 22 measures of language-related skills, and 37 measures from the neuropsychological battery. This yielded a total of 5253 correlations among the 103 measures. Except for the correlations involving the neuropsychological measures, which were already age-corrected, the correlations given in Appendix A are partial correlations, in which the effects of age were partialed out. The correction for age effects was necessary because the correlation between tests would be increased by the extent to which test performance jointly improved with age.

For the purpose of the present chapter, we will consider only those correlations in Appendix A that involved the Durrell measures and the 39 tests of reading-related skill. With a sample of 88 subjects, any correlations higher than .20 are statistically significant $(p < .05)$. By this criterion, virtually all of the 47 reading measures were positively related for this sample, the few nonsignificant correlations mostly involving picture naming and visual scanning for consecutive rectangles.

The occurrence of statistically significant positive correlations does not, however, guarantee a strong relationship between tests. Another way of looking at the strength of positive correlations is the proportion of variance among subjects that the two tests have in common. The common variance between tests is estimated by squaring the correlation coefficient. A correlation of .20, although statistically significant, indicates only 4% common variability between two tests. A correlation of .50 is needed for .25 common variance, .70 for .50 common variance, .80 for .66 common variance, and .90 for .80 common variance between two tests for the present sample of subjects.

We will not discuss the correlations between tests in detail, because there are too many, but simply alert the reader to the usefulness of referring to Appendix A whenever there is a question of the extent to which any two measures are related for the sample of 88 subjects. At this point, we will only mention certain highlights from the 946 correlations involving the 5 standardized and 39 reading-related measures:

1. The standardized reading achievement measures from the Durrell were highly correlated, in the range of .80–.90, with the sentence comprehension test and the four measures of oral word, phrase, and sentence reading. The correlations among the four oral reading measures were above .90, and the correlations between these tests and the sentence comprehension test were in the .80–.90 range. This provided another indication that the overall reading skill of most subjects in the present sample did not go beyond the level of orally reading one word at a time.

2. Most of the remaining measures of reading-related skills were also substantially correlated with the standardized reading measures. Correlations involving oral letter reading and spelling were in the .60–.80 range, those involving auditory–visual matching in the .50–.80 range, visual matching in the .40–.80 range, and visual scanning in the .30–.60 range. Thus, even the tests that could be accomplished by direct visual matching or scanning required the types of skill measured by standard reading achievement tests.

3. The 31 measures of reading skill that were used for statistical classification showed two major correlational trends: There tended to be higher correlations between tests that involved the same task (i.e., visual matching to sample or oral reading); and correlations tended to be higher between tests involving the same type of stimulus (i.e., letters, syllables, or words. These patterns of intercorrelation suggested that the tests were

to some extent measuring the separate operation of component skills for reading letters, syllables, or words, and were also measuring the separate operation of component skills for the visual perception, letter–sound association, and oral reading of text.

Conventional R Factor Analysis of Reading Test Relationships

The correlational trends among the 31 measures of reading skill were examined further by conventional R factor analysis. The computational procedure was the same as that described for Q factor analysis in the next section, except that the factor analysis was based on correlations between tests rather than on correlations between subjects. An analysis that yielded four factors gave the most information about correlational trends. The factor loadings of the 31 tests on each of the four factors are given in Table 7.1. The four factors can be interpreted very easily. With only one exception, the tests with loadings above .40 on Factor 1 involved word and syllable reading skills as opposed to letter and number skills; all of the tests with loadings above .40 on Factor 2 involved visual matching or visual scanning; on Factor 3, all but one of the tests with loadings above .40 involved letter or number reading; and all but one of the tests with loadings above .40 on Factor 4 were oral reading tests.

The relations between tests revealed by R factor analysis gave a further indication of the component skills measured by the 31 reading tests. Skills for word and syllable reading were differentiated from skills for reading letters on Factors 1 and 3; visual perception skills were differentiated, on Factor 2, from skills that required recoding to spoken form; and skills that involved oral reading were differentiated from those that involved other modes of reading response on Factor 4. The component skill dimensions of stimulus type and response mode seemed to be fairly well distinguished by the 31 reading tests. The test battery should, therefore, be sensitive to differences among subjects on these aspects of component reading skill.

Statistical Classification of the Reading Test Results

Following the preliminary analyses of the average trends and the relations between reading tests, the main analyses for classifying subjects into different types of reading disabilities were carried out using the percen-

TABLE 7.1

Summary of the Results of an R Factor Analysis of the Thirty-One Reading Tests for the Sample of Eighty-Eight Subjects.[a]

TESTS	FACTORS			
	1	2	3	4
Visual Matching: Numbers	19	35	79	28
Upper-case letters	28	32	78	26
Upper & lower-case letters	29	32	71	34
Familiar CVC words	39	49	64	28
Familiar CVCC words	48	51	54	20
CVC syllables	61	53	37	21
CCC letter strings	34	41	49	19
Auditory-visual Matching: Letters	44	6	62	20
Familiar CVC words	72	26	43	19
Familiar CVCC words	74	27	29	31
CV syllables	64	16	34	42
CCV syllables	68	31	24	28
CVC syllables	58	6	30	25
CVCC syllables	57	23	37	39
Oral reading: Upper-case letters	28	22	44	75
Lower-case letters	29	23	48	73
Upper & lower-case letters	19	20	37	79
Letters in sentences	30	15	46	71
Random words	59	26	17	66
Two-word phrases	65	29	15	62
Seven-word phrases	62	27	11	65
Sentences	66	31	14	59
Meaningless syllables	43	19	-5	62
Visual scanning: Number	9	62	59	13
Letter	16	59	58	12
Two letters	15	77	41	22
Letter in syllable	19	76	40	6
Word	41	74	13	18
CVCC syllable	47	74	5	14
CCCC letter string	1	75	11	33
Unspaced word	32	69	33	28

[a] Factor loadings are given for each test for each factor (decimal points omitted).

tile scores of the 88 subjects on the 31 reading tests. To allow for as many as five different types of reading disabilities, three-, four-, and five-factor solutions by the Q Technique were calculated by the SPSS computer program, principal factoring without iteration, (PAI), employing the principal component solution with a varimax rotation (Nie, Hull, Jenkins, Steinbrenner, & Bent, 1975). The first solution classified reading test profiles into three types, the second into four types, and the third into five types.

Factors 1–3 in all three solutions closely resembled those found for the reading problem sample of the previous study (Doehring & Hoshko, 1977a). The factors emerged in the same order as before, Factor 1 being characterized by oral reading difficulty, Factor 2 by auditory–visual association difficulty, and Factor 3 by difficulty with syllables and words as compared to letters and numbers. Figure 7.2 shows the factor score profiles for these three factors, with the three-, four-, five-factor solutions plotted together. Positive factor scores indicate relatively good performance and negative factor scores indicate relatively poor performance.

Factor 1 featured relatively good visual and auditory–visual matching and a very poor oral reading, with visual scanning intermediate. The factor score profiles for the three solutions were almost identical. Within tasks there was no strong trend, apart from exceptionally poor oral syllable reading. Factor 1 seems to represent difficulty in reading aloud printed material ranging from single letters to sentences, but with no severe deficit in silent reading. Poor performance on visual scanning relative to visual matching suggests a more general difficulty in carrying out sequential visual–motor activities. The type of reading disability defined by this factor will be designated as Type O oral reading deficit.

The factor score profiles for the three solutions were also almost identical for Factor 2. Visual scanning was best, visual matching next best, oral reading poor, and auditory–visual matching even poorer. There was no striking trend within tasks, except that auditory–visual letter association was very poor. This factor appeared to involve difficulty in the types of silent reading skills that require the association of the spoken equivalents of printed letters, syllables, and words. It is noteworthy that auditory–visual letter matching, the poorest skill in this factor, was very close to normal for the group as a whole (Figure 7.1). Visual scanning was better than was visual matching, indicating that there was no generalized visual–motor difficulty. The reading disability defined by this factor will be designated as Type A association deficit. The basic difficulty could involve intermodal association between visual–verbal and auditory–verbal stimuli, or could be restricted to the auditory–verbal aspect.

The factor score profiles for the three solutions were also similar for Factor 3, the only large discrepancies occurring for the auditory–visual matching of single letters and four-letter words. On each task, the tests involving letters and numbers were best and the tests involving syllables and words were worst. The only exceptions were visual scanning for a consonant string and for an unspaced word, both of which were probably done even by most normal subjects in letter-by-letter units rather than in syllable and word units. The visual matching tests tended to be highest and the visual scanning tests to be lowest, but there was not a great deal of overall difference among the four tasks in this respect. This factor

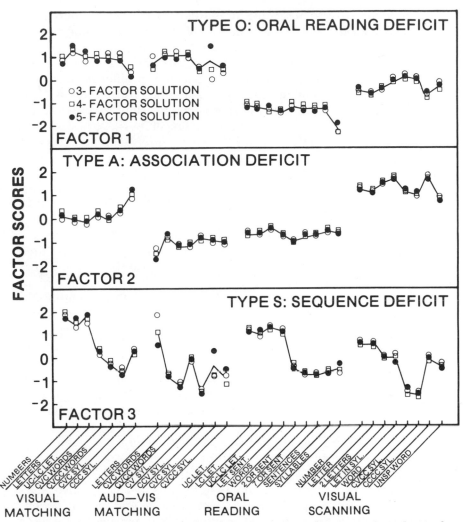

FIGURE 7.2. *Factor scores obtained from analyses of the reading test results of the 88 subjects by three-, four-, and five-factor solutions with the Q technique of factor analysis. The average trends are indicated by solid lines.*

clearly reflected difficulty in responding to pronounceable sequences of letters as units. The type of reading disability defined by this factor will be designated as Type S sequence deficit. The difficulty with sequences could be restricted to the visual–verbal sequences on each task, or could extend to auditory–verbal sequences as well.

The fourth factor in the four-factor solution and the fourth and fifth factors in the five-factor solution, which are not shown in Figure 7.2, did not seem to define types of reading disabilities. Factor 4 of the four-factor solution and Factor 5 of the five-factor solution had the same profile, with extremely good auditory–visual letter matching and intermediate factor scores on the remaining tests. This probably reflected special attention to learning letter names, as the individual tests profiles of the six subjects with high loadings on these factors had nothing else in common. The remaining factor, Factor 4 of the five-factor solution, featured an extremely low factor score for the visual matching of four-letter words, and once again the individual profiles of the nine subjects with high loadings on this factor were otherwise quite different.

Comparison with the Previous Study

The factor score profiles for the three factors identified in this study were remarkably similar to those found for the sample of 34 children with reading problems in the previous study. This can be seen in Figure 7.3, where the factor scores from the three-factor solution of the present study are plotted together with those from the three-factor solution for the reading problem group of the previous study. The factor scores were almost identical for Factors 1 and 2, except that oral letter reading was as poor as oral word, phrase, and sentence reading in the present study. This suggests a more general oral reading deficit in the first two factors in this study, with oral syllable reading being worst in Factor 1 of both studies. For Factor 3, the same discrepancy occurred in both samples between visual and auditory–visual letter matching and the matching of syllables and words but, in the present study, oral letter reading was also superior to oral word, phrase, sentence, and syllable reading, and visual number and letter scanning was superior to scanning for normally spaced words and pronounceable syllables. As compared with the factor score profiles of the reading problem sample in the previous study, then, Factor 1 in the present sample involved a more general oral reading deficit, Factor 2 essentially the same silent reading deficit, and Factor 3 a more general deficit in responding to pronounceable sequences of letters as units.

The similarity of the factor score profiles in the two studies could not have occurred by chance. Three definite profiles of reading disabilities were found in samples from two different cities (Montreal and Ottawa) and two different sources (children attending a summer reading program and referrals to a neuropsychology clinic) by the use of a completely objective classification procedure. The close agreement between the reading disability profiles of the two different samples of subjects is perhaps the most important finding of the present study.

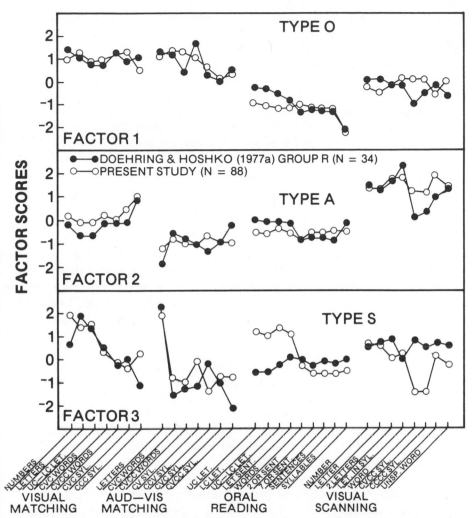

FIGURE 7.3. *Comparison of the factor score profiles of the 88 subjects of the present study with those of 34 subjects with reading problems from the previous study. Factor scores were derived from three-factor solutions by the Q technique of factor analysis.*

Classification of Subjects into the Three Types of Reading Disabilities

The factor score profiles in Figures 7.2 and 7.3 show the patterns of reading skill deficits that characterized the subjects whose reading test profiles had contributed to the definition of each factor. These subjects can be identified in terms of their factor loadings. Those with high load-ings on a particular factor will have a test score profile similar to the fac-tor score profile defining that factor. A high loading on a particular fac-tor can, therefore, be used to classify a subject as having the type of reading disability defined by that factor.

An arbitrary decision must be made as to what constitutes a high enough factor loading for classification into a particular type of reading disability. In the previous study, subjects were classified according to the factor on which they had the highest loading for the three-factor solu-tion, providing the loading was .50 or more. In the present study, a more stable estimate of the profile classification was obtained by averaging the loadings for the three-, four-, and five-factor solutions, and, as a conse-quence, the minimum loading for classification was reduced from .50 to .40. This procedure also eliminated the possibility of bias in the selection of a particular factor solution.

Another arbitrary decision in statistical classification relates to the classification of subjects with high loadings on more than one factor. We chose to maximize the number of subjects classified into the three types of reading disabilities by classifying a subject with more than one loading above .40 into the type defined by the factor for which he or she had the highest loading. To obtain "purer" reading disability types we could have excluded such subjects, and perhaps classified them instead as having "mixed" types of reading disabilities. Future investigators who have ac-cess to more refined tests and classification procedures may wish to use more complex classification systems, but the aim in the present study was to arrive at stable classifications of reading skill deficits, and then to analyze their interactions with deficits of nonreading skills.

Table 7.2 lists the subjects classified by these criteria into the three types of reading disabilities. Within each type, subjects are ranked ac-cording to the size of the loading on the factor defining that type. There were 33 subjects whose highest factor loadings were .40 or more on Fac-tor 1, and who were therefore classified as having Type O oral reading disability. The 22 subjects who had their highest loading on Factor 2 were classified as having Type A association disability, and the 17 sub-jects who had their highest loading on Factor 3 were classified as having Type S sequence disability.

The loadings of the 16 subjects who were not classified into any of the types are ranked according to age in Table 7.2. Even if the criterion for group selection had been reduced to .30, 11 of the subjects would still have remained unclassified. If the same criterion had been used in this as in the previous study (i.e., the highest factor loading beyond .50 on the three-factor solution), 2 fewer subjects would have been classified into

TABLE 7.2

Age, Sex, and Mean Factor Loadings (Decimal Points Omitted) of Subjects Classified into Each Type of Reading Disability, on the Basis of the Highest Mean Factor Loadings Above .40 on the Q Factor Analyses of Thirty-One Reading Tests for Eighty-Eight Subjects, and also for Unclassified Subjects [a]

			Factors						Factors						Factors		
S	Age	Sex	1	2	3	S	Age	Sex	1	2	3	S	Age	Sex	1	2	3
Type O						Type A						Type S					
01	13	M	90	5	-20	A1	12	F	-13	90	-21	S1	10	M	9	-5	80
02	14	M	84	9	-8	A2	12	M	8	87	-14	S2	9	M	9	42	74
03	14	M	84	25	-1	A3	14	F	46	81	7	S3	12	M	31	23	73
04	11	M	83	-6	-2	A4	10	M	3	77	-25	S4	14	M	15	49	70
05	13	M	80	9	13	A5	11	F	38	74	26	S5	10	M	15	-2	64
06	13	M	80	36	20	A6	8	F	17	71	22	S6	10	M	21	24	63
07	15	M	79	0	13	A7	9	M	6	70	10	S7	10	F	41	3	62
08	13	M	76	48	5	A8	13	M	42	67	38	S8	8	M	16	32	62
09	14	M	75	11	39	A9	11	M	42	67	22	S9	16	M	19	4	61
010	11	F	74	30	20	A10	8	M	2	65	36	S10	11	M	54	-13	59
011	15	M	72	-12	39	A11	12	M	33	63	29	S11	13	M	1	-9	57
012	12	M	70	-30	29	A12	12	F	40	62	43	S12	10	F	22	16	55
013	13	M	62	-6	34	A13	11	M	6	62	54	S13	22	M	40	29	54
014	11	F	62	-2	-12	A14	8	F	-13	59	14	S14	13	M	26	40	52
015	12	M	59	40	3	A15	12	M	39	59	21	S15	8	M	5	-21	46
016	13	M	59	31	54	A16	14	M	33	58	49	S16	10	M	38	7	44
017	12	M	59	35	34	A17	11	M	12	57	21	S17	13	M	10	32	42
018	11	F	58	32	9	A18	14	M	4	57	13						
019	11	M	57	16	17	A19	10	M	26	57	-42						
020	17	M	57	47	32	A20	27	M	29	56	42						
021	9	M	57	11	25	A21	11	M	42	45	25						
022	13	M	57	51	26	A22	9	M	32	44	-21						
023	10	M	55	-2	41												
024	15	F	55	26	9	Unclassified Subjects											
025	10	M	54	-14	50												
026	12	F	51	3	25	U1	8	M	-1	-53	20	U9	10	F	-15	-75	-22
027	13	M	50	-16	44	U2	8	M	6	22	11	U10	10	F	11	-53	9
028	11	M	46	-25	9	U3	9	M	-39	3	-16	U11	10	F	5	10	-55
029	16	M	45	31	10	U4	9	M	-8	-35	-6	U12	13	M	11	38	31
030	14	M	44	18	11	U5	9	M	37	38	8	U13	13	M	22	-1	14
031	11	M	43	-40	40	U6	9	M	8	29	35	U14	14	M	28	10	8
032	20	M	43	18	16	U7	9	M	22	21	13	U15	14	M	30	-76	24
033	15	M	41	31	18	U8	10	F	31	39	37	U16	14	M	17	16	10

[a] Members of type O are ranked according to Factor 1 loadings; those of Type A according to Factor 2 loadings, and those of Type S according to Factor 3 loadings.

each type. Thus, the three types would have included about the same number of subjects even if a more liberal or a more conservative selection criterion had been used. The proportion of unclassified subjects (16 of 88) was somewhat higher than it was in the previous study (3 of 34 in the reading problem sample and 5 of 31 in the mixed problem sample), but 7 of the 16 unclassified subjects in this study were normal or near-normal in reading. As in the previous study, therefore, the majority of subjects with reading problems could be classified into one of three types.

There were a few more subjects with loadings above .40 on two or more factors in this study, 23 of 88 or 26%, as compared with 7 of 34 (21%) and 4 of 31 (13%) in the previous samples. These subjects can be classified as having mixed types of reading disabilities. The possible mixed types of reading disabilities in this study are OA, OS, AS, and OAS. There was an even distribution of the dual classifications, with 8 subjects of Type OA, 7 each of Types OS and AS, and 1 of Type OAS. The statistical classification did not, therefore, reveal a complete separation of the three types of reading disabilities.

As in the previous study, there were relatively few subjects with high negative factor loadings. Only seven (four of whom were unclassified) had negative loadings beyond −.40, five on Factor 2 and two on Factor 3. This is in contrast to the results for normal readers (Doehring, Hoshko, & Bryans, 1979), in which there were almost equal proportions of subjects with high positive loadings and high negative loadings.

There was no definite trend with regard to sex. Each of the three types included some female subjects, with the highest proportion (6 of 22) in Type A and the lowest (2 of 17) in Type S. Five of the 33 Type O subjects were female, as were 4 of the 16 unclassified subjects.

The members of Type O tended to be the oldest, with a mean age of 13.3 and only four members younger than 11. The members of Types A and S tended to be about a year younger, Type A having a mean age of 12.3 with nine younger than 11, and Type S having a mean age of 12.2 with nine younger than 11. The unclassified subjects tended to be considerably younger, with a mean age of 10.9 and only five older than 10. In the reading problem group of the previous study, the mean ages were 12.1 for Type O, 13.1 for Type A, 12.7 for Type S, and 9.4 for the three unclassified subjects. Thus, there were no consistent age trends among the three types for the two studies, but the unclassified subjects tended to be younger.

The classification of subjects into different types of reading disabilities on the basis of their factor loadings is both objective and arbitrary. Subjects with the highest loadings will have a reading skill profile that most closely resembles the factor score profile, and there is a gradual decrease in the distinctiveness of profiles with lower loadings. The information in Table 7.2 suggests that the three types of reading disabilities cannot be explained as a function of age or sex. The relatively large proportion of subjects with high dual loadings does not conform to Benton's (1975) requirement that we find homogeneous types of reading disabilities, but does agree with the common finding of mixed types of acquired alexias in

brain-damaged adults (Hecaen & Kremin, 1976). Although these individual classifications are provisional and to some extent arbitrary, they
provide a concrete basis for further examination of the nonreading at-
tributes of the subjects classified into each type of reading disability.

Average Performance of Subjects with Each Type of Reading Disability

The individual classifications can be used to determine the average
reading test performance of subjects within each type, providing a less
abstract representation of the pattern of reading skill deficit than the factor score profiles. To make the average profiles even more meaningful,
we converted them from percentiles to grade-equivalent scores, assuming
for calculational purposes that the average age per school grade would be
6.5 at Grade 1.0, 7.0 at Grade 1.5, etc., and that the three oldest subjects
were in Grade 12. By these criteria, the average expected grade levels
were 7.7 for the 33 Type O subjects, 6.4 for the 22 Type A subjects, and
6.3 for the 17 Type S subjects.

Figure 7.4 shows the average reading skill profiles for the three types
of reading disabilities relative to their average expected grade levels. The
average normal reader would have the flat profile indicated by the
dotted line at the expected grade level for each type. Deviations from
the dotted line indicate both the pattern and the relative severity of
reading deficit. The profiles cannot be exactly the same as the factor
score profiles in Figure 7.2, as all subjects did not have maximum
loadings on the factors that defined the groups. However, the essential
trends are the same. Visual matching and auditory–visual letter matching were least impaired for Type O subjects, being only about 1 year
below expected grade level, with oral reading skills more than 4 years
below and oral syllable reading approaching a minimum. For Type A
subjects, visual matching and visual scanning were impaired by 2–3
years, and auditory–visual matching and oral reading were more than 4
years below expected grade level. For Type S, there was a discrepancy of
about 2 years between tests involving single letter or number reading and
tests in which words or syllables could read as units.

The comparison of Figures 7.2 and 7.4 is very instructive. The factor
score profiles of Figure 7.2 represent the most complete differentiations
of the types of reading disabilities that can be achieved by factor analysis,
and Figure 7.4 shows how closely the average profiles of subjects
classified into each type of reading disability approached the factor score
profiles. The differences between the factor score profiles in Figure 7.2

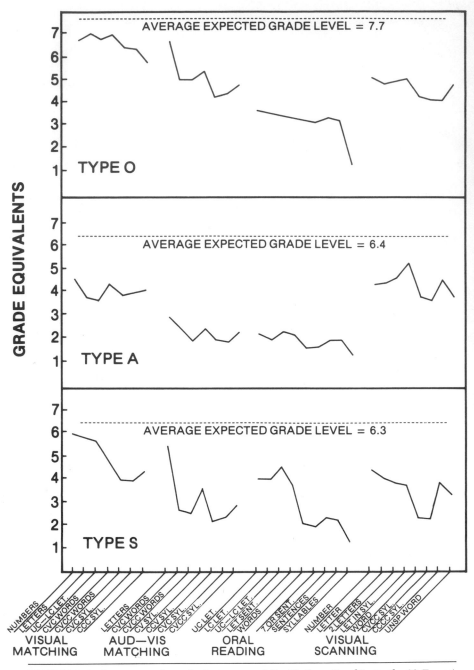

FIGURE 7.4. *Average grade-equivalent scores of the 33 Type O subjects, the 22 Type A subjects, and 17 Type S subjects. An average normal reader would have the flat profile shown by the dotted line at the average expected grade level.*

and the average grade-equivalent profiles in Figure 7.4 reflect, in part, the presence of subjects with high loadings on more than one factor and, hence, "mixed" types of reading disabilities (Table 7.2). We can speculate at this point that the three types of reading disabilities are additive rather than independent, some subjects (e.g., Subjects 01 to 04 in Table 7.2) having a relatively pure form of a single type of reading disability, and others having a mixture of two (e.g., Subjects A11 and A16) or even three (Subject A12) types.

The average profiles also provide a rough estimate of the severity of each type of reading disability. There was an average retardation of more than 4 years in the most deficient skills within each type, indicating that the average subject classified into each type had severe reading disability of that type. Except for some of the visual matching skills in Types O and S, even the least impaired reading skills tended to be retarded by more than 1 year. This is not at all surprising, considering the interactive nature of reading skill development. An initial difficulty with one aspect of reading achievement can have widespread effects, indirectly hampering the acquisition of other component reading skills. Furthermore, the performance of one type of skill, such as oral reading, can be directly impaired by a deficit in another skill, such as letter–sound association. Thus, the average profiles of reading skill deficits clearly indicate the type and the extent of reading skill impairment associated with each type of reading disability.

We also calculated the average performance of the subjects of each type for the eight standardized reading achievement measures and the eight additional measures of reading-related skills, as shown in Table 7.3. All three types averaged more than 2 years below expected grade levels on all standardized achievement tests, with greater reading impairment on the Durrell oral and silent reading tests than on the Durrell word recognition and word analysis tests and the WRAT reading test. Durrell listening comprehension was less impaired than the four Durrell reading measures in Types A and S, but not in Type O; and WRAT arithmetic was less impaired than WRAT reading in Types A and S but not in Type O. Spelling was the most impaired of the WRAT measures for all three types.

All three types also showed substantial impairment on most of the remaining measures of reading-related skills. Type O subjects averaged about 2 years retardation on the nonverbal scanning measures, 3 years retardation on the oral naming measures, 4 years on the spelling measures, and 5 years in sentence comprehension. Type A subjects averaged 1.3–3.2 years behind in the naming and scanning measures and more than 4 years behind on the sentence comprehension and spelling

TABLE 7.3

Average Grade-Equivalent Scores of Subjects Classified into the Three Types of Reading Disability on the Standardized Achievement Tests and the Eight Additional Tests of Reading-Related Skill

Test	Type of Reading Disability		
	O	A	S
Average expected grade for age	7.7	6.4	6.3
Durrell: Oral reading	3.8	2.2	3.1
Silent reading	3.9	2.2	3.0
Listening comprehension	4.7	3.8	4.2
Word recognition	5.0	2.8	3.5
Word analysis	5.2	3.0	3.7
Wide Range Achievement: Reading	5.4	3.5	3.6
Spelling	4.4	3.1	3.1
Arithmetic	5.4	4.2	4.0
Reading-Related Skills: Color naming	4.3	3.0	4.5
Picture naming	4.5	3.9	5.4
Visual scanning for rectangles	5.3	3.9	5.1
Visual scanning for figures	5.8	5.1	4.9
Sentence comprehension	2.7	1.7	2.1
Oral spelling	3.4	1.9	2.3
Written spelling	3.2	2.1	2.2
Spelled-Out Words	3.9	2.3	2.8

measures. Type S subjects averaged only .9–1.8 years behind on the naming and scanning measures, 3 years behind in sentence comprehension, and over 4 years behind on two of the three spelling measures. Although the average trends of the eight standard reading measures and the eight remaining measures of reading-related skills for the three types of reading disabilities are not immediately interpretable, they do indicate a generalized impairment of skills tested, with some differences in the patterns of impairment among the three types of reading disabilities, notably the relatively less impaired color and picture naming of Type S subjects.

Reading Skill Profiles of Individual
Subjects of Each Type

Another perspective for interpreting the statistical classifications is provided by the individual profiles of reading skill deficits of the subjects classified into each of the three types. These are shown in the most complete, clear, and compact form that we could devise in Tables 7.4, 7.5, and 7.6, which give the grade-equivalent scores for the eight standard achievement measures and the 39 measures of reading-related skills relative to the normal grade for age of each subject classified into Types O, A, and S reading disabilities. In all cases, grade equivalents are given to the nearest grade. Within each type, the subjects are ranked according to their factor loadings (Table 7.2). The test ceiling (i.e., the highest grade for which test norms were available), is given at the left of each table, and the letter c within the body of the table indicates that the subject scored at the ceiling for that test.

Careful study of Tables 7.4, 7.5, and 7.6 reveals that the reading profiles of the highest-ranked subjects within each type do closely resemble the factor score profiles of Figure 7.2. In Table 7.4, Subjects 01 to 05 scored close to the expected grade for their age in visual matching, almost as close in auditory–visual matching, somewhat lower in visual scanning, and 4 or more years below the expected grade level on most oral reading tests. The five highest-ranked subjects of Type A (Table 7.5) scored at or below Grade 2 level on most of the auditory–visual matching tests and on all of the oral reading tests, with most visual matching and visual scanning scores being 1 or more years above the Grade 2 level; and the five highest-ranked subjects of Type S (Table 7.6) showed consistently higher scores on the tests involving numbers and letters than on the tests involving syllables and words. These distinctive patterns of reading skill deficits are not nearly as evident in the five lowest-ranked members of each type. The reading skill profiles of subjects with high loadings on more than one factor (Table 7.2) reflect the mixed types of reading deficits (e.g., Subject A 11, Table 7.5, has a profile that combines the features of Types A and S, and Subject S10, Table 7.6, has a profile that combines the features of Types S and 0).

For completeness, the reading test profiles of the 16 unclassified subjects are shown in Table 7.7. Some (Subjects U5, U6, U8, U12, and U14) had profiles somewhat resembling one of the types of reading disabilities. Others (Subjects U1 and U2) were probably unclassified because they were young and close to the lower limit of many tests, and still others (Subjects U9, U10, U11, U13, U15, and U16) because they were near-normal on most tests. Poor visual matching suggested possible visual

TABLE 7.4

Grade-Equivalent Scores of Subjects of Type O (oral reading deficit) on the Durrell and the Wide Range Achievement Tests and on the Thirty-Nine Tests of Reading-Related Skills[a]

Type O Rank:		1	2	3	4	5	6	7	8	9	10	11	12	13	14	15	16	17	18	19	20	21	22	23	24	25	26	27	28	29	30	31	32	33	Mean
Grade for age:		8	9	9	6	8	8	10	8	9	6	10	7	8	5	7	8	7	6	6	12	4	8	5	10	5	7	8	6	11	9	5	12	10	7
DURRELL oral	6	5	3	5	4	5	3	3	4	2	3	3	4	3	3	2	4	3	4	2	3	2	3	3	c	2	0	4	4	4	5	3	c	3	3
silent	6	c	3	5	c	5	3	3	4	3	3	4	4	4	3	2	4	3	4	2	3	1	3	4	4	2	0	4	4	4	4	3	c	3	3
listening	6	c	c	c	c	c	3	c	c	5	3	c	5	5	3	5	5	3	3	5	3	3	3	3	5	5	3	4	4	-	3	5	c	3	4
word rec.	6	c	4	c	c	c	5	c	c	3	3	c	5	5	3	2	5	4	5	3	4	2	4	4	c	4	1	5	4	c	c	5	c	4	5
word anal.	6	c	4	c	c	c	5	c	c	3	3	c	5	5	3	2	c	5	c	4	4	4	5	4	c	4	1	5	5	c	c	5	c	4	5
WRAT reading	19	7	4	9	8	7	5	5	7	4	2	4	5	3	3	3	6	4	7	5	5	3	5	4	7	3	-	6	5	6	5	5	6	4	5
spelling	19	6	3	5	5	8	4	4	5	3	2	4	4	3	1	2	4	4	6	3	3	2	3	3	6	4	-	4	5	4	5	5	4	4	4
arithmetic	19	7	7	7	9	5	7	6	4	5	2	5	6	6	4	4	3	6	5	5	6	3	4	3	4	6	3	-	6	4	4	6	4	5	5
V MATCH NU	10	8	5	c	7	8	c	6	7	8	c	8	c	c	8	3	c	8	7	5	7	6	7	c	c	8	7	c	6	5	c	5	7	8	7
LE	10	c	7	c	8	c	c	8	9	c	9	c	c	9	c	5	8	8	6	5	5	9	9	8	c	5	6	c	4	9	9	6	7	7	7
UL	10	7	5	c	7	c	8	8	c	6	8	c	c	7	4	4	c	9	6	6	5	9	9	7	8	c	7	8	c	4	7	8	8	6	7
W3	10	9	7	c	7	9	8	7	8	7	8	8	8	6	4	3	7	c	7	4	7	7	7	7	9	5	7	c	5	6	c	6	6	7	7
W4	10	9	7	9	8	8	9	7	6	8	8	6	7	7	3	2	9	9	8	3	6	7	8	8	9	7	5	9	5	7	7	5	7	6	6
S3	10	7	7	c	7	7	8	6	8	6	8	6	5	6	5	3	8	8	6	4	5	5	4	8	c	5	6	7	5	8	c	4	8	5	6
CC	10	6	5	c	6	7	c	5	8	5	5	8	4	5	5	3	9	8	7	5	8	1	8	5	c	6	c	c	4	1	7	3	7	6	6
AV MATCH LE	10	c	5	c	8	c	c	6	5	c	7	c	c	9	8	3	7	6	7	1	8	5	4	c	c	8	8	c	5	7	c	8	6	c	7
W3	10	6	6	c	6	6	c	5	4	9	5	7	c	5	3	3	5	5	5	4	4	3	5	5	4	4	5	c	7	3	5	6	4	7	5
W4	10	8	7	c	8	c	9	6	4	3	5	4	7	7	8	3	4	4	c	2	2	2	8	7	c	4	1	c	4	4	8	4	4	8	5
S2	10	8	c	8	8	c	8	7	7	7	5	c	7	6	5	2	6	6	7	4	6	3	7	1	c	6	1	c	5	4	7	6	6	5	5
CV	10	7	5	9	4	c	5	7	6	2	4	7	8	4	4	3	5	1	9	3	4	3	4	7	7	1	9	1	4	4	9	5	4	4	4
S3	10	9	5	c	7	6	5	6	5	6	7	c	7	1	1	4	4	1	6	2	4	4	2	4	c	8	1	9	2	4	1	5	5	4	4
S4	10	9	7	c	8	7	6	5	5	7	1	5	8	1	4	5	4	5	6	2	4	3	2	9	4	5	6	c	5	2	8	3	4	5	5
NAMING CO	10	4	6	c	5	7	5	8	9	7	3	2	6	6	2	4	2	2	5	1	4	5	3	4	9	9	3	5	4	4	9	9	1	4	4
PI	10	1	3	8	6	5	6	9	7	7	2	c	6	3	1	2	2	2	4	1	9	3	5	9	9	6	1	9	2	5	7	4	3	6	6
ORAL READ UC	10	3	5	5	3	4	4	4	4	3	3	6	5	3	2	1	5	2	4	1	4	3	5	7	6	4	1	6	4	5	6	5	4	6	6
LC	10	4	4	6	4	4	3	3	3	5	4	4	4	2	1	1	5	3	4	1	3	2	4	6	6	5	2	6	3	3	7	6	5	5	4
UL	10	3	2	8	4	4	4	3	2	3	1	6	4	3	2	2	6	3	8	1	4	2	4	8	6	5	1	6	3	6	6	4	3	4	3
LS	10	3	3	4	2	5	4	2	3	4	2	5	7	3	1	1	5	2	4	3	3	2	3	5	7	3	2	5	5	4	6				3
WR	10	5	2	4	4	4	2	3	3	2	2	5	7	2	2	1	3	2	3	2	2	2	3	7	2	1	8	4	3	6	3	8	6		3
2W	10	4	3	6	5	5	2	3	4	2	1	4	3	2	3	1	3	2	3	2	2	2	5	6	2	1	7	4	2	6	3	6	5		3
7W	10	5	3	8	4	4	2	4	3	2	3	4	4	3	3	1	3	2	3	2	2	2	6	2	1	6	3	6	3	7	6	3	7	6	3
WS	10	4	3	6	3	4	3	3	3	2	3	5	4	3	3	1	3	2	5	2	3	2	2	5	7	2	2	5	5	3	6	3	6	3	3
SY	10	2	1	2	2	2	1	2	1	1	1	1	1	1	1	1	1	1	1	1	2	2	2	2	1	1	6	1	1	2	1	2	2	5	1
comprehension	10	3	3	5	5	5	3	3	4	2	1	3	3	3	2	1	3	2	3	2	2	2	2	3	4	2	1	4	3	3	4	3	3	3	3
spelling S1	10	5	3	5	4	7	4	2	5	2	1	3	3	3	2	4	2	4	3	3	3	2	3	3	c	3	1	3	4	3	7	6	4	6	4
S2	10	6	6	5	4	7	5	3	5	2	3	6	2	1	2	2	2	2	6	2	3	2	2	5	7	2	1	2	2	3	5	4	4	2	3
S3	10	6	2	4	3	7	4	2	4	4	3	5	3	2	4	1	6	1	5	9	3	4	4	3	c	5	1	2	4	2	8	8	6	7	4
VIS SCAN RE	10	6	7	6	5	4	7	9	6	6	7	5	4	4	4	1	9	5	7	1	7	5	7	9	9	3	9	5	c	6	/	1	4	c	5
F1	10	7	4	7	6	7	9	7	7	5	5	6	5	4	4	7	3	8	7	3	c	6	5	8	8	c	4	c	7	3	5	5	4	7	8	6
NU	10	6	4	7	4	7	7	6	6	5	6	6	6	4	4	3	8	5	8	4	6	1	7	7	7	3	7	6	5	4	6	4	6	6	5
LE	10	5	6	6	4	7	8	7	3	5	4	6	6	3	2	4	7	5	7	3	6	4	7	6	5	5	6	7	3	4	6	3	4	5	5
2L	10	5	5	c	4	8	8	6	6	4	5	5	4	4	3	3	6	6	8	2	8	3	8	9	7	2	8	8	2	7	7	3	5	6	5
LS	10	5	6	c	6	6	9	7	6	5	6	5	3	5	3	5	5	8	2	5	3	6	6	9	4	6	6	2	6	7	3	5	6		5
WD	10	8	4	8	6	4	4	4	7	4	5	6	4	3	4	3	4	3	6	2	4	3	5	8	c	3	1	4	3	6	7	3	4	4	4
SY	10	7	5	c	5	c	5	3	6	3	4	3	4	2	5	3	3	4	7	2	4	3	5	7	c	2	2	3	3	8	8	4	4	4	4
о)	10	7	3	c	6	5	9	2	c	4	5	4	6	1	1	5	5	5	6	3	5	4	6	4	c	2	1	4	5	5	6	4	7	5	4
UW	10	8	5	6	4	8	8	3	8	6	5	4	5	2	3	3	6	4	5	3	5	5	7	c	5	5	5	4	4	7	8	4	5	6	5

[a] Test ceilings are given in the left-hand column, and scores at the ceiling are designated by the letter c in the body of the table. Mean grade levels are given in the right-hand column.

94

TABLE 7.5

Grade-Equivalent Scores of Subjects of Type A (association deficit) on the Durrell and the Wide Range Achievement Tests and on the Thirty-Nine Tests of Reading-Related Skills[a]

	Ceiling	1	2	3	4	5	6	7	8	9	10	11	12	13	14	15	16	17	18	19	20	21	22	Mean
Type A Rank:																								
Grade for age:		7	7	9	5	6	3	4	8	6	3	7	7	6	3	7	9	6	9	5	12	6	4	6
DURRELL oral	6	2	2	3	2	2	2	1	1	0	0	1	3	1	1	4	3	2	c	3	1	2	2	2
silent	6	3	2	2	1	2	1	1	1	1	0	1	3	1	1	4	3	2	c	3	1	2	2	2
listening	6	2	3	4	5	5	3	-	5	3	3	5	3	3	3	5	4	3	c	5	c	3	3	3
word rec.	6	4	2	4	2	3	2	1	2	0	1	1	5	1	1	5	5	2	c	4	1	3	3	2
word anal.	6	4	2	4	2	3	2	1	3	0	1	1	5	3	1	5	5	2	c	4	1	3	3	3
WRAT reading	19	5	3	5	1	3	2	1	-	-	2	-	5	2	2	4	8	1	7	-	1	3	3	3
spelling	19	4	3	3	2	3	2	1	-	-	1	-	4	2	2	2	5	1	7	-	2	3	2	3
arithmetic	19	5	1	4	3	3	3	2	-	-	3	-	6	5	2	6	5	2	8	-	3	4	3	4
V MATCH NU	10	2	1	c	1	5	3	3	7	5	3	6	6	6	2	c	c	3	6	3	c	3	4	4
LE	10	1	1	7	1	4	2	1	9	5	1	2	9	4	1	c	8	2	6	1	9	7	5	3
UL	10	2	3	8	1	7	3	1	4	3	2	1	5	3	2	c	8	2	9	1	7	4	6	3
W3	10	3	3	6	2	7	3	1	5	3	1	2	5	3	1	c	7	4	7	3	c	4	3	4
W4	10	3	2	7	2	4	2	1	4	3	0	2	7	2	1	8	6	4	6	4	8	4	3	3
S3	10	4	4	8	2	5	3	0	4	4	2	3	8	2	1	7	6	3	7	5	0	4	3	4
CC	10	4	3	8	3	5	3	0	4	4	3	3	6	4	1	c	7	4	7	3	0	3	3	4
AV MATCH LE	10	1	0	5	0	1	1	1	7	1	1	3	7	1	3	5	9	1	2	2	5	4	6	2
W3	10	2	1	4	1	2	1	1	3	1	1	2	5	0	1	2	4	2	4	4	0	3	2	2
W4	10	1	1	3	0	1	1	0	1	0	0	1	3	1	0	4	2	1	2	3	0	2	6	1
S2	10	3	1	2	1	3	1	1	3	1	1	2	4	1	1	4	2	0	5	3	0	2	1	2
CV	10	2	1	2	1	1	1	0	1	1	0	1	2	1	1	5	5	1	2	4	0	2	0	2
S3	10	1	0	2	1	1	1	0	2	1	0	1	5	2	0	3	2	2	4	1	0	2	0	1
S4	10	1	1	2	1	1	1	0	1	1	1	1	3	4	1	5	4	2	4	1	0	2	1	2
NAMING CO	10	4	1	1	1	3	5	0	1	1	0	1	7	5	1	6	5	1	8	3	7	1	4	2
PI	10	3	1	0	2	5	7	5	2	0	0	4	4	5	1	9	8	2	8	9	7	3	1	4
ORAL READ UC	10	2	1	1	1	2	1	1	1	1	1	1	6	2	1	5	6	1	5	2	1	3	1	2
LC	10	1	0	2	1	2	1	0	2	0	0	0	6	3	0	4	5	1	4	0	1	3	1	1
UL	10	2	1	1	1	2	1	0	2	0	1	1	5	4	3	6	5	3	5	0	0	2	2	2
LS	10	2	1	2	1	2	1	0	2	0	1	1	4	2	1	2	4	2	3	3	1	2	1	2
WR	10	2	1	1	1	1	1	0	1	1	1	1	2	1	1	4	2	1	4	1	1	1	1	1
2W	10	2	1	1	1	1	1	0	1	1	1	1	2	1	1	5	2	1	5	2	1	2	1	1
7W	10	2	2	1	1	1	1	0	1	1	1	1	2	1	1	4	2	1	8	2	1	2	2	1
W5	10	2	1	2	1	1	1	1	1	1	1	1	2	1	1	3	2	1	6	2	1	2	2	1
SY	10	1	1	1	1	1	1	0	1	1	1	1	1	1	1	2	1	4	1	1	1	1	1	1
comprehension	10	2	1	2	1	1	1	0	1	1	1	2	1	1	2	2	1	3	0	2	2	1		1
spelling S1	10	3	2	2	1	2	1	0	1	1	1	2	5	1	1	2	2	1	5	1	3	1	1	1
S2	10	3	2	2	1	2	1	0	1	1	1	1	6	1	1	2	7	1	6	1	1	2	1	2
S3	10	4	1	3	2	2	1	0	1	1	1	2	3	1	1	3	4	1	4	4	1	3	2	2
VIS SCAN RE	10	1	1	7	1	5	1	1	7	7	1	5	7	8	4	c	6	5	6	8	6	3	1	4
F1	10	4	2	2	2	6	3	2	9	3	5	6	8	6	5	c	7	2	6	4	6	2	3	5
NU	10	5	2	7	3	3	3	3	8	3	1	4	8	5	2	7	7	2	5	4	5	2	5	4
LE	10	4	2	3	2	3	1	2	6	4	3	4	c	4	2	7	8	2	6	5	4	4	5	4
2L	10	6	3	c	1	4	4	1	7	3	3	3	8	4	4	6	7	3	7	4	7	3	5	4
LS	10	6	4	c	1	5	4	2	c	4	3	5	8	4	3	9	c	3	3	5	5	5	3	5
WD	10	6	2	c	2	5	2	2	3	1	1	1	9	3	1	c	6	2	6	5	3	5	3	3
SY	10	6	2	c	2	4	1	2	5	2	1	2	5	2	3	7	5	2	7	3	4	3	2	3
CC	10	8	5	c	2	5	2	7	6	2	1	3	7	5	4	c	7	2	7	2	6	2	1	4
UW	10	5	3	c	2	3	1	1	5	3	1	2	7	2	2	7	5	2	7	4	2	4	1	3

[a] Test ceilings are given in the left-hand column, and scores at the ceiling are designated by the letter *c* in the body of the table. Mean grade levels are given in the right-hand column.

95

TABLE 7.6

Grade-Equivalent Scores of Subjects of Type S (sequence deficit) on the Durrell and the Wide Range Achievement Tests and on the Thirty-Nine Tests of Reading-Related Skills[a]

Type S Rank:		c	1	2	3	4	5	6	7	8	9	10	11	12	13	14	15	16	17	Mean
Grade for age:			5	4	5	9	5	5	5	3	11	6	8	5	12	8	3	5	8	6
DURRELL	oral	6	3	2	2	2	2	3	3	1	3	2	5	2	3	3	2	4	4	3
	silent	6	2	2	2	3	2	3	3	1	3	2	4	1	4	2	2	3	5	3
	listening	6	5	3	5	3	4	3	3	3	5	4	c	3	c	3	8	5	5	4
	word rec.	6	4	2	2	2	3	2	2	1	4	2	c	2	5	3	2	c	4	3
	word anal.	6	4	3	3	2	4	3	2	1	4	3	c	2	c	3	2	c	4	3
WRAT	reading	19	5	2	2	2	3	2	2	1	4	2	4	2	7	5	3	5	4	3
	spelling	19	2	2	2	2	2	2	2	2	3	2	3	2	5	3	2	5	4	3
arithmetic		19	3	3	2	5	4	3	3	3	2	4	5	3	6	2	3	6	4	4
V MATCH	NU	10	7	5	c	c	6	6	6	2	7	c	c	3	7	8	4	6	6	6
	LE	10	5	7	c	c	6	4	7	4	7	9	c	3	6	3	2	5	6	6
	UL	10	5	6	7	8	8	4	6	4	7	c	6	3	8	5	4	7	6	6
	W3	10	4	4	7	9	3	4	6	2	6	7	8	1	6	4	2	7	7	5
	W4	10	3	3	5	8	2	4	3	1	4	4	5	1	7	3	2	6	8	4
	S3	10	4	2	5	4	2	4	4	1	4	3	5	2	4	4	2	8	9	4
	CC	10	4	3	3	8	2	6	5	2	6	3	7	4	4	3	2	c	8	4
AV MATCH	LE	10	c	2	c	5	8	4	6	1	3	c	9	c	8	2	7	7	7	6
	W3	10	2	2	1	1	2	2	3	2	5	5	6	2	4	3	2	4	5	3
	W4	10	1	2	1	2	2	3	3	1	8	3	4	1	5	1	2	5	4	3
	S2	10	5	3	1	3	4	3	4	2	6	3	7	2	6	4	2	5	4	4
	CV	10	2	1	1	1	2	4	1	1	1	3	7	1	4	2	2	5	4	2
	S3	10	3	1	1	3	3	2	1	2	1	c	1	1	2	2	1	4	2	2
	S4	10	3	2	1	5	3	5	2	1	1	9	5	2	4	2	1	4	2	3
NAMING	CO	10	1	4	7	6	9	6	2	1	6	8	3	7	3	6	3	7	c	5
	PI	10	3	9	5	7	3	5	3	3	c	6	6	8	6	8	3	8	c	5
ORAL READ	UC	10	5	4	4	6	6	3	2	1	7	4	8	6	5	4	2	6	6	4
	LC	10	4	4	3	5	6	4	2	1	6	4	7	8	5	3	2	8	8	4
	UL	10	5	3	3	7	6	5	5	2	8	5	c	8	4	3	3	8	9	5
	LS	10	4	4	2	5	3	3	9	2	5	4	7	6	4	3	2	5	5	4
	WR	10	2	1	1	3	1	2	2	1	2	1	8	6	3	2	2	4	6	2
	2W	10	2	2	1	1	2	3	2	1	2	2	7	4	2	2	2	3	5	2
	7W	10	2	2	1	2	2	3	2	1	2	1	6	4	3	2	2	4	7	2
	W5	10	3	2	1	2	2	3	1	1	2	2	4	5	3	2	2	4	6	2
	SY	10	2	1	1	1	1	1	1	1	1	2	1	2	1	1	1	1	1	1
comprehension		10	2	2	2	2	2	2	2	1	3	2	3	2	3	2	2	3	5	2
spelling	S1	10	2	2	2	2	2	2	3	2	3	3	3	2	3	2	2	3	4	2
	S2	10	2	2	2	2	1	2	2	1	2	2	5	1	3	2	1	4	2	2
	S3	10	2	4	2	2	2	2	1	2	2	4	4	2	7	1	3	7	3	3
VIS SCAN	RE	10	5	8	7	9	4	7	3	c	7	7	9	5	8	3	3	5	1	5
	F1	10	5	5	2	9	2	5	4	2	4	6	c	7	7	5	3	7	c	5
	NU	10	5	6	5	8	2	5	3	3	4	4	7	4	6	3	2	4	7	4
	LE	10	5	5	5	6	1	4	3	2	4	4	7	7	5	3	2	7	6	4
	2L	10	3	4	3	8	4	4	3	2	4	3	5	7	8	4	3	7	c	4
	LS	10	4	4	5	5	5	3	2	2	4	4	6	5	5	3	2	5	7	4
	WD	10	2	3	2	2	2	1	3	2	3	2	1	4	4	2	2	4	8	2
	SY	10	2	2	1	3	3	2	3	1	2	2	4	3	3	3	2	3	1	2
	CC	10	2	3	1	c	4	4	4	2	2	5	7	4	7	4	2	4	9	4
	UW	10	4	3	2	6	5	5	2	1	4	3	6	5	4	4	2	5	7	3

[a] Test ceilings are given in the left-hand column, and scores at the ceiling are designated by the letter *c* in the body of the table. Mean grade levels are given in the right-hand column.

TABLE 7.7

Grade-Equivalent Scores of Unclassified Subjects on the Durrell and the Wide Range Achievement Tests and on the Thirty-Nine Tests of Reading-Related Skills[a]

SUBJECT		1	2	3	4	5	6	7	8	9	10	11	12	13	14	15	16
Grade for age:		3	3	4	4	4	4	4	5	5	5	5	8	8	9	9	9
DURRELL oral	6	1	0	3	2	1	1	1	3	3	4	5	1	c	5	c	c
silent	6	1	0	3	3	2	1	0	3	3	3	4	1	4	5	c	c
listening	6	3	3	3	3	4	5	4	4	3	3	5	4	4	c	c	c
word rec.	6	3	0	3	3	3	3	2	2	5	4	c	1	c	c	c	c
word anal.	6	3	1	3	3	3	3	3	2	4	4	5	1	c	c	c	c
WRAT reading	19	2	1	-	-	3	2	1	2	5	4	5	1	9	6	8	6
spelling	19	1	2	-	-	2	2	2	2	4	3	5	2	6	4	8	3
arithmetic	19	2	2	-	-	3	5	2	2	4	3	4	1	6	6	6	6
V MATCH NU	10	1	1	2	2	4	3	2	4	4	5	4	3	8	c	c	c
LE	10	1	1	2	1	3	2	1	4	4	5	4	2	8	c	c	5
UL	10	1	1	1	1	1	3	2	4	4	3	5	2	8	c	c	8
W3	10	1	2	3	1	5	2	2	3	4	5	6	3	7	c	9	c
W4	10	1	1	2	3	4	2	2	2	5	4	6	3	7	c	c	7
S3	10	2	1	3	2	4	3	3	3	5	4	6	3	8	c	9	7
CC	10	1	4	1	1	·5	1	2	4	2	6	5	1	6	1	8	8
AV MATCH LE	10	2	1	2	7	6	3	3	6	3	8	5	6	8	c	c	c
W3	10	2	2	2	2	4	2	2	2	3	4	6	1	2	c	c	c
W4	10	1	1	1	2	3	2	1	3	5	5	7	1	c	7	c	c
S2	10	2	1	3	2	1	2	1	1	5	6	6	1	8	7	c	1
CV	10	1	1	2	2	1	1	2	4	6	3	6	1	6	6	c	c
S3	10	1	4	1	1	1	3	1	5	4	6	4	1	6	6	c	1
S4	10	1	1·2	2	1	2	2	1	5	3	7	1	7	5	c	9	
NAMING CO	10	1	2	2	1	1	2	1	5	4	2	4	5	5	7	c	5
PI	10	7	1	2	4	2	5	1	1	5	1	6	1	3	8	c	c
ORAL READ UC	10	1	1	2	1	1	3	1	1	4	4	5	1	5	5	c	7
LC	10	1	1	1	1	2	1	1	2	4	7	5	1	4	6	9	7
UL	10	2	1	1	1	1	2	1	2	4	4	7	1	7	7	9	9
LS	10	2	1	2	1	1	1	1	3	4	4	4	1	4	5	c	5
WR	10	1	1	2	2	1	1	1	1	6	4	4	1	c	9	c	6
2W	10	1	1	2	2	2	1	1	1	5	4	5	1	6	5	9	6
7W	10	1	1	2	2	1	1	1	2	5	7	7	1	7	7	c	7
WS	10	1	1	2	2	2	1	1	1	6	7	4	1	4	7	8	8
SY	10	1	1	2	2	1	1	1	1	5	1	7	1	8	7	c	1
comprehension	10	1	1	2	2	2	1	1	2	2	2	4	1	3	4	5	4
spelling S1	10	1	1	2	3	2	1	2	3	4	1	3	1	4	3	8	5
S2	10	1	1	2	2	2	1	1	1	5	1	2	1	6	6	5	1
S3	10	2	3	1	3	1	1	2	2	5	3	4	1	4	8	c	5
VIS SCAN RE	10	1	2	5	2	1	5	2	6	7	8	5	3	7	c	c	3
F1	10	1	2	2	3	3	5	3	5	3	4	6	3	7	c	7	7
NU	10	1	1	2	1	3	4	2	7	3	1	4	3	6	c	c	7
LE	10	1	2	3	2	3	2	2	5	3	2	4	3	5	c	c	7
2L	10	1	2	1	1	1	4	2	5	3	3	8	2	7	c	7	8
LS	10	1	1	3	2	3	1	2	5	2	5	5	3	c	c	5	6
WD	10	1	1	2	1	3	2	1	2	3	3	8	1	4	7	5	4
SY	10	1	2	2	3	3	1	1	2	2	4	6	2	5	9	6	c
CC	10	1	1	3	2	5	5	1	4	2	3	6	3	4	6	7	8
UW	10	1	1	1	3	3	4	1	2	2	4	8	1	8	8	6	7

[a] Test ceilings are given in the left-hand column, and scores at the ceiling are designated by the letter *c* in the body of the table.

perception problems in three subjects (U3, U4, and U7), and poor sentence comprehension relative to normal reading suggested comprehension problems in five subjects (U9, U10, U13, U15, and U16). However, these trends, although interesting, were revealed by subjective inspection of the individual profiles rather than by statistical classification. As previously mentioned, a factor that did not define a reading disability subtype (Factor 4 of the four-factor solution and Factor 5 of the five-factor solution) involved relatively good auditory–visual letter matching. Subjects U4, U5, U8, and U12 had high loadings on this factor and did show the trend for superior letter name matching.

We also compared the individual profiles of members of the same family. There has always been a great deal of interest in the possibility that reading disability is hereditary (Hallgren, 1950; Owen, 1978). If there is more than one type of reading disability, members of the same family could have the same type. The largest family group tested included five subjects, three of whom were triplets. They did not all have the same profile of reading skill deficit. One triplet (S7) and one other sibling (S10) were classified into Type S, but their profiles were not very similar. The remaining two triplets (U9 and U10) and the other sibling (U15) were unclassified. They were near normal on the 31 reading skill tests and the standard reading tests, but all three were relatively poor in sentence comprehension.

The other family members consisted of six pairs of siblings. Four of the pairs were classified into Group O and had profiles typical of that group. Those of two pairs of brothers (Subjects O11 and O12 and Subjects O23 and O33) were almost identical in both pattern and absolute magnitude; those of one pair of brothers (Subjects O5 and O31) had the same pattern but different overall levels; and those of one pair of brothers (Subjects O14 and O17) were similar on all tasks except visual matching. The other two pairs were brother–sister pairs (Subjects S8 and U11, and Subjects A20 and O18) who did not have similar profiles, both sisters being much closer to normal in the majority of reading skills.

The individual profiles of reading skill deficits shown in Tables 7.4–7.7 provide an explicit indication of the extent to which individual subjects exhibit the different types of reading disabilities. As would be expected, subjects with the highest loadings on a given factor have the profiles most similar to the factor score profile for that factor, and subjects with high loadings on more than one factor have profiles that reflect the characteristics of two of three different factor score profiles. The individual profiles of unclassified subjects indicate that some were not statistically classified because they were too young and others because they were near-normal in reading. There was also a suggestion that visual perception deficits and comprehension deficits might emerge in differently composed or larger samples, and some indication of how special training in one particular skill (letter naming in this instance) might affect statistical classification. Three pairs of siblings had similar patterns of Type 0 reading disability, and there was also a suggestion of a familial comprehension deficit. These various trends show the potential value of analyzing individual profiles after they have been objectively classified into different types of reading disabilities.

The Effect of Additional Tests on Statistical Classification

To determine whether different statistical classifications would occur when the naming, nonverbal scanning, sentence comprehension, and spelling tests were included, the scores of all 39 of the tests of reading-related skills were used in three-, four-, and five-factor solutions by the Q technique. We were specifically interested in finding out whether the oral reading deficit in Type 0 involved a general naming difficulty, and whether sentence comprehension would have the same close relationship to oral word reading as it did in the previous study (Doehring, 1977).

The factors associated with Types A and S appeared in all three factor solutions for the 39 tests, and most subjects of Types A and S had high loadings on the corresponding factors. The Type A and Type S subjects tended to be relatively good in color and picture naming. The results for Type 0 subjects were more complex. Although Type 0 was well preserved in the three- and four-factor solutions, most of the Type 0 subjects were classified into three different factors in the five-factor solution, 18 having their highest loading on a factor in which color and picture naming were much better than oral reading, 7 having their highest loading on a factor in which naming and oral reading were at the same low level, and 5 having their highest loading on a factor in which color and picture naming were even worse than oral reading. This demonstrated that the oral reading problem in Type 0 was often associated with a more general naming difficulty.

As before (Doehring, 1977), sentence comprehension was at exactly the same level as was oral word reading in all factor score profiles, and no factor defining a specific comprehension disorder emerged. Spelling tended to be slightly better than comprehension, with no large differences among spelling tests for the three types of reading disabilities. Rectangle and figure scanning tended to be at the same level as number and letter scanning for Types 0 and A, but higher than the remaining visual scanning tests for Type S.

The inclusion of nonreading tests in statistical classifications did not eliminate the different types of reading disabilities, but did indicate that some types may be subdivided by being associated with different patterns of nonreading deficits. The analyses of language and neuropsychological tests provided further information in this regard.

Stability of Statistical Classifications

As the use of statistical classification procedures is relatively new, a number of questions can be raised about its effectiveness. How reliable are the results? How are they affected by the number of subjects, the number types of tests, the ages of subjects, the inclusion of normal readers, the criteria for selecting subjects with reading disability, or the type of statistical classification procedure used? Some of the questions regarding the inclusion of normal readers and the use of alternative statistical procedures were answered in connection with the previous study, and some have already been answered in the present study. The earlier analyses indicated that the reading disability classifications are not exaggerations of normal reading skill profiles, are not changed by the inclusion of normal readers, and can be derived by completely different statistical procedures (Doehring, Hoshko, & Bryans, 1979). The same types of reading skill deficits were found in the present sample that had been found in the reading problem sample of the first study, demonstrating the replicability of three types of reading disabilities. For the present results, it was shown that the same types of reading disabilities emerge with three different factor solutions, that the average reading skill profiles of subjects of each type resemble the abstract factor score profiles, and that the reading disability types were largely preserved when additional tests were included in statistical classifications. All of these findings constitute direct evidence that the statistical classifications actually do reveal characteristic differences in the reading skill deficit of the subjects tested.

To learn about other aspects of the stability of the classifications, we assessed the effects of retests, smaller samples, different age ranges, different selection criteria, and classification by cluster analysis, as described in the following section. Those readers who are not interested in the details of these additional analyses may wish to go directly to the summary and preliminary discussion at the end of this chapter.

RELIABILITY OF REPEATED TESTS

Among the 88 subjects, 18 had been given the reading tests a second time. The time between tests was 7 months for 1 subject, 9 months for another, and 1 year or more for the other 16. All 18 had been classified into one of the three reading groups, with 4 having factor loadings beyond .40 on more than one factor. To assess the stability of the patterns of deficit for individual subjects, the two test profiles of the 18 subjects were visually compared, and the scores on the two sets of tests were correlated. In every case, the two profiles were similar. By visual inspection, exactly the same classification would have been made of both profiles for every subject, including 10 subjects classified as Type 0, 5 as Type A, and 2 as Type S. The correlations between the two sets of tests for a given subject can be interpreted in the same way as the correlation between two administrations of a single test to a group of 31 subjects, with a high correlation indicating a similar pattern of scores. In all but 3 of the 18 subjects, the correlations were statistically significant ($P < .01$), with nine correlations between .45 and .65, and six above .75. Thus, the reading test profiles and the reading disability classifications were quite stable in the majority of subjects tested twice.

STATISTICAL CLASSIFICATION OF SMALLER SAMPLES

Another way of estimating the reliability of classification is to see if the same types of reading disabilities occur when the sample is split into sub samples. The statistical classification of smaller samples also satisfies the requirement of some statisticians (cf. Nunnally, 1967) that the number of subjects should not be too large relative to the number of tests in Q factor analysis. An original sample of 94 subjects, which included the 88 subjects used in the main analysis plus 6 children younger than 8 years old who were not used for the main analysis, was divided into samples of 32, 31, and 31 subjects matched in age. A three-factor solution by the Q technique was calculated for each subsample. The three types of reading disabilities were clearly evident in each of the three subsamples. The Type 0 profile was Factor 1 in the first sample and Factor 2 in the other two samples, the Type A profile was Factor 3 in the first sample and Factor 1 in the other two samples, and the Type S profile was Factor 2 in the first sample and Factor 3 in the other two samples. Of the 88 subjects classified into one of the three types in the main analysis, 56 were classified into the same type in the subsample analysis, an agreement of 78%. The occurrence of the same types of reading disabilities in four independent samples (including the reading problem sample of the first study) provides a very strong demonstration of the replicability of three types of reading disabilities.

THE EFFECTS OF AGE ON STATISTICAL CLASSIFICATIONS

The average age of Type 0 subjects was 1 year more than Type A and S subjects, but all three types included subjects ranging in age from 8 to adult (Table 7.2), and Type 0 subjects had the lowest average age in the previous study. This suggested that the types of reading disabilities did not depend on age. Because the possibility that the pattern of reading disability does vary with age has been a matter of considerable theoretical interest (Satz, Taylor, Friel, & Fletcher, 1978), however, we directly assessed the effects of age by statistical classification of subsamples of 31 subjects 8–10 years old, 28 subjects 11–13.5 years old, and 29 subjects 13.6–27 years old. The reading test scores of each subsample were factor analyzed by a three-factor solution. The three types of reading disability emerged very clearly in each age group. For the 8–10-year-olds, Factor 1 resembled Type S, Factor 2 Type A, and Factor 3 Type 0; for the 11–13.5-year-olds, Factor 1 resembled Type A, Factor 2 Type 0, and Factor 3 Type S; and for the 13.6–27-year-olds, Factor 1 resembled Type 0, Factor 2 Type A, and Factor 3 Type S. The proportion of subjects classified into the same type of reading disability for the subsamples as for the entire sample was somewhat lower than had been the case for the three age-matched samples. The classifications were the same for the main sample and the subsamples in 44 cases, a 61% agreement. The lower rate of agreement was largely a result of relatively poor agreement of Type 0 classifications in the youngest age sample and Type S classifications in the oldest sample. This does provide a faint suggestion that the Type S deficit is most clearly evident in younger subjects and the Type 0 deficit in older subjects.

SUBSAMPLES SELECTED BY MORE STRINGENT CRITERIA OF READING DISABILITIES

One of the greatest potential advantages of the statistical classification procedure is that the usual exclusionary definitions of reading disabilities are unnecessary. If reading disability is a distinct unitary disorder, all children with that disorder should be classified into a unique subtype, thus providing an objective definition of the disorder. However, some readers may not feel comfortable in drawing inferences from statistical classifications involving a few subjects who did not meet the usual exclusionary criteria for developmental dyslexia, because they are accustomed to the traditional experimental design in which a rigidly defined sample is essential. To satisfy any doubts in this regard, we statistically classified three subsamples selected according to successively more stringent criteria of reading disability, using three-factor solutions by the Q technique. The three types of reading disabilities clearly emerged in all three subsamples, and there was consistent agreement in the classification of individual subjects.

A subsample that met the usual criterion of reading retardation and was closer to the usual age range included 50 subjects aged 9–15 who were at least 2 years behind expected grade for age on the reading part of the WRAT. All but 8 were classified into one of the three types of reading disabilities, and 86% were classified as having the same type of reading disability as in the 88-subject sample.

A subsample that also met the usual criterion of intelligence included 43 subjects aged 9–15 with PIQs of 90 or above and 2 or more years of reading retardation on the WRAT. All but 4 were classified into one of the three types and there was 74% agreement with the original classification.

A more age-restricted subsample included 36 children aged 10–14 with PIQs of 90 or above and at least 2 years behind in reading on the WRAT. All but 2 were classified into one of the three types, with 71% classified into the same type as in the original classification.

These results agree with our earlier results (Doehring, Hoshko, & Bryans, 1979) in showing that the reading disability classifications remain quite stable regardless of the composition of the sample. The three types of reading disabilities emerge in samples selected according to the usual exclusionary criteria of reading disabilities, as well as in less-stringently selected samples. This aspect of the stability of statistical classifications is important for future applications.

STATISTICAL CLASSIFICATION BY CLUSTER ANALYSIS

As in the previous study (Doehring, Hoshko, & Bryans, 1979), we analyzed the 31 reading test scores of the 88 subjects by several different cluster analysis procedures (Wishart, 1975) to determine whether the same types of reading disabilities would be obtained by a different statistical classification technique. Once more, the best agreement with the Q technique classifications was found for the four-cluster solutions by McQuitty's similarity analysis, using squared Euclidean distance coefficients. Of the 72 subjects who had been classified into the three types of reading disabilities in the present study, 57 were classified into three corresponding clusters. All but 3 of the 33 members of Group O were classified into one cluster, all but 4 of the 22 members of Group A into a second cluster, and all but 5 of the 17 members of Group S into a third cluster. Of the 12 misclassified subjects, 7 had their next highest positive loading on the factor that corresponded to the cluster into which they had been misclassified. The agreement of 79% between the two classification methods is even better than the agreement of Q technique classifications between the three age-matched subsamples and the total sample of 88 subjects. Although the lack of guidelines for choosing among the many different varieties of cluster analyses precluded its use as the primary technique for statistical classification, it was found once more that the McQuitty technique of cluster analysis provided very satisfactory confirmation of the Q technique classifications.

Summary and Preliminary Discussion

In the present study, we used the Q technique of factor analysis to classify 88 subjects, most of whom had severe reading problems, into three different types of reading disabilities on the basis of their scores on 31 tests of reading-related skills. The 33 subjects classified into Type 0 tended to be poorest on all oral reading tests and also to have difficulty on visual scanning tests. The 22 subjects of Type A tended to be poorest on all tests involving the matching of printed and spoken materials, and also on all oral reading tests. The 17 subjects of Type S tended to have much more difficulty on all tasks in reading words and nonsense syllables than in reading letters and numbers.

There was considerable evidence for the stability of the reading disability classifications. Essentially the same three types of reading disabilities had been found in a sample of 34 children with reading problems in a previous study (Doehring & Hoshko, 1977a). For the present sample, the same three types of reading disabilities were evident when three-, four-, and five-factor solutions were used for factor analysis, and when the reading skill deficits were expressed in terms of abstract factor score profiles, the average profiles of subjects of each type, and the individual profiles of subjects of each type. The three types also emerged when subjects were retested, when the total sample was divided into three subsamples matched in age, and three subsamples of different ages, when subjects who did not meet the usual criteria for reading disabilities or developmental dyslexia were excluded from the sample, and when the classification was done by cluster analysis rather than by Q-technique factor analysis.

Despite the consistency of the classifications, it cannot be concluded that there are only three types of reading disabilities, and that all subjects within each type have exactly the same patterns of reading and nonreading deficits. A number of subjects were statistically classified into more than one type and had profiles characteristic of the combined types, suggesting some form of continuity between types. Statistical classifications carried out with additional tests of nonreading skills suggested that Type 0 oral reading problems might be further subdivided in terms of the presence or absence of naming problems. Although all three types emerged in each of the three subsamples of different ages, the Type 0 classifications were least stable in the youngest, and Type S, the least stable in the oldest subsample, suggesting a possible effect of age on the typologies. Inspection of the individual profiles of unclassified subjects indicated that other types of reading disabilities such as comprehension problems and visual perception disorders might be found in different samples of reading problems.

Further speculation about the characteristics of each type of reading disability will be deferred until their possible interactions with linguistic and neurological deficits are considered.

The Interaction of Reading and Language Deficits

8

Having identified three stable types of reading disabilities, we were ready to look for interactive patterns of language deficit. On the basis of previous research (Chapter 4), it can be predicted with virtual certainty that any sample of subjects with reading problems will include some with significant deficiencies of language functioning. The linguistic deficiencies could be either the cause or the result of reading difficulty, or both. As there is insufficient evidence at present to draw valid conclusions about the cause-and-effect relationships, it is best to view concurrent reading and language deficits as interactive (Doehring & Aulls, 1979). The persons having interactive reading and language deficits will not necessarily be classified as having a disorder of spoken language, because linguistic deficiencies such as difficulty in segmenting phonemes may hamper reading acquisition but may not noticeably affect spoken language.

The search for interactive language deficits must be made with appropriate measures. A well-validated set of tests based on a comprehensive, generally accepted language theory is needed. As was the case for the reading measures, available tests and theories did not meet these requirements. The language tests that were used represented our best guess as to what measures would be sensitive to the types of language deficit that occur in reading disabilities. An important outcome of the analysis of language test results will be to arrive at suggestions regarding the types of language measures needed for further research.

The reading tests were designed on the assumption that reading involves several component skills rather than one skill, because there is no way that differential patterns of deficit could be found in a unitary skill.

The same is true for language skills. The type of theory that is espoused in designing a language test battery must almost necessarily involve the assumption that there are component abilities rather than a unitary language ability. If there were a unitary language ability, language deficiency could differentially affect reading disabilities only in the sense that one type of reading disability might interact with language deficiency and other types would interact with nonlinguistic deficiencies such as visual perceptual disorders. We preferred to explore the possibility that different types of language deficit might be involved in different types of reading disabilities.

Guesses as to exactly how language deficiencies interact with reading deficiencies also depend, of course, on exactly what component skills are said to be involved in reading. Code-oriented reading theories would postulate that printed words are always or almost always recoded into phonological form, with all subsequent language processing at the lexical, syntactic, and semantic levels taking place through the spoken language system (Foss & Hakes, 1978). According to these theories, any differential effects of language deficiencies on reading disabilities would have to involve language abilities at or below the level of phonological recoding, and deficiencies at the lexical, syntactic, or semantic level would have to be generalized disorders of both spoken and written language. Meaning-oriented reading theories would postulate that readers can directly access the meaning of words or even larger units of text without phonological recoding. According to these theories, any differential effects of language deficiencies on reading disabilities would have to involve language deficits at or above the lexical level. More eclectic theories might postulate that phonological recoding is necessary during the early stages of reading acquisition and for the reading of difficult or unfamiliar words, or that skills for phonological recoding and more direct access of meaning operate in parallel during reading. Both the reading and language test batteries were designed to accommodate the eclectic view of reading. We anticipated that reading disabilities would more likely involve lower-level reading skills, and allowed for the possibility that reading disabilities were more likely to interact with lower-level rather than with higher-level language skills.

Another theoretical complication has to do with the interactive effects of language development. Because not all language abilities are fully developed when the child is learning to read, interactive language and reading deficits can involve developmental lags in language abilities. There has been a great deal of interest in language development for a number of years, but few of the theoretical issues have yet been resolved. The language measures reflect P.G. Patel's particular theoretical interest in how reading acquisition and language development interact with brain maturation (Patel, 1977, 1981, in press). Although his inferences about these interactions are highly speculative, they provide a theoretical basis for a neurolinguistic approach to reading disabilities, as discussed in the following section.

Neurolinguistic Development about Age Seven

The area of the brain comprising the junction of the parietal, temporal, and occipital lobes was the last to evolve and matures relatively late, around age 7 (Luria, 1970; Yakovlev & Lecours, 1967). The functions associated with this area are complex simultaneous and spatial syntheses involving visual, tactile, vestibular, and auditory analyzers (Luria, 1966). Luria (1966, 1970) categorized the language disorders associated with injuries to this area as semantic aphasias. Some of the language abilities that emerge around age 7 are quite similar to those that are impaired in semantic aphasia, suggesting a connection between the developing language abilities and maturation at the temporal–parietal–occipital junction in the language dominant hemisphere.

The language disorder in semantic aphasia involves impairment of complex simultaneous processing of logicogrammatical and spatiotemporal relationships such as "father's brother" and "the circle under the triangle." Some of the specific symptoms associated with semantic aphasia are visuospatial disorders, constructional apraxia, acalculia, and finger agnosia (Luria, 1970). The factor underlying these symptoms is said to be "a disturbance of the capacity to unify individual stimulations into a single simultaneous pattern [p. 226]" even though there is adequate understanding of individual words.

The patterns of linguistic breakdown associated with focal lesions in the temporal–parietal–occipital region of the left hemisphere are similar to the "developmental shifts" (Whyte, 1965) or "cognitive pendulums" (Nelson & Nelson, 1978) that have been observed in psycholinguistic development around the age of 7. At this stage, the child's language appears to change from unanalyzed, iconic, situation-bound to more abstract, symbolic, and categorical utterances at the phonological, morphophonemic, lexical, and syntactic–semantic levels of linguistic functioning. One might speculate that as the "association area of the association areas" begins to operate around the age of 7 (Critchley, 1953; Geschwind, 1965; Luria, 1966), the child becomes able to process linguistic structures epilinguistically (i.e., independently from situational cues).

The linguistic changes occurring at the phonological level around age 7 relate to the ability to perceive the linguistic units within utterances. The sentence, which was previously perceived as a whole, can be segmented into phrases, words, syllables, and phonemes, and these linguistic units can be blended to create syllables, words, phrases, and sentences (Karpova, 1977). This ability is of obvious importance for reading acquisition, as the child must be able to segment utterances into phrases, words, syllables, and phonemes to identify their counterparts in written language (Bruce, 1964; Elkonin, 1973; Fox & Routh, 1975; Liberman, Shankweiler, Fischer, & Carter, 1974; Rosner & Simon, 1971). The ability emerges as children engage in various kinds of language games that involve rhyming, syllabication, and the use of nonsense words (Kirshenblatt-Gimblett, 1976; Wolfenstein, 1954). Phonemic segmentation abilities have been described by the terms "linguistic awareness" (Mattingly, 1972), "metalinguistic awareness" (Read, 1978), and "metacognitive awareness" (Clark, 1978), but such terms also encompass a number of other abilities (Hakes, Evans, & Tunmer, 1980; Sinclair, Jarvella, & Levelt, 1978); and phonemic segmentation may better be characterized simply as access to linguistic segments rather than conscious awareness of linguistic activity (Mattingly, 1980).

Another aspect of the emerging categorical use of language is the acquisition of specific morphophonemic rules (Palermo, 1978; Vaughn-Cooke, 1977). Phonemes are units of speech sounds and morphemes are units of meaning. Morphophonemic rules describe how the pronunciation of a morpheme can vary as a function of the phonemes that precede or follow it in a word. In the spoken words *divine* and *divinity*, *grateful* and *gratitude*, and *meter* and *metric*, the child must know the morphophonemic rules that vary the pronunciation but not the meaning of the morphemic unit as its grammatical function changes; and in the spoken words *bugs*, *books*, and *busses*, the child must know the morphophonemic rules that vary the pronunciation of the final sound while preserving its underlying meaning of pluralization. The ability to abstract and apply morphophonemic rules is particularly important for reading, because written words reflect morphophonemic structure in complex ways (Chomsky, 1970; Chomsky & Halle, 1968; Mattingly, 1980; Venezky, 1970). For example, the underlying morpheme is preserved at the expense of sound–letter correspondence in the printed form of *divine* and *divinity*, and in *ducks* and *pigs*.

At the lexical level, "the mental filing system for words" (Francis, 1972) seems to undergo considerable change around age 7. Children begin to associate words on a paradigmatic basis as members of the same grammatical class, rather than syntagmatically as belonging to the dif-

ferent grammatical classes of adjacent words in the undifferentiated utterance (Brown & Berko, 1960; Entwistle, 1966). These changes in word
associations seem to reflect a change in the structure of long-term
memory from an entirely episodic, situationally organized form to a more
abstract, categorical semantic memory (Petrey, 1977; Tulving, 1972), in
which words are organized into "semantic fields" (Luria & Vinogradova,
1959; Marshall & Newcombe, 1966; Weigel & Bierwisch, 1970). The
ability to respond to words as abstract linguistic units rather than as inex-
tricable parts of a total utterance enables children to retrieve words
rapidly from semantic memory by a process that can be termed automatic lexical access. This ability would be of obvious use in reading an
unfamiliar text that did not include the situational interpersonal context
of spoken language (Olson & Nickerson, 1978).

Development beyond the stage of treating utterances as undifferentiated wholes also involves the acquisition of rules for analyzing the syntactic–semantic structure of utterances. This is indicated by children's
ability to understand passive sentences (Slobin, 1966), to differentiate
correct from incorrect syntactic-semantic usage (McNeill, 1970), to
understand complex syntactic–semantic relationships in sentences containing words such as *ask* and *tell* (Chomsky, 1969; Kessel, 1970), and to
use metaphors (Gardner, 1974). These abilities for processing syntactic–semantic structure epilinguistically involve the kind of logicogrammatical relationships that are impaired in semantic aphasics, and are
important for understanding the "schooled language" (Olson, 1975) of
written texts.

The parallel between developmental shifts in language abilities and
the maturation of the temporal–parietal–occipital region may also be extended to cognitive development. Piaget postulated a stage of concrete
operational thought beginning at about age 7, when the child becomes
able to deal with the dynamic nature of events by simultaneously coor-
dinating several different dimensions in a situation (Ginsberg & Opper,
1969; Waller, 1977). Current linguistic thinking suggests that the semantic properties of spatial and temporal terms are related to such cognitive
strategies (Clark, 1974). Thus, cognitive and linguistic abilities may be
going through an important stage of interactive development during the
years when children are learning to read. These changes could take the
form of a complex reorganization that involves temporary disruption of
behavior (Carey & Diamond, 1980; Cromer, 1976) rather than a smooth
transition from situation-bound to context-free linguistic processing. Gibson (1971) described developmental shifts in reading acquisition in much
the same manner.

The language abilities that enable the child to go beyond the illocutionary stage of perceiving utterances as unified semantic wholes must be of great importance for learning to understand written language, which not only lacks the situational cues that are usually available in spoken language, but also is quite different from spoken language in syntactic–semantic structure (Olson, 1977). Children who have not completed the normal developmental shifts in language abilities may encounter great difficulty in learning to deal with written text. It is possible that such difficulties are not uniform across all levels of linguistic functioning, and that there are individual differences in patterns of linguistic impairment that correspond to individual differences in patterns of reading skill impairment.

These speculations about neurolinguistic development, which are based on Patel's (1977, 1980, in press) "systematization of induction," served as guidelines for the selection of language tests. The test battery described in the following section was designed to sample the linguistic abilities that emerge during the developmental shifts just described, including the segmentation and blending of phonemes, the acquisition of morphophonemic rules, the formation of semantic memory, the use of syntactic rules, and the understanding of complex logicogrammatical and spatiotemporal relationships.

Description of Language Tests

The battery of language tests was selected from a variety of different sources, as no appropriate test battery was available. The battery includes several tests on which children with reading disabilities had been particularly impaired in a previous study (Doehring, 1968). The tests do not systematically assess separate categories of language ability. Some tests sample more than one aspect of language, and some language abilities are sampled by more than one test. However, the present set of tests was sufficiently comprehensive and detailed to reveal any major areas of language weakness.

Insofar as possible, a uniform procedure was followed for administrating and scoring the language tests. All except the Cartoon Description Test were scored in terms of latency of response when the error rate was sufficiently low. The criterion for low error rate was based on the distributions of errors of a sample of normally achieving children. Latency was expressed in terms of median latency on tests that had a series of separate items, with errors classified as infinitely long latencies, and in terms of total time on tests involving a sequence of spoken responses rather than separate items. All spoken responses were tape-recorded.

PHONEMIC SEGMENTATION-BLENDING TESTS

In view of the probable importance of abilities at the phonemic level, we obtained five different measures of the ability to differentiate phonemes within syllables and words. The two most direct measures were obtained with a procedure devised by Bruce (1964), in which the subject had to blend the sounds of a syllable or a word from which a phoneme had been deleted. Less direct measures were provided by two word games, Pig Latin and Ubby Dubby, which require the subject to segment and blend words at a particular phonemic boundary. The most indirect measure was rhyming words, where the subject had to find words having the same combination of phonemes at the end. Some or all of these measures should be sensitive to language difficulty at the phonemic level.

Sound Deletion. The Sound Deletion Test was adapted from that of Bruce (1964), but using different items that included linguistically possible nonsense words. It was presented as a word game. On each trial a word or nonsense syllable was spoken by the tester, who then spoke one of the sounds in the word or syllable. The subject had to say the word or syllable that remained after the sound had been deleted. Three practice trials were given (*nest* with *s* deleted, *fairy* with *y* deleted, and *hill* with *h* deleted). Then eight trials with words and eight with syllables were given in the following order (deleted sound in parentheses): *plate (p), card (d), stand (t), lost (s), lawn (n), cold (c), went (n), scream (s), noral (l), misk (s), fepity (f), silp (p), lant (n), gathod (d), zalp (l), and snat (s).* The word and the nonsense syllable trials were scored separately, with median response latency calculated when there were two or fewer errors on the eight trials, and total errors counted when there were three or more errors. Adequate performance in segmenting and blending syllables demonstrates the ability to segment phonemes in the absence of morphemic cues.

Pig Latin. The tester explained the Pig Latin game to the subject with an example *(bat–atbey)* of how the first sound in the word is moved to the end and followed by *ey*. Three practice items *(mat–atmey, dog–ogdey,* and *doll–olldey)* were then given, followed by ten test trials using the words *loss, nurse, that, think, friend, judge, room, land, neat,* and *sing.* Responses were scored in terms of median latency when there were three or fewer errors, and otherwise in terms of total errors.

Ubby Dubby. The tester explained the Ubby Dubby test as a game in which the syllable *ab* was put before the middle vowel sound in each word, giving one example *(boy–baboy)* and three practice trials *(nut–nabut, sheet–shabeet,* and *ring–rabing).* Then ten test items *(soon, sock, chair, candy, pen, book, lamp, store, toy,* and *cup)* were given on tape. Median latency was calculated when there were three or fewer errors, and otherwise total errors were recorded.

Rhyming. Rhyming ability was tested because it had been found to be very deficient in an undifferentiated sample of children with reading disability (Doehring, 1968). On the Rhyming test the subject was asked to give as many words as possible that rhymed with each of four words *(go, tree, car, write).* When the subject stopped on each trial, there was one prompt ("Any more?"). Two examples were given *(day:* "may, way, pay, or any word that sounds like day" and *sweet:* "heat, neat, seat, or any word that has the same sound"). Responses were scored in terms of median time for saying six rhyming words when six or more rhyming words were given on at least three of the four trials. Otherwise, total errors were counted by subtracting the number of correctly rhymed words from six on each of the four trials.

SERIAL NAMING

In a previous study (Doehring, 1968), an undifferentiated group of children with reading disability was very deficient on a test of serial word-finding responses adapted from Schuell, Jenkins, and Jimenez-Pabon (1964). This test was included in the present study to assess the ability to rapidly retrieve sequences of words stored serially rather then semantically. The three measures obtained were the serial naming of numbers, days, and months.

Counting to 20. The subject was asked to count to 20, and was scored in terms of the total time required. All subjects were accurate enough to eliminate an error criterion.

Naming Days of the Week. The subject was asked to name the days of the week, and was scored in terms of total time, with no error criterion necessary.

Naming Months of the Year. The subject was asked to name the months of the year in correct order. Responses were scored in terms of total time if there were two or fewer errors, and otherwise in terms of total errors. Any month omitted or given out of order was counted as an error.

SHORT–TERM VERBAL MEMORY

Reading obviously requires some form of short-term memory, as the exact meaning of words in sentences cannot be determined until the complete sentence has been read (Lashley, 1951). Reading disability could involve a deficiency in short-term verbal memory (Shankweiler, Liberman,

Mark, Fowler, & Fischer, 1979). To test this, we devised a word repetition test of the type used by other investigators (cf. McNeill, 1970). The subjects were required to repeat unrelated words, randomly ordered words from sentences, grammatically correct but meaningless sentences, and simple meaningful sentences. Subjects who use syntactic structure to aid short-term memory should repeat meaningless sentences better than unrelated or randomized words, and those who use syntactic–semantic structure should repeat meaningful sentences better than meaningless sentences.

The subject was asked to repeat a series of 16 tape-recorded sequences of five words exactly as they had been spoken. There were 4 sequences containing unrelated words (UW), 4 containing randomly ordered words from a meaningful sentence (RW), 4 grammatically correct but meaningless sentences (AS), and 4 meaningful sentences (MS). They were presented in the following order:

> *Pretty shining raincoats attract children* (MS)
> *Cats closed stop doors some* (RW)
> *Pastry foxes many open worry* (UW)
> *Serious public raindrops debate houses* (AS)
> *Empty bottles litter public highways* (MS)
> *Nervous apples watch greasy kites* (AS)
> *Progress fathers hamper many backward* (RW)
> *College outside happy supply easy* (UW)
> *Carry helpful many empty rabbits* (UW)
> *Pupils teachers disturb noisy sincere* (RW)
> *Many college students study language* (MS)
> *Worried sunny pastry supplies children* (AS)
> *Relax mornings workers pleasant Sunday* (RW)
> *Parties rivers litter feeling houses* (UW)
> *Empty smokers consult foolish gardens* (AS)
> *Open markets attract many flies* (MS)

Separate scores were calculated for the four different types of word sequences. Median latency was calculated when there were three or fewer errors on VA or AS sequences, four or fewer errors on RW sequences, and five or fewer errors on MS sequences. Otherwise, total incorrect words on all four sequences were counted as the error score.

COMPREHENSION

Previous research (Doehring, 1977) had suggested that reading comprehension was limited by poor word-reading skills in all types of reading disabilities, but the possiblity of a generalized comprehension deficit in at least one type of reading disability could not be ruled out. A measure of the syntactic–semantic skills necessary for the complex simultaneous processing of spatiotemporal relationships was provided by the Token test (Whitaker & Noll, 1972), which requires the subject to carry out simple spoken instructions regarding colored geometric figures.

An array of 20 tokens, white, yellow, blue, green, or red in color, large or small in size, and circular or square in shape was placed before the subjects. On each trial, the subject was given a spoken instruction to point to or to rearrange one or more tokens. The test was given in six sets of increasingly difficult items. In the sixth set, testing was terminated after four consecutive items were failed. The test items were exactly the same as those used in the Neurosensory Center Comprehensive Examination for Aphasia (Spreen & Benton, 1969) and consisted of 7 trials in Part A (Example: "Show me a red one."); 4 in Part B ("Show me the green circle."); 4 in Part C ("Show me the small blue square."); 4 in Part D ("Take the white square and the green circle."); 4 in Part E ("Take the small blue circle and the large yellow square."); and 16 in Part F ("Put the red circle between the yellow square and the green square."). Median latency was calculated on Parts A to E when there was 1 error or no errors, and on Part F when there were 4 or fewer errors. Errors were scored in terms of total incorrect parts of instructions (e.g., pointing to a large blue circle in response to "Show me the small blue square" would be counted as 2 errors). There were 7 possible errors on Part A, 8 on Part B, 12 on Part C, 16 on Part D, 24 on Part E, and 84 on Part F.

OTHER SYNTACTIC–SEMANTIC SKILLS

Other syntactic–semantic skills that were tested included morphophonemic knowledge, complex syntactic usage, semantic fields, and knowledge of complex syntactic–semantic relationships.

Morphophonemic Knowledge. The correct use of word endings to indicate tense, number, and possession involves both phonemic and morphemic knowledge. To test this type of morphophonemic ability, the subject was required to generate word endings in response to pictures. The subject was tested on 12 items of morphophonemic knowledge of the type used in the Berko (1958) and Berry-Talbott tests (Berry, 1966). Knowledge of how to form plurals (Pl) was tested in six trials, past tense (PT) on three trials, and third person singular (TPS) on two trials. The subject was told that the tester would present some funny pictures, tell something about the pictures, and then ask the subject to finish a sentence about the pictures. On each trial, the subject was shown a picture of the type used on the Berko and Berry-Talbott tests and asked to supply the missing word in a statement that demonstrated a particular form of morphophonemic knowledge. Two practice items were given:

This is a wug; now there is another one; there are two of them; there are two wugs (P1) and *This is a nid who knows how to gutch; he did the same thing yesterday; what did he do yesterday? He gutched* (PT). Then 12 trials were given using the same types of pictures and the same types of verbal instructions as did the Berko and Berry-Talbott tests to elicit the following word endings: *fops* (P1), *gishes* (TPS), *spuzzes* (P1), *ludded* (PT), *flitched* (PT), *zills* (P1), *nazzes* (TPS), *votches* (P1), *quiffed* (PT), *gans* (P1), *rets* (P1), *natted* (PT). Responses were scored in terms of median latency when there was one error or no error, and otherwise in terms of total errors.

Complexity of Syntactic Usage. The ability to use complex grammatical rules was tested by analyzing spoken descriptions of cartoons. The subject was asked to tell the stories represented in each of three cartoon strips. The cartoons had no written captions and showed simple sequences of action involving two boys, their father, and their dog. When there were fewer than 4 utterances for a given cartoon strip, the tester said "Tell me more." If there were fewer than 15 utterances by the end of the third cartoon strip, the first cartoon strip was presented again and the tester asked the subject to "Tell me something more about this one." This was the only test that could not be scored in terms of latency. The total set of utterances was scored by the developmental sentence scoring technique of Lee (1974), in which the syntactic complexity of each utterance was scored according to the use of eight categories of grammatical form: indefinite pronoun or noun modifier, personal pronoun, main verb, secondary verb, negative, conjunction, interrogative reversal in questions, and wh-questions. The developmental sentence score (DSS) was obtained by dividing the total score by the number of utterances. The scores of the present subjects cannot be related to the norms reported by Lee (1974) because the cartoon description differed from the language sample recommended by Lee for DSS scoring. However, the DSS measure should reveal any striking deficiencies in grammatical usage by the present subjects.

Semantic Fields Test. Knowledge of semantic relationships of words (Francis, 1972; Petrey, 1977) was tested by a word association procedure of the type employed by Brown and Berko (1960). The subject had to give 2 associated words for each of 10 stimulus words. On each trial, the subject was told to close his or her eyes, repeat a word spoken by the tester, and say two other words that go with the stimulus word. Prompting was used whenever necessary to obtain two words. The stimulus words were *house, store, school, cook, chair, ink, car, nickel, desk,* and *child.* Responses were counted as incorrect if the grammatical category of the response word was not the same as that of the stimulus word, and were scored in terms of median latency when there were two or fewer errors. Otherwise, the score was the total number of incorrect or omitted words.

Syntactic–Semantic Relationships in Sentences. Knowledge of complex syntactic–semantic relationships was assessed by the Ask and Tell test of Chomsky (1969), given in the form described by Kessel (1970). The subject was required to point to one of a pair of pictures that showed the semantic–syntactic relationship described in a test sentence. Each of the 12 trials involved some variation of a boy or a girl either asking the other a question or telling the other to do something (Examples: "The boy asks the girl which pencil to sharpen." "The girl tells the boy which picture he should move."). The tester spoke the sentence, and the subject had to choose the picture that corresponded to the sentence. Responses were scored in terms of median latency when there were three or fewer errors on the 12 trials, and otherwise in terms of total errors.

ORDER OF PRESENTATION

The tests were presented in the following order: Ask & Tell, Serial Naming, Rhyming, Morphophonemics, Token, Sound Deletion, Pig Latin, Ubby Dubby, Semantic Fields, Cartoon Description, and Oral Repetition.

Language Test Performance of Normally Achieving Children

Normative data were obtained for the 22 language measures by administering them to 10 normally achieving children per grade from kindergarten through Grade 6, a total of 70 children. The children were selected from the same schools and according to the same criteria of normal achievement as the normative sample used for the tests of reading-related skills (Doehring, 1976a). They were neither too low nor too high in school achievement, were in the normal grade for their age, had English as their first language, and had no hearing problems or uncorrected visual problems.

The language scores of the normal subjects gradually increased from the lower to the higher grades on all tests except serial naming of numbers, which reached a very early latency limit. Within each grade, the scores tended to be quite variable. On most of the measures, the best score in Grades 2 or 3 was almost as high as the best score in Grades 5 or 6. Thus, the skills measured tended to be quite well developed in some normally achieving children in the lower grades.

To give some idea of the relative difficulty of the tests, we have estimated the grades at which responses become highly accurate and then the grades at which the highly accurate responses approach a stable speed of response. The accuracy limit is defined as the highest grade in which two or fewer subjects exceeded the criterion of errors for a test. The latency limit is defined as the grade where the latency of accurate responses approached a lower limit. On the Cartoon Description Test, where responses were scored in terms of relative complexity rather than accuracy and latency, the limit of learning is defined as the grade in which the Developmental Sentence Score approached an upper limit.

The estimates of accuracy and latency limits are shown in Table 8.1. The accuracy limit was reached in the lowest grades on the simplest serial naming tests and the simplest parts of the Token test. Otherwise, the accuracy limit was reached in Grade 3 or above, and was not reached at all on the rhyming test and three of the word repetition tests. The latency limit for serial naming of numbers was approached in Grade 1 and the Cartoon Description scores approached a limit in Grade 3, but the latency limit on the remaining measures was not approached before Grade 5.

The use of latency as well as accuracy to score the language tests enabled us to extend the estimate of normal performance up to the higher grades for the majority of language measures. The variability within grades and the overlap of scores from grade to grade suggested that there was a wide range of individual differences in the acquisition of the language abilities that were sampled by the tests.

Calculation of Percentile Scales

As before, the scores of the subjects with reading problems were expressed in terms of percentiles based on the performance of the normally achieving subjects. The percentile scores for the language tests are not directly comparable to those for reading-related skills because the language test percentiles were based on 10 subjects each from Kindergarten and Grades 1 to 6, whereas the reading test percentiles were based on an older sample of 10 subjects each in Grades 1, 1.5, 2, 2.5, 3, 4, 6, 8, and 10. A single distribution of error and latency scores of the 70 normally achieving subjects was made for each language test, with the highest percentile assigned to the shortest latency and the lowest to the largest number of errors. The error criteria were those given in the descriptions of the tests, with the Cartoon Description percentiles based on the Developmental Sentence Scores rather than on error and latency scores.

TABLE 8.1

Estimates of the Grades at Which Accuracy and Latency Limits Were Achieved on the Language Measures by Normal Subjects from Kindergarten through Grade 6[a]

Language Measure		Accuracy Limit		Latency Limit
Phonemic Segmentation:				
Sound Deletion in Syllables		4		5
Sound Deletion in Words		4		5
Pig Latin		5		none
Ubby Dubby		3		none
Rhyming		none		none
Serial Naming:	Numbers	K		1
	Days	1		none
	Months	5		none
Oral Repetition:				
Unrelated Words		none		none
Random Words from Sentences		none		none
Meaningless Sentences		none		none
Sentences		4		5
Token Test:	A. One word	K		5
	B. Two words	K		5
	C. Three words	K		5
	D. Four words	K		5
	E. Six words	5		none
	F. Complex	5		none
Synt-Sem.:	Morphophonemics	5		none
	Cartoon Description (DSS)		(3)	
	Semantic Fields	4		5
	Ask & Tell	6		none

[a] The accuracy limit was achieved at the highest grade where two or fewer of the ten subjects exceeded the error criterion for a test, and the latency limit was achieved at the grade where the distribution of latencies approached a lower limit. The entry "none" indicates that the limit was not reached by Grade 6. For the Cartoon Description Test, where responses were not scored in terms of accuracy or latency, the grade at which the distribution of scores approached an upper limit is given.

This procedure enabled us to put all language test scores on the same scale, and to evaluate language test performance in relation to that of normally achieving subjects.

Average Performance of the Eighty-Eight Subjects with Reading Problems

The average performance of the entire sample of 88 subjects on the 22 language measures was examined first, to evaluate their overall language proficiency as a group. This was accomplished by plotting their average grade-level equivalent scores, as shown in Figure 8.1. These averages were calculated in the same way as those for the reading tests (Figure 7.1), but must be considered even rougher estimates because the grade-level norms were derived from a more restricted sample of normal subjects. In general, the subjects with reading problems were about as impaired in language skills (Figure 8.1) as they were in reading skills (Figure 7.1). Their worst performance was on the Morphophonemics and Cartoon Description tests, in which they scored at about the level of normal first graders. They were about 5 years behind their average expected

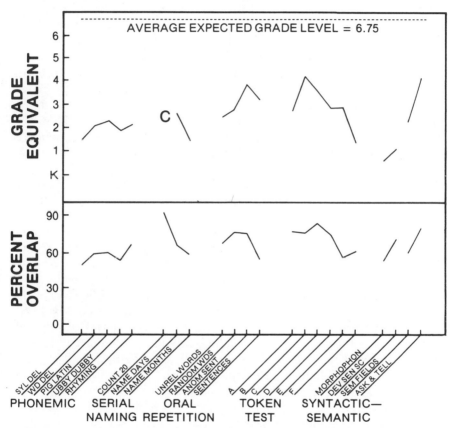

FIGURE 8.1. *The top graph shows the mean grade-equivalent scores of the 88 subjects on the 22 language measures. The average age of the 88 subjects was 12 years, 3 months, corresponding to an expected grade level of 6.75. The letter c indicates that the average score was at the ceiling of the test norms. The bottom graph shows the percentage of subjects from the reading problem sample who scored within the same range as normal readers of their own age.*

grade level of 6.75 in phoneme deletion in syllables, serial naming of months, and Token test F; and 3–4 years behind on the remaining phonemic segmentation tests, naming days, repeating unrelated words and randomized words in sentences, Token tests A, C, and D, and Semantic Fields. They were 2–3 years behind in repeating meaningless and meaningful sentences, on Token tests B and C, and on the Ask and Tell test. Counting to 20 was at the test ceiling (see Table 8.1).

The pattern of language deficit suggested that the greatest difficulty was at relatively low levels of language skill (i.e., phonemic segmentation–blending, serial naming, and morphophonemic knowledge). The language skills closest to normal involved the higher levels of semantic knowledge. Oral repetition problems were greater when there were no syntactic or semantic cues (unrelated words and random words), indicating that any difficulty in verbal memory during reading was not primarily the result of poor skills for using grammer and meaning to structure the verbal input. Likewise, average performance was considerably better on the Ask and Tell than on the phonemic segmentation-blending tests, suggesting relatively less impairment at higher linguistic levels. Thus, the linguistic deficits within an undifferentiated sample of reading problems tended to involve linguistic skills at and below the level of single words, as suggested by previous research on sentence comprehension (Doehring, 1977). More detailed interpretation of the group averages would not be appropriate, because of the wide range of ages and reading problems in the sample.

The average percentage of subjects who scored within the normal range for their ages was calculated in the same manner as before (Figure 7.1), as shown in the bottom graph of Figure 8.1. This could be done only for subjects in the age range from 8 to 11, as the normally achieving sample extended only to age 11 and the reading problem sample did not include subjects younger than 8. In contrast to the results for reading tests, in which there was less than 50% overlap on the majority of the oral reading tests (Figure 7.1), the reading problem and normal groups overlapped by at least 50% on all language tests. Within the 8–11 age range, then, over half of the subjects with reading problems had language skills comparable to those of normally achieving subjects. This suggests that reading disability does not invariably involve a general language deficit, leading one to expect the amount and type of language deficit to vary in different types of reading disabilities.

Before presenting the language test results for each type of reading disability, we will describe the relationships among the language tests, and then the relationships between the language tests and the reading tests.

Relationships among Language Measures

The relationships among the 22 language measures were examined for the same reason that we had examined the relationships among reading tests, to estimate the extent to which component skills had been tested and to provide a foundation for interpreting individual differences. The age-corrected correlations among the 22 language measures for the 88 subjects are shown in Appendix A. The reader is referred to the previous chapter for a discussion of the rationale for interpreting the statistical significance and percentage of common variance.

Although 77% of the 231 correlations among the 22 language tests were statistically significant, only 18 (4%) were higher than .40, indicating that only a few tests had a common variance greater than 16%. Almost all of the higher correlations involved measures of the same type. All 4 of the oral repetition tests were moderately correlated with each other (.54–.70); but not with any of the other tests. All of the phonemic segmentation tests except Rhyming were reasonably well correlated with each other (.29–.62), and Naming Days was correlated .50 with Naming Months. The 4 syntactic–semantic measures were not highly correlated (.07–.34); and of the 15 correlations among the 6 Token test measures, only 2 were greater than .32. The only correlations greater than .40 between different types of measures were correlations of .45 between Pig Latin and Cartoon Description, .42 between Rhyming and Naming Months, .44 between Rhyming and Morphophonemics, .41 between Naming Days and Token Test E, .42 between Naming Months and Token Test C, and .51 between Token Test D and Ask and Tell.

The patterns of correlation suggested fairly independent measures of phonemic segmentation–blending; verbal short-term memory (oral repetition), and serial naming, but not much consistency within the other categories of language ability. An R factor analysis was next carried out to obtain more information about these relationships, using the computational procedure described in the previous chapter.

CONVENTIONAL R FACTOR ANALYSIS OF LANGUAGE TESTS

An R factor analysis yielding four factors gave the most information about correlational trends among the language tests. The factor loadings of the 22 language measures on each of the four factors are shown in Table 8.2. Factor 1 appeared to involve the comprehension of instructions, with high loadings on all 6 parts of the Token test, and on the Ask and Tell test. The second factor involved verbal short-term memory, with high loadings on the 4 oral repetition tests. Factor 3 involved phonemic segmentation–blending, with high loadings on all phonemic segmenta-

TABLE 8.2

Summary of the Results of an R Factor Analysis of the Twenty-Two Language Measures for the Eighty-Eight Subjects[a]

					Factors		
Tests			1	2	3	4
Phonemic Segmentation:						
	Sound Deletion in Syllables		01	33	66	06
	Sound Deletion in Words		36	19	73	-06
	Pig Latin		10	15	65	47
	Ubby Dubby		37	15	76	18
	Rhyming		04	09	-06	79
Serial Naming:	Numbers		41	16	-62	-11
	Days		38	13	21	45
	Months		44	01	16	61
Oral Repetition:						
	Unrelated Words		17	79	05	14
	Random Words from Sentences		13	85	08	01
	Meaningless Sentences		04	78	18	28
	Sentences		19	75	17	24
Token Test:	A.	One word	69	05	09	-17
	B.	Two words	57	03	-08	09
	C.	Three words	60	21	14	29
	D.	Four words	63	13	11	21
	E.	Six words	67	24	13	29
	F.	Complex	57	44	10	01
Synt-Sem.:	Morphophonemics		07	31	11	67
	Cartoon Description (DSS)		32	21	22	43
	Semantic Fields		44	0	31	17
	Ask & Tell		65	13	03	19

[a] Factor loadings are given for each test (decimal points omitted).

tion–blending tests except Rhyming. Factor 4, with high loadings on Rhyming, Naming Months, and Morphophonemics, could not be interpreted in a simple manner.

The R factor analysis suggests a useful organization of language skills for the present purposes. Reading disabilities associated with a comprehension problem should involve Factor 1 skills; those associated with verbal short-term memory problems should involve Factor 2 skills; and those associated with difficulty in segmenting words into phonemes should involve Factor 3 skills.

Correlations with Reading Tests

Age-corrected correlations between the language tests and the four standardized reading measures from Durrell test (Appendix A) give some idea of how the language skills were related to more global reading skills.

Correlations of the Durrell tests with the four syntactic–semantic measures were low (.09–.32) and correlations with the first four phonemic segmentation–blending measures were relatively high (.36–.71), indicating that reading achievement of the 88 subjects was related to phonemic level rather than to higher-level language skills.

The majority of the 858 age-corrected correlations between the 22 language and the 39 reading-related measures were statistically significant (.21 or more, Appendix A). The percentages of significant correlations were 62% for visual matching, 60% for auditory–visual matching, 62% for oral reading, 68% for sentence comprehension, 65% for spelling, and only 33% for visual scanning. However, only 14% of the correlations were greater than .40, and none was larger than .70. The highest correlations were between the first 4 phonemic segmentation tests and auditory–visual matching, oral reading, and comprehension and spelling. Correlations with the 4 syntactic–semantic measures were uniformly low, as were correlations with the 4 oral repetition measures. This suggested once again that the reading skills of the 88 subjects were most closely related to phonemic-level language abilities. It is also noteworthy that language-related skills were more highly correlated with visual matching than with visual scanning.

These descriptions of the performance of the sample as a whole on the language tests, and of the relationship between language and reading tests provide a basis for interpreting the linguistic correlates of the three types of reading disabilities.

Average Language Test Scores of the Three Types of Reading Disabilities

The average language test scores of the subjects classified into the three types of reading disabilities provide the most direct indication of the interaction of linguistic deficits with the reading disabilities. The average language test scores for each type of reading disability are shown in Figure 8.2. Grade-equivalent scores were calculated by the same procedure that was used for the average reading test scores. It is immediately apparent that the language test profiles of the three types were not as sharply differentiated as were their reading test profiles (Figure 7.4). The only notable discrepancy between the profiles was in developmental sentence scoring on the Cartoon Description Test, which was the lowest score for Types A and S, but not for Type O. Otherwise, all three types were about 5 years below expected grade level on the phonemic segmentation tests, Naming Months, Token test F, and Morphophonemics, and showed the same general pattern of better performance on the two oral

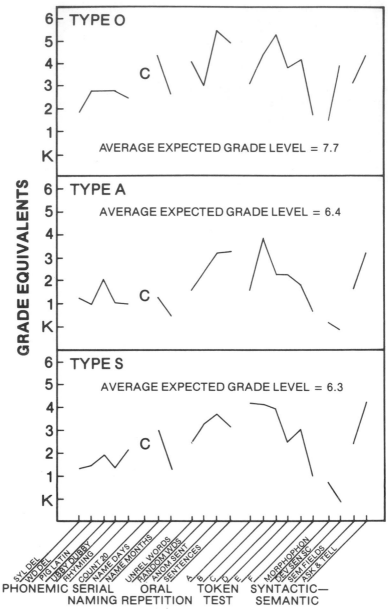

FIGURE 8.2. *Average grade-equivalent scores on the language tests for the three types of reading disabilities. The letter* c *indicates that the average score was at the test ceiling.*

repetition tests involving sentences, increasingly poor performance on Token tests C–F, and relatively poor performance on the Ask and Tell test. Even the best performances were 2 or more years below expected grade level, although the results of several tests for Type O subjects approached the test limits.

The language test profiles do not show the different patterns of deficit that we had expected to be associated with the three types of reading disabilities. The only discrepancy that is clearly evident in Figure 8.2 is the consistently poor cartoon descriptions of Type A and Type S subjects, with Type O subjects tending to be much better on this sentence grammar measure. Otherwise, the three types showed the same general pattern of being more impaired in phonemic-level abilities than in higher-level linguistic skills.

Even though the language test profiles in Figure 8.2 did not reveal striking differences between the three types of reading disabilities, it is possible that some subtle combination of language skill deficits might differentiate the reading disabilities. We investigated this possibility by the use of discriminant analysis (Nie et al., 1975), a statistical procedure that estimated the extent to which the three types of reading disabilities could be differentiated by the best possible weighted combination of language test scores. The results were consistent with the lack of difference between profiles in Figure 8.2. Only 45 (56%) of the 72 subjects of the three types were correctly classified by the optimal weighted scores, with 67% correctly classified as Type O, 41% as Type A, and 53% as Type S. By chance, one would expect 38% of Type O, 25% of Type A, and 19% of Type S subjects to be correctly classified. The somewhat higher-than-chance percentages of correct classifications may largely reflect differences in overall levels of test performance rather than differential patterns of test scores, as the Type O subjects averaged 1 year older than the Type A and S subjects. Without these age differences, the optimal weighted scores would have been even more similar and there would have been even fewer correct classifications of reading disability types on the basis of the language test scores.

In the previous chapter, it was stated that the finding of the same three types of reading disabilities in two different samples of subjects was perhaps the most important finding of this study. The absence of distinctive patterns of language deficits for the three types of reading disabilities is another major finding of this study. This does not mean that none of the reading disabilities are differentially related to language problems. We next explored the possibility that there was a more complex relationship between reading disability and language deficit by examining the language skill profiles of individual subjects, then analyzing the types of language disabilities that emerged from a Q factor analysis of the language test results, and finally analyzing the types of combined reading and language disabilities that emerged from a Q factor analysis of the combined reading and language test batteries.

Language Skill Profiles of Individual Subjects

Language test results for the individual subjects in Types O, A, and S are given in Tables 8.3, 8.4, and 8.5. They are presented in the same form as the individual reading results (Tables 7.4–7.6), as the nearest grade equivalent of the percentile score for each test. Within each type, subjects are ranked according to their factor loadings on the reading test analyses (Table 7.2). The test ceilings (c) given at the left of the tables are

TABLE 8.3
Grade-Equivalent Scores of Subjects of Type O (oral reading deficit) on the Twenty-Two Tests of Language-Related Abilities[a]

	c	1	2	3	4	5	6	7	8	9	10	11	12	13	14	15	16	17	18	19	20	21	22	23	24	25	26	27	28	29	30	31	32	33	Mean
Type O Rank		1	2	3	4	5	6	7	8	9	0	1	2	3	4	5	6	7	8	9	0	1	2	3	4	5	6	7	8	9	0	1	2	3	
Grade for Age		8	9	9	6	8	8	10	8	9	6	10	7	8	5	7	8	7	6	6	12	4	8	5	10	5	7	8	6	11	9	5	12	10	7
Phonemic:	5	1	k	2	4	c	1	1	1	3	k	1	2	1	1	k	2	1	2	3	2	3	k	k	c	k	k	2	3	4	c	c	2	1	2
DW	5	5	4	c	c	c	3	c	c	1	k	c	k	2	k	k	3	1	3	3	2	1	k	3	c	k	1	2	1	4	c	4	c	3	3
PL	6	6	k	c	3	c	3	1	3	2	1	2	1	1	1	2	5	2	c	c	1	4	3	1	c	1	2	k	1	4	1	5	3	5	3
UD	6	2	3	c	4	c	2	2	3	1	2	3	1	1	2	2	4	c	4	4	4	3	1	2	c	1	2	c	1	c	1	3	2	5	3
RH	6	3	k	3	4	2	3	k	2	3	4	3	4	3	4	k	3	k	c	4	c	c	c	c	1	4	k	c	5	1	1	1	2	2	2
Naming: NU	1	c	c	k	k	c	c	c	c	c	c	c	c	c	c	c	c	k	c	k	k	c	c	c	c	k	c	c	c	k	c	c	c	k	c
DA	6	4	c	2	5	c	c	c	c	k	4	c	c	3	c	c	5	c	c	c	4	c	2	1	c	3	k	c	k	k	c	c	5	1	4
MO	6	3	4	3	2	2	3	c	c	k	3	c	c	k	c	1	3	k	3	2	3	c	k	c	c	1	k	c	3	k	3	k	3	c	3
Repetition: UW	6	4	5	c	2	4	k	1	3	c	c	1	1	1	3	c	c	1	1	4	1	1	3	4	3	k	3	1	c	c	5	2	c	3	4
RW	6	c	5	3	2	2	k	5	k	c	4	2	k	1	5	c	c	3	2	c	k	3	4	k	4	2	k	1	c	4	c	2	c	k	3
AS	6	c	c	c	3	2	k	c	c	c	k	k	c	3	c	c	c	3	2	c	k	4	c	4	c	2	k	c	c	c	c	4	c	k	c
MS	5	c	3	c	2	c	k	5	3	c	c	c	c	1	1	c	c	1	k	4	2	3	4	3	3	4	1	c	2	2	2	4	c	1	c
Token Test: A	5	1	4	4	k	c	2	4	k	3	k	c	3	2	2	4	k	3	3	k	c	3	4	c	3	3	4	3	1	c	c	1	k	k	3
B	5	c	c	4	1	2	c	c	1	c	c	c	2	c	3	k	1	c	c	k	c	c	1	c	k	3	c	3	2	4	k	2	1	c	4
C	5	c	c	c	3	c	c	c	k	c	c	1	1	1	3	c	c	c	c	1	1	1	3	3	c	c	3	c	k	c	c	2	2	2	2
D	5	c	c	c	k	c	c	c	k	3	2	k	k	3	3	k	2	c	3	4	2	4	c	c	3	1	c	c	2	k	k	c	c	c	4
E	6	c	5	c	k	3	4	c	3	c	1	5	1	c	k	3	3	c	c	3	4	3	4	c	5	3	k	5	3	4	c	4	4	5	4
F	6	c	4	1	1	3	k	k	k	c	1	k	1	1	k	1	3	1	1	3	c	3	3	1	3	k	k	3	k	c	2	1	3	4	2
Synt–Sem: MO	6	3	k	2	3	2	2	2	c	k	1	2	2	2	1	5	4	1	2	c	1	2	2	k	c	2	2	2	3	k	1	1	2	k	2
DS	3	c	c	c	k	c	c	2	1	c	c	1	1	c	c	c	c	c	c	c	c	c	1	k	c	1	1	c	c	c	k	c	c	c	c
SF	5	c	2	c	4	c	4	4	4	k	1	3	c	c	c	k	3	4	3	3	4	1	3	1	3	2	2	4	1	k	c	1	4	3	3
AT	6	3	c	c	3	c	c	c	2	c	c	2	1	c	5	4	2	5	4	5	4	4	1	c	3	1	4	4	c	c	c	3	1	3	4

[a] The test ceilings listed in the left-hand column and designated by the letter c in the body of the table represent the grade at which normal readers ceased to improve. The letter k is used to indicate performance at or below kindergarten level.

TABLE 8.4.

Grade-Equivalent Scores of Subjects of Type A (letter-sound association deficit) on the Twenty-Two Tests of Language-Related Abilities[a]

		1	2	3	4	5	6	7	8	9	10	11	12	13	14	15	16	17	18	19	20	21	22	Mean
Type A Rank		1	2	3	4	5	6	7	8	9	0	1	2	3	4	5	6	7	8	9	0	1	2	Mean
Grade for Age		7	7	9	5	6	3	4	8	6	3	7	7	6	3	7	9	6	9	5	12	6	4	6
		c																						
Phonemic:	DS	5	1	1	k	1	2	2	1	1	k	2	k	3	1	1	1	2	1	c	k	k	1	1
	DW	5	1	1	k	1	2	k	k	1	k	1	k	2	1	1	2	2	3	4	2	k	k	1
	PL	6	k	3	4	k	3	3	k	k	k	k	c	1	1	4	4	k	c	4	2	2	k	2
	UD	6	4	1	2	k	3	2	k	1	k	2	k	2	1	1	2	4	k	5·3	k	k	k	1
	RH	6	k	2	c	k	k	k	k	k	k	k	c	1	k	1	5	k	4	k	k	5	1	1
Naming:	NU	1	k	c	c	c	c	c	k	c	c	c	c	k	c	c	c	c	c	k	c	c	c	c
	DA	6	1	k	k	k	c	k	k	k	1	2	3	c	4	k	4	c	k	c	2	k	1	1
	MO	6	c	1	c	k	1	2	k	k	k	k	2	k	k	k	3	k	c	k	k	k	k	1
Repetition:	UW	6	k	1	1	1	c	4	k	3	k	4	1	3	3	2	c	c	k	3	c	k	k	2
	RW	6	2	4	4	2	3	2	1	c	k	1	c	1	1	5	c	c	k	4	c	k	5	2
	AS	6	2	k	2	k	c	c	c	4	k	1	c	5	2	2	c	c	k	c	c	k	c	3
	MS	5	c	k	c	1	3	c	2	c	k	2	3	c	2	2	c	c	k	c	3	3	3	3
Token Test:	A	5	1	4	4	k	1	k	c	4	3	k	k	c	c	c	k	1	2	c	k	k	c	2
	B	5	2	2	c	1	2	k	k	k	3	2	c	3	c	3	c	5	5	c	2	2	4	
	C	5	4	c	c	k	c	k	k	2	k	3	k	c	c	1	c	2	k	c	5	k	2	2
	D	5	4	2	c	k	2	2	k	4	k	1	1	c	4	k	c	c	k	3	2	k	k	1
	E	6	1	k	5	k	1	k	k	2	k	3	k	c	c	1	c	c	k	1	2	1	c	2
	F	6	3	1	3	k	3	k	k	2	k	k	1	1	1	k	3	3	k	k	1	c	3	1
Syntac-Sem.	MO	6	4	k	2	k	2	k	1	k	k	k	k	1	k	k	k	2	k	3	1	2	1	k
	DS	3	c	c	k	k	k	1	k	k	k	1	k	c	k	k	c	1	1	c	k	c	k	k
	SF	5	4	1	c	3	4	1	k	k	k	3	1	4	c	1	1	3	k	1	4	2	1	2
	AF	6	c	5	c	1	3	5	k	c	1	3	3	c	c	k	5	4	1	3	2	c	k	3

[a] The test ceilings listed in the left-hand column and designated by the letter *c* in the body of the table represent the grade at which normal readers ceased to improve. The letter *k* is used to indicate performance at or below kindergarten level.

the grades at which the normally achieving subjects reached a limit, or the highest grade (6) for which normative data were available. The letter *c* within the body of the table indicates that the subject scored at or above the ceiling for normally achieving subjects on that test, and the letter *k* indicates that the subject scored at or below kindergarten level.

The generally poor performance of all three types on the phonemic segmentation tests and the Morphophonemic test (MO) can easily be seen, as well as the very poor cartoon descriptions (DS) of Type A and Type S subjects. However, some subjects of each type (01, 03, 05, A10, A12, S1, S8) had much less language impairment, another demonstration that language impairment was not highly predictive of the type of reading disability. We will refer again to the individual results when interpreting the results of the Q factor analyses of language tests.

TABLE 8.5

Grade-Equivalent Scores of Subjects of Type S (letter sequence deficit) on the Twenty-Two Tests of Language-Related Abilities[a]

		1	2	3	4	5	6	7	8	9	10	11	12	13	14	15	16	17	Mean
Type S Rank		1	2	3	4	5	6	7	8	9	0	1	2	3	4	5	6	7	
Grade for Age		5	4	5	9	5	5	5	3	11	6	8	5	12	8	3	5	8	6
Phonemic:	DS	5[c]	3	k	1	k	4	1	k	1	3	1	5	3	1	3	k	1	1
	DW	5	1	k	k	1	c	k	k	k	1	4	3	1	1	2	1	4	1
	PL	6	3	k	2	k	1	1	1	k	4	1	1	k	c	2	4	1	2
	UD	6	k	k	k	k	2	k	k	k	2	2	4	k	4	3	3	c	1
	RH	6	3	1	c	k	k	k	4	k	c	c	k	4	k	2	k	k	2
Naming:	NU	1	c	c	c	c	c	c	c	c	c	k	c	c	c	c	k	c	c
	DA	6	k	k	c	c	3	c	k	k	c	4	2	k	c	2	k	c	3
	MO	6	1	k	k	c	k	k	k	k	5	3	k	1	c	2	2	1	1
Repetition:	UW	6	c	k	c	1	c	4	k	k	1	5	k	k	c	5	1	1	3
	RW	6	c	2	c	k	c	2	2	4	3	1	1	1	c	2	k	c	3
	AS	6	c	k	4	k	c	3	4	k	c	5	k	4	c	c	k	c	4
	MS	5	3	1	3	k	3	3	1	k	c	2	1	3	c	3	1	c	3
Token Test:	A	5	1	c	3	c	c	2	k	2	c	c	4	k	4	3	c	1	4
	B	5	5	k	c	c	c	c	2	3	c	3	c	k	c	c	k	k	4
	C	5	c	1	k	c	c	k	c	1	c	c	c	2	c	k	k	c	4
	D	5	3	k	k	c	2	k	3	k	k	c	k	c	c	2	k	c	3
	E	6	1	k	k	c	4	4	3	k	c	c	1	3	5	5	1	1	3
	F	6	2	2	k	3	c	k	1	k	k	4	k	1	c	2	1	2	1
Syntac-Sem.	MO	6	c	k	3	k	1	k	k	k	1	2	k	k	5	2	k	k	1
	DS	3	1	k	k	k	k	k	2	k	1	k	k	k	c	c	c	1	k
	SF	5	1	c	3	3	c	3	k	k	2	4	1	3	c	c	k	1	3
	AF	6	5	3	2	5	c	k	4	2	4	c	k	5	c	c	4	2	4

[a] The test ceilings listed in the left-hand column and designated by the letter *c* in the body of the table represent the grade at which normal readers ceased to improve. The letter *k* is used to indicate performance at or below the kindergarten level.

Statistical Classification of the Language Test Results

Another method of studying the interaction between language deficit and reading disability was to determine whether the 88 subjects could be classified into different types of language disabilities by a Q factor analysis of their language test scores. Different types of language disabilities, like the different types of reading disabilities, would be defined by characteristic profiles of language skill deficits. Then a determination could be made of the types of reading disabilities that were represented among the subjects classified into each type of language disability. If a particular type of reading disability were the result of a particular type of language disability, then all the subjects classified into one type of reading disability would also be classified into one type of language disability. The preceding analyses of language test results indicated that no such perfect correspondence between reading disability and language disability would be found, but more complex relationships between reading and language deficits might exist.

We used three-, four-, and five-factor solutions to factor analyze the language percentiles of the 88 subjects by the Q technique. Each solution yielded only two stable factors. Factor 1 of the three-factor solution corresponded to Factor 2 of the four- and five-factor solutions, and Factor 2 of the three-factor solution corresponded to Factor 1 of the four- and five-factor solutions. The remaining factors contained few subjects with high loadings and were not consistent from one solution to another. Only the two major factors will be interpreted.

Figure 8.3 shows the factor scores that defined the two types of language deficits. The factor scores from the three-, four-, and five-factor solutions were fairly consistent. Both types of language deficits involved low scores on the first four phonemic segmentation tests and on the Morphophonemics test, and relatively good scores on the Ask and Tell test. Type 1 language deficit was differentiated by poor scores on all four of the oral repetition tests. Type 2 language deficit was characterized by relatively good scores on all four oral repetition tests, and generally poorer scores on the Serial Naming and Token tests.

The oral repetition problem that differentiated Type 1 from Type 2 was not the result of higher-level syntactic–semantic deficiencies in verbal short-term memory, as performance was somewhat worse in repeating unrelated words and randomized words from sentences. This aspect of the Type 1 language deficit could indicate a generalized short-term memory deficit rather than a linguistic deficit per se. The deficiencies on the Serial Naming and Token tests in Type 2, although not as marked as the verbal repetition deficit of Type 1, may reflect a joint difficulty in rapid retrieval of stored sequences and rapid spatiotemporal associations. Both types of language deficits showed the phonemic and morphophonemic deficiencies that characterized all three types of reading disabilities.

CORRESPONDENCE BETWEEN THE LANGUAGE DISABILITIES AND THE READING DISABILITIES

To determine the correspondence between the two types of language deficits and the three types of reading disabilities, we classified subjects into the two types of language deficits, using the same criterion that we had used for reading disability classifications. Subjects with their highest

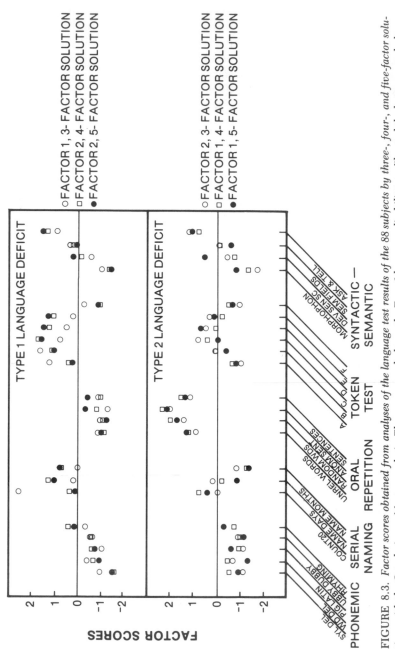

FIGURE 8.3. *Factor scores obtained from analyses of the language test results of the 88 subjects by three-, four-, and five-factor solutions with the Q technique of factor analysis. The upper graph shows the Type 1 language disability profile, and the bottom graph shows the Type 2 language disability profile.*

average loading above .40 on the Type 1 factors (Figure 8.3) were classified as language deficit Type 1, and those with their highest loading above .40 on the Type 2 factors were classified as language deficit Type 2.

Only 51 of the 88 subjects were classified into the two types of language deficits, as compared with 72 subjects classified into the three types of reading disabilities. The 23 subjects classified into Type 1 included 7 females and 16 males with an average age of 12.75. There were 28 subjects of Type 2, including 6 females and 22 males with an average age of 12.0.

Although there was nothing approaching a perfect correspondence between any of the types of language disabilities and any of the types of reading disabilities, the reading disability types were not equally represented in each type of language disability. The 23 subjects with language deficit Type 1 (poor Oral Word repetition) included 12 (36%) of the 33 members of reading disability Type O, 5 (23%) of the 22 members of Type A, and 4 (24%) of the 17 members of Type S. The 33 subjects with Type 2 language deficit (poorer Serial Naming and Token test performance) included only 7 (21%) Type O subjects, but 9 (41%) Type A and 7 (41%) Type S subjects.

These joint classifications suggest a weak relationship between Type O reading disability and Type 1 language deficit. About one-third of the subjects with oral reading deficits also had relative difficulty in repeating orally presented word strings. Smaller proportions of subjects with the other two types of reading disabilities had such difficulty. These trends can be seen by inspecting the individual language test results in Tables 8.3–8.5. There was also a weak relationship between Type 2 language deficit and reading disability Types A and S. About 40% of the subjects with association deficits and the subjects with sequence deficits were relatively poor in Serial Naming and Token test performance, but relatively good in Oral Word repetition. These trends can also be seen by inspecting the individual language test results in Tables 8.3–8.5. At this point, there appeared to be evidence of both a generalized language deficit centered on lower-level linguistic skills in all three types of reading disabilities, and certain specific patterns of language deficits complexly associated with the reading disabilities.

OTHER ANALYSES OF LANGUAGE TEST RESULTS

The stability of Q technique classifications was evaluated as before by analysis of subsamples of different ages and by cluster analysis, and the results of siblings were also compared for the language tests. To determine the effects of age on the language test scores, the same procedure was used that had been used for the reading tests. The 88 subjects were divided into groups of 31 subjects 8–10 years old, 28 subjects 11–13.5 years old, and 29 subjects 13.6–17 years old. The language test scores of each group were factor analyzed by a three-factor solution. The factors defining the two language disability types emerged very clearly in each age group as either Factor 1 or Factor 2, with the third factor not revealing any clear pattern apart from the common tendency for phonological and syntactic deficit. The majority of subjects were classified into the same type in the age subsamples as in the 88-subject analysis, with 36 of 51 (71%) of the subjects from the two language disability types classified into the same types in the smaller samples. Thus, the patterns of language test deficit did not change with age in the subjects with reading problems. In all three age ranges, there was a generalized phonemic segmentation and morphophonemic deficit, with some subjects being particularly poor in Oral Word repetition and others being relatively poorer in Serial Naming and Token test performance.

Cluster analyses of the language test results were also carried out in the same way as before. Once again, very good agreement was obtained between the Q technique classifications and McQuitty's similarity analysis with squared Euclidean distance coefficients. The three-cluster solution by McQuitty's method classified 16 of the 23 members of language deficit Type 1 into one cluster, and 24 of the 28 members of language deficit Type 2 into another cluster. This agreement of 78% between the two methods was almost exactly the same as that obtained for the reading test classifications.

The individual profiles of siblings were compared for the language tests in the same way that they had been compared for the reading tests. Even though there were only two types of language deficits, there was very little agreement in the language deficit classifications of siblings, and in no case was there close similarity between their language test profiles. Among the five members of the same family, two were classified into Language Type 1, one into Type 2, and two were unclassified, with no noticeable similarity among test profiles. For the six cases of two siblings each, there were only two in which both siblings were classified into the same type of language disability, Type 1 in both instances. Even in these cases, there was no consistent similarity between the profiles. Contrary to the reading test results, then, there were no pairs of siblings with very similar profiles of language skill deficit.

STATISTICAL CLASSIFICATION OF THE COMBINED READING AND LANGUAGE TESTS

Another way to determine joint reading–language classifications was by statistically classifying the 88 subjects by a Q factor analysis of the 39 tests of reading-related skills (including the comprehension, spelling, color, and picture naming, and nonverbal scanning tests) together with the 22 language tests. We used three-, four-, five-, and six-factor solutions, as more factors might emerge with 61 tests. The five-factor solution was the most interpretable in relation to the factors obtained by the separate factor analyses of the 31 reading tests (Figure 7.2) and the 22 language tests (Figure 8.3). The factor scores for the 61 tests on the five factors are listed in Table 8.6.

The reading test profile for Factor 1 was most like that of Type A reading disability, but with auditory–visual matching even poorer than oral reading. Higher letter skills on all but the visual matching tests suggested some resemblance to the Type S profile. Color and picture naming were good, and comprehension and spelling were at the same level as oral word reading. The language test profile for Factor 1 resembled that of Type 2 language deficit, with good oral repetition and poor phonemic segmentation, serial naming, comprehension, and syntactic skills, but the language deficiencies were not as severe as the reading deficiencies. The reading disability and language deficit classifications of the 33 subjects whose highest loadings were above .40 on Factor 1 confirmed these trends, as they included 16 of the 22 members of reading disability Type A and 9 of the 17 members of Type S, along with 22 of the 28 members of language deficit Type 2. This indicated even more strongly than did the Q factor analyses of the language test scores alone that many subjects in reading disability Types A and S shared a common pattern of language deficit, featured by poor performance in phonemic segmentation, rapid naming of stored sequences, following instructions, morphophonemic knowledge, and syntactic usage, but not in short-term verbal memory.

The reading test profile for Factor 2 showed the poor oral reading skills of Type O, along with the better number and letter skills of Type S reading disability. Color and picture naming were relatively good, with comprehension and spelling as poor as oral word reading. The language profile resembled that of Type 1 language deficit, with the poorest scores on the first four phonemic segmentation tests and the four oral repetition tests. Of the 18 subjects whose highest loadings were above .40 on Factor 2, 12 were members of reading disability Type O and 16 were members of language deficit Type 1. This provides another indication of a possible subdivision of Type O reading disability, with about one-third of its members being deficient in verbal short-term memory in addition to having the common phonemic segmentation problem and deficient morphophonemic knowledge.

The three remaining factors were more tenuous, having fewer subjects with high loadings. Of the six subjects with high loadings on Factor 3, five were members of reading disability Type O and three were members

TABLE 8.6

Factor Score for the Thirty-Nine Reading-Related and Twenty-Two Language Measures as Derived from a Five-Factor Q Technique Solution for the Eighty-Eight Subjects.

		FACTOR SCORES				
	TESTS	1	2	3	4	5
READING-RELATED SKILLS						
Visual Matching:	Numbers	0.6	1.7	0.8	0.6	0.9
	Letters	0.0	1.7	0.8	0.6	1.2
	Upper-Lower Case Letters	−0.1	1.7	0.7	0.3	0.7
	CVC Words	−0.1	0.8	0.7	1.1	0.5
	CVCC Words	−0.4	0.7	0.8	1.3	0.4
	CVC Syllable	0.0	0.2	1.4	1.1	0.2
	CCC String	0.4	0.1	0.5	1.1	0.5
Aud.-Vis. Match.:	Letter	−0.3	1.9	0.2	0.5	0.9
	CVC Words	−1.1	0.8	1.1	0.2	0.5
	CVCC Words	−1.4	0.4	0.5	0.7	0.8
	CV Syllable	−1.14	0.8	1.3	−0.5	1.1
	CCV Syllable	−0.9	−0.9	0.2	0.7	0.6
	CVC Syllable	−1.5	0.4	−0.3	−0.7	0.6
	CVCC Syllable	−1.2	0.0	−0.4	0.2	1.1
Oral Read./Name:	Colors	0.1	0.7	−0.8	−0.1	0.3
	Pictures	0.7	0.0	−0.5	−0.2	0.8
	Upper-Case Letters	−0.5	0.0	−0.6	−0.3	1.3
	Lower-Case Letters	−0.7	−0.2	−0.7	−0.2	1.2
	Upper-Lower Case Letters	−0.4	−0.1	−0.9	0.1	1.1
	Letters in Sentence	−0.5	−0.2	−0.8	−0.5	1.1
	Random Words	−1.1	−1.1	−0.4	0.0	0.8
	Two-Word Phrases	−1.0	−1.2	−0.5	0.0	0.5
	Seven-Word Phrases	−1.0	−1.2	−0.5	−0.1	0.5
	Sentences	−0.9	−1.2	−0.3	−0.2	0.5
	Syllables	−0.9	−1.7	−1.4	−0.5	−0.1
Visual Scanning:	Rectangles	0.8	−0.2	−0.3	1.7	−0.6
	Figure	1.4	−0.4	0.1	1.9	−0.4
	Number	0.0	−0.8	0.7	1.2	−0.7
	Letter	0.2	−1.1	0.4	1.7	−0.8
	Two Letters	1.2	−0.9	0.3	1.2	−0.8
	Letter in Syllable	0.2	−0.2	0.0	1.5	−0.4
	Word	−0.9	−0.9	−0.6	−0.2	−0.1
	Syllable	−0.7	−0.8	−0.1	−0.1	−0.2
	Consonant String	−1.0	−1.0	0.1	0.4	−0.4
	Unspaced Words	−0.4	−0.9	0.3	−0.2	0.2
Sentence Comprehension		1.4	0.1	−0.1	0.4	1.4
Spelling:	Oral Spelling	1.3	0.3	0.2	1.3	−0.2
	Written Spelling	0.9	−0.1	0.2	1.2	−0.4
	Spelled-Out Word	0.9	0.1	−0.3	1.0	−0.2
LANGUAGE ABILITIES						
Phonemic:	Syllable Deletion	0.2	−1.6	−0.5	−0.9	−0.2
	Word Deletion	−0.2	−1.2	−0.4	0.4	0.6
	Pig Latin	−0.6	−0.8	0.8	0.2	−2.5
	Ubby Dubby	−0.7	−0.8	−0.1	0.3	−1.3
	Rhyming	−0.9	1.2	0.0	−2.6	−0.4
Serial Naming:	Count 20	3.1	0.8	−3.7	−1.4	1.1
	Name Days	−0.6	1.7	0.3	−1.2	0.3
	Name Months	−1.1	0.9	−0.4	−0.8	−0.8

(*continued*)

TABLE 8.6 (*continued*)

	TESTS	FACTOR SCORES				
		1	2	3	4	5
Oral Repetition:	Unrelated Words	1.7	-1.2	1.1	-1.6	-0.1
	Random Words	2.3	-1.9	1.7	-1.5	0.8
	Meaningless Sentences	1.8	-0.6	2.9	-2.2	1.0
	Sentences	1.4	-0.7	1.5	-1.6	0.2
Token Test:	A	0.4	0.8	-2.9	0.6	-0.8
	B	1.2	1.0	-1.5	0.1	-1.0
	C	0.3	1.5	0.3	-0.7	-0.2
	D	0.1	0.9	-0.1	0.1	-1.9
	E	-0.5	1.7	-0.1	-1.1	-0.6
	F	0.2	-0.7	-1.2	-0.7	-0.9
Synt.-Sem.:	Morphophonemics	-0.7	-0.7	-0.3	-2.0	-1.4
	Cartoon Description	-0.8	1.0	1.0	-1.0	-3.9
	Semantic Fields	0.6	-0.1	-0.7	-0.3	-0.6
	Ask & Tell	1.1	1.5	0.0	-0.3	-1.7

of language deficit Type 2, with the other three being unclassified as to language disability. The reading profile for Factor 3 featured poor oral reading, color naming, and picture naming. The only severe language deficits were in serial naming of numbers and following simple instructions on the Token test. This reading–language pattern suggested oral reading difficulty associated with difficulty in rapid word retrieval, another subdivision of Type O reading disability. Factors 4 and 5 will not be interpreted, as many of the subjects with high loadings on these factors were unclassified as to language or reading disability.

On separate Q technique classifications for the three subsamples of different ages there was as much agreement between the age subsamples as there had been for the separate analysis of reading and language tests. However, the reading–language classifications of siblings, like the language classifications, showed less similarity between siblings than did the reading classifications. The agreement between Q factor analysis classifications and cluster analysis classifications of the 61 reading and language tests was not as good as the agreement for the separate analyses of reading and language tests.

The results of the statistical classifications of combined reading and language tests must be interpreted with caution, because differences between the test batteries probably affected the classifications, but the theoretical implications of the findings are important and should not be disregarded. The reading skill deficit that defined one type of reading disability may be associated with two different patterns of language deficits, and two different types of reading disabilities may be associated with the same type of language deficit.

Summary and Preliminary Discussion

To investigate the interaction of linguistic deficits with the three types of reading disabilities, language abilities that are still developing during the early school years were tested. The 22 language measures sampled abilities for phonemic segmentation and blending, rapid naming of simple stored sequences, short-term verbal memory, following spoken instructions, use of morphophonemic rules, use of syntactic structures, paradigmatic word associations, and knowledge of complex syntactic–semantic relationships. The tests were first given to 70 normally achieving children from Kindergarten through Grade 6, and scored in terms of both accuracy and latency to obtain an estimate of normal ability against which the language abilities of the subjects with reading problems could be compared. Most of the language skills measured continued to develop during the early years of school, with a great deal of variability within and between grades.

The greatest average deficiencies of the entire sample of 88 subjects with reading problems were in phonemic segmentation–blending, serial naming of months, following complex instructions, morphophonemic knowledge, and syntactic usage, where the sample averaged 5 years below expected grades for their ages. They were also 2 or more years behind on the remaining skills, with knowledge of complex syntactic—semantic relationships closest to normal. There was, however, considerable variability, with 50% of the subjects scoring within the normal range for this ages. Examination of the relationships among the language tests for the 88 subjects indicated that several different types of language skills were being measured, the most clearly identified being phonemic segmentation, verbal short-term memory, and comprehension of instructions. The phonemic segmentation–blending tests were most highly correlated with the reading achievement tests and the 31 tests of reading-related skills, supporting the previous indications that the reading disabilities tended to involve deficits in lower-level skills.

The generalized deficiency of the reading problem sample on the language tests, coupled with the variability from test to test and from subject to subject, suggested that different patterns of linguistic deficit might indeed be found for the different types of reading disability. However, all three types of reading disabilities had the same general pattern of average language test scores, with the greatest difficulty in phonemic segmentation–blending, naming months, following complex instructions, and morphophonemic knowledge, and the least difficulty in oral sentence repetition, following simple instructions, and understanding syntactic–semantic relations in sentences. The only discrepancy was a severe deficit in syntactic usage for reading disability Types A (association deficit) and S (sequence deficit) but not O (oral reading deficit). Even when discriminant function analysis was used to calculate optimum weighted language scores, the three types of reading disabilities could not be clearly differentiated solely on the basis of their language test performance.

The final steps in exploring the relationship between reading disability and language deficit were Q factor analyses of the language tests alone and of the combined reading and language tests. The results suggested a complex relationship between reading disability and language disability, with reading disability Type O (oral reading deficit) associated with two different types of language deficits (short-term verbal memory deficit and word retrieval deficit), and a single pattern of language deficit (relatively poor serial naming and following instructions) associated with the remaining two types of reading disabilities.

Although the detailed analyses of language skills did not reveal clear-cut linguistic correlates of the three types of reading disabilities, they did provide some grounds for suggesting even more complicated models of reading disabilities. A given type of reading disability may be associated with more than one type of language deficit, and a given type of language deficit may be associated with more than one type of reading disability. The findings regarding language deficit are much more tentative than those regarding reading disability, because they have not yet been replicated, but they do open very interesting avenues for further exploration. There is little doubt that the majority of subjects with reading problems were deficient in language skills. Although the small sample of normally achieving subjects may not have provided a fair standard of comparison for the diverse sample of subjects with reading problems, the majority showed a definite weakness in phonemic segmentation–blending, serial naming, morphophonemic knowledge, and syntactic usage (Tables 8.3–8.5). These results support contentions that reading disability involves language deficit (Vellutino, 1978), and that there are particular difficulties in phonemic segmentation–blending abilities (Liberman & Shankweiler, 1979) and syntactic abilities (Vogel, 1975) in reading disabilities. However, the relatively milder impairment of higher-level semantic–syntactic skills suggests that most subjects did not have a generalized language disorder. It should also be noted that these results do not permit us to conclude that the reading problems were caused by the language deficits. Failure to master the mechanics of reading could contribute to any or all of the language deficits that were found. The reading and language deficits must be interpreted in interactive rather than cause-and-effect terms.

The language test results will be discussed in more detail after the neuropsychology results have been presented in the next chapter.

The Interaction of Reading and Neuropsychological Deficits

9

The neuropsychological test results provided the final basis for studying the interaction between reading and nonreading deficits. The measures were representative of the types that have been used in previous neuropsychological investigations of reading disability (cf. Doehring, 1968; Rourke, 1978). The neuropsychology battery included a wide range of measures of perceptual, motor, cognitive, and linguistic skills. The majority of the measures have been well standardized (Trites, 1977) and are suitable for quantitative analysis. However, the tests were developed for neuropsychological diagnosis, and their usefulness for assessing different types of reading disabilities has yet to be established.

The interaction of reading and neuropsychological deficits was analyzed by the same methods that had been used to analyze the interaction of reading and language deficits. The neuropsychological test results for the sample as a whole were examined first with respect to average levels of performance, variability, intercorrelations, and correlations with the reading and language measures. Then the pattern of neuropsychological deficit for each type of reading disability was analyzed in terms of average test scores and by discriminant analysis. Finally, Q factor analyses of the neuropsychology results were carried out to determine if statistical classifications corresponding to the types of reading disabilities would occur. In addition, R. L. Trites and C. A. M. Fiedorowicz made a clinical evaluation of the amounts and types of possible cerebral dysfunction in individual subjects.

On the basis of previous research, in which reading disability was investigated as a unitary disorder, we might expect to find a wide range of nonreading deficits in subjects with reading disability, including deficits of visual perception, auditory perception, memory, language, cognition, motor functioning, and intermodal integration. As described in Chapters 3 and 4, some writers (cf. Vellutino, 1979) have attempted to reduce the confusion about the scope of nonreading deficits by arguing that there is really only one basic deficit, whereas others (cf. Mattis, 1978) have defined different types of reading disabilities in terms of different patterns of nonreading deficits. Still others (cf. Petrauskas & Rourke, 1979) have improved on the latter strategy by using statistical methods to define reading disabilities in terms of nonreading deficits. However, none of these attempts have completely overcome the problems of inadequate sampling and test selection, subjective classification methods, and lack of a detailed analysis of reading skill deficits. Our analysis of the neuropsychological deficits in subjects with reading disability shares some of the problems of previous studies, being less than ideal with respect to subject sampling and the range of abilities tested, but no previous study has systematically applied quantitative methods to determine the interaction of reading and nonreading deficits.

The Trites Neuropsychological Test Battery

All subjects had been given a 6–8-hour battery of neuropsychological tests developed by the second author (Trites, 1977), many of which were taken from batteries developed by Halstead, Reitan, and Klove (Halstead, 1947; Klove, 1963; Reitan, 1959). The tests had been standardized on a Canadian population by R. L. Trites for use in the clinical evaluation of children and adults referred to the Neuropsychology Laboratory of the Royal Ottawa Hospital (Trites, 1977). Many of the tests had been validated on adult neurological populations (cf. Reitan & Davidson, 1974; Stuss & Trites, 1977), and some validation studies have also been conducted on a school-aged population. To illustrate the value of the test battery in studying children with reading disabilities, one validation study will be described in some detail.

In an extensive long-term evaluation of the type of learning difficulties that some children experience when immersed in a second language for their education, Trites and Price (1976) compared the complete neuropsychological test profiles of 32 children who were failing in a second language program with two other groups of children for whom language of instruction was possibly implicated in their learning difficulty, and five groups of children for whom language of instruction was presumably not a factor because they were being educated in their first language. The latter five groups were selected to represent more "traditional" problems of children; namely reading disability, hyperactivity with learning difficulties, behavioral and personality problems with learning difficulties, "minimal brain dysfunction" with learning difficulties, and French-speaking children with reading difficulties in their French language program. There were 32 children in each group, and all the comparison groups were matched as closely as possible in terms of age and sex. All children in each of the eight groups had difficulty in school (i.e., a hyperactive child who was not experiencing difficulty in school would not have been included in the study). Strict inclusion criteria were established for each of the eight groups. For example, all children in the reading disability group had at least average Full Scale IQ on the WISC, no evidence of gross neurological or psychiatric disorder, no evidence of inadequate home or school opportunity, and, in most cases, a family history of reading disability. Interested readers can consult the original report for the selection criteria for the other seven groups (Trites & Price, 1976; Trites & Price, 1978–1979).

Descriptive information for the eight groups in terms of age, WISC Full Scale IQ, sex, and handedness is presented in Table 9.1. One initial goal of the study was to assess the ability of the neuropsychological test battery to differentiate the eight groups of children, all of whom shared in common a difficulty in school achievement. On the basis of factor analysis, the large number of neuropsychological test variables were reduced to 14 factors: PIQ, academic achievement, VIQ, auditory perception, visual perception, resting steadiness, vertical movement accuracy, movement coordination, lateral preference, vertical movement speed, movement steadiness, and speed of movement. The factor scores were used as new dependent variables in a discriminant function analysis. Using the eight groups of subjects as independent variables, the 14 factor scores were subjected to a stepwise discriminant function analysis in an attempt to establish test score patterns that would differentiate subjects in the eight groups. The eight-group discriminant function analysis yielded a Wilks Lambda of .4608 (p = .0000, df = 70), indicating that the eight groups could be accurately classified. The significant differences between groups could be accounted for on the basis of three discriminant functions. A statistically significant number of subjects was correctly classified in each of the eight groups. The percentage of cases correctly classified is shown in Table 9.2.

This study demonstrated the validity of the neuropsychological test battery for assessing various kinds of learning problems. The ability of the test score profile to differentiate between different kinds of problems was further illustrated by two-group discriminant functions. For example, in comparing the children failing in French immersion with the

TABLE 9.1

Age, WISC FSIQ, Sex, and Lateral Dominance of the Nine Groups

	Age			WISC FSIQ			Sex		Dominance	
Groups	Mean	SD	t-probability[a]	Mean	SD	t-probability	Males	Females	Left	Right
French immersion	7.0	1.2		104.3	10.6		22	10	9	23
Anglophones in francophone schools	8.2	1.7	0.002**	97.7	12.5	0.028*	26	6	8	24
Ethnic groups in anglophone schools	8.0	1.5	0.007**	95.3	13.7	0.005**	24	8	1	31
Francophones in francophone schools	8.4	1.1	0.000**	94.0	10.7	0.000**	27	5	2	30
Reading disability	8.3	1.0	0.000**	104.8	8.5	0.836	22	10	10	22
Hyperactive	7.2	1.7	0.533	101.3	9.7	0.244	30	2	5	27
Behavior and personality problems	7.8	1.1	0.019*	101.8	11.5	0.373	24	8	5	27
Minimal brain dysfunction	7.8	1.6	0.058	96.9	10.2	0.006**	21	11	9	23
French immersion success	7.1	1.8	0.947	103.1	15.1	0.843	6	2	1	7

* p < .05.
** p < .01.
[a] The t-tests referred to involve the comparison of the French immersion group with each of the eight comparison groups.

TABLE 9.2

Percentage of Cases Correctly Classified in the Discriminant Function Analysis of the Eight Groups

Group	Percentage correctly classified
French immersion	34.4
Anglophones in francophone schools	18.8
Ethnic groups in anglophone schools	31.3
Francophones in francophone schools	62.5
Reading disability	43.8
Hyperactive	18.8
Behavior and personality problems	28.1
Minimal brain dysfunction	46.9

reading disability group, 71.9% of the French immersion children were correctly classified and 75% of the reading disability group were correctly classified, indicating that these two groups of children had distinctly different neuropsychological test profiles. The important aspects of this study were cross validated in a subsequent year of study (Trites & Price, 1977). Not only has the neuropsychological test battery proven to be useful in differentiating between various learning difficulty groups, but the power to discriminate within-group variables has been demonstrated. For example, the identifying characteristics of hyperactive children who respond to stimulant medication were discriminated from those of hyperactive children who are poor responders to the stimulant medication (Trites, Brandts, & Blouin, 1980).

The behaviors tested by the Trites Neuropsychological Test Battery include attention, perception, memory, intellectual ability, language ability, concept formation, sensory and motor skills, personality, and achievement. The test battery and the forms of certain tests vary somewhat for young children aged 5–8, older children aged 9–14, and adults. Some of the tests most relevant to the present study are listed in Table 9.3, where they are categorized according to types of tests. It should be noted that the majority of verbal measures are Verbal subtests of the WISC, the revised WISC (WISC–R), or the WAIS, and many of the visual measures are Performance subtests of the Wechsler tests (Wechsler, 1949, 1955, 1974). The majority of tactile and motor tests are given separately to each hand or foot, to permit inferences about possible lateralized cerebral dysfunction. Certain tests, such as the Aphasia Screening test and the sensory imperception measures, yield scores that are useful for clinical diagnosis but are difficult to analyze for research purposes.

TABLE 9.3
Tests from the Trites Neuropsychological Battery That Were Most Relevant to the Present Study[a]

Test	Young (5–8)		Older (9–14)		Adult (15 +)	
Verbal: Wechsler Verbal	(WISC)	6	(WISC)	6	(WAIS)	6
Peabody Picture Vocabulary		1		1		—
Aphasia Screening	K	—	A	—	A	—
Verbal Concept Formation				23	A	23
Visual: Trail Making			M	2	A	2
Halstead Category	K	1	M	1	A	1
Wechsler Performance	(WISC)	6	(WISC)	6	(WAIS)	5
Raven Progressive Matrices	K	1	M	1		
Right–Left Discrimination	K	1	A	1	A	1
Knox Cube		1		1		1
Developmental Drawings		1		1		
Auditory: Seashore Rhythm		1		1		1
Tactile–Perceptual: Finger Agnosia	KRL	2	ARL	2	ARL	2
Fingertip Number Writing	RL	2	RL	2	RL	2
Fingertip Symbol Writing	RL	2	RL	2	RL	2
Roughness Discrimination	KRL	2	ARL	2	ARL	2
Tactile Form Recognition	RL	2	RL	2	RL	2
Tactual Performance Test	KRL	6	MRL	6	ARL	6
Motor–Speed: Finger Tapping	KRL	2	ARL	2	ARL	2
Foot Tapping	RL	2	RL	2	RL	2
Strength: Dynamometer Grip Strength	KRL	2	ARL	2	ARL	2
Steadiness: Vertical Groove	RL	2	RL	2	RL	2
Horizontal Groove	RL	2	RL	2	RL	2
Holes Steadiness	KRL	2	ARL	2	ARL	2
Resting Steadiness	KRL	2	ARL	2	ARL	2
Maze Coordination	RL	2	RL	2	RL	2
Accuracy: Grooved Pegboard	RL	2	RL	2	RL	2
Lateral dominance		4		4		4
Achievement: Reading, Spelling, Arithmetic		3		3		3
Sensory imperception		16		16		16

[a] The number of measures obtained from each test is given for each of the three age ranges. Special forms are indicated by K for young range, M for older range, and A for adult age range. The initials RL indicate that a separate score was obtained for each side of the body.

The Trites Neuropsychological Test Battery had been given to the majority of subjects for diagnostic purposes before the reading and language batteries were administered. Not all of the test results could be used for the quantitative analyses, because some subjects had not been given the complete battery and quantifiable data were not available for all tests. The tests used for quantitative analyses are listed in Table 9.4. These were 7 measures of verbal ability, 13 measures of visual skill, 7 measures of tactile skill, and 12 measures of motor skill. Many of the measures involve more than one type of skill. For example, the WISC Digit Span test is also a measure of verbal short-term memory, the WISC Coding, WISC Maze, Knox Cube, Developmental Drawings, Steadiness, and Grooved Pegboard tests could be classified as visual–motor tests, and the Tactual Performance and Maze Coordination tests could be classified as tactual–motor tests. Among the 37 measures, there were 2 tactile and 6 motor tests for which separate scores were obtained for the dominant and nondominant hand or foot, a total of 16 lateralized measures. Separate forms were used for younger subjects on the Raven Progressive Matrices, Halstead Category, and Tactual Performance tests; and there were separate norms for males and females on the Dynamometer test. The tests used for quantitative analyses are described in the following section.

Description of Neuropsychological Tests

The neuropsychological tests used for quantitative analyses are briefly described in what follows. Where no reference is given, a more detailed description of the test can be found in Trites (1977).

WECHSLER INTELLIGENCE SCALE FOR CHILDREN (WISC)

Only subjects who had been given the original WISC (Wechsler, 1955) or the revised WISC (Wechsler, 1974) were included in the data analyses. The 12 WISC subtests are assigned scaled scores based on different normative samples at each age. The six Verbal subtests include Information—an assessment of elementary knowledge by a series of factual questions; Comprehension—a series of questions that require an evaluation of verbally formulated problem situations; Digit Span—the spoken repetition in forward or backward order of progressively longer strings of digits; Arithmetic—the mental solution of increasingly difficult arithmetic problems; Similarities—a verbal concept formation task in which the common characteristics of pairs of words are named; and

TABLE 9.4

The Thirty-Seven Measures from the Trites Neuropsychological Battery That Were Used for Quantitative Analyses[a]

Verbal measures	WISC	Information	
		Comprehension	
		Arithmetic	
		Similarities	
		Vocabulary	
		Digit Span	
	Peabody Picture Vocabulary test		
Visual measures	WISC	Picture Completion	
		Picture Arrangement	
		Block Design	
		Object Assembly	
		Coding	
		Maze	
	Knox Cube		
	Raven Progressive Matrices (2 forms)[b]		
	Halstead Category (2 forms)[b]		
	Developmental Drawings		
	Right–left Discrimination		
Tactile measures	Tactual Performance Total (2 forms)[b]		
		Memory [b]	
		Location [b]	
	Tactile Form Recognition		Dominant
			Nondominant
	Finger Agnosia		Dominant
			Nondominant
	Motor measures		Dominant
			Nondominant
	Foot Tapping[b]		Dominant
			Nondominant
	Maze Coordination		Dominant
			Nondominant
	Grooved Pegboard		Dominant
			Nondominant
	Holes Steadiness		Dominant
			Nondominant
	Dynamometer Grip Strength [b,c]		Dominant
			Nondominant

[a] Seven of the measures were not used in all analyses. Three tests had separate forms for younger subjects, and the Dynamometer test had separate norms for males and females.

[b] Not used in analyses involving 82 subjects.

[c] Separate norms for males and females.

Vocabulary—spoken definitions of increasingly difficult words. The six Performance subtests include Picture Arrangement—the sequential arrangement of picture cards to make a story; Picture Completion—the identification of a missing part in each of a series of line drawings; Block

Design—the arrangement of colored blocks to form designs that match those on printed cards; Object Assembly—arrangement of pieces to form pictures; Coding—writing in symbols that match a series of digits; and Maze—drawing paths through a series of printed mazes.

OTHER TESTS

The Peabody Picture Vocabulary Test (Dunn, 1965) is a measure of receptive vocabulary skills in which the subject chooses one of four pictures that matches a spoken word on a series of trials of increasing difficulty. The Knox Cube Test (Arthur, 1947), is a measure of visual attention span and memory in which the examiner touches a row of blocks in a different order on each trial and the subject has to touch the blocks in the same order. The Raven Progressive Matrices Test (Raven, 1960, 1965) is a measure of visual conceptual–spatial ability where an incomplete visual design is presented and the subject has to select a design part from a set of alternatives to complete the design, in a series of trials of increasing difficulty. The Developmental Drawings Test is a measure of the ability to copy line drawings of 11 simple geometric figures. The Right–Left Discrimination Test consists of 12 items in which right–left orientation is assessed with reference to the subject's own body and that of the examiner, who sits opposite; testing is done both with eyes open and with eyes closed. The Halstead Category Test (Reitan, 1959) is a measure of nonverbal abstraction and concept formation ability; multiple choice items are presented via slide projection, and immediate feedback is given by a bell for correct choices and a buzzer for incorrect choices; a number of subtests of increasing complexity are given. The Tactual Performance Test (Reitan, 1959) is a measure of psychomotor problem-solving ability, in which tactual–motor speed, memory, and spatial skills are involved. The Total Time score is the total time required for placement of blocks of different sizes and shapes in a form board with the preferred hand, the nonpreferred hand, and both hands, with the subject blindfolded; the Memory score is the number of blocks drawn correctly from memory following completion of the task; and the Location score is the number of blocks drawn in the correct spatial location with respect to their position on the form board.

TESTS IN WHICH SEPARATE SCORES WERE
OBTAINED FOR THE TWO HANDS

On the measures of lateralized tactual, perceptual–motor, and motor ability, a separate score was obtained for the dominant hand and the nondominant hand (there were 75 right-handed and 13 left-handed subjects, including 7 left handers of Type O, 3 of Type A, and 1 of Type S reading disability). The Finger Agnosia Test (Reitan, 1959) is a measure of finger localization in which each finger is touched behind a screen and a correct localization is requested; each finger is touched several times over the series of trials. The Tactile Form Recognition Test (Reitan, 1959) is a measure of stereognosis where the subject has to identify plastic geometric shapes presented behind a screen by touch alone. The Grooved Pegboard Test (Reitan, 1959) is a measure of fine manipulative skills involving visual–motor speed and accuracy; the subject has to place grooved pegs into a board as fast as possible with each hand. The Maze Coordination and Holes Steadiness tests are part of a motor steadiness battery developed at the Neuropsychology Laboratory, University of Wisconsin. The Maze Coordination Test is a measure of movement coordination that involves visual–motor skills; the subject moves a stylus through a maze that has no blind alleys; the number of times the stylus touches the side of the path and the total duration of contacts are electrically recorded; the task is done twice with each hand. The Holes Steadiness Test is a measure of kinetic tremor in which the subject attempts to hold a stylus without touching the sides of holes of varying diameter during 15-sec trials; the frequency and duration of contacts are electrically recorded on two trials for each hand. The Finger Tapping Test (Reitan, 1959) is a measure of motor speed; the subject taps a mechanical or electrical counter as fast as possible with the index finger of each hand; several 10-sec trials are given with each hand. The *Foot Tapping Test* is a measure of motor speed in which the subject presses a foot pedal attached to an electrical counter as rapidly as possible; several 10-sec trials are given with each foot. The Dynamometer Grip Strength Test is a measure of grip strength measured by the subject squeezing a hand dynamometer as hard as possible; at least two trials are given with each hand.

SELECTION OF SUBJECTS AND TESTS FOR
QUANTITATIVE ANALYSES

Several different sets of tests and subjects were used for the quantitative analyses. A total of six subjects were eliminated from all quantitative analyses, including five adult subjects (07, 020, 032, A20, and S13) who had not been given the WISC, Peabody, Raven Progressive Matrices, or Developmental Drawings, and one subject (S3) who had verified brain damage and had been retested with the neuropsychological battery several times. The remaining 82 subjects were used in the analyses of 30 measures, where the 7 measures from the Raven Progressive Matrices, Halstead Category, Tactual Performance, and Foot Tapping tests were not included because of some missing scores for 17 of the subjects. These 17 subjects were eliminated from analyses that used all of the 37 measures listed in Table 9.2 for the remaining 65 subjects. Certain analyses were also carried out with a subsample of 36 subjects who met more stringent criteria of reading disabilities, as will be described.

Age Norms of Neuropsychological Tests

The reading tests were scored in terms of percentiles derived from a single sample of normal subjects of varying ages, and the language tests were scored in terms of percentiles derived from a second normal sample. The scoring of neuropsychological tests was more complicated. Scores on the six Verbal and the six Performance subtests of the WISC were expressed in terms of scaled scores based on age norms, in which the average score of normal subjects at each age is 10, with a standard deviation of 3. The Peabody Picture Vocabulary and Knox Cube tests were scored in terms of mental age norms and converted to quotients equivalent to the intelligence quotient by dividing mental age (MA) by chronological age (CA); the average score of normal subjects would be 100 and the standard deviation for the Peabody Picture Vocabulary Test is 15. The remaining tests were all converted to T scores based on a large sample of approximately 5000 subjects referred to the Neuropsychology Clinic of the Royal Ottawa Hospital, with separate norms for each age (a computer program for T score conversions is available from R. L. Trites). The average T score of the clinic sample is 50 and the standard deviation is 10. Thus, the 37 measures derived from the neuropsychological test battery are all age-corrected, and can be evaluated with reference to an average score at each age. However, the age norms of the WISC, Peabody Picture Vocabulary and Knox Cube tests are based on samples of normal subjects, and the age norms of the remaining tests are based on a sample of referrals to a neuropsychology clinic. Because of the differences in age norms and the differences in the tests and the subjects used for the various analyses, the neuropsychology results must be interpreted with much more caution than the reading and the language test results.

Average Performance on the Neuropsychological Tests

The average performance of the total sample (minus those subjects who had not taken all of the tests or whose results could not be used) on the 37 measures from the neuropsychological battery was examined first.

Figure 9.1 shows the average scores for 82 subjects on 30 tests and for 65 subjects on the remaining 7 tests. The tests are grouped according to the scoring scales used, with 12 WISC subtests first, followed by the Peabody and Knox quotients and the 23 measures using T scores. Among the latter measures, the 7 nonlateralized measures are presented first, followed by the 8 tests for which separate scores were obtained for dominant and nondominant hands. The lateralized tests have been grouped somewhat differently than they are in Table 9.4, with the first 2 tests (Finger Agnosia and Tactile Form Perception) classified as perceptual, the next three (Grooved Pegboard, Maze, and Holes Steadiness) as perceptual–motor, and the final three (Finger Tapping, Foot Tapping, and Dynamometer Grip Strength) as predominantly motor.

For the reading tests (Figure 7.1) and the language tests (Figure 8.1) we evaluated average proficiency in terms of the discrepancy from the expected level of performance of normal subjects of the same average age, and variability of performance in terms of the average percentage of overlap between the reading problem sample and normal sample at each age. For the neuropsychological measures shown in Figure 9.1, we can directly evaluate proficiency on the WISC, Peabody Picture Vocabulary, and Knox Cube tests relative to the average performance of normal samples, and proficiency on the remaining measures relative to the average performance of neuropsychology clinic referrals. Variability of performance is indicated by the width of the standard deviation on each side of the mean, within which 68% of the scores fall.

On the WISC, the group average was generally typical of that for reading disability samples (Vernon, 1971), with all but one Verbal subtest slightly below normal and all but one Performance subtest slightly above normal, the lowest Verbal subtest being Digit Span and the lowest Performance subtest being Coding. The highest Verbal subtest score was obtained on Similarities, a measure of verbal concept formation. All subtests except Digit Span were within one standard deviation of normal performance. The group average for the Peabody Picture Vocabulary Test coincided with the normal average of 100, and the Knox Cube average was about 15 points above normal, with a very large standard deviation. Six of the nonlateralized tests were above average, and the seventh (Right–Left Discrimination) was average with reference to the clinic referral sample. On the lateralized measures, performance was below the average of the clinic sample on both Finger Agnosia measures, and above average on the remaining measures. The dominant hand was relatively less proficient on the Tactile Form Recognition Test, and the nondominant hand was relatively less proficient on the Grooved Pegboard, Maze Coordination, Holes Steadiness, and Finger Tapping tests

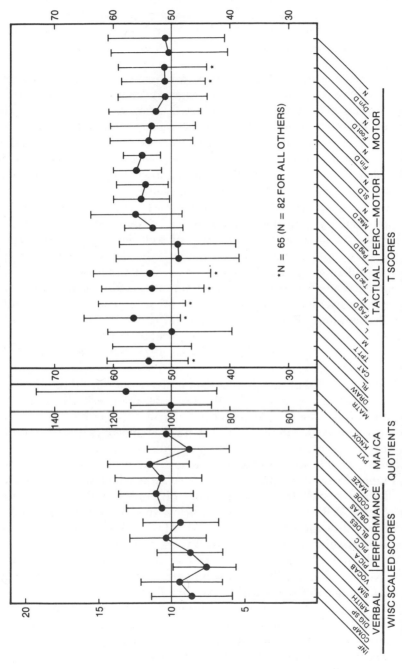

FIGURE 9.1. *Means and standard deviations for samples of 65 and 82 subjects on 37 neuropsychological tests.*

(because the tests were scored in terms of the average of the clinic sample rather than absolute proficiency, both dominant and nondominant hand scores would be 50 for an average clinic referral; i.e., the usual superiority of dominant over nondominant hand is eliminated by this method of scoring).

Interpreted within a clinical frame of reference, the present sample could be said to perform above the average expected for clinical referrals in many areas. The lower scores on heavily weighted Verbal tests were probably due to a poor fund of general information rather than to a primary linguistic deficit (i.e., poor performance may not have been due to an inherent inability in verbal expression, but to the secondary effects of not being able to read and to acquire knowledge). Both verbal and nonverbal concept formation skills were above average. Visual attention–memory span (Knox Cube Test) was well developed, but auditory attention–memory span (Digit Span) was moderately short. Copying of letter forms (Coding) was slow in spite of well-developed motor skills. Despite a few mild asymmetries on the lateralized tests, there were no strong lateralizing signs, and there was no clear indication of cerebral dysfunction. The poor bilateral Finger Agnosia performance was in contrast to above average performance on the other tactual measure (Tactile Form Recognition). Finger localization difficulty has been previously reported as a good predictor of reading problems (Benton, 1975; De-Hirsch, Jansky, & Langford, 1966; Rourke, 1978; Satz, Taylor, Friel, & Fletcher, 1978).

Although the present sample included subjects who would be classified as having reading disabilities by the usual selection criteria, some investigations have used more stringent criteria. To permit comparison with such studies, a sample that met more stringent selection criteria with regard to intelligence, reading retardation, and age range was selected to provide some indication of how our results compared with such studies. This subsample included 36 subjects who had been given all 37 of the neuropsychological tests, had a PIQ of 90 or above, a reading grade on the WRAT 2 or more years below their expected grade level, and were within the age range of 9–15. Most of the subjects excluded were younger subjects with less than 2 years reading retardation on the WRAT (the majority were, however, 2 or more years below expected grade level on one of the Durrell reading measures). The subsample of 36 subjects included 15 from reading disability Type 1, 10 from Type 2, and 6 from Type 3. Because we will be primarily concerned with these 31 subjects in the subsequent analyses, their averages are shown in Figure 9.2. The means and standard deviations of the neuropsychological tests were very similar to those of the larger sample.

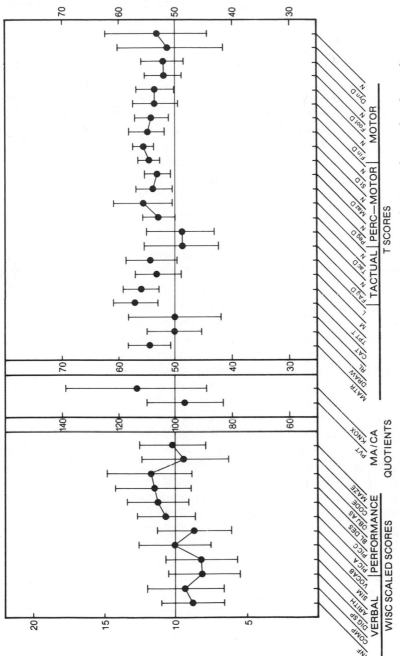

FIGURE 9.2. Means and standard deviations of 37 neuropsychological measures for a sample of 36 subjects selected according to more stringent criteria of reading disability.

In general, both the larger sample of subjects with reading problems and the smaller sample that met more stringent age, IQ, and WRAT reading achievement criteria showed the usual WISC pattern, with all Verbal subtests except Similarities tending to be slightly below average and all Performance subtests except Coding tending to be slightly above average. They were slightly below average on the Peabody Picture Vocabulary Test and above average on the Knox Cube Test. Their performance relative to a sample of clinic referrals on the remaining 23 measures was near or above average, with no consistently large descrepancies between dominant and nondominant hands. Although there was no clear indication of cerebral dysfunction, clinical evaluation of the overall pattern of deficit suggested that possible left-hemisphere involvement in the temporal–parietal region could not be ruled out, particularly for the smaller sample.

Relationships among Neuropsychological Test Scores

As before, we examined the relationships among the 37 neuropsychological measures to estimate the extent to which component skills had been tested and to provide a foundation for later interpretations of individual differences. The correlations among 30 neuropsychological measures for 82 subjects and 7 neuropsychological measures for 65 subjects are given in Appendix A. For correlations involving 82 subjects, .22 is significant at the 5% level and .28 at the 1% level; and for 65 subjects, .25 is significant at the 5% level and .31 at the 1% level. Only 23% of the 666 correlations among the 37 neuropsychological tests were statistically significant, as compared with over 90% of the reading and 77% of the language test intercorrelations, and only 4% of the neuropsychological test intercorrelations were greater than .40. This would be expected, as the reading tests and the language tests involved much more homogeneous skills. The majority of the higher correlations involved the WISC subtests, the Peabody Picture Vocabulary Test and the Raven Progressive Matrices Test. Among the remaining tests, the only high correlations were between Tactual Performance Memory and Location and between the dominant and nondominant hands on the lateralized tests. The Knox Cube, Halstead Category, Tactual Performance Total Time, Developmental Drawings, and Right–Left Discrimination tests were not highly correlated with any measures. Among the neuropsychological measures, then, there was some interrelationship among verbal and nonverbal intelligence measures and between hands on lateralized tests, but otherwise relatively independent skills. R factor analyses were next carried out to get a clearer idea of these patterns.

Conventional R Factor Analyses of Neuropsychological Tests

R factor analyses were calculated for the set of 30 tests for 82 subjects and the set of 37 tests for 65 subjects, using three-, four-, and five-factor solutions. The four-factor solutions were most interpretable for both analyses, which are summarized in Tables 9.5 and 9.6. Factor 1 in both analyses was clearly a verbal factor, with high loadings on WISC Information, Comprehension, Similarities, and Vocabulary subtests, and also on the Peabody Picture Vocabulary Test. Factor 2 in both analyses could be interpreted as a spatial factor, with high loadings on WISC Block Design and Object Assembly, Progressive Matrices, the Tactual Performance measures, and the Finger Agnosia and Tactile Form Recognition measures. Factor 3 in the first analysis and Factor 4 in the second analysis were perceptual–motor factors, with high loadings on both hands for the three lateralized perceptual–motor tests. Factor 4 in the first analysis and Factor 3 in the second analysis had high loadings on the lateralized motor tests. Thus, both factor analyses quite clearly showed a verbal factor, a spatial factor, a perceptual–motor factor, and a motor factor. These four types of measures seemed well enough represented to be sensitive to individual differences in the further analyses. Reading disabilities associated with verbal deficits should involve Factor 1 skills; those involving visual–spatial deficits should involve Factor 2 skills; and those involving perceptual–motor or motor deficits should involve the respective Factors 3 and 4 of the two analyses.

Correlations with Standardized Reading Tests

Correlations between the neuropsychological tests and the standard reading achievement measures (Appendix A) were quite low, none exceeding .41. For the four Durrell reading measures, only the WISC Information, Comprehension, and Similarities tests had correlations in the .31 to .41 range. Correlations between the reading achievement tests and the tests of reading-related skills tended to be much higher, as did many of the correlations between the reading achievement tests and the language measures. Only certain neuropsychological measures directly involving verbal skills, then, were moderately correlated with reading achievement measures in the present sample of subjects.

TABLE 9.5

Summary of the Results of an R Factor Analysis of Thirty Neuropsychological Tests for Eighty-Two Subjects [a]

	Tests	Factors			
		1	2	3	4
WISC Verbal:	Information	75	18	−13	07
	Comprehension	71	16	02	08
	Digit Span	25	43	09	22
	Arithmetic	56	42	−01	−07
	Similarities	80	−11	−08	16
	Vocabulary	86	03	−06	05
Performance:	Picture Arrangement	51	04	18	−05
	Picture Completion	29	39	−04	05
	Block Design	24	57	18	−20
	Object Assembly	29	54	21	−13
	Coding	27	21	13	05
	Maze	15	45	26	−33
	Peabody Picture Vocabulary	78	05	−01	02
	Knox Cube	03	30	14	−34
	Developmental Drawings	03	10	38	03
	Right–Left Discrimination	02	−03	11	10
Lateralized Tactual:	Finger Agnosia—dominant	−06	74	10	−09
	Recognition Nondominant	13	74	−01	02
	Tactile Form Recognition—dominant	−08	40	00	23
	Nondominant	−01	41	05	23
Perceptual–Motor:	Grooved Pegboard—dominant	22	26	62	−10
	Nondominant	−09	25	59	−12
	Maze—dominant	01	−02	69	−26
	Nondominant	−05	04	73	−03
	Steadiness—dominant	−07	−06	65	47
	Nondominant	−08	03	68	37
Motor:	Finger Tapping—dominant	11	14	13	58
	Nondominant	00	00	−01	68
	Dynamometer Grip Strength—dominant	15	24	−02	69
	Nondominant	06	30	−04	62

[a] Factor loadings are given for each test (decimal points omitted).

Correlations between Neuropsychological and Reading-Related Skills

Whereas the majority of correlations between the language tests and the tests of reading-related skills were significant, only a small proportion of the 1443 correlations between the 37 neuropsychological measures and the 39 measures of reading-related skills were significant. The only cor-

TABLE 9.6

Summary of the Results of an R Factor Analysis of Thirty-Seven Neuropsychological Tests for Sixty-Five Subjects[a]

		Factors			
	Tests	1	2	3	4
WISC Verbal:	Information	75	13	00	05
	Comprehension	75	− 09	03	11
	Digit Span	34	15	06	22
	Arithmetic	58	29	− 05	17
	Similarities	71	10	25	− 27
	Vocabulary	83	− 03	14	− 04
Performance:	Picture Arrangement	24	18	07	11
	Picture Completion	38	29	10	15
	Block Design	26	62	− 19	20
	Object Assembly	31	44	− 16	44
	Coding	35	− 04	05	41
	Maze	11	25	− 30	45
	Peabody Picture Vocabulary	70	19	07	− 12
	Knox Cube	06	− 24	− 07	56
	Progressive Matrices	34	50	02	26
	Developmental Drawings	23	11	32	23
	Right–Left Discrimination	00	− 04	− 09	16
	Halstead Category	37	22	09	24
Tactual Performance:	Total Time	17	62	25	19
	Memory	05	66	01	17
	Location	04	71	− 06	21
Lateralized Tactual:	Finger Agnosia—dominant	20	37	− 14	49
	Nondominant	25	51	− 04	26
	Tactile Form Recognition—dominant	− 15	29	15	14
	Nondominant	06	54	16	07
Perceptual–Motor:	Grooved Pegboard—dominant	23	02	09	66
	Nondominant	− 06	− 03	07	67
	Maze–dominant	− 13	15	23	45
	Nondominant	− 18	37	39	47
	Steadiness—dominant	− 33	08	62	31
	Nondominant	− 33	21	52	35
Motor:	Finger Tapping—dominant	16	− 23	67	− 01
	Nondominant	09	− 07	67	− 11
	Foot Tapping—dominant	17	11	69	02
	Nondominant	20	19	64	− 15
	Dynamometer Grip Strength—dominant	29	29	40	− 11
	Nondominant	19	36	33	− 07

[a] Factor loadings are given for each test (decimal points omitted).

relations of .40 or higher were between WISC Coding and Color Naming
(.43), Oral Reading of Upper-Case Letters (.42), Oral Reading of Lower-
Case Letters (.48), and Oral Reading of Unrelated Words (.40). Other-
wise, there were 3 correlations in the .30–.40 range involving the 7
Visual Matching tests and WISC Arithmetic, Similarities, Coding, and
Raven Progressive Matrices; 13 involving the 11 Oral Reading tests and
WISC Arithmetic, Similarities, and Coding; 6 involving the 10 Visual
Scanning tests and WISC Coding and Arithmetic; 2 involving the Sen-
tence Comprehension test and WISC Arithmetic and Similarities; and 8
involving the 3 Spelling tests and WISC Information, Arithmetic,
Similarities, Object Assembly, and Raven Progressive Matrices. As the
few moderate correlations that did occur tended to center around WISC
Coding and Arithmetic, it may be inferred that the reading skills of the
subjects tended to be related to lower-level visual–verbal skills rather
than to higher-level language skills or to complex visual–perceptual skills.
Nor were there substantial correlations between reading skills and neuropsychological tests involving sequencing, spatial orientation, or lateralized skills.

Correlations between Neuropsychological and Language Tests

Only a small proportion of the 814 correlations between the 37 neuropsychological tests and the 22 language tests were significant. The only
correlations exceeding .40 were between WISC Arithmetic and Pig Latin
(.43), and between Morphophonemics and WISC Vocabulary (.40) and
Peabody Picture Vocabulary (.48). The only correlations between .30
and .40 were 5 involving the 5 phonemic segmentation measures and
WISC Arithmetic and Similarities; 11 involving the 4 oral repetition
measures and WISC Information, Comprehension, Digit Span, Arithmetic, Similarities, and Vocabulary, and the Peabody Picture Vocabulary,
Halstead Category, and Tactual Performance tests; 4 involving the 6
Token Tests and WISC Information, Arithmetic, and Coding; and 12 involving the 4 syntactic–semantic tests and WISC Information, Comprehension, Similarities, Arithmetic, Picture Arrangement, and Coding, and
the Peabody Picture Vocabulary Test. As would be expected, then, the
most verbal of the neuropsychological tests (i.e., the WISC Verbal
subtests plus the Coding subtest and the Peabody Picture Vocabulary
Test, were most highly correlated with the language tests, but none of the
correlations were high).

The relatively low interrelations among the neuropsychological measures, and between the neuropsychological measures and the reading and language measures suggested that the neuropsychological measures sampled a wide range of independent abilities, and might thus be sensitive to any gross deficiencies of nonreading skills in the three types of reading disabilities.

Average Neuropsychological Scores for the Three Types of Reading Disabilities

The average neuropsychological test scores for each type of reading disability provided the most direct indication of whether any or all of the reading disability types were associated with particular patterns of deficiency on the neuropsychological tests. Figure 9.3 shows the averages for the 30 subjects of Type O, the 21 of Type A, and the 15 of Type S from the sample of 82 subjects for 30 tests; and for the 25 subjects of Type O, the 14 of Type A, and the 11 of Type S from the sample of 65 subjects for the remaining 7 tests. As the neuropsychological tests were scored in terms of age norms, absolute levels of performance could be directly compared to provide a more precise indication of differences between types. This is most easily done by plotting the results for each type against each other type, as is shown in Figure 9.4. The top pair are those of types O and A. Both types showed the same general pattern of difference between WISC Verbal and Performance subtests; Type O was generally superior to Type A, with the exception of poorer performance on Digit Span. Type O was considerably superior on the Peabody Picture Vocabulary and Knox Cube tests. Performance was comparable on the Halstead Category, Tactual Performance, Raven Progressive Matrices, Developmental Drawings and Right–Left Discrimination tests. On the lateralized tests, Type A was quite deficient on the Finger Agnosia and Finger Tapping tests, and showed some trend toward dominant hand deficiencies relative to Type O.

The comparison of Types A and S in the middle graph of Figure 9.4 once again shows the WISC Verbal–Performance difference for both types, with Type S better on all Verbal subtests except Information and Digit Span, and on all Performance subtests except Picture Completion and Block Design, for which comparable scores were obtained. Type S was also superior on the Peabody Picture Vocabulary and Knox Cube tests, but poorer on the Raven Progressive Matrices, Right–Left Discrimination, Halstead Category, and Tactual Performance tests. On the lateralized tests, Type S was better on the Pegboard, Steadiness,

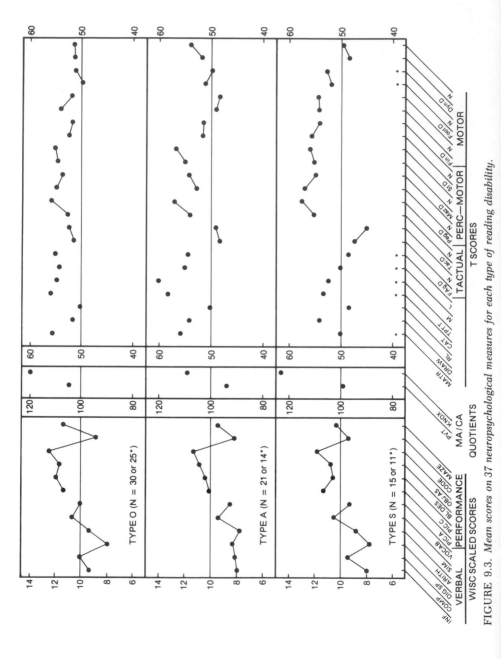

FIGURE 9.3. Mean scores on 37 neuropsychological measures for each type of reading disability.

162

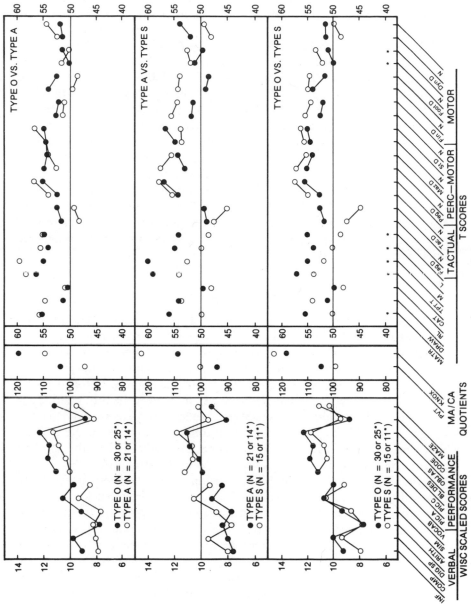

FIGURE 9.4. Comparisons of neuropsychological test profiles between different reading disability types.

Finger Tapping, and Foot Tapping tests, and Type A was better on the Finger Agnosia (nondominant hand) and Dynamometer Grip Strength tests. Type S showed some tendency for nondominant deficiencies relative to the Type A trend toward dominant hand deficiencies.

The comparison of Types O and S in the bottom graph of Figure 9.4 shows that Type O was slightly superior to Type S on half of the WISC subtests, and comparable on the other half. Type O was superior to Type S on the Peabody Picture Vocabulary, Raven Progressive Matrices, Right–Left Discrimination, Halstead Category, and Tactual Performance tests, and Type S was better on Developmental Drawings. On the lateralized tests, Type S was very deficient on the Finger Agnosia Test and slightly deficient on the Dynamometer Grip Strength Test, and was equal or superior to Type O on the remaining tests.

The average scores on the 37 tests for the more stringently selected sample of 15 Type O, 10 Type A, and 6 Type S subjects are shown in Figure 9.5. The trends are essentially the same, but not quite as consistent as those for the larger samples, probably because of the relatively small number of subjects.

CLINICAL EVALUATION OF AVERAGE PROFILES

Clinical interpretations suggested that Type O subjects tended to be the least impaired, with WISC scores comparable or superior to those of Types A and S. Auditory attention–memory span (Digit Span) was short relative to visual attention–memory span (Knox Cube). Concept formation ability was particularly good for nonverbal stimuli. Letter copying (Coding) was slow even though motor skills were generally good. It is also notable that only Type O subjects tended to perform well on the Finger Agnosia Test. There were a few mild asymmetries on the lateralized tests, but performance levels were generally within the clinical average and there was no evidence of cerebral dysfunction.

Type A was the most impaired group. WISC subtest scores were generally lower than those of Types O and S. Auditory attention–memory span was short; and visual attention–memory span, although above average, was considerably shorter than that of the other types. Psychomotor problem solving and nonverbal concept formation skills were well developed, but verbal concept formation skills (Similarities) were below average. Dominant hand asymmetries on the Finger Agnosia, Tactile Form Recognition, Grooved Pegboard, Maze Coordination, and Dynamometer Grip Strength tests would be consistent with an interpretation of left-hemisphere dysfunction.

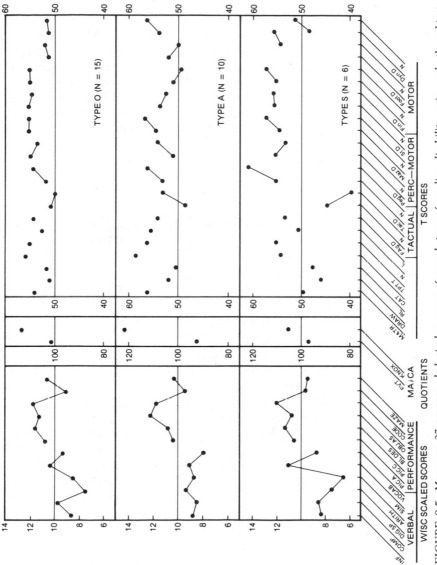

FIGURE 9.5. Means on 37 neuropsychological measures for each type of reading disability, using only the subjects selected by more stringent criteria.

The predominant deficit of Type S subjects appeared to be spatial in nature. Performance on the Raven Progressive Matrices, Right–Left Discrimination, and Tactual Performance tests tended to be poor in comparison with the other types. Auditory attention–memory span was short but visual attention–memory span was well developed. Although verbal and nonverbal concept formation skills were at or above average, nonverbal concept formation skills on the Raven Progressive Matrices and Halstead Category tests were lower than those of the other types. There were a number of asymmetries on the lateralized tests, but no consistent pattern emerged. The predominant spatial deficit in conjunction with low Finger Agnosia scores, particularly on the nondominant side, could be compatible with an interpretation posterior dysfunction, particularly in the right hemisphere.

Statistical Differentiation of Reading Disability Types

As the neuropsychological results were scored relative to age norms, we could also make direct statistical comparisons of the three types of reading disabilities on each test. The significance levels of differences among the types (OAS) and between each pair of types (OA, AS, OS) are shown in Table 9.7 for the sample of 82 subjects for 30 tests and for the sample of 65 subjects for the remaining 7 tests, and in Table 9.8 for the more stringently selected sample of 36 subjects. All significance levels are based on simple analyses of variance derived from the discriminant analyses that will be discussed in the following section. As the significance levels of the analyses of the pairs of groups were not adjusted to allow for the effects of multiple comparisons, they somewhat overestimate the actual probability of a difference between types on individual tests, although multivariate analyses might have revealed highly significant differences for subsets of tests taken together. With such a large number of tests, the interpretations of significant differences must, in any case, be extremely cautious.

For the larger samples of subjects in Table 9.7, the only statistically significant differences among the three types (OAS) were for WISC Comprehension, Peabody Picture Vocabulary, Finger Agnosia (nondominant), Grooved Pegboard (dominant), and Finger Tapping (nondominant). On the pairwise comparisons of types, Type O was significantly better than Type A on three WISC subtests (Comprehension, Picture

Completion, and Maze), a result consistant with the general superiority of Type O on WISC measures, as indicated by the graphic results of Figure 9.4. A significantly higher Peabody Picture Vocabulary score for Type O was further evidence of superiority on verbal intelligence measures. The only significant difference between Types O and A on the remaining measures was a significantly higher score for Type O on Finger Tapping with the dominant hand. Nondominant finger tapping approached significance, suggesting an overall inferiority in finger tapping for Type A rather than a lateralized deficit. For this comparison of types, then, Type A was shown to be particularly deficient on several measures of verbal and nonverbal intelligence, and also on a measure of simple motor speed. The comparison of Types A and S did not reveal comparable significant differences on the WISC or Peabody Picture Vocabulary tests, even though the mean differences were in the same direction, but finger tapping was deficient in Type A for both dominant and nondominant hands, and Type S was deficient on the Raven Progressive Matrices Test. The comparison of Types O and S revealed only a deficiency of Type S for the Raven Progressive Matrices and Finger Agnosia tests in the nondominant hand. For the largest samples of subjects, then, the univariate significant differences among types suggested less proficiency on intelligence measures—particularly verbal intelligence—for Type A, accompanied by consistent deficiency of Type S on the Raven Progressive Matrices Test, and an indication of Finger Agnosia in Type S.

The significance tests for the more stringently selected samples (Table 9.8) show fewer significant differences. The trend for IQ deficiencies in Type A disappeared, but their deficiency in Finger Tapping was still evident and Type S was still deficient on the Raven Progressive Matrices. The only new deficiencies to appear were in WISC Arithmetic for Type S relative to Type A and in Developmental Drawings for Type S relative to both Types O and A.

The overall results for these univariate significance tests provide a definite suggestion of deficient motor speed in Type A and a deficiency in certain complex visual–conceptual skills (Raven Progressive Matrices) in Type S, with less consistent suggestions of a general deficiency in intelligence test measures for Type A and Finger Agnosia in Type S. These results are in accordance with those of the language tests in failing to support the possibility of a general language deficiency in Type O, and also give no indication of motor deficiency or especially poor short-term memory (on the WISC Digit Span subtest) in Type O. Type S was not outstandingly deficient on tests involving sequencing (WISC Coding, Knox Cube), but did give some indication of a weakness in complex

TABLE 9.7

Mean Scores for **Thirty** Subjects of Type O, Twenty-One of Type A, and Fifteen of Type S on Thirty Neuropsychological Measures, and for Twenty-Five Subjects of Type O, Fourteen of Type A, and Eleven of Type S on the Seven Remaining Measures[a]

	Means			Significance levels			
	O	A	S	OAS	OA	AS	OS
WISC Verbal (10 = normal average)							
Information	9	8	8	.13	.11	.98	.06
Comprehension	10	8	9	.05	.02	.24	.32
Digit Span	8	8	8	.78	.64	.54	.71
Arithmetic	9	8	9	.23	.09	.34	.64
Similarities	11	9	11	.15	.09	.16	.92
Vocabulary	10	8	9	.14	.06	.47	.28
WISC Performance (10 = normal average)							
Picture Arrangement	11	10	11	.12	.07	.15	.95
Picture Completion	12	10	11	.11	.04	.79	.19
Block Design	12	11	11	.52	.36	.86	.33
Object Assembly	12	11	12	.37	.13	.49	.61
Coding	9	8	9	.41	.34	.27	.57
Maze	11	10	10	.07	.02	.29	.30
MA/CA quotients (100 = normal average)							
Peabody Vocabulary	105	94	99	.03	.01	.27	.19
Knox Cube	120	109	123	.33	.19	.20	.72

T scores (50 = average for clinic referrals)

Raven Progressive Matrices [b]		56	56	50	.06	.94	.04	.03
Developmental Drawings		52	54	54	.49	.27	.91	.32
Right–Left Discrimination		50	50	48	.85	.90	.60	.67
Halstead Category [b]		57	58	53	.21	.49	.07	.21
Tactual Performance: [b]								
Total Time		55	57	52	.16	.24	.12	.23
Memory		54	55	50	.36	.75	.21	.22
Location		55	54	49	.16	.77	.15	.06
Lateralized Tactual								
Finger Agnosia	D	51	48	48	.49	.32	.87	.30
	N	52	49	44	.05	.25	.19	.02
Tactile Form Recognition	D	53	54	55	.46	.50	.61	.18
	N	55	57	58	.70	.32	.88	.43
Lateralized Perceptual–Motor								
Grooved Pegboard	D	55	52	56	.05	.06	.06	.30
	N	54	54	55	.54	.93	.37	.30
Maze	D	55	54	55	.43	.59	.25	.35
	N	55	57	56	.63	.33	.78	.61
Steadiness	D	53	52	56	.29	.78	.10	.23
	N	52	52	54	.72	.86	.41	.52
Lateralized Motor								
Finger Tapping	D	54	49	54	.06	.03	.04	.98
	N	52	48	54	.05	.06	.02	.44
Foot Tapping [b]	D	50	51	52	.60	.64	.60	.32
	N	51	50	53	.63	.61	.32	.57
Dynamometer Grip Strength	D	52	52	48	.48	.98	.30	.24
	N	52	54	50	.38	.38	.15	.51

[a] The significance levels for mean differences among the three types (OAS) and between each pair of types (OA, AS, OS) are also shown, as determined from analyses of variance carried out as part of discriminant analyses.

[b] Means for twenty-five Type O, fourteen type A, and eleven Type S subjects.

TABLE 9.8

Mean Scores for Fifteen Subjects of Type O, Ten of Type A, and Six of Type S Who Were Selected by Stringent Criteria of Reading Disability, with Significance Levels for Differences among the Three Types and between Each Pair of Types

	Means			Significance levels			
	O	A	S	OAS	OA	AS	OS
WISC Verbal (10 = normal average)							
Information	9	9	8	.84	.88	.59	.57
Comprehension	10	9	9	.40	.25	.99	.27
Digit Span	8	9	7	.15	.09	.18	.70
Arithmetic	8	9	7	.23	.81	.18	.04
Similarities	10	9	11	.28	.23	.20	.50
Vocabulary	9	8	9	.49	.26	.61	.64
WISC Performance (10 = normal average)							
Picture Arrangement	11	10	11	.77	.56	.78	.82
Picture Completion	11	11	11	.82	.48	.68	.81
Block Design	11	12	11	.63	.45	.33	.76
Object Assembly	12	12	12	.96	.76	.80	.97
Coding	9	9	10	.87	.88	.76	.53
Maze	10	10	9	.52	.69	.43	.29
MA/CA quotients (100 = normal average)							
Peabody Vocabulary	101	91	97	.22	.07	.49	.50
Knox Cube	112	121	105	.47	.42	.18	.58

T scores (50 = average for clinic referrals)

	D/N							
Raven Progressive Matrices		54	56	50	.16	.36	.01	.22
Developmental Drawings		51	52	46	.05	.67	.01	.05
Right–Left Discrimination		49	50	53	.73	.81	.51	.45
Halstead Category		56	59	54	.50	.37	.25	.70
Tactual Performance:								
Total Time		55	56	55	.86	.62	.77	.93
Memory		52	56	51	.47	.32	.32	.67
Location		54	53	53	.94	.77	.97	.77
Lateralized Tactual								
Finger Agnosia	D	50	48	44	.58	.67	.56	.32
	N	50	53	39	.10	.52	.06	.12
Tactile Form Recognition	D	52	53	55	.50	.70	.48	.19
	N	54	56	61	.30	.55	.45	.06
Lateralized Perceptual–Motor								
Grooved Pegboard	D	55	51	55	.14	.07	.20	.77
	N	53	53	53	.94	.82	.79	.90
Maze	D	55	54	54	.57	.32	.94	.35
	N	55	56	57	.55	.60	.57	.29
Steadiness	D	55	53	56	.68	.47	.45	.78
	N	54	52	56	.34	.38	.15	.43
Lateralized Motor								
Finger Tapping	D	55	50	54	.35	.18	.22	.91
	N	54	49	57	.07	.06	.03	.48
Foot Tapping	D	51	52	57	.66	.74	.52	.38
	N	52	50	56	.36	.55	.16	.31
Dynamometer Grip Strength	D	51	53	48	.66	.71	.40	.47
	N	52	56	51	.40	.28	.18	.75

visual skills. There was no single neuropsychological measure that directly reflected the types of intermodal integration deficits that might be involved in Type A.

Discriminant Analysis of
Neuropsychological Measures

In addition to determining the differences among the three types of reading disabilities on individual neuropsychological tests, we wanted to find out whether the types were characterized by particular patterns of neuropsychological test scores. This type of analysis can be accomplished by discriminant analysis (Tatsuoka, 1971), where the best possible combination of weighted scores for differentiating a given number of groups by a given set of measures is computed by a procedure that combines analysis of variance and multivariate correlational analysis. We had used discriminant analysis in attempting to differentiate the three types of reading disabilities by the 22 language measures, but did not achieve a good discrimination. Even though age differences among the three types were not controlled for by the percentile scores, only 56% of the 72 subjects could be correctly classified by the best possible combination of weighted scores on the 22 language measures. Because comparable discriminant analyses of neuropsychological measures resulted in a much higher percentage of correct classifications of reading disability types despite the fact that age effects had been eliminated by the scoring methods, we carried out an extensive set of discriminant analyses of the neuropsychological results.

The results of the discriminant analyses must be interpreted with the greatest of caution, because the mathematical objective of discriminant analysis—to force particular groups of subjects to be as statistically distinct as possible—does not completely coincide with our aim of reliably determining the patterns of neuropsychological deficit that characterize each type of reading disability. The results of discriminant analysis permit us to make some inferences about the extent to which the reading disability types can be distinguished by neuropsychological test results. However, these inferences must be provisional, because chance variations in test scores are used as much as actual differences in the skills tested to achieve the mathematical separation of groups. A similar problem arises in the interpretation of factor analyses, which we solved by replicating the Q technique classifications of reading disabilities, as described in Chapter 7. Findings regarding the neuropsychological measures will also have to be replicated by further reasearch.

To provide some basis for evaluating the present discriminant analyses, we carried out several sets of analyses that yielded both liberal and conservative interpretations regarding the amount and type of distinction between reading disability types. Liberal interpretations were obtained from analyses that used a large number of tests, and conservative interpretations from analyses using a small number of tests relative to the number of subjects. All analyses were done by the SPSS DISCRIMINANT program (Nie et al., 1975) using a stepwise method of selecting the neuropsychological measures that best discriminated the reading disability types. The largest increase in Rao's V served as the criterion for controlling the stepwise selection, with selection terminating when the F-to-enter value was less than an F-to-remove value of at least 1.0. Four different combinations of subjects were analyzed. The most liberal interpretations were provided by two analyses using 30 tests for the maximum sample of 82 subjects and the maximum set of 37 tests for 65 subjects. The most conservative interpretation was provided by an analyses of 8 tests for the maximum sample of 82 subjects. This analysis involved the ratio of more than 10 subjects per test needed for conservative interpretation of discriminant analyses. The analysis used 2 tests with high loadings on each of the factors defined by the R factor analyses summarized in Tables 9.5 and 9.6 to best represent the factorial structure of the abilities sampled by the neuropsychological measures. The 8 tests thus selected included the WISC Similarities and Vocabulary subtests (verbal factor), the WISC Block Design and Object Assembly subtests (visual–spatial factor), the Maze (nondominant) and Steadiness (nondominant) tests (perceptual–motor factor), and the Finger Tapping (nondominant) and Dynamometer (dominant) tests (motor factor). A second conservative analysis, which used the 12 WISC subtest scores for the 82 subjects, had a ratio of almost 7 subjects per test.

The relative power of the four discriminant analyses to differentiate each pair of reading disability types is given in Table 9.9, which lists significance levels for differences between Types O and A, A and S, and O and S, as derived from the four stepwise discriminant analyses. The significance levels were obtained from F tests of the Mahalonobis distance between groups (Statistic 5, SPSS DISCRIMINANT program). Type O was significantly different from Type A in all analyses; Type A was differentiated from Type S only by the two liberal analyses; and Type O was differentiated from Type S only by the WISC analysis. These results indicate that the patterns of neuropsychological test scores that

TABLE 9.9

Significance Levels for Differences among Types of Reading Disability Obtained by Stepwise Discriminant Analyses, Using Several Different Samples of Subjects and Sets of Neuropsychological Tests

	Types of reading disability compared		
	OA	AS	OS
1. 30 tests, 82 subjects	.001	.001	.43
2. 37 tests, 65 subjects	.001	.001	.29
3. 12 WISC subtests, 82 subjects	.01	.43	.40
4. 8 tests selected by R factor analysis, 82 subjects	.03	.45	.03

distinguish Types O and A can be interpreted with the most confidence.

Table 9.10 gives more details about the discrimination between reading disability types on the four analyses. The percentages of correct classification into each type and of total correct classifications are shown for analyses that discriminated all three types at the same time and for additional analyses that discriminated only two types at a time from the total sample of 65 or 82 subjects. The latter analyses, although less valid statistically, lead to more exact specification of differences between types. The percentage of correct classifications exceeded that obtained for the 22 language measures even when only the 12 WISC subtests were used. For the first two sets of analyses all three types were well discriminated, with Type A always discriminated the best. The three types were differentiated fairly well by the 12 WISC tests, with Types O and A discriminated best. On the 8 selected by R factor analysis, Types A and S were discriminated quite well, but Type O was not, particularly with respect to Type S. Almost all classifications were considerably in excess of chance, which would be 37% for Type O, 26% for Type A, and 18% for Type S in the sample of 82 subjects.

The three types of reading disabilities were differentiated quite well by patterns of neuropsychological test scores even when small subsets of tests were used. Although discriminant analyses must be interpreted with caution, the three types did appear to differ in their patterns of strengths and weaknesses on the 37 neuropsychological tests, and also on the 12 WISC subtests by themselves and on 8 tests selected by R factor analysis. This evidence for the discriminating power of the neuropsychological tests supports the previous inferences about neuropsychological differences between the three types.

TABLE 9.10

Percentages of Correct Classifications of Each Type of Reading Disability Obtained from Stepwise Discriminant Analyses Using Several Different Samples of Subjects and Sets of Neuropsychological Tests[a]

		Types of reading disability		
	Types classified	O	A	S
1. 30 tests, 82 subjects:	OAS	77	91	73
30 in Type O, 21 in Type A, 15 in Type S	OA	93	95	
(see Figure 9.4 and Table 9.5)	AS		95	93
	OS	93		93
2. 37 tests, 65 subjects:	OAS	80	93	82
25 in Type O, 14 in Type A, 11 in Type S	OA	100	100	
(see Figure 9.4 and Table 9.5)	AS		100	100
	OS	100		91
3. 12 WISC subtests, 82 subjects as in 1	OAS	67	62	50
	OA	77	86	
	AS		67	73
	OS	57		60
4. 8 tests selected by R factor analyses (WISC	OAS	30	67	60
Sim, WISC Voc, WISC BD, WISC OA,	OA	63	71	
Maze N, Stead N, Fin tap N, Dyn D),	AS		81	87
82 subjects as in 1	OS	47		67

[a] Discriminant classifications are shown for all three types (OAS) and for each pair of types (OA, AS, and OS).

Neuropsychological Test Profiles of Individual Subjects

Neuropsychological test results for individual subjects in Types O, A, and S are given in Tables 9.11, 9.12, and 9.13. They are not as easy to read as the individual results for reading and language tests, which had been given in age-equivalent scores. Scaled scores are given for WISC subtests, MA/CA quotients for Peabody Vocabulary and Knox Cube test scores, and T scores for the remaining measures. The tendency for the highest ranked Type O subjects to have low Digit Span scores is quite striking, as are the generally low Verbal subtest scores of many Type A subjects. The Finger Tapping deficiency of Type A is not too marked in the individual results, except with respect to the larger proportion of above average performances in types O and S. The Finger Agnosia and Progressive Matrices deficiencies of Type S subjects were also more set off

TABLE 9.11
Individual Neuropsychology Results for Thirty Type O Subjects [a]

TYPE O	1	2	3	4	5	6*	8*	9*	10*	11*	12*	13*	14*	15	16*	17*	18	19	21	22	23	24*	25*	26*	27*	28*	29*	30*	31*	33*
INF	14	11	13	10	7	8	9	7	13	8	11	9	9	10	8	9	11	14	9	8	7	6	10	6	11	11	5	10	8	7
COMP	8	9	8	12	9	9	12	11	13	10	10	9	12	6	16	12	8	12	8	13	15	6	12	9	11	14	6	10	9	5
DIG SP	5	6	7	9	10	4	7	8	6	6	11	6	7	9	9	7	10	8	11	9	10	11	9	5	7	8	8	10	10	8
ARITH	14	8	11	12	13	11	10	10	9	6	11	10	7	7	12	11	9	17	11	10	9	11	6	4	12	10	5	9	8	7
SIM	12	11	15	12	10	11	9	10	12	13	13	10	11	9	13	11	9	14	12	10	11	5	11	7	12	11	8	10	11	8
VOCAB	10	10	15	12	6	7	10	7	9	9	12	12	11	9	13	12	7	14	13	10	9	8	13	8	13	12	6	8	10	6
PIC AR	14	12	11	15	12	12	14	11	13	10	9	11	11	11	13	13	9	11	15	11	14	13	11	9	9	11	6	12	11	8
PIC COM	15	7	18	14	10	14	11	13	13	14	17	14	14	12	11	11	12	11	5	14	12	14	11	12	9	15	11	12	10	8
BL DES	15	9	10	10	11	11	12	12	13	14	12	11	11	9	11	11	12	18	13	12	12	14	6	10	11	13	9	11	11	7
OBJ AS	12	9	13	7	10	15	14	13	10	12	14	14	10	10	14	10	7	18	16	13	13	9	8	10	14	13	11	19	16	8
CODING	8	12	10	12	11	11	9	9	11	12	10	11	8	5	12	8	7	7	11	7	8	9	9	11	11	10	9	14	10	14
MAZE	9	12	10	6	9	10	18	7	7	7	9	8	11	5	9	8	13	11	11	7	8	10	9	11	11	10	9	14	13	9
PPVT	13	12	28	21	22	98	03	96	09	12	12	93	03	16	15	03	86	46	09	89	98	01	07	80	09	01	89	99	06	80
KNOX	15	14	21	99	27	83	13	28	47	69	14	50	74	26	42	74	34	63	52	97	98	92	74	87	05	63	06	08	63	45
MATR	–	62	67	60	57	65	58	53	53	53	62	50	53	45	56	53	–	64	57	53	46	57	–	42	57	50	64	63	49
DRAWING	45	54	43	47	53	56	56	43	53	53	49	48	53	45	51	49	58	55	57	62	54	56	55	63	42	57	46	53	56	44
R-L DIS	58	12	57	42	43	43	58	43	41	58	56	49	59	53	43	56	42	59	26	57	59	49	49	58	44	57	33	55	60	58
CATEGORY	–	60	66	51	47	46	56	65	45	54	55	–	56	–	65	56	–	66	57	70	57	61	54	–	44	57	43	62	57	56
TPT TOT	–	58	58	54	44	58	51	50	58	59	50	–	60	–	55	60	–	66	57	56	51	57	50	–	44	51	54	58	56	59
MEM	–	46	62	63	56	54	53	56	53	53	48	–	48	–	55	48	–	70	57	63	40	59	48	–	57	43	67	56	56	40
LOC	–	49	59	67	54	54	49	39	63	64	45	–	55	–	55	55	–	78	60	66	55	50	60	–	36	46	65	65	46	50
F AGN D	57	45	45	58	36	49	49	45	45	45	60	51	48	41	60	48	54	41	57	58	54	58	57	57	17	60	58	58	56	54
F AGN N	58	50	46	60	46	58	50	45	44	39	60	55	60	54	60	60	55	55	57	54	60	58	55	58	23	55	58	58	55	38
TAC D	55	54	54	56	56	56	54	51	45	54	49	58	52	55	45	52	50	48	48	60	61	51	50	55	43	45	46	56	44	59
TAC N	57	53	58	71	50	56	53	58	52	54	50	59	58	57	53	58	50	53	47	59	64	53	50	56	43	36	53	56	57	56
PEG D	57	53	55	52	56	59	54	55	53	51	56	52	55	49	57	55	64	51	53	58	60	56	59	53	58	52	45	58	55	54
PEG N	56	49	51	54	57	54	53	54	52	53	53	51	49	57	58	49	55	52	52	57	61	57	53	59	53	47	43	54	54	54
MAZE D	55	55	46	54	54	54	41	56	56	53	56	47	54	54	58	54	55	53	56	56	57	57	59	59	59	47	54	54	62	59
MAZE N	53	57	59	56	59	51	35	58	58	53	38	43	54	50	59	54	55	55	60	56	58	59	59	55	51	52	53	56	53	54
STD D	43	56	61	31	41	61	34	59	59	48	50	49	57	40	53	57	61	53	55	58	58	57	57	62	51	44	51	61	58	54
STD N	49	55	59	42	47	61	35	57	47	47	46	46	54	37	57	57	58	59	55	59	59	60	54	60	51	44	52	60	57	53
FIN D	55	51	49	43	58	61	51	57	51	50	73	65	62	58	54	62	59	51	40	72	66	54	53	53	46	35	52	62	57	54
FIN N	50	44	61	41	53	58	52	50	50	50	75	57	54	53	48	54	52	55	37	60	52	57	55	52	45	36	53	56	54	52
FOOT D	–	50	56	51	41	53	41	43	51	45	59	–	44	–	48	44	–	54	44	69	54	57	57	–	45	55	54	46	56	40
FOOT N	–	48	54	54	44	45	41	49	55	52	60	–	48	–	46	48	–	72	54	54	51	54	58	–	45	51	51	45	47	48
DYN D	45	51	57	46	51	46	47	42	52	52	69	61	47	46	80	47	55	72	61	49	40	63	64	44	37	51	58	58	47	47
DYN N	46	49	64	47	55	46	47	49	43	49	70	56	43	45	78	43	52	52	61	47	40	61	65	38	35	50	48	56	47	69

[a] The first 12 measures are WISC Scaled Scores. The next 2 measures are Peabody Vocabulary and Knox Cube Quotients, where quotients over 100 are underlined, with only the last 2 digits given. The remaining measures are T scores. Subjects who met more stringent reading disability criteria are designated by an asterisk.

TABLE 9.12

WISC Scaled Scores, Peabody Vocabulary and Knox Cube Quotients (quotients over 100 are underlined, with only the last two digits given), and T Scores (all remaining measures) for Fifteen Subjects of Type S [a]

TYPE A	1 *	2 *	3 *	4	5	6	7	8 *	9	10	11	12 *	13 *	14	15 *	16	17 *	18	19 *	21 *	22
INF	10	6	11	9	7	9	3	6	1	7	4	11	12	11	11	11	4	11	12	6	5
COMP	12	4	11	6	6	10	8	5	2	8	7	14	9	12	9	11	6	12	9	6	3
DIG SP	6	7	11	6	5	9	8	7	4	9	7	13	10	11	9	8	5	8	14	10	5
ARITH	10	6	9	4	9	7	7	7	4	10	5	8	11	8	14	10	1	12	10	10	3
SIM	15	9	8	15	10	10	7	5	5	8	6	12	6	11	10	15	7	12	11	7	6
VOCAB	11	3	9	11	10	10	9	6	1	7	6	11	10	15	8	12	6	10	12	3	6
PIC AR	12	4	8	10	10	12	7	10	7	11	10	13	15	15	9	11	11	8	10	11	7
PIC COM	11	12	9	9	11	10	8	11	11	11	9	11	14	12	9	10	10	7	11	10	12
BL DES	13	13	13	7	13	11	9	12	6	12	11	8	16	11	13	13	10	4	11	12	11
OBJ AS	13	9	14	7	10	12	11	10	12	14	9	15	12	13	10	11	11	10	10	12	11
CODING	11	4	6	8	10	11	10	10	4	6	3	19	11	5	9	6	6	9	9	7	5
MAZE	9	13	13	7	10	11	6	10	6	11	10	9	11	11	8	11	8	7	8	12	9
PPVT	08	71	04	99	06	10	88	79	82	88	89	77	12	12	91	18	71	91	01	96	88
KNOX	95	09	07	92	49	79	83	21	84	91	96	34	02	65	44	14	51	79	99	44	49
MATR	63	51	62	–	–	–	–	50	–	63	47	55	57	55	67	52	51	–	54	53	–
DRAWING	54	47	50	55	51	57	67	50	66	57	48	48	55	60	58	53	49	39	51	54	60
R-L DIS	59	57	33	57	59	36	38	57	46	49	57	36	42	42	59	57	46	56	47	59	60
CATEGORY	67	66	57	–	–	–	–	57	–	53	63	53	69	52	53	60	50	–	62	56	–
TPT TOT	60	54	55	–	–	–	–	59	–	53	58	55	63	61	65	64	33	–	64	54	–
MEM	63	63	60	–	–	–	–	56	–	65	49	57	63	40	63	63	40	–	43	48	–
LOC	66	62	45	–	–	–	–	54	–	67	59	24	62	42	60	62	39	–	52	50	–
F AGN D	54	41	58	38	42	31	60	50	54	57	49	57	54	57	60	58	24	29	33	54	56
N	49	55	58	35	54	57	40	50	28	43	42	57	49	57	60	60	38	40	50	60	55
TAC D	48	46	54	54	57	56	58	50	40	61	50	63	64	59	48	48	46	53	52	59	61
N	50	39	51	52	52	60	59	54	71	62	51	64	87	60	54	55	43	53	57	60	61
PEG D	51	39	58	43	54	52	56	40	56	56	46	52	56	60	57	58	56	57	48	54	54
N	49	42	57	44	52	56	59	55	56	62	52	56	55	52	57	51	55	53	47	61	53
MAZE D	51	53	52	54	53	54	54	55	56	55	55	53	56	55	57	58	57	55	46	56	58
N	51	56	55	51	57	54	56	59	57	65	58	51	58	58	60	59	60	55	54	57	58
STD D	48	52	59	49	42	54	53	53	44	59	51	58	57	58	54	52	54	51	39	59	47
N	43	48	55	47	47	60	52	53	44	62	49	57	54	59	53	47	52	52	42	63	46
FIN D	56	43	44	53	41	49	59	50	62	44	35	49	48	38	58	43	60	57	51	45	53
N	45	42	44	38	43	50	57	50	54	47	40	47	47	42	56	49	43	59	57	58	42
FOOT D	46	38	53	–	–	–	–	51	–	41	52	60	55	45	60	55	52	–	52	54	–
N	58	39	45	–	–	–	–	54	–	47	51	49	57	47	58	55	40	–	53	51	–
DYN D	55	55	53	50	35	65	66	28	54	50	54	65	48	44	71	58	54	52	53	46	31
N	59	51	56	52	39	66	61	51	56	51	55	63	47	40	74	57	57	51	60	45	45

[a] Those who met more stringent reading disability criteria are designated by an asterisk.

from the other types by a lack of high scores than by a large number of very low scores. Individual trends on the remaining tests were difficult to discern because of differences in the scoring scales.

Case History Information

Some of the available case history information for subjects of each type and unclassified subjects is summarized in Table 9.14. Although information obtained from interviews may be unreliable, any marked differences

TABLE 9.13

WISC Scaled Scores, Peabody Vocabulary and Knox Cube Quotients (quotients over 100 are underlined, with only the last two digits given), and T Scores (all remaining measures) for Fifteen Subjects of Type S [a]

TYPE S		1	2	4	5	6	7	8	9 *	10 *	11 *	12 *	14 *	15	16	17 *
INF		9	6	7	6	9	7	10	6	9	10	7	8	9	7	9
COMP		12	9	9	11	9	5	13	4	10	10	7	10	10	10	10
DIG SP		9	6	9	5	11	6	7	7	10	5	4	12	9	10	7
ARITH		8	9	11	12	9	7	12	6	6	6	5	7	16	10	9
SIM		11	10	9	11	10	10	10	11	9	12	8	15	13	9	11
VOCAB		12	11	7	8	9	7	13	7	7	9	7	11	12	6	11
PIC AR		11	14	9	11	12	12	13	9	10	11	11	13	13	9	10
PIC COM		10	15	8	5	11	4	14	10	8	12	11	12	11	14	14
BL DES		11	10	6	13	15	5	10	9	12	14	9	7	13	13	14
OBJ AS		11	14	9	11	11	6	15	11	9	18	9	8	14	15	17
CODING		7	11	9	12	10	6	7	8	8	14	7	7	8	10	15
MAZE		12	13	8	9	10	9	13	10	14	9	8	7	12	14	7
PPVT		14	06	93	97	06	01	12	00	01	77	79	18	99	90	05
KNOX		34	68	42	34	06	07	39	83	37	81	93	01	75	15	32
MATR		54	46	45	–	–	43	–	53	51	59	41	41	–	64	52
DRAWING		63	62	44	61	58	55	64	45	50	45	51	39	64	65	45
R–L DIS		21	57	24	53	60	49	49	58	57	42	46	57	68	24	57
CATEGORY		59	56	47	–	–	45	–	48	46	63	49	54	–	53	67
TPT TOT		46	64	45	–	–	36	–	59	52	51	52	58	–	52	58
	MEM	40	58	48	–	–	40	–	59	63	55	40	40	–	63	47
	LOC	50	52	45	–	–	36	–	64	56	51	45	40	–	34	62
F AGN	D	36	60	60	48	51	37	57	53	54	54	12	33	54	48	58
	N	44	45	44	38	50	37	57	54	44	49	6	24	59	54	55
TAC	D	49	52	57	52	69	52	61	54	61	59	56	53	58	53	48
	N	50	57	56	56	68	52	58	55	66	87	56	82	57	56	55
PEG	D	54	60	54	55	54	47	60	56	64	55	54	45	56	59	59
	N	54	58	55	58	52	52	53	58	53	48	50	50	52	60	57
MAZE	D	56	60	51	58	60	53	54	53	56	56	56	49	60	56	53
	N	54	58	55	59	59	53	43	55	61	61	59	51	61	58	56
STD	D	53	59	55	45	70	58	55	59	61	62	57	59	46	58	39
	N	42	54	52	48	71	54	44	55	62	61	56	54	46	53	51
FIN	D	62	49	52	45	55	64	62	59	62	45	54	56	45	50	50
	N	63	42	52	60	42	58	53	65	62	52	54	62	47	54	46
FOOT	D	49	48	49	–	–	47	–	57	50	53	59	54	–	57	51
	N	49	51	52	–	–	43	–	61	55	52	57	62	–	52	46
DYN	D	46	59	66	34	51	48	41	54	43	59	44	46	47	42	44
	N	46	67	63	30	57	47	48	53	45	61	49	41	44	40	54

[a] Those who met more stringent reading disability criteria are designated by an asterisk.

among subtypes should be evident. All groups showed a sizable incidence of pregnancy or delivery complications, head injuries, mild emotional problems, childhood speech problems, grades repeated, and current educational problems. None had an outstandingly high or low incidence of problems. On the basis of the neuropsychological results, one might expect Type O subjects to have the lowest and Type A subjects the highest incidence of problems of birth, development, and education. However, there appeared to be a uniformly high incidence of such problems throughout the sample.

TABLE 9.14
Summary of Case History Information for Subjects with Each Type of Reading Disability and Unclassified Subjects[a]

	Type of reading disability			
	Oral (N = 33)	Associative (N = 22)	Sequential (N = 17)	Unclassified (N = 16)
Pregnancy complications	24 (8)	27 (6)	6 (1)	31 (5)
Prematurity	3 (1)	9 (2)	24 (4)	31 (5)
Delivery complications	24 (8)	32 (7)	47 (8)	50 (8)
Convulsions	12 (4)	9 (2)	0 (0)	6 (1)
Head injuries	27 (9)	36 (8)	47 (8)	19 (3)
Mild emotional problems	52 (17)	36 (8)	76 (13)	50 (8)
Delayed speech	12 (4)	18 (4)	6 (1)	25 (4)
Childhood speech problems	27 (9)	41 (9)	41 (7)	25 (4)
Grades repeated	39 (13)	50 (11)	71 (12)	38 (6)
Current educational problems	70 (23)	68 (15)	47 (8)	44 (7)

[a] Percentages of occurrence are given to facilitate comparisons, with actual frequency in parentheses.

Statistical Classification of the Neuropsychological Test Results

The statistical classification of language test results yielded interesting information about the interaction of reading and language deficits. We hoped that statistical classification of the neuropsychological results would prove to be equally helpful. Factor analyses by the Q technique were carried out on the first four sets of neuropsychological test data that had been used for discriminant analyses (i.e., 30 tests for the maximum sample of 82 subjects, the maximum set of 37 tests for 65 subjects, 37 tests for the 36 subjects selected by stringent criteria of reading disability, and the 12 WISC subtests for 82 subjects). As in the analyses of reading and language tests, we used three-, four-, and five-factor solutions for each analysis. It was necessary to convert the scores on each measure to standard scores prior to the analyses, because the use of several scoring scales for the neuropsychological tests would otherwise result in spuriously high intercorrelations of the individual test profiles of subjects.

The Q-technique factor analyses were interpreted in the same way as before. Factor score profiles were plotted to identify the profile of neuropsychological deficit associated with each factor, and then the number of subjects with high loadings one each factor was determined.

The results of the first three sets of analyses proved to be uninterpretable. In contrast to the analyses of the reading and language test results, where types of reading disabilities could be defined by factor scores of less than -1.0, the factor score profiles for the neuropsychological tests showed almost no large deviations from zero for any type of skill. The WISC subtests in particular fell almost exactly along the zero line. Even if there had been interpretable factor score profiles for the first three sets of analyses, there was no correspondence at all between the factor loadings and the reading disability classifications of the subjects. For each factor there tended to be as many subjects with high negative loadings as high positive loadings, much more similar to the unsystematic reading test classifications of normal readers (Doehring, Hoshko, & Bryans, 1979) than to the consistently high positive loadings derived from the Q technique analyses of reading and language tests in the present study.

The reasons for the lack of interpretable results for the first three sets of factor analyses were not immediately apparent, unless the standardization of test scores had not adequately equated the neuropsychological tests with respect to scoring scales. The results for the separate analysis of the 12 WISC subtests were interpretable, perhaps because of the common scoring scales. The factor score profiles of the three factors that emerged from these analyses are plotted in Figure 9.6. None was as uniformly represented by the three different solutions as were any of those for the reading tests (Figure 7.2), but the Factor 1 profile, as shown in the upper graph of Figure 9.6, was relatively consistent. All Verbal subtests except Digit Span and Arithmetic were low for all three-factor solutions, with Coding also low for the four- and five-factor solutions, and Picture Arrangement somewhat low for all three-factor solutions. The Factor 2 profile from the three- and four-factor solutions and the Factor 3 profile from the five-factor solution, as shown in the middle graph of Figure 9.6, had a low score for the Digit Span test on all three-factor solutions, but the remaining scores were quite variable. The Factor 3 profile for the three- and four-factor solutions and the Factor 5 profile for the five-factor solution, as shown in the bottom graph of Figure 9.6, had a very low Coding score, with the profiles for the three- and four-factor solutions being very similar and the profile for the five-factor solution profile being otherwise quite dissimilar.

Like the results for the other three sets of neuropsychological measures, there were almost equal numbers of subjects with high positive and high negative loadings on the WISC subtest analyses. However, there was some correspondence between the WISC classifications and the reading disability classifications for the first two factors of Figure 9.6. In all three-factor solutions for the first factor, which was characterized by

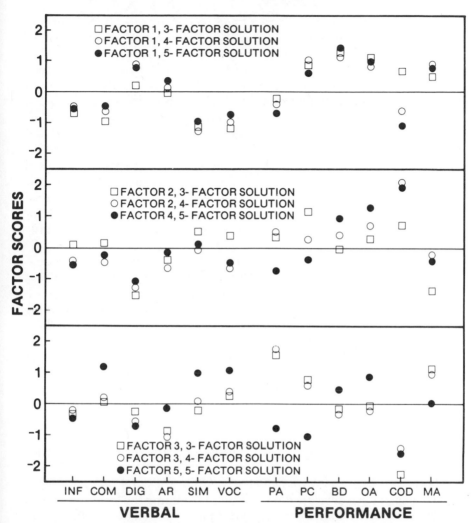

FIGURE 9.6. *Factor scores obtained from analysis of the WISC subtest scores of 82 subjects by three-, four-, and five-factor solutions with the Q technique of factor analysis.*

low factor scores on Information, Comprehension, Similarities, and Vocabulary, 8 of the 21 subjects of Type A had high positive factor loadings. This demonstrated some agreement between the result of Q factor analyses and the findings of the previous analyses of neuro-psychological tests. For the second factor, which was characterized by low Digit Span score, 7 of the 30 subjects of Type O had high positive loadings for the three-factor solution. This provided a weak confirmation of the relationship between Type O and poor short-term verbal memory on the oral word repetition test in the Q factor analysis of combined reading and language test results. Inspection of individual results further revealed that 4 (06, 010, and 013) of the 7 Type O subjects with high loadings on the WISC factor with poor Digit Span had also been classified into the reading–language factor that was characterized by poor oral and word repetition, thus establishing a tenuous connection between the Q factor analyses of reading, language, and neuropsychological test results.

Because the reading and language tests had not been scored in terms of age norms, Q factor analyses of the combined neuropsychological, reading, and language test results could not be carried out. The overall results of the Q factor analyses of neuropsychological tests were disappointing, as only the analyses involving the WISC subtests were partially interpretable. These results did support the other indications of particularly deficient verbal skills in Type A subjects and did suggest a deficiency on short-term memory for digits in certain Type O subjects that corresponded to their deficit in oral word repetition on the language test battery. However, the noninterpretable analyses involving the remaining tests failed to confirm the deficiencies of Type A subjects in Finger Tapping and of Type S subjects in complex visual–conceptual skills on the Raven Progressive Matrices and Finger Agnosia tests. In our present state of knowledge about statistical classification, we cannot conclude that there were no subtypes of neuropsychological deficit, but simply that the analyses failed to reveal any consistent profiles of deficit.

Clinical Judgments of Cerebral Functioning

Beginning with the work of Reitan and his associates, clinical neuropsychologists have developed methods for estimating the location, extent, and type of cerebral lesions in individual patients from the results of standard test batteries. The validity of these estimates has been confirmed by neurological and neurosurgical evidence for both adults (Reitan, 1959, 1964) and children (Reitan, 1974). Estimates of the probability of cerebral dysfunction in a single group of children with reading disability had been made by Ralph Reitan and Hallgrim Klove as part of an earlier study (Doehring, 1968). The same general rationale was used by the clinical neuropsychologists among us (Trites and Fiedorowicz) to estimate the probability of cerebral dysfunction in subjects from the present study.

The judgments of probable cerebral dysfunction were based on the results of the neuropsychological battery (Table 9.1), but without reference to reading or personality test results or case history information. To provide a perspective for judging the relatively mild indications of cerebral dysfunction that might be expected in children with reading disability (Doehring, 1968), the test results for 13 male and 3 female normal readers who were not clinic referrals but had been tested as part of a study involving second language acquisition (Trites & Price, 1977) were examined, along with those of 87 of the 88 subjects of the present study (subject S3, who had verified brain damage, was excluded). Each subject was classified into one of four mutually exclusive categories: no cerebral dysfunction, left hemisphere dysfunction, right hemisphere dysfunction, or bilateral brain dysfunction. Within each of the three dysfunction categories it was necessary to include a "cannot rule out" subcategory for cases where the evidence was particularly equivocal. A judgment of mild or moderate was also made to estimate the severity of dysfunction, and a judgment of anterior or posterior was made whenever possible to indicate the predominant area of dysfunction within hemispheres.

The ratings were made independently by the two judges, without knowledge of the reading disability classifications of the subjects. Agreement was close enough that a single set of ratings was achieved, with the few instances of disagreement resolved by consultation with a third clinical neuropsychologist. The ratings of the judges are summarized in Table 9.15. Their judgments tended to be somewhat stringent, as indicated by three judgments of possible cerebral dysfunction among the 16 normal readers. However, these were equivocal "cannot rule out" estimates. In contrast, the neuropsychological test results of 62 of the 87 subjects of this study gave some indication of cerebral dysfunction. In agreement with previous studies (Doehring, 1968; Rourke, 1978), the evidence suggested mild rather than moderate or severe dysfunction in almost all cases.

Chi-square tests revealed no significant differences in the location or severity of cerebral dysfunction among the three types of reading disabilities. The proportion of subjects with estimated dysfunction was about the same in each type, and the estimated incidence of lateralized right- and left-hemisphere dysfunction was essentially equal for each type, with a consistently higher incidence of bilateral than lateralized dysfunction. The only notable discrepancies were a larger proportion of bilateral deficit in the Type S subjects. Unlike previous studies (cf. Doehring, 1968), there was not a higher incidence of estimated left- than of right-hemisphere dysfunction in the present study.

The clinical judgments of neuropsychological test results did suggest a much higher than normal incidence of mild cerebral dysfunction, but

TABLE 9.15

Judgments of Cerebral Dysfunction in Subjects Classified into the Three Types of Reading Disabilities as Compared with Unclassified Subjects and Normal Readers, Including Estimates of Relative Severity, Right–Left–Bilateral Lateralization and Anterior–Posterior Localization [a]

| | | Estimated cerebral dysfunction | | | | | | | |
| | | Lateralization | | | | Localization | | Severity | |
Reading disability classification	N	None	Right	Left	Bilateral	Anterior	Posterior	Mild	Moderate
O	33	11	6	5	11 (9)	3	3	21	1
A	22	7	4	4	7 (4)	1	2	12	3
S	16	5	1	1	9 (5)	1	4	11	0
Unclassified	16	3	3 (1)	3 (1)	7 (4)	2	3	12	1
Normal readers	16	13	0	1 (1)	2 (2)	0	0	3	0

[a] The number of equivocal "Cannot Rule Out" judgements included in the estimates of lateralization are given in parentheses.

there was no consistent lateralization or anterior–posterior localization either for the sample as a whole or for any of the three types of reading disabilities, apart from a suggestive trend for more bilateral and posterior dysfunction in Type S subjects. The fact that the three types of reading disabilities were differentiated by the univariate and discriminant analyses of neuropsychological test results indicated that there were clear-cut neuropsychological differences; and the clinical appraisal of the mean profiles suggested where these differences might lie. However, the classification of each individual neuropsychological profile by blind clinical judgments did not support the results of the other analyses. As this was the first study to integrate neuropsychological and reading data, the neuropsychologist judges had no previous experience in making differential clinical classifications within a reading problem sample. Now that the neuropsychological profiles of the three types have been provisionally differentiated, further research is needed in which clinical neuropsychologists attempt to classify subjects into the three types of reading disabilities by blind analysis of neuropsychological profiles.

Summary and Preliminary Discussion

A battery of neuropsychological tests was administered to determine the extent to which neuropsychological deficit interacted with each type of reading disability, and to estimate the types of brain dysfunctions that might be associated with the reading disabilities. The 37 neuropsychological measures sampled a variety of perceptual, motor, cognitive, and linguistic skills. The WISC, Peabody Vocabulary, and Knox Cube tests were scored in terms of standardized age norms, and the remaining 23 measures were scored in terms of standardized T scores derived from a large sample of referrals to a neuropsychology clinic. Not all subjects had been given all tests. Data analyses for 30 of the tests included 82 of the subjects, and those for the remaining 7 tests included 65 subjects. Certain analyses were also carried out with a sample of 36 subjects selected according to more stringent criteria of reading disabilities. Their results were found to be equivalent to those of the larger sample in all analyses, demonstrating that the present results were applicable to the populations of disabled readers that are usually studied.

The sample as a whole tended to be slightly below normal on verbal tests and slightly above normal on nonverbal tests. On perceptual and motor tests where separate scores were obtained for each hand, there was no consistent indication of lateralized deficit. A clinical appraisal of the overall profile revealed no clear evidence of cerebral dysfunction for the sample as a whole, but increasing signs of left-hemisphere dysfunction were evident in the smaller sample. The intercorrelations among neuro-psychological tests tended to be much lower than those for the reading and language tests, and R factor analyses revealed a definite structuring of the tests into verbal, spatial, perceptual–motor and motor factors. Correlations with the standardized reading tests, the 39 tests of reading-related skills, and the 22 language tests tended to be low, with the highest correlations occurring for the WISC subtests.

Of greatest interest were the neuropsychological test profiles associated with each type of reading disability. All three types tended to have verbal skills somewhat below normal and nonverbal skills somewhat above normal. Type O subjects showed no major deficiency relative to the other types, tending to be highest on the majority of tests; Type A subjects scored below the other two types on the WISC, Peabody, Knox Cube, and Finger Tapping tests, but higher on the Halstead Category and Tactual Performance tests; and Type S subjects scored below the other two types on the Raven Progressive Matrices, Right–Left Discrimination, Finger Agnosia, and Dynamometer Grip Strength tests. There was no consistent lateralized impairment, except for a slight trend toward poorer dominant hand performance in Type A subjects.

Clinical interpretations of the average neuropsychological profiles suggested no clear evidence of cerebral dysfunction in Type O subjects, despite relatively poor auditory attention–memory span and slow copying on a coding test; in Type A subjects, a number of asymmetries in dominant hand performance, along with relatively poor verbal concept formation skills and relatively poor auditory and visual attention–memory span were consistent with an interpretation of left-hemisphere dysfunction; and relatively poor performance by Type S subjects on the Raven Progressive Matrices, Right–Left Discrimination, and Tactual Performance tests, along with a marked deficiency in nondominant finger localization, would be compatible with posterior cerebral dysfunction, particularly of the right hemisphere.

Statistical comparisons of the three types on individual tests revealed that the only significant differences occurred on the WISC Comprehension, Peabody Vocabulary, Finger Agnosia, Pegboard, and Finger Tapping tests. On pairwise comparisons, Type A was inferior to Type O on the Comprehension, Picture Completion, and Maze subtests of the WISC, and also on the Peabody Vocabulary, and Finger Tapping tests; Type A subjects were inferior to Type S subjects on the Finger Tapping tests; and Type S subjects were inferior to Type O subjects on the Progressive Matrices and Finger Agnosia tests. Discriminant analysis revealed that the three types could be quite well differentiated by patterns of test scores even when small subsets of tests were used, providing additional evidence that there might be characteristic patterns of neuropsychological deficits associated with each type of reading disability. Analysis of case history information suggested a relatively high incidence of pregnancy and delivery problems, head injuries, mild emotional problems, speech problems, and educational problems in all three types of reading disabilities. Factor analysis of the results for all 37 neuropsychological tests by the Q technique did not differentiate any characteristic profiles of neuropsychological deficit. However, analyses of the 12 WISC subtests by themselves did differentiate a subtype characterized by generalized Verbal subtest deficit, into which eight subjects with Type A reading disability were classified; and a subtype characterized by poor Digit Span, into which seven subjects with Type O reading disability were classified, four of whom had also been classified into the reading–language subtype with poor oral word repetition. The reasons for the failure to find subtypes of neuropsychological deficits when all tests were used were not immediately evident, but the finding of two WISC subtypes, one of which corresponded to a subtype derived from the other test batteries, did demonstrate some interaction among the reading, language, and neuropsychological deficits.

Finally, clinical judgments of possible cerebral dysfunctions were made on the basis of individual test results without reference to reading status, in comparison with a small sample of normal readers. Ratings of possible cerebral dysfunction were made for 62 of 87 subjects from the reading problem sample, as compared with only three of 13 control subjects. Except for a larger proportion of estimated bilateral deficit and posterior dysfunction in Type S subjects, however, there was very little indication of any difference in the relative incidence, localization, or severity of cerebral dysfunction among the three types of reading disabilities.

Type O subjects appeared to be the least impaired on the neuropsychological tests but, once again, a small subset of Type O subjects was found deficient on a measure of verbal short-term memory. Type A subjects tended to be most impaired, particularly in cognitive skills, linguistic skills, and speed of finger tapping; and a small subset of Type A subjects were particularly deficient in verbal skills. Type S subjects tended to be most impaired on a test of visual nonverbal conceptualization and a test of finger localization. These patterns of results were suggestive of possible left hemisphere dysfunction in Type A reading disability and posterior dysfunction involving the right hemisphere in Type S reading disability. The relationship between the neuropsychological results and the reading and language test results will be discussed further in Chapter 10.

Overall Evaluation of Interactive Deficits

10

The most straightforward method of studying the interaction of reading, language, and neuropsychological deficits in subjects with reading disabilities would have been to put all the results into a single analysis. This would have involved the statistical classification of 88 subjects with respect to almost 100 measures (39 reading, 22 language, and 37 neuropsychological). Because the present study was, to our knowledge, the first attempt to systematically assess different types of reading disabilities in terms of a wide range of reading and nonreading skills, it seemed best to proceed one step at a time, first analyzing the reading-related skills to replicate the patterns of reading skill deficits that had been previously identified (Doehring & Hoshko, 1977a), and then attempting to determine how these reading disabilities interacted with patterns of language deficits and patterns of neuropsychological deficits. This step-by-step approach facilitated the interpretation of the findings. A single analysis would have confronted us with too many interactions at the same time, and the differences between scales of measurement and normative data from one test battery to another could have confused the interpretation of the interactions. Having completed the separate analyses, we will now attempt a joint evaluation of the results of the three test batteries.

Average Performance of the Total Sample

At the outset, we were somewhat concerned that the present sample of subjects might not be entirely representative of reading disability samples selected by very strict criteria of intelligence and reading retardation.

However, the results of more stringently selected subsamples showed the same trends as did the entire sample. We were also concerned about the wide age range in this sample, but analysis of samples of different ages did not reveal any consistent age effects. The present sample of reading problems can, therefore, be considered reasonably similar to samples tested in other investigations of reading disability.

Estimates of the relative impairment of the entire sample on the measures from each battery were shown in Figures 7.1 for the reading tests, 8.1 for the language tests, and 9.1 for the neuropsychological tests. Because of the differences in scoring scales and test norms, differences between the reading, language, and neuropsychological batteries must be interpreted with caution. With these reservations in mind, it appears that most reading and language abilities were moderately to severely impaired, with visual matching skills least impaired. There seemed to be less impairment on the neuropsychological tests, with many visual skills and several verbal skills at a normal level. Although linguistic deficit was a major feature of the impairment on nonreading tasks, some of the higher-level language abilities such as those assessed by the Ask and Tell test and the WISC Similarities, Comprehension and Vocabulary tests were less impaired than the lower-level language abilities such as those assessed by the Morphophonemics, Phonemic Segmentation-Blending, Cartoon Description (Developmental Sentence Scoring), and WISC Digit Span tests. Likewise, the greatest reading impairment was in orally decoding nonsense words, which was more deficient than the reading of whole words on the standardized achievement tests. The sample as a whole, then, appeared to have a severe decoding problem accompanied by great difficulty in certain basic language skills. Nonreading impairment was far from uniform from subject to subject, with many subjects scoring within the normal range on the language and neuropsychological tests. There was also considerable variability of performance on many reading measures.

Relationships among Measures

The measures of reading-related skills tended to be highly correlated with each other and with the standardized reading measures. The language measures tended not to be correlated with each other, and not highly correlated with the reading tests. Among the language measures, the phonemic segmentation measures were most highly correlated with reading measures; and the syntactic–semantic measures, two of which were the most severely impaired language measures, were not highly correlated with the reading measures. The correlations among the neuro-psychological tests tended to be low and nonsignificant, as did the correlations between the neuropsychological measures and the language and reading measures; and the few moderate correlations with reading measures tended to involve intelligence test measures.

Within each test battery, the measures exhibited a well-defined structure, as revealed by R factor analysis. The factors identified for the reading tests (Table 7.1) included word and syllable reading, visual matching and scanning, letter and number reading, and oral reading; those identified for language measures (Table 8.2) included comprehension, verbal short-term memory, and phonemic segmentation–blending; and those identified for neuropsychology tests (Tables 9.5 and 9.6) included verbal, spatial, perceptual–motor, and motor ability. The occurrence of a definite factor structure within each test battery suggested that different aspects of reading could be evaluated in relation to different levels of linguistic functioning and different aspects of neuropsychological functioning.

The Identification of Types of Reading Disabilities

Our strategy for evaluating the interactive reading, language, and neuropsychological deficits was to begin by objectively identifying the different types of reading skill deficits. This first step went according to plan. We found the same three types of reading disabilities that had been identified in the reading problem sample of the previous study (Doehring & Hoshko, 1977a). The 33 subjects statistically classified into one type, designated as Type O (oral reading disability), tended to be much poorer in their oral reading skills for letters, syllables, and words than in their silent reading skills for the visual and auditory–visual matching of letters, syllables, and words. The 22 subjects statistically classified into a second type, designated as Type A (associative reading disability), tended to be very poor on all auditory–visual matching tests, even one involving the matching of printed letters and spoken letter names, and were also poor on the oral reading tests. The 17 subjects classified into a third type, designated as Type S (sequencing reading disability), were much poorer in reading syllables and words than in reading single letters on all four tasks (visual matching, auditory–visual matching, oral reading, and visual scanning). Only 16 subjects were unclassified.

The reading disability types were not homogeneous and mutually exclusive; a number of subjects exhibited characteristics of more than one type. However, a variety of different analyses showed the classifications to be extremely stable; they were not altered by variations in sample size, criteria of reading disability, age, test–retest effects, or type of statistical classification method. The three reliably differentiated types of reading skill deficits provided a solid foundation for evaluating interactive impairment on the language and neuropsychological measures.

Interactive Linguistic and Neuropsychological Impairment

The consistent factorial structures of the language and neuropsychological batteries led us to hope that their relationships to the reading disabilities would not be completely unsystematic, but any number of interactions were possible. Among the simplest would be a completely different type of language disability for each type of reading disability, and a different type of neuropsychological deficit associated with each type of language disability. With such simple interactions, the origin of the reading disabilities might be traced through underlying language deficits to distinct neurological origins, always bearing in mind that some of the nonreading deficits could be the result rather than the cause of the reading disabilities. Another simple interaction could be a case where one type of reading disability was not linguistic in origin, but corresponded to a profile of nonverbal deficit on the neuropsychological tests, and the two remaining reading disabilities corresponded to different profiles of language deficits.

The interactions that did occur were not as simple as those just described. To the extent that the test batteries actually sampled component abilities within each domain, characteristic patterns of deficits in the acquisition of component reading skills were not associated in such a simple manner with characteristic patterns of language and neuropsychological deficits. The interactions that emerged from the various forms of data analysis were complex, but very interesting. Our interpretation of these interactions must be considered provisional, because no replication studies have yet been carried out, and also because there is not a unitary theoretical framework for defining the abilities measured by the tests. We will describe the interactions separately for each type of reading disability.

ORAL READING DISABILITY (TYPE O)

The reading skill deficit of Type O subjects on the 31 tests of reading-related skills was restricted to oral reading, and was thus less widespread than that of Type A subjects, which extended to auditory–visual match-

ing, and that of Type S subjects, which extended to all reading tests except those involving isolated letters and numbers. Type O subjects also
tended to be less impaired on the standardized achievement tests, at least
relative to Type A subjects, and their neuropsychological test performances tended to be closer to normal than those of Type A and Type S
subjects. However, they were about as impaired as Types A and S on the
language measures, and the case history information (Table 9.14) suggested that they came from the same at-risk population as did the other
types. These results did not confirm the speculation in the previous study
(Doehring & Hoshko, 1977a) that Type O reading disability might correspond to a language subtype identified by Mattis (1978) and by others.
What emerged from the further analyses of this least impaired form of
reading disability was definite evidence that it is not homogeneous, but is
itself divided into subtypes.

There were several kinds of evidence for subtypes within Type O. A
Q-technique factor analysis of all 39 reading-related measures, as
described in the section on the effects of additional tests on statistical
classification in Chapter 7, suggested that the reading problems of Type
O subjects were associated with moderate to severe color and picture
naming difficulty in 12 subjects, and were definitely not related to naming problems in 18 subjects; a Q factor analysis of the 61 combined
reading and language measures (Table 8.6) indicated that the oral
reading deficits of 12 Type O subjects were associated with poor verbal
short-term memory on a test involving oral repetition, and those of 5
Type O subjects were associated with relatively good verbal short-term
memory but poor color and picture naming; and a Q factor analysis of
the 12 WISC subtests from the neuropsychology battery (Figure 9.6) indicated that 7 Type O subjects had particularly poor Digit Span scores.
Further examination of individual Q factor classifications revealed some
encouraging concordance in the subtypes of oral reading disabilities
emerging from these different test batteries. Of the Type O subjects, 4
were classified as having a verbal short-term memory deficit on both oral
word repetition tests of the language battery and on the Digit Span test of
the neuropsychological battery. Test batteries in which short-term
memory tests were more systematically integrated with the other tests
might have shown more concordance with respect to a verbal short-term
memory deficit.

These results suggest that a single type of reading disability may interact with at least two different types of nonreading problem—difficulty
in the rapid retrieval of names and difficulty in the immediate recall of
unrelated digits or words. The sizable proportion of oral reading problems that were not associated with either naming or short-term memory

difficulty might be found to interact with a third, as yet undiscovered, problem. Both the naming and the short-term memory deficits have an expressive language component, as both involve sequential oral responses. Poor visual scanning relative to visual matching in Type O subjects (Figure 7.2) suggests a more general motor deficit, because visual scanning, unlike visual matching, involves the rapid sequential underlining of target items. However, the absence of a marked deficit of Type O subjects on any of the lateralized motor tests of the neuropsychological battery indicates that they do not have a generalized motor deficit. A third subtype of oral reading disability might involve a specific problem of motor control for the types of synchronized movements involved in speech and writing.

ASSOCIATIVE READING DISABILITY (TYPE A)

Type A subjects had particular difficulty in rapidly associating printed and spoken letters, syllables, and words. Their reading deficit was more widespread than that of Type O subjects in the sense that it encompassed both auditory–visual matching and oral reading, and more widespread than that of Type S subjects in the sense that it included letters as well as word and syllable deficits. Type A subjects were also more deficient than Types O and S subjects on the standardized reading achievement tests.

Taken at face value, the theoretical implications of this type of reading disability seem quite clear. A higher-level neural center, such as the left angular gyrus, which integrates graphic and phonemic associations could be defective; or the deficiency could originate at the phonemic level, involving a difficulty in segmenting the speech stream into the phoneme-sized units that are necessary for letter–sound associations; or there could be an even more basic difficulty in the perception of complex auditory stimuli. Unfortunately, the test results do not provide a clear-cut basis for selecting one of these alternative explanations.

The Type A deficit did not appear to be a result of purely visual difficulty, because visual matching was better than auditory–visual matching and there was no outstanding visual deficit on the neuropsychological tests. Nor was there positive evidence that this reading disability was differentiated from the others by a particularly severe phonemic segmentation–blending problem. In such a case, auditory–visual syllable matching should have been much more impaired than auditory–visual letter name matching, which does not require phonemic segmentation, and it was not (Figure 7.2); nor were Type A subjects any more deficient than the other reading disability types on the phonemic segmentation–blending measures of the language battery (Figure 8.2). The analyses of language tests did not single out Type A subjects at all. Their only real distinction on the language tests, which was shared by Type S subjects, was a lack of the short-term memory problems seen in certain Type O subjects. The neuro-psychological tests did, however, differentiate Type A from Type O and Type S subjects (Figure 9.4 and Table 9.7). The Type A subjects tended to be lower on the IQ measures and slower in finger tapping with both hands. Clinical evaluation of the Type A profile suggested more intellectual impairment than the Types O and S profiles, and the total pattern of neuropsychological test results was consistent with an interpretation of left-hemisphere dysfunction. The Q factor analysis of WISC subtests further suggested, that there might be a subtype of Type A subjects who were particularly deficient on the Verbal subtests of the WISC, but the case history information (Table 9.14) did not differentiate Type A from the other types.

We are left with several unresolved findings regarding Type A reading disability. The apparent ruling out of purely visual, phonemic, or auditory nonverbal perception deficits could suggest a specific associative deficit rather than a deficit restricted to one particular modality. It is not at all clear, however, how generalized intellectual deficit on the WISC, gross motor deficit on the finger tapping tests, and generally poor reading achievement could be related to a specific associative deficit. Nor is it clear how the associative deficit should be best interpreted. Some authors (cf. Mattingly, 1978; Vellutino, 1979) would interpret the auditory–visual matching deficit as a problem in associating visual and linguistic information rather than a difficulty in associating visual and auditory stimuli. More detailed testing of visual nonverbal–auditory verbal, visual verbal–auditory nonverbal, and visual nonverbal–auditory nonverbal associations might provide more information.

SEQUENTIAL READING DISABILITY (TYPE S)

Type S reading disability was clearly defined in this study. Letter and number reading were superior to word and syllable reading on all four tasks. The distinction was not simply between isolated letters and physically contiguous letters in syllables and words, because Type S subjects were also relatively less impaired in visual scanning for a consonant string (Figure 7.2). The problem could result from a difficulty in learning to recognize orthographic regularity, a purely phonological difficulty in segmenting spoken syllables and words, a more complex phonological recoding difficulty that did not extend to single letters and numbers, or a generalized difficulty in dealing with serial order.

The Type S reading problem was more general than those of Types O and A in the sense that it involved a visual deficit as well as auditory–visual and oral reading deficits. However, the Type S subjects tended to be less impaired on standardized achievement tests than did Type A subjects, suggesting that the sequencing difficulty had less severe practical consequences than did the associative difficulty. The reason for this is not clear.

No clues as to the specific nature of the Type S deficit were gained from the analyses of language tests, where Type S subjects shared a lack of verbal short-term memory problems with Type A subjects. The possibility of a phonological deficit seems unlikely, because syllable reading was no more impaired than whole word reading, which could have been done without recourse to phonological recoding (Figure 7.2), and because Type S subjects were not outstandingly deficient on phonemic segmentation tests (Figure 8.2). Deficiencies in visual–conceptual and spatial ability and in finger localization on the neuropsychological tests (Figure 9.4 and Table 9.7), coupled with a suggestion of bilateral posterior cerebral dysfunction in both the clinical interpretation of the Type S neuropsychological profile and the blind clinical evaluation of neuropsychological results, did raise the possibility of a higher-level deficit in both the verbal and nonverbal visual processing of Type S subjects. More detailed assessment of the processes in question could result in statistical classifications that show a direct correspondence between Type S reading disability and some sort of visual deficit.

OTHER POSSIBLE TYPES OF READING DISABILITIES

The types of reading disabilities identified by statistical classification procedures depend in part on the criteria for selecting subjects and the types of reading skills tested. It is entirely possible that other types would have been revealed by statistical classification if we had used different tests or a different sample of subjects. It is also possible that certain types of reading disabilities occur so infrequently that they would not often be identified by statistical classification methods. It may always be best to carefully inspect the individual test profiles of unclassified subjects to assess these possiblities. Inspection of the reading skill profiles of the 16 unclassified subjects in the present study revealed two possible additional types of reading disabilities, as will be discussed.

Most previous studies of reading disability subtypes have identified a visual perception type, which is usually rare. In the present study, Type S reading disability could involve a visual processing problem, or it may be that an apparent type of visual perception problem identified by statistical classification of one sample of subjects in the previous study (Doehring & Hoshko, 1977a) but not in the present study corresponds to the visual perception subtypes reported by previous investigators. Visual perception problems of this type may have occurred in the present sample, but not frequently enough to be identified as a separate factor in the Q factor analysis. Inspection of the individual reading skill profiles of unclassified subjects (Table 7.7) did reveal several (U1, U2, U3, U4) whose visual matching skills were as poor as their other reading skills, but all of their reading skills approached a minimum, rendering any interpretation rather questionable.

A type of reading problem that has often been reported (cf. Huttenlocher & Huttenlocher, 1973), but is not usually classified as a reading disability, is poor comprehension of oral reading. The statistical classifications that included the sentence comprehension tests (see the section on the effects of additional tests on statistical classification in Chapter 7) did not differentiate a comprehension disorder, perhaps because there was only one explicit measure of comprehension. For almost all subjects, sentence comprehension was impaired to the same degree as was oral word reading, suggesting that comprehension was limited by the extent to which individual words could be read (Doehring, 1977). Examination of the individual profiles of unclassified subjects (Table 7.7) did reveal five (U9, U10, U13, U15, U16) whose sentence comprehension was poorer than their oral reading. Those subjects were not notably deficient in listening comprehension on the Durrell Achievement Test or the Token test, but did tend to be quite poor on the Cartoon Description and Morphophonemic tests. Their relatively poor Sentence Comprehension scores could have been the result of a specific language problem at the syntactic level. However, the most outstanding characteristic of these subjects was their generally near-normal level of reading and language skills. Such subjects would probably not be selected for single-syndrome studies of severe reading disabilities, but would be included in single-syndrome studies that use reading comprehension as the criterion of poor reading (cf. Perfetti & Hogaboam, 1975), thus adding to the ambiguity of single-syndrome research. Statistical classification studies could resolve such ambiguities and clarify the somewhat controversial status of reading comprehension problems by objectively differentiating them from other types of reading disabilities in terms of patterns of reading and nonreading deficits, provided that a sufficient number of comprehension measures were included for classification purposes.

Relation to Previous Research

It is useful to compare the present results with those of other investigators, as long as it is kept in mind that inferences are limited by differences in tests and in samples of subjects. The results will first be compared to previous investigations of reading disability as a unitary disorder, and then to types of reading disabilities described by others.

If the present sample had been compared to a control group of normal readers on individual tests, many significant differences would have been found. The findings of certain reading disability studies that tested only a limited range of abilities would have been supported, but the conclusions regarding unitary causes of reading disabilities that have emerged from such studies would have been obviated by the wide range of deficits. The language battery used in the present study revealed a widespread linguistic deficit, plus additional impairment of nonreading abilities tested by a neuropsychological battery. For the sample as a whole, the results support Vellutino's (1979) contention that reading disability is not a unitary disorder caused by deficits in visual perception, visual memory, intersensory integration, or serial order recall. Nor could the results be explained in terms of unitary deficits in attention or auditory perception. The widespread deficiency of the sample as a whole in linguistic abilities does seem to conform to Vellutino's verbal processing theory, which states that reading disability can result from deficits in the semantic, syntactic, or phonological components of reading. In the present sample, the impairment of phonological and syntactic components appeared to be greater than the impairment of semantic components. Although there was a consistent phonological-syntactic deficit in the sample as a whole, there were differences in the patterns of linguistic and nonlinguistic deficits in the different types of reading disabilities and in individual subjects, conditions that argue against a single pattern of linguistic deficit as the cause of a unitary type of reading disability. It is perhaps more useful to ask whether there appear to be unitary causes of the three types of reading disabilities identified in this study. We will briefly survey the three types of reading disabilities to see whether any unitary explanations might be appropriate.

Because Type O reading disability may itself be divided into several subtypes, unitary explanations can be sought for each subtype. Explanations that cite short-term memory or storage problems as causal factors (cf. Farnham-Diggory & Gregg, 1975) would fit one subtype of oral reading disability, and those that stress naming or retrieval problems (cf. Wolf, 1981) would fit the other. If the remaining oral reading disabilities were, as speculated, the result of a specific form of motor involvement, explanations that postulate verbal apraxias in speaking and writing (Myklebust, 1978) might be appropriate.

For Type A reading disability, explanations in terms of intermodal integration difficulties are the most plausible, but research that attempts to isolate the causal effects of such problems has been plagued with methodological problems (Blank & Bridger, 1967; Bryant, 1975; Vellutino, 1979). Most investigators have not adequately controlled for the possibility that apparent cross-modal deficits are actually the result of deficits within one of the modalities tested; and the cross-modal tasks used often bear too little relation to the types of cross-modal skill involved in phonological recoding during reading. With better testing methods, a more definite link might be established with this type of reading disability. However, the intellectual and motor deficits of Type A subjects would still have to be explained.

Several unitary explanations of Type S reading disability are possible, including difficulties in the perception of temporal patterns (Bakker & Schroots, 1981), regularly recurring sequences of letters (Venezky & Massaro, 1979), or regularly recurring sequences of phonemes (Liberman et al., 1977). The pattern of neuropsychological deficit in Type S subjects, which raised the possibility of visual–spatial or conceptual difficulty associated with posterior bilateral cerebral dysfunction, would support the hypothesis of a visual pattern perception problem encompassing both verbal and nonverbal abilities. However, further research is needed to clarify the exact distinction between alternative hypotheses.

It is difficult to see how the observed patterns of deficit in the different types and subtypes of reading disabilities could have been caused by a single basic problem in any of the unitary processes that have been studied by various investigators. However, where strong evidence has been found for the association of certain abilities with reading disabilities in single syndrome studies (cf. Fisher, 1979; Liberman & Shankweiler, 1979; Tallal, 1980), the abilities should be tested in further multiple-syndrome studies.

RELATION TO OTHER READING DISABILITY TYPOLOGIES

The types of reading problems identified in the present study do not correspond exactly to any of the typologies proposed by other writers. A consideration of the discrepancies could suggest the types of research needed to resolve the lack of agreement between studies.

With regard to the earlier typologies, Type O reading disabilities might be included among Ingram's (1960) auditory–linguistic deficiencies, Type A might relate to his deficiency in relating visual symbols to their linguistic equivalents, and Type S to his visuospatial deficiencies, but closer agreement is difficult to establish, because his types were not based on explicit patterns of deficits. Agreement with the two types described by Kinsbourne and Warrington (1963) was not close. All three of our types had the lower Verbal IQ that helped to define their language subtypes, although Type S did have the finger localization deficit that helped to define their visual–spatial type. Similar difficulty is encountered in relating our three types to the auditory and visual dyslexias of Johnson and Myklebust (1967) and Pirozzolo (1979).

Although Boder's (1971, 1973) dyslexia types were based on reading-related skills, direct comparisons are difficult, because she primarily used qualitative analysis of spelling errors for classification. Type S reading disability could involve some sort of visual problem, as does Boder's dyseidetic dyslexia, but Type S subjects should have had relatively less difficulty reading nonsense syllables than in reading whole words if they conformed to dyseidetic dyslexia, and they did not. All three of our types seemed to have the phonetic analysis–synthesis deficit of Boder's dysphonetic dyslexia. The apparent lack of correspondence between our types and those of Boder was confirmed by a master's thesis study carried out by Eva Rhynas (1981) under the supervision of R. L. Trites. She found no consistent agreement between the two typologies. Each of our three types had approximately the same proportion of subjects who had been classified as dyseidetic or dysphonetic by a method that closely approximated Boder's method. The most likely explanation for the discrepancy between our types and hers is that there were too few of Boder's dyseidetic dyslexics to be statistically classified in our sample, and that Boder's dysphonetic dyslexia can actually be subdivided into our three types of dyslexia.

Comparisons with the subtypes reported by Mattis *et al.* (1975) and Mattis (1978) are more promising. Subjects classified as having Mattis' language disorder syndrome had naming difficulty characteristic of one of the Type O subtypes, and also the verbal short-term memory difficulty that characterized the other Type O subtype, suggesting that the Mattis language disorder might itself be subdivided. If the remaining Type O subjects could be characterized as having difficulty in rapid repetitive speech and writing movements, there would be an obvious correspondence with Mattis' articulation and graphomotor disorder syndrome. Type S might correspond to the temporal sequencing deficit tentatively proposed by Mattis (1978). Mattis' remaining visuospatial–perceptual disorder syndrome could relate to the unclassified visual perception problems in our sample, or possibly to Type S reading disability, as the Mattis visuoperceptual syndrome included poor scores on the Progressive Matrices test. Mattis' second study agreed with ours in finding mixed types of reading disability. However, none of Mattis' types corresponded to Type A reading disability.

The reading disabilities described by Denckla (1977, 1979) are similar to those of Mattis, and in some ways agree even more closely with our types. The possible subtypes of Type O might agree with anomic repetition disorder (Type O naming subtype), verbal memorization disorder (Type O verbal short-term memory subtype), and articulation and graphomotor disorder (remaining Type O subjects); and Type S could relate to her dysphonemic sequencing disorder or her correlational (sequential–simultaneous) dyslexia. Once again, Type A reading disability did not correspond to any of Denckla's types.

Several writers have suggested possible reading disability types on the basis of literature reviews. Benton (1975) suggested an intersensory integration disorder similar to Type A reading disability, a disorder in the perception of temporal order that could correspond to our Type S, and basic linguistic disorders that could include our Type O subtypes. Vernon (1977, 1979) also suggested several classifications related to difficulties at different stages of reading acquisition. Her first type (difficulty in perception and memory for complex forms) or fourth type variable grapheme–phoneme correspondence) could correspond to our Type S, her second type (auditory–linguistic disorder with poor visual memory) to the short-term memory subtype of Type O, and her third type (grapheme–phoneme association difficulty) to our Type A. Myklebust (1978) also divided reading disabilities into several major types. His inner language dyslexia would fit the comprehension problems that were not identified by statistical classification in our study; his auditory and visual dyslexias were the same as those discussed earlier by Johnson and Myklebust (1967); and he also postulated an intermodal dyslexia that corresponded to our Type A, which he further subdivided into auditory–intermodal and visual–intermodal dyslexia according to which modality is primarily involved. It should be noted that Kinsbourne has also discussed other types of reading disabilities in addition to the two types originally proposed by Kinsbourne and Warrington (cf. Kinsbourne, 1975, 1976).

Multiple reading disabilities can also be interpreted with reference to the types of acquired alexias in brain-damaged adults that were discussed in Chapter 3. The oral repetition deficit of one subtype of Type O might correspond to the severe impairments of oral reading and oral word repetition in certain types of aphasia; the naming deficit of the second Type O subtype could correspond to the naming deficit in Wernicke's or fluent aphasia; and the possible verbal apraxia in remaining Type O subjects could correspond to the speech dysfluencies in Broca's or nonfluent aphasia. Types A and S, do not, however, appear to correspond to any of the acquired alexias.

RELATION TO OTHER STATISTICAL CLASSIFICATIONS

The statistical classifications obtained by other investigators did not completely match our classifications. There was discrepancy between our results and those of Rourke and his colleagues (Fisk & Rourke, 1979, Petrauskas & Rourke, 1979) because they found several different types with Q technique classifications of an entire battery of neuropsychological tests, and we did not, even though the test batteries were somewhat similar. We only obtained interpretable factors when we analyzed the results for the 12 WISC subtests by themselves. Because of the relatively new application of statistical classification techniques to neuropsychological test results, these discrepancies must probably be resolved by further research. Whatever the explanation of the discrepancy, some comparisons can be made with the subtypes of Rourke and his colleagues. Our Type S subjects had finger localization difficulties like those of Petrauskas and Rourke's Type 2 and Fisk and Rourke's Type A. In all three instances, the relative incidence was about 20%. Type S reading disability could also be related to Petrauskas and Rourke's Type 3; and Type O reading disability could bear some relationship to Type 1 of Petrauskas and Rourke, or Type B of Fisk and Rourke, but none of their subtypes showed any obvious correspondence to our Type A reading disability. It was more difficult to make comparisons with the subtypes defined by the remaining statistical classification study, that of Satz, Morris, and Darby (1980), because they used very few tests in their cluster analyses. Their Subtype 2 (naming–verbal fluency disorder) could correspond to our Type O naming subtype, and their Subtype 3 (global language and perception disorder) could correspond to our mixed types and those of Boder and Mattis. However, their Subtypes 1 (global language impairment), 4 (visual perceptual–motor), 5 (unexpected absence of deficit) do not completely match any of our types or subtypes.

CONCLUSIONS REGARDING RELATIONSHIPS
TO OTHER TYPOLOGIES

It is interesting to compare our types to those found by others, but Satz and Morris (1980) are undoubtedly correct in cautioning against basing any definite conclusions on the correspondence between different typologies. We will not draw any specific conclusions, but can offer several generalizations. The general language disorder described by several writers was not found. Either our sample did not contain a sufficient number of such cases for statistical classification, or (more likely) the so-called general language disorders are themselves heterogeneous, including subtypes with naming disorders, short-term memory disorders, and other subtypes of language disorders. Type S disorders did not correspond to the type of visuoperceptual disorders postulated by a number of writers, because VIQ did not tend to be higher than PIQ in Type S subjects. Type A disorders were mentioned as a logical possibility by several writers, but were not directly identified in previous studies, perhaps because tests that could be used to define such disorders were not given. The types of reading disabilities identified depend on the number and types of tests, the population sampled, and the method of classification. As testing, sampling, and classification methods evolve, it seems likely that more rather than fewer reading disability types will emerge.

Provisional Interpretation

Any interpretation of the present results must be provisional, because this is the first study in which objective classifications were based upon joint assessment of reading and nonreading skills. The previous chapters have described the experimental design, subject selection, testing, data analyses, and preliminary interpretations. Interpretations in relation to previous research were made in this chapter. We have exerted every effort to base interpretations directly on the experimental observations, and to clearly label any speculative interpretations. These attempts to specify the operational basis of all interpretations have necessarily restricted generalizations. We will not claim to have solved the riddle of dyslexia, but simply to have made substantive progress toward a reasonable explanation. Some general conclusions are possible:

1. The present results do not contradict the assertions of many previous writers that reading disabilities tend to involve deficits of the basic mechanics of reading, language, and cognition rather than higher-level deficiencies of comprehension and inference. Poor reading comprehension seemed to be a direct function of difficulty in reading syllables and words; and higher-level abilities seemed less impaired on the language tests (cf. Ask and Tell test) and neuropsychological tests (cf. Category test).

2. Although it might seem reasonable on theoretical grounds to assume that these basic deficiencies exclusively pertain to the recoding of print to speech, this does not appear to be the case. Reading acquisition may also be impaired by difficulty in retrieving names, temporarily stor-

ing words, processing related sequences of words, and other basic deficiencies.

3. The present study was designed to determine what type of nonreading deficit interacted with each pattern of reading skill deficit. It now appears that more than one type of nonreading deficit can interact with a particular pattern of reading skill deficit, suggesting that the interactions of reading and nonreading deficits are more complex than we had originally anticipated.

4. We did not discover systematic changes in types of reading disabilities as a function of age, although no definite conclusions in this regard are possible. Further research is also needed to study possible interactions of sex and hereditary factors with different types of reading disabilities.

5. We have tentatively concluded that oral reading problems may interact with at least three different types of nonreading deficits: difficulty in retrieving names, poor short-term verbal memory, and difficulty in formulating the coordinated movements needed for speaking and writing. Auditory–visual association problems definitely seem to involve difficulty in rapidly associating written and spoken verbal material, but interactive nonreading deficits logically related to this problem were not found, perhaps because appropriate tests were not included. Sequential problems in reading syllables and words appear to interact with difficulty in both verbal and nonverbal visual pattern perception, along with other deficits compatible with posterior bilateral cerebral dysfunction.

6. Some of the observed nonreading deficits could be the result rather than the cause of reading disabilities. The use of the term interaction explicitly allows for this possibility. Additional research designs will be required to evaluate the causal relationships between reading and nonreading deficits.

7. We have not ruled out the possibility that differences between reading disabilities may be at least partially a result of differential reading experience. That issue will be explored more fully in the next chapter.

8. Perfetti and Lesgold (1979) have suggested that lack of automatization of basic reading skills may serve as a hindrance, causing poor readers to concentrate their limited attention span on the basic skills at the expense of higher-level comprehension skills. Our results suggest that there can be several different kinds of hindrances stemming from processes basic to reading, including difficulties in conceptualizing visual patterns, rapidly associating visual patterns with spoken words, retrieving the spoken names of printed words, temporarily storing spoken words in short-term memory during reading for comprehension, and formulating the motor patterns needed for oral reading and writing.

Suggestions for Further Research

Different results might be obtained in further research by alterations of experimental design, subject selection, test selection, or data analyses. Some specific considerations in this regard will be mentioned in what follows, and more general issues will be discussed in Chapter 11.

EXPERIMENTAL DESIGN

The design used for the present experiment may not have been complex enough to deal adequately with the interactions that were found. Instead of defining the basic typology in terms of patterns of reading skill deficits, it might be more appropriate to define reading disabilities in terms of interactive patterns of reading and nonreading deficits. On the basis of our experience in this study, such analyses would best be done with tests that had a common scale and normative population. In any case, there seems no reason to go back to the simpler designs where a reading disability is defined as a unitary disorder because the present approach is not subject to the methodological criticisms that have been leveled at single-syndrome designs (cf. Doehring, 1978; Valtin, 1978–1979).

The choice of design will also continue to depend on theories of reading, language, and cognition. A fully interactive analysis of reading and nonreading deficits would be much easier to interpret if the tests were based on a single integrated theory of reading, language, and cognition. Designs should incorporate the idea of interactive relationships rather than simple cause-and-effect relationships between reading and nonreading abilities. The main uncontrolled variable in virtually all reading disability research designs is the amount and type of prior reading experience. Suggestions regarding designs that would control this variable are given in the next chapter.

SUBJECTS

A good theoretical case can be made for testing unselected samples of reading problems, along with a reasonable sample of normal readers, as subjects with the same type of reading disability should be grouped together regardless of whatever other patterns of deficits are present. However, we do not yet know enough about the subject populations, the tests, and the statistical classification methods to be completely free in selecting subjects. Even though we found no age effects, it is probably best to test enough subjects within restricted age ranges to classify them in different age groups, and also to test enough subjects who meet strict criteria of reading disabilities to carry out separate analyses of severe reading problems.

Many of the improvements that could be made in the test batteries would involve more detailed examination of certain classes of skills. For example, more systematic assessment of naming disorders is needed to differentiate accuracy, latency, and other factors that are involved in naming. Some compromise is necessary between the demands of comprehensive testing and the practical limitations of testing time. Tests that more directly assess reading capabilities might be found, and more carefully designed spelling, writing, and comprehension measures should be included. Better criterion measures for reading connected text should also be obtained, particularly those that include qualitative analyses of oral and silent reading errors.

A more comprehensive and well-integrated battery of language tests would be very desirable, including more direct tests of language abilities. For example, a master's thesis study carried out by Patrick Brown (1980) under the supervision of P. G. Patel showed that the subjects of the present study tended to make correct use of bound morphemes in their spontaneous speech on the Cartoon Description test even though they made many errors on the Morphophonemic test. Much thought should also be given to the best ways of testing the apparent deficits in naming, verbal short-term memory, and articulatory–graphomotor abilities. The processes involved in abilities at the phonemic, graphemic, phonological, orthographic, and morphophonemic levels should be tested in a more integrated manner; and higher-level language abilities should be tested more systematically if we wish to identify comprehension reading disabilities in future studies.

The choice of different neuropsychological tests is more difficult, because these tests are intended to assess sensory, motor, perceptual, and cognitive skills and, at the same time, provide inferences about the location and severity of possible cerebral dysfunction. As the abilities assessed by the language and neuropsychological batteries overlap, a single battery of nonreading tests that samples an adequate range of language and nonlanguage abilities would be preferable. A single battery that incorporates both reading and nonreading tests would be even more desirable.

Satz and Morris (1980) have made extensive suggestions about data analysis strategies, and different methods of analysis have been compared in the present and a previous study (Doehring, Hoshko, & Bryans, 1979). Many of our data analysis attempts have been by trial and error, because statistical consultants had not had sufficient experience with the present applications to make informed suggestions. Now that more use is being made of statistical classification techniques, we may be in a better position to obtain help from mathematical statisticians. The types of problems for which we need guidance are the possible effects of differences in the distributional properties of different tests, and the criteria for choosing the most appropriate statistical classification methods. Methods of multivariate analyses might be found that are more appropriate for classifying subjects in terms of similarity of test profiles before determining how they differ on measures that were not used for classification.

We hope that the present study will provide some useful guidelines for future investigators. A major shortcoming that became apparent during the analysis of the present results was the inability to conclude whether a given pattern of deficit was the result of differences in reading experience rather than to the differences in basic processes that reading disability studies are designed to find. This Problem will be discussed in Chapter 11.

Training Deficient Reading Skills

11

Some writers are optimistic about the application of research findings to the practical treatment of reading problems, whereas others say that any practical applications are far in the future (Resnick & Weaver, 1979). There may be some gap between theory and practice in the sense that hasty, incautious applications of research findings should be avoided. For example, one should not advise the teacher that reading disabilities could be cured by remediation of language deficits that might actually be the result rather than the cause of the reading problem, and one should not recommend a specific form of training for all reading disabilities when it may be appropriate for only one type.

Even if we had found unambiguous interactions of reading, language, and neuropsychological deficits, we could not have provided teachers with immediate practical guidelines for dealing with the reading problems. Under these circumstances, it would seem reasonable to conclude that our research was simply intended to add new information about the nature of reading disabilities, and leave any practical applications to others. However, the analyses of the present results suggested to us that further research on training the deficient reading skills would be useful for the theoretical interpretation as well as for the practical treatment of the different types of reading disabilities. Systematic training of the reading skills that were tested could help to indicate the extent to which patterns of reading skill deficit reflect differences in reading experience rather than differences in nonreading abilities and neurological functioning.

The exact methods to be used for training research are not immediately evident. A number of factors must be taken into consideration, some of which will not become clear until the results of training research have been carefully analyzed. In this chapter, we will discuss some practical and theoretical issues in training research, and then describe our own preliminary efforts in this direction.

The Gaps among Research, Theory, and Practice

The idea of a gap between theory and practice is really too simple as applied to reading disability. "Practice" in remedial reading instruction must involve the application of a theory. In this sense, the gap is between the working theory of the teacher and other theories. The working theory of the teacher can be defined by the instructional operations used to improve the reading skills of poor readers. These operations are partly dictated by standard remedial methods and partly derived from the teacher's own experience. Regardless of the exact origin of the remedial approach, it is a working theory about the nature of the reading problem and the most effective method of treatment. The teacher's experience is not an infallible guide for the construction of the theory, because one person cannot try out all methods with all types of reading problems. Even if this were possible, there are too many uncontrolled variables to permit definite conclusions regarding the best method for each type of reading disability. Those who have developed the method or methods that the teacher uses may have had more opportunity to assess the validity of the theory that defines the method, but very few are able to supply more than rudimentary evidence in this regard, because the evaluation of treatment methods is difficult and expensive.

Because the teacher cannot be certain of arriving at the most effective working theory through experience, it would be helpful if the working theory could be evaluated by research. However, the immediate goal of most reading disability research has been to test hypotheses about deficient nonreading abilities rather than hypotheses about the most effective training method, under the assumption that the nature of reading disability must be understood before treatment methods can be evaluated. The gap between the theories evaluated by reading disability research and the working theories of reading teachers is what most writers refer to when they discuss the gap between theory and practice. This gap between theories can be closed when a particular theory of reading disability has been sufficiently confirmed that hypotheses about training can be tested.

Has any reading disability theory been sufficiently confirmed by research that training methods can be derived from it? To our knowledge, none have. The gap between reading disability research and theory is as large as the gap between reading disability theories and working remedial theories. This is not the result of a lack of theories. It is easy to construct a theory of reading disability on the basis of psychological, linguistic, and neurological theories, plus practical experience and pure speculation. Such theories abound in professional journals and in the popular press. The difficulty lies, as we have taken such great pains to point out in the preceding chapters, in designing research that adequately tests the theories. As studies using the single-syndrome paradigm to assess nonreading deficits have not closed the gap between research and theory, we used a multiple-syndrome approach to assess both reading and nonreading deficits.

We have encountered two related problems in using the multiple-syndrome approach to close the gap between research and theory. The first problem is in determining the cause-and-effect relationships involved in reading and nonreading deficits, and the second is in determining the extent to which the patterns of reading skill deficit are associated with differential reading experience rather than with deficiencies in nonreading abilities. There is a gap between the inferences that can be made on the basis of our experimental observations and the conclusions that we would like to reach about the origins of different types of reading disabilities. The teacher is faced with very similar problems of appraising cause-and-effect relationships and the effects of previous reading experience when diagnosing reading disabilities, making decisions about which reading or nonreading abilities should be trained, and evaluating the outcome of training. The teacher's difficulties could be considered a gap between theory and practice. Research on the training of deficient skills, if properly designed, could help to close the research–theory gap of the scientist, the theory–theory gap between the scientist and the practitioner, and the theory–practice gap of the practitioner.

Design of Research That Integrates Theory and Practice

Research that incorporates training procedures into a comprehensive assessment of relevant abilities is needed to close the gaps between research, theory, and practice. If reading and nonreading skills are evaluated before and after the systematic training of deficient skills, more definite conclusions can be reached about the nature of the different types of reading disabilities, closing the gap between research and theory.

Then hypotheses about practical training of the different types of reading disabilities can be formulated, closing the gap between reading disability theories and the working theories of reading teachers; and the successful testing of these hypotheses could directly benefit the disabled readers by closing the gap between the working theory and practice. Because of the interactive nature of reading disabilities, the effects of instructional and other experiences must be taken into consideration whenever the abilities involved in reading are studied. A common research paradigm is needed for the scientific explanation of reading disabilities and the practical evaluation of the effects of instruction.

The conclusions derived from our research are strongly supported by several recent critical analyses of learning disability theory, research, and practice. Wong (1979) felt that learning disability theories and research were hampered by a lack of perspective, a division between those with a neuropsychological orientation toward the study of deficits in underlying processes and those with an educational orientation toward the analysis of tasks for remedial teaching purposes. She concluded that future progress requires an integration of the two approaches. Torgeson (1979) also contrasted process-oriented and task-analytic approaches to learning disabilities. He pointed out that the psychological processes studied as possible causes of learning disabilities are theoretical constructs largely derived from information-processing models that conceive of human cognition as occurring in a series of discrete stages. As most of these processes cannot be directly observed, it is difficult to obtain valid measures of the processes and to specify the relationship between deficient processes and classroom performance (see also Ohnmacht & Weiss, 1976). The task analysis approach makes no inferences about processing deficits, but provides remedial information directly relevant to the learning disability, assuming that failure to attain skills necessary for reading is the result of a lack of appropriate practice. Like Wong, Torgeson advocated an integration of process-oriented and task-analytic approaches, beginning with an analysis of the task into component skills and then a development of diagnostic tests to assess the processes required to learn the skills. Special procedures could then be developed and evaluated for dealing with individual differences.

Arter and Jenkins (1979) and Coles (1978) were more concerned with the direct application of process-oriented theories. Arter and Jenkins (1979) criticized in detail remedial methods based directly on process-oriented theories that purport to strengthen basic processes such as psycholinguistic or perceptual–motor abilities rather than directly teach remedial skills. The authors questioned the evidence that educationally relevant psychological abilities exist and can be measured, that existing tests of these abilities are reliable and valid, that treatment methods can be generated from patterns of deficit to improve weak abilities, and that either the improvement of deficient processes or the exclusive use of intact processes can improve academic achievement. They concluded that there is a gap between theory and practice in the sense that prescriptive teaching based on process-oriented theories does not appear to benefit children with learning problems, and advocated that teachers should be encouraged to create variations in task-oriented instructional procedures until there is more satisfactory research evidence for process-oriented instructional methods. Coles questioned both the construct validity and the empirical basis of process-oriented learning disabilities test batteries. His major criticism was that such diagnostic procedures permit only a biological interpretation of learning disabilities, focusing remedial efforts on the supposed neurological deficiency, whereas many learning disabilities may be, at least partially, the result of experiential factors.

The present research method conformed quite well to the recommendations of Wong and Torgeson that process-oriented and task-analytic approaches to learning disabilities should be integrated. The reading battery was based on an analysis of the reading acquisition process (Doehring, 1976a), the language battery was based on an analysis of language acquisition processes relevant to reading (Patel, 1977), and the neuropsychological battery was based on analyses of abilities that might be affected by neurological dysfunction in children and adults (Trites, 1977). In our efforts to integrate the analyses of deficiencies in performance of the reading task and basic neuropsychological and linguistic deficits, we came to recognize the need for an extension of the research approach to include procedures for training deficient skills. The extended research approach could provide the type of research evidence sought by Arter and Jenkins, and permit an evaluation of the effect of experience, as recommended by Coles.

Training of Reading and Nonreading Skills

As stated previously, there has been much dissatisfaction with the results of training nonreading abilities such as linguistic and perceptual–motor skills that are supposedly prerequisite to reading (Arter & Jenkins, 1979; Wong, 1979). However, the idea of training deficient nonreading skills should not be abandoned. As Arter and Jenkins pointed out, the nonreading abilities in question may not have been adequately defined, because they were based on theoretical constructs whose validity was not well established. If the process-oriented and task-analytic approaches can be successfully integrated, it should be possible to construct a battery of tests in which nonreading abilities are more logically related to component reading skills. In such a case, reading disabilities could be described in terms of a single pattern of reading–nonreading deficit, and the effects of training both reading and nonreading skills could be evaluated. This could be one of the most important outcomes of combining the process-oriented and task-analytic approaches.

Training to Strengths and to Weaknesses

The task analysis approach assumes that specific reading deficits are the result of inadequate practice, and that extra instruction in the deficient skills will eliminate the problem (Torgeson, 1979). Process-oriented approaches have made two conflicting assumptions about training, that the training of deficient nonreading skills will eliminate reading problems, and that reading acquisition will be facilitated by matching reading instruction to the strong or intact abilities of the poor readers (Arter & Jenkins, 1979). Those who advocate training deficient nonreading skills seem to be assuming that nonreading deficiencies of neurological origin can be eliminated by training, and those who advocate training through intact abilities seem to be assuming that nonreading deficiencies of neurological origin are irreversible and will not be improved by direct training. These assumptions must be reexamined with research based on more satisfactory theoretical constructs. It is not all clear whether neurological deficits associated with reading disabilities involve gross abnormalities or simply variations in neurological structure and function, or both. Even if this were known, the extent to which the deficits could be eliminated by training would still be unknown, as would the extent to which reading disability might be the result of the interaction of neurological deficits and experiential deficits. Reading disability research that incorporates training must obtain evidence about the extent to which reading and nonreading deficits can be eliminated by training, and then use this information in a further attempt to determine the neurological or experiential origins of the deficits.

Transfer of Training

One of the hallmarks of normal reading acquisition is the interactive development of component reading skills. There is reason to suspect that reading disability is characterized by a lack of generalization of the new skills that are learned (Guthrie, 1973). In carrying out reading disability research that incorporates training, special attention must be paid to transfer of training. It may be found that the lack of generalization is restricted to the reading and nonreading deficiencies that characterize each type of reading disability. If so, a careful study of transfer of training should provide important information about the nature of reading disabilities.

If transfer of training is to be adequately studied, the integrated assessment–training research methods should be based on interactive theories of reading acquisition. Information–processing models that postulate independent component processes are probably inadequate (Guthrie, 1978). Interactive models of reading that take into consideration the joint operation of perceptual, linguistic, and cognitive processes in reading acquisition (cf. Levy, 1980; Stanovitch, 1980) are more suitable for assessing transfer of training.

Training Strategies

A great deal of attention has been paid to methods of teaching reading over the years (Chall, 1967). The main difference of opinion still relates to the necessity of teaching decoding skills (Resnick & Weaver, 1979). Those who view reading as translation from print to speech emphasize the teaching of the correspondence between printed symbols and spoken language. Those who view reading as a separate, autonomous form of language emphasize that reading instruction must focus on deriving meaning from text (Resnick, 1979a). It is necessary to consider the code-oriented and meaning-oriented views of reading instruction when planning methods for overcoming the reading and nonreading deficiencies that characterize different types of reading disability. Code-oriented teaching strategies are most likely to be effective, as our results and those of most other investigators suggest that reading disabilities are not the result of deficiencies in higher-level cognitive and linguistic abilities, and that any higher-level deficits that do exist may be secondary to lower-level deficits. Rosner (1979) differentiated beginning readers into those who are easy to teach, requiring little formal instruction in basic decoding skills; and those who are hard to teach, requiring extended drill and practice in basic skills. Instructional methods that emphasize reading as language are probably more suitable for the easy-to-teach; and those that emphasize reading as translation are probably more suitable for the hard-to-teach, including children with reading disabilities. Suggestions for training strategies to be used in combined assessment–training research might be obtained from programs designed to teach skills needed for reading as translation, as described by Bateman (1979), Beck and Block (1979), and Williams (1979).

There might be some question as to whether exclusive reliance should be placed on code-oriented training programs in studying different types of reading disabilities. Because of the interactive nature of reading acquisition (Doehring & Aulls, 1979), children with certain types of reading disabilities might benefit from the training of higher-level skills. However, Pflaum and Pascarella (1980) found that training in higher-level skills for using context in reading benefitted only those learning-disabled children who had already acquired basic reading skills. It is probably best to restrict the instructional aspects of assessment–training research to lower-level coding and word recognition skills, using subjects who have not been able to acquire basic reading skills.

Design of Further Reading Disability Research

In designing reading disability research to meet the related needs of theory and practice, it seemed best for us to begin by determining the effects of training the reading skills that defined the three types of reading disabilities. After assessing the changes that occur in the patterns of reading skill deficit as a result of training, we can design further research on the effects of training both reading and nonreading deficits. This next research step is based on the idea that more definite conclusions can be reached about the effects of training if the reading skills trained are those defined by the original task analysis. Work on a training device was begun at a time when we optimistically assumed that the present research would close the gap between theory and practice to the extent that the device could be used for practical training. The computer-assisted instructional device that was produced is quite flexible and we still have hopes that it will be of direct practical use. Before describing the development and preliminary use of the method of computer-assisted instruction in component reading skills, we will briefly review previous applications of computer-assisted instruction in teaching reading.

COMPUTER–ASSISTED INSTRUCTION IN READING

Mason and Blanchard (1979) reviewed the different ways that computers have been used to assess and teach reading skills. The majority of computer education projects have been in mathematics and the physical sciences, with relatively few involving reading, perhaps because special features such as spoken stimuli and touch-sensitive screens are often needed for reading instruction. However, a number of computer-assisted instruction programs have been designed to teach various aspects of reading, and we can expect more in the future. We will briefly describe a few programs that are most similar to ours, and the reader can consult the review by Mason and Blanchard (1979) for further information.

Some of the earliest and most thoroughly designed and tested programs were those of Atkinson and his colleagues at Stanford University (see also Fletcher, 1979). They designed very detailed programs for teaching letter identification, sight–word vocabulary, spelling patterns, phonics, word comprehension, and sentence comprehension. Children trained with the computer acquired reading skills faster than non-computer-trained children. The drill-and-practice approach of computer-assisted instruction seemed uniquely suited to bringing about the rapid, automatic reading skills needed for fluent reading, and would seem particularly appropriate for hard-to-teach children with reading disabilities.

Another program was based on the "talking typewriter" devised by Omar Khayyam Moore a number of years ago. Prentice-Hall Developmental Learning Centers developed a computerized electric typewriter that responds to a key press by giving a 1-sec spoken message that can be a letter name, a letter sound, or other information. In one phase of operation, no key can be depressed unless it is an appropriate response at that point in the program. A variety of reading instructional programs are possible, including the teaching of letter–sound correspondences and blending. Favorable results have been achieved with preschool children, adult illiterates, and poor readers in elementary schools. (IBM has developed a talking typewriter for blind typists, as reported in the popular press, where a speech synthesizer speaks letter names, words, or lines of text as they are typed.)

A widely used computer system called PLATO (Programmed Logic for Automatic Teaching Operation) with more varied stimulus and response capabilities was developed at the University of Illinois. Visual stimuli are generated by the computer or projected from a random-access slide projector onto a screen, and auditory stimuli can be rapidly retrieved from a phonograph record by a random-access system. The subject responds by typing or by touching a visual stimulus on the screen. A wide variety of reading instruction can be given with this device. Several interesting programs that use PLATO were developed at the University of Delaware. Oral reading skills are taught by having PLATO orally read a line while the child listens without seeing the text, and then orally read while the child silently reads; finally, the child orally reads and can ask PLATO for an oral prompt whenever difficulty is encountered. A program for teaching sight words presents an animated story using the word to be taught, and then a multiple-choice procedure to teach word recognition and spelling. Semantic skills are taught by having the child touch the screen to move words into "cages" that contain other words in the same category, with the computer indicating errors and giving prompts when requested.

An ingenious animated instructional system developed at the University of New Hampshire teaches beginning reading skills to the handicapped. The only stimuli are words and line drawings presented on a touch-sensitive screen. The child touches a noun in a list of nouns to produce a pictured representation of the noun and a list of verbs. Touching a verb produces an appropriate action of the pictured noun. The child can also select a string of words to make a sentence, and an animated computer sequence illustrates the meaning of the sentence.

A system developed at Brigham Young University to teach critical reading skills to college freshmen used the informational and motivating properties of color television in a random-access video cassette system that can be stopped or run frame by frame. A special keyboard contains keys that the student can press to obtain an example of a rule to be taught, practice materials, available options, and progress to date. Mason and Blanchard point out that use of video disks controlled in the same way as computer memory disks would facilitate the use of televised material during computer-assisted instruction.

The Computer Curriculum Corporation of Palo Alto has a series of drill and practice programs that were derived from the original Stanford work on computer-assisted instruction in reading. The lowest level is for Grades 3–6. In one type of program, simple sentences with a missing word are selected. The student selects the missing word from three choices and is immediately reinforced. The computer adjusts the difficulty level up or down as a function of the child's success, and the class of deleted word is systematically varied to give practice in grammer, word meaning, literal comprehension, and inferential comprehension. These programs contain excellent guidelines for the further development of comprehension training programs.

Mason and Blanchard (1979) give many other examples of computer systems for teaching reading skills, and emphasize the future prospects for computer-assisted instruction. Within a decade many homes will have microcomputers for controlling household appliances and communication facilities, record keeping, recreation, and self-education. Schools will also use microcomputers for instruction and record keeping, relieving the teacher from time-consuming paper work and repetitive drills. Some reading texts will be accompanied by a computer disk containing diagnostic tests and practice exercises. Some children will have personal computers that become an integral part of their education, and micro-computers and instructional television on video disks can be used in-terdependently for remedial teaching and literacy training.

The rapid growth of microcomputer technology provides a stimulating context for designing computer-assisted instruction systems for different types of reading disabilities. One such program is being developed by Knights and Hardy (1978). It is interesting to note that the programs described by Mason and Blanchard and the Knights and Hardy program are intended for practical teaching rather than for research. The research that has been done compared computerized and conventional instruc-tion, but provided no information about the exact variables that con-tributed to reading acquisition. The type of training research that we en-visage would, in its initial phase, investigate the effects of training reading skills that define particular types of reading disabilities. The training would continue until the limits of rapid, accurate responding are approached, whereas most practical instructional programs appear to use accuracy alone as a criterion for learning. Computer-assisted instruction, like other forms of instruction, cannot be applied indiscriminately to meet all teaching and research needs. Programs must be specially de-signed to achieve the joint goal of obtaining more information about the natures of reading disabilities and the most effective methods of dealing with each type.

RATIONALE FOR COMPUTER–ASSISTED INSTRUCTION OF COMPONENT READING SKILLS

The reading test battery used in our research was based on knowledge available in the early 1970s about the component skills of reading (Doehring, 1976a). An attempt was made to construct quantitative tests that would sample the actually deficient reading skills, and reading disability was defined in terms of basic coding and word recognition skills rather than in terms of higher-level syntactic and semantic skills. Not only did this seem appropriate to what was known about reading dis-abilities, but it was much easier to devise tests that sampled skills for reading isolated letters, syllables, and words than to devise a test battery that systematically sampled the skills defined by more meaning-oriented theories of reading (cf. Goodman & Goodman, 1979; Smith, 1979).

Intensive training of the component reading skills that were tested in the present study should help to overcome a very undesirable uncon-trolled variable in all studies of this type (i.e., differences in previous reading experience). The patterns of reading deficit that remain after in-tensive training may suggest which types of reading disabilities involve intractable deficits of neurological origin, and the rate at which rapid, automatic reading responses are achieved may provide some indication of the extent to which trainable reading deficits are the results of previous experience or of neurological deficit. The assessment of skills for reading connected text before and after training should indicate how much practical benefit was associated with improved reading skills for each type of reading disability. Further training research involving a wider range of reading and nonreading abilities could be designed on the basis of the results of the initial training research.

DESIGN OF THE COMPUTER–ASSISTED
INSTRUCTIONAL PROGRAM

The matching-to-sample tests, which were originally adminstered by means of a rather inflexible system controlled by digital logic modules, were most easily adapted for computer-assisted instruction. A basic difference between the tests and the training programs was that a variety of different items had to be available for training to a criterion of automaticity, whereas the tests required only a small number of items presented in a fixed order. The solution to this problem was to assemble a large pool of items for each type of skill, and randomly select the items during training. This would permit training to continue until the learning criterion had been achieved, with no need to prepare many different lists of items. An important advantage of this type of computer-assisted instruction for both research and practical instruction is that a great deal of highly structured training can be presented in a short time (Guthrie, Martuza, & Seifert, 1979). A microcomputer system was developed by Eric Covington and Humphrey Brown to accomplish this purpose, and also to present training in oral reading skills.

The core of the computer training system is a central processor with a speed of operation adequate for training purposes. Because the working memory of the central processor is not large enough to store all of the training programs, a flexible disk memory system provides additional memory to store the training programs and to keep a record of the subject's responses. Visual stimuli are presented on a television screen, with a real-time clock used to time stimulus presentation and response latency. On matching-to-sample tasks, the subject has to touch the visual choice that matches the sample. The response interrupts an invisible matrix of light beams that covers the choice stimuli, and the speed and accuracy of the responses are recorded by the computer.

Spoken materials are essential to training, because auditory–visual matching-to-sample is the one task in the reading test battery that can directly teach sound–letter correspondences. Because the quality of speech produced by available speech synthesizers was inadequate for auditory samples, tape-recorded natural speech was converted to digital form by an analog-to-digital converter and recorded on flexible disks, from where it can be retrieved and converted back to spoken form by a digital-to-analog converter during auditory–visual matching-to-sample training. The flexible disk memory is taxed to capacity to store the digitized auditory samples, with an entire disk needed for each training program, and the changing of disks to go from one auditory–visual matching program to another slows down training. The use of the higher quality synthesized speech that is now becoming available would require much less disk memory and greatly improve the efficiency of training.

The remaining components of the training system include a standard cathode ray tube (CRT) terminal, consisting of a keyboard and a cathode ray screen, and a line printer. The CRT terminal is used to enter new programs into the computer, call up stored programs for training purposes, and control the computer operations during training. The screen of the CRT terminal displays information about the speed and accuracy of the subject's responses, as well as the training programs. The programs, the training stimuli, and the response data can also be printed by the line printer.

The stimulus displays and computer control operations were programmed in machine language by Juhan Leemat and the actual training programs were written in BASIC language by George Pandi. The structure of the training programs was directly taken from the reading skill tests, but using randomly selected items instead of the original fixed sequences of items. The computerized matching-to-sample procedure is more elaborate. On the original matching-to-sample tests, the sample and the choice stimuli were presented at the same time, and visual matching could be accomplished by direct physical comparison. Another aspect of reading skill can be assessed by presenting the sample and the choice stimuli at different times, where direct physical matching is not possible. For both the visual and the auditory–visual matching-to-sample training programs, the temporal relationship of the sample and the choice stimuli is varied. Each time a program is presented, the operator decides whether the sample is to be presented before, at the same time, or after the choice stimuli, specifying the exact interval of time between the sample and the choice stimuli.

In addition to controlling the temporal sequence of the sample and the choices, the operator can also vary the duration of the stimuli, the duration of a plus sign that serves as a signal of correctness, the duration of a period during which the correct choice is displayed following an incorrect choice, and the time interval between training trials. All temporal durations during a training session can be varied. One can begin training

by providing unlimited time for the subject to study the visual sample
and choices before touching the choice that matches the sample, and then
giving an unmistakably long signal of correctness, a long period in which
the correct response is displayed after an error, and a sufficient interval
between trials for the subject to prepare for the next set of stimuli. As the
subject becomes more proficient, all durations can be reduced, except
perhaps the interval between the sample and the choices, providing rapid
training (up to 100 trials/min for visual matching-to-sample) that keeps
pace with increasing skill and staves off boredom. This feature should be
very useful for training skills to the point of automaticity (LaBerge &
Samuels, 1974). The computer keeps a complete record of what stimuli
were presented and how rapidly and accurately the subject responded to
each, and computes descriptive statistics such as means, medians, and
distributions of response latencies. An example of a visual matching-to-
sample trial is given in Figure 11.1.

The auditory–visual matching-to-sample programs are the same as the
visual matching programs except that training cannot be quite as rapid.
The duration of the auditory sample (usually about .5 sec) is fixed by the
length of the spoken letter name, word, or syllable, and the time between
trials cannot be less than the time needed (about 1 sec) to locate the
auditory sample on the flexible disk. With the present system, the maxi-

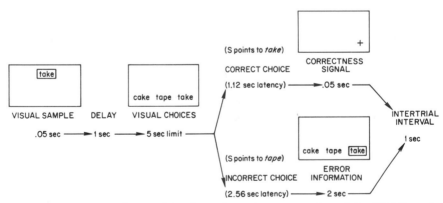

FIGURE 11.1. *Example of a delayed visual matching-to-sample trial for CVCV words,*
where the visual sample is presented for .05 sec, there is a delay of 1 sec, and the three visual
choices are displayed until the subject touches the choice word judged to match the sample,
with a 5 sec time limit for responding. If the choice is incorrect, or the subject fails to respond
within 5 sec, a box appears around the correct choice for 2 sec. Then a new item is randomly
selected and presented after a 1 sec intertrial interval. The number of trials and the duration
of the sample, the delay between the sample and the choices, the response latency, the cor-
rectness signal, the error information, and the intertrial interval are recorded in the com-
puter's memory.

mum rate of training in auditory matching to sample is probably about 30 trials/min. An example of an auditory matching-to-sample trial is given in Figure 11.2.

The matching-to-sample procedure can also be used for training in word and sentence comprehension. Although the sentence comprehension test (Doehring, 1977; Doehring & Hoshko, 1977b) was not used in the primary statistical classification of reading disabilities, it would obviously be of value to assess the effect of training the more basic skills on comprehension, and also of being able to give simple training in rapid comprehension. For word comprehension, a visual sample is presented with three choice words, one of which has the same meaning as the sample. The subject must comprehend the word meaning to make the correct matching-to-sample response. In sentence comprehension, a sentence with a missing word is presented with three choice words, one of which is the word that completes the sentence. The subject must comprehend the meaning of the sentence to choose the correct word. Temporal durations and sequences are controlled in the same way as the visual matching-to-sample programs. An example of a comprehension trial is given in Figure 11.3.

Oral reading skills do not lend themselves as easily to computer programming as matching-to-sample skills. The original oral reading tests were given by showing the subject a card with the test materials printed

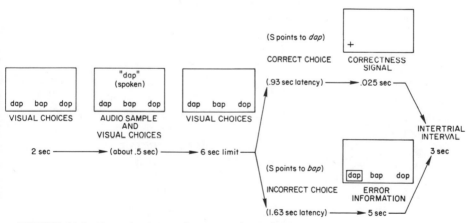

FIGURE 11.2. *Example of an auditory–visual matching-to-sample training trial for CVC syllables where the subject can "preview" the visual choices before the auditory sample is presented. The visual choices are presented for 2 sec prior to the spoken sample, which lasts about .5 sec, and remain on until the subject makes a correct or incorrect choice or the 6 sec time limit expires. The number of trials and the duration of the visual choice preview, response time limit, correctness and error information, and intertrial interval can be varied. The visual choices can also be presented at the same time or after the auditory sample.*

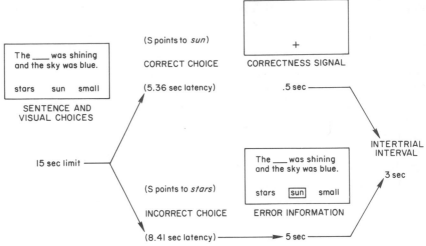

FIGURE 11.3. *Example of a sentence comprehension training trial in which the sentences and choices are presented at the same time. The subject touches the choice that best completes the sentence and immediately receives information about correctness. Previewed or delayed presentation of the choices is also possible. As in visual matching-to-sample, the number of trials and the duration of the sample sentence, the interval between the sentence and choice words, the correctness signal, the error information, and the intertrial interval can be varied from one training run to another.*

on it, asking him or her to read the stimuli aloud as rapidly as possible, and tape-recording the response for later analysis. The stimulus materials for oral reading can be displayed on the computer's television screen, but the microcomputer system is not capable of analyzing the subject's oral responses and providing immediate information about correctness. Pending further advances in computer technology, we have designed a rather crude training system where the operator presses a key on the CRT terminal to present the stimulus materials on the television screen and begin timing the response, the subject reads the material aloud as rapidly and accurately as possible, and the operator terminates the response timing by typing in the number of errors. Then the operator tells the subject how many errors were made. The computer records the stimuli presented, the number of errors, and the time required for oral reading (i.e., the time between the two key presses of the operator), and also carries out preliminary data analyses such as errors per trial, median latency, and distribution of latencies.

Computer training programs were not written for the visual scanning tests, because the tests are not central to the interpretation of the reading disabilities and the skills measured do not seem as basic as are those measured by the other tests in the battery. However, some types of reading disabilities may benefit from training in careful scanning, and we may add training in visual scanning to future training programs.

TRAINING PROGRAMS

A large number of items were compiled for each training task and incorporated into a series of 45 training programs. Details of the programs are given in Table 11.1.

The visual matching programs use most of the syllables and words that we could find with regular sound–letter correspondences for the most frequent combinations of consonants and vowels in two-, three-, and four-letter words and syllables (there are not enough regularly pronounced two-letter words for a training program). Incorrect choices are meaningless syllables for syllable matching and meaningful words for word matching, with the two incorrect choices differing by only one letter from the correct choice. A number of words and syllables could not be used as samples because minimally different choices were not available. There is also a training program for common words with irregular

TABLE 11.1

Preliminary Programs for Computer-Assisted Instruction, with the Number of Randomly Accessible Items Indicated for Each of the Forty-Five Programs. All Syllables and Words except the Irregular Words Have Regular Sound–Letter Correspondences.

Types of stimuli		Visual matching	Auditory–Visual matching	Oral reading	Comprehension
Letters[a]:	Names	52	52	52[c]	
	Sounds		52		
CV & VC	Syllables[b]	114	80	113	
CVC:	Syllables	148	79	173	
	Words	136	79	149	
CVVC:	Syllables	78	78	108	
	Words	133	79	204	
CVCV:	Syllables	75	75	168	
	Words	34	34	34	
CCVC:	Syllables	76	76	76	
	Words	37	37	159	
CVCC:	Syllables	60	58	60	
	Words	143	80	143	
Irregular words		124	76	124	75[d]
Two-word phrases			73		
Three-word phrases			78		
Sentences			57		75

[a] Both upper- and lower-case letters are used.
[b] C = consonant; V = vowel.
[c] The same program is used for oral letter names and oral letter sounds.
[d] Both regular and irregular words are included.

sound–letter correspondences, where the incorrect choices are other words of the same length. Because the stimulus items in each category are fairly exhaustive, training in simultaneous and successive visual matching-to-sample could lead to automatic recognition of single letters and a large number of one-syllable words and spelling patterns.

The auditory–visual matching programs include the same types of stimuli as the visual matching programs. An important addition to the auditory–visual tasks that had been used in the reading test battery is a program for matching letter sounds with single letters (because many consonants cannot be pronounced in isolation, the vowel sound "uh" was added to all consonants). Some of the auditory–visual programs include fewer stimulus items than the visual programs, because only 80 auditory samples can be stored on the flexible disks. The auditory–visual programs can provide intensive training to automaticity in sound–letter corre- spondences for single letter names and letter sounds, common spelling patterns in meaningless syllables, and regular and irregular words. These are the types of sound–letter correspondences taught in a less intensive manner by most code-oriented training programs.

The oral reading programs contain as many or more stimulus items as the visual matching programs, because minimally different incorrect choices are not needed. The oral reading items can be presented in series of any desired length up to the capacity of the television screen (about nine items for most programs). Oral reading speed and accuracy can be systematically increased by starting with single items and increasing the number of items as speed and accuracy improve. With the oral reading programs, training can be given in reading phrases and sentences as well as isolated words.

The comprehension programs are much more preliminary in nature than the other programs. For word comprehension, sample and choice words were selected for which the correct choice is similar in meaning to the sample and the incorrect choices are not; and for sentence compre- hension, one word was deleted from simple sentences and that word plus two inappropriate words were used as choices. Larger sets of items will be needed for systematic training in comprehension. Computer-assisted instruction in comprehension should be a very important aspect of fur- ther training research.

TRAINING PROCEDURES

The procedure for operating the training programs is quite simple. No previous experience with computers is needed. The operator first selects a disk containing the programs for a particular task. The visual matching- to-sample, auditory–visual matching-to-sample, oral reading, and comprehension programs are recorded on separate disks. Each disk also contains the necessary operating language. The operator inserts the disk into the disk drive and types a simple instruction that enters BASIC programming language and the training program into the working memory of the central processor. After the programs have been entered, the computer asks the operator to select the training material (e.g., CVVC syllables), and to specify the training conditions (the number of trials, the interval between trials, the duration of the sample, the delay between the sample and choice stimuli, the duration of positive reinforcement, and the duration of error information). When the necessary information has been entered, the operator types RUN to run the program. The first stimulus item is presented and the subject makes the first response. From then on, the subject interacts with the computer (and the operator, in the case of oral reading programs) to finish the training run. Each training item is randomly selected from the total pool of items for the program.

After the preselected number of training trials have been completed, the computer prints a summary, giving the number of trials and the number of correct responses, errors, and nonresponse trials, along with the experimental conditions for that run. It then asks the operator if he or she wishes other information such as the median latency of correct responses, the distribution of correct latencies, or a trial-by-trial listing of the stimulus items, responses, and response latencies. The operator is also given the option of storing any or all of this information on a second disk, printing it out on the line printer, or both. When a run is completed, the operator can repeat the same program, changing the number of trials or the timing as a function of the subject's performance, shift to another type of material with the same task, or change to a different task. Changing from one task to another (or from one program to another for auditory–visual matching) requires entering the new program into working memory, which takes 1–2 min because of the relative slowness of the microcomputer. Technological improvement in computer speed or in the programming efficiency is needed to reduce the delay between training runs.

PRELIMINARY RESEARCH

The first study using the computer-assisted instruction system was master's thesis research carried out by Gary Johnston (1981) under the supervision of R. L. Trites. Subjects were 12 children, ranging in age from 8 to 18, with reading disabilities. They were divided into three matched groups of 4 subjects each, including a nontrained control group, a group that received 7.5 hours training (1.5 hours per day over 5 days) in visual matching-to-sample of four-letter CVCC nonsense syllables, and a group receiving 12 hours training in visual matching-to-sample of four-letter CVCC words. The Reading subtest of the WRAT was administered before and after training, and at corresponding times for the control group. All subjects were also given a pretraining and posttraining test using the computer-assisted instructional programs, in which 15 trials each were given with simultaneous and delayed visual and auditory–visual matching and in oral reading of letters (including both letter names and letter sounds for auditory–visual matching and oral reading), three-letter nonsense syllables and words, and four-letter CVVC nonsense syllables and words, and also in the oral reading of phrases and sentences.

Training was given in as many as 20 blocks per training session, with most blocks consisting of 15 training trials. Training began with simultaneous matching and continued until 90 % accuracy was achieved, and then changed to a delay condition with a long visual sample and a minimal delay between the visual sample and the three visual choices. Each time that 90 % accuracy was achieved, the sample duration was decreased and the delay between sample and choice stimuli was increased. Training was begun at a relatively easy level on each training session, and task difficulty was gradually increased until the 90 % accuracy criterion could not be achieved, or until the sample had been decreased to .01 sec and the delay to 3 sec, and then training was terminated with several blocks of easier trials to avoid frustration. A few subjects did so well that fewer than 20 blocks per session were given.

Most subjects were able to reach the 90 % accuracy criterion with a .01 sec sample and a 3 sec delay, demonstrating a great deal of proficiency in perception and memory for printed syllables and words. On the pre- and posttests for the trained materials, the median response latency of the nonsense syllable group decreased significantly from 1.34 to 1.12 sec, as compared to a nonsignificant decrease from 1.34 to 1.24 sec for the word group. The control group had nonsignificant decreases from 1.79 to 1.77 sec for syllables and from 1.50 to 1.41 sec for words. There was considerable variability in median response latencies in all groups, ranging from .6 sec to 2.7 sec.

Reading scores (WRAT) increased nonsignificantly by .4 years in the nonsense syllable groups, .3 years in the word group, and .2 years in the control group. In addition to their significant decrease in response latency on the trained material, the nonsense syllable group showed considerable evidence of transfer of training, with significant pre–post training decreases in response latencies for visual matching of three and four-ietter (CVCC) nonsense syllables and for the oral reading of words, phrases, and sentences. The word training group also showed significant decreases of latencies for the oral reading of letters, words, phrases, and sentences. There were no significant changes in latencies over the two tests for the control group.

Because of the preliminary nature of the study, the limited training period, and the small number of subjects, no definite conclusions are possible regarding the efficacy of computer-assisted instruction of deficient reading skills in subjects with reading disabilities. However, the results are very encouraging. Even when limited training was given on a visual matching task that could be accomplished with minimal reading skills, there was not only evidence of increased proficiency on the skills trained, but also a definite indication of transfer of training to the visual matching of other types of stimuli and, more important, to oral reading. These effects appeared to be greater for a group trained with nonsense syllables than for a group trained with words, suggesting that training in coding skills may be more helpful than training in whole word recognition. Even stronger training and transfer-of-training effects should be found when subjects are trained on the more demanding auditory–visual matching-to-sample task. Unfortunately, it was not possible to determine the interaction of training effects with the types of reading disabilities, as we have not as yet developed a method for classifying subjects on the basis of performance of the computer assisted instructional tasks.

This preliminary study demonstrated that computer-assisted instruction of children with reading disabilities could be successfully accomplished, with good prospects that there would be not only an improvement of the skills trained, but generalization of the trained skills to untrained skills and to the actual reading of texts. Johnston noted the importance of carefully changing task difficulty in accordance with the subject's performance to minimize boredom from continuing easy tasks and frustration from repeated errors on difficult tasks. This prevented him from giving exactly the same training to all subjects, an important problem to be considered in the design of further research.

FURTHER RESEARCH

Johnston's (1981) preliminary study provided valuable suggestions for further research. Although the use of a microcomputer system made it possible to design programs in which there can be a delay between the sample and the choice stimuli, this potentially valuable feature will not be used in initial training research. All matching-to-sample training will be restricted to simultaneous matching, to permit direct comparison with the previous classifications of reading disabilities, to provide more uniform training, and to make it practical to train a wider range of

reading skills. In subsequent research, however, it should be very interesting to determine whether the use of delayed matching enhances the
training effects and helps to define other types of reading disabilities.

Even when training is restricted to simultaneous matching, several
alternative research designs are possible. Training only the deficient skills
that define each type of reading disability might indicate the extent to
which these particular deficiencies are irreversible. For practical purposes, the most efficient training system might be to train the least impaired skills first, not beginning to train the most deficient skills until
there has been maximum opportunity for transfer of training. However,
the most appropriate initial step toward the goal of obtaining more valid
inferences about the interaction of behavioral and neurological deficits
might be to give uniform training in visual and auditory–visual
matching-to-sample and oral reading to the point where the limits of
learning for each type of reading skill can be determined. Then, assessment of the remaining patterns of reading skill deficit for each type of
reading disability should provide the information needed for planning
the next step of research. Even in the initial research, measures of skills
for reading continuous text should be obtained before, during, and after
training; and information will be needed about the limits of learning of
normal readers for each skill to estimate the normal range of individual
differences in accuracy and latencies of reading responses.

When sufficient information has been obtained from the initial
studies, more elaborate studies can be planned. Designs that involve the
assessment of transfer of training will provide important information for
the theoretical purpose of understanding reading disabilities and the
practical purposes of finding the most efficient training procedures.
Single-subject research designs (Herson & Barlow, 1976; Guralnick,
1978) may prove to be the most appropriate for this purpose. It will also
be necessary to reanalyze the reading task at some point to define a new
set of component reading skills that conforms more closely to the actual
skills used in reading continuous text, and then to design procedures for
assessing and training these skills. Similar efforts should be made to
analyze the nonreading abilities that contribute to reading acquisition
and to design assessment and training procedures for nonreading skills
that are integrated with the programs for assessing and training reading
skills.

If these stages of research can be successfully completed, the time may
come when the gap between research, theory, and practice has closed
sufficiently that practical training effects can be studied by systematically
comparing computer-assisted instruction with the best available remedial
programs. This will constitute progress of the type described by Resnick

(1979b) as a joining of cognitive psychology and learning psychology to create a cognitive psychology of learning. If successful, this new psychology will be able to specify the interaction between the learner and the environment, and will be particularly attentive to individual differences. It will have to create a new kind of logic to answer the new questions that are raised, and in so doing may change the nature of cognitive psychology and the psychology of learning.

These are indeed praiseworthy aims, but we are not yet sure how to begin. A certain amount of trial-and-error will be necessary to find the most appropriate research strategies. Training research of this type is long, difficult, and expensive, and may pose ethical questions with regard to the short-term interests of the children who are trained and the long-term interests of all children with reading disabilities. The most important feature of our research is that we have gone beyond the point of speculation and have begun to carry out research that combines assessment and training. We hope that others will be encouraged to embark on similar efforts.

Future Prospects

12

Our research was the first that used statistical methods to classify different types of reading disabilities in terms of both reading and nonreading deficits. The deficits were more complex than we had anticipated. The three types of reading disabilities that were reliably defined by differential patterns of reading skill deficits did not interact in a simple manner with patterns of deficits on batteries of language and neuropsychological tests. There seemed to be two or perhaps three types of nonreading deficits associated with one type of reading disability, and the nonreading deficits associated with the other two types of reading disabilities were not easy to interpret.

This research did not, then, solve the mystery of reading disability. Theories, tests, and statistical methods have not evolved to the point where final answers can be expected. However, we can confidently identify three types of reading disabilities and describe a number of interesting linguistic and neuropsychological characteristics of each type; and we have gained considerable insight regarding directions for further work. In this final chapter we will first draw some provisional conclusions about types of reading disabilities, and will then discuss a number of issues that should be considered in future research.

Types of Reading Disabilities

When reading disabilities are defined in terms of the interaction of reading, nonreading, and neurological variables, several models are possible. Among the simplest would be those in which each pattern of reading skill deficit (R) is associated with one particular pattern of nonreading deficit (N) and one particular neurological dysfunction (B), as shown in Figure 12.1A. The nonreading deficit could involve language or nonlanguage abilities and the neurological dysfunction could occur in one or more locations within the brain. If all reading disabilities took this form, they would be relatively uncomplicated, much like unitary explanations of reading disabilities. However, a specific pattern of reading skill deficit would correspond to each pattern of nonreading deficit–neurological dysfunction, and cause-and-effect relationships would not be specified, as indicated by the bidirectional arrows. More complex interactions could occur where two or more combinations of nonreading deficit–neurological dysfunction were associated with a single pattern of reading skill deficit, as shown in Figure 12.1B, or two or more patterns of reading skill deficits were associated with a single pattern of nonreading deficit–neurological dysfunction, as shown in Figure 12.1C.

The types of reading disabilities that were actually identified could be described in terms of the models in Figures 12.1A and 12.1B. Type O reading disability seemed to fit the interaction in Figure 12.1B, where a severe difficulty in oral reading was associated with two or three different patterns of deficits on the language and neuropsychological tests. Types A and S reading disabilities could fit the simple model in Figure 12.1A, where each would be associated with a particular pattern of nonreading deficit–neurological dysfunction.

As the reading disabilities are empirically defined in terms of a given set of measures, the addition of new measures could result in a further differentiation of patterns of reading deficits, nonreading deficits, or neurological dysfunctions. For example, additional reading tests might reveal three different patterns of reading skill deficits within Type O, resulting in three separate reading disabilities that fit the model in Figure 12.1A, instead of a single reading disability with three subtypes that fits the model of Figure 12.1B. Additional nonreading tests might also reveal

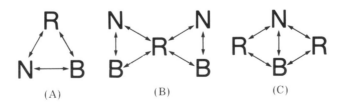

FIGURE 12.1. *Examples of three different models for explaining the interactions between patterns of deficits in reading skills (R), nonreading abilities (N), and brain functioning (B).*

several different combinations of nonreading deficit–neurological dysfunction associated with Type A reading disability, making the model of Figure 12.1B more appropriate for this type of reading disability.

These models provide a simple, operational statement of current evidence about reading disabilities, but at least one complication is unavoidable. As discussed in the previous chapter, differences in educational experience could affect the patterns of reading skill deficits. Some reading disability models that take into account various interactive effects of experience are shown in Figure 12.2. The model of Figure 12.2A is one in which the pattern of reading skill deficit is not affected by different reading experiences, whereas the model of Figure 12.2B is one in which differences in reading experience do result in different patterns of reading skill deficits for a given pattern of nonreading–neurological deficit. These additional possibilities could complicate the interpretation of our results. Even more complex models could easily be envisaged, where different reading experiences could affect the development of nonreading skills such as morphophonemic knowledge.

We do not have enough information about the differential reading experiences of our subjects to make a confident choice among the alternative models presented here or those described by previous writers (Applebee, 1971; Wiener & Cromer, 1967); nor do other investigators. If a severe reading disability remains after the best possible remedial training, differential effects of reading experience might be ruled out. However, it is difficult to determine how many disabled readers receive optimal training. Experiential differences should be controlled more explicitly in future research. Some possible methods for doing this were discussed in Chapter 11 and will be discussed again in a later section of this chapter. If reading disabilities are found to vary as a function of

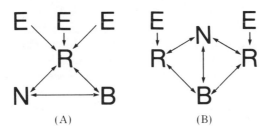

(A)   (B)

FIGURE 12.2. *Examples of two different models for explaining the interactions involving deficits in reading skills (R), nonreading abilities (N), and brain functioning (B), as well as differences in reading experience (E).*

reading experience, concepts of reading disabilities must be modified to take account of these interactive effects. A broader concept of reading disability that specifies the interaction of organismic and environmental variables would be more in accordance with current theories of cognitive development (cf. Fischer, 1980). Before any further discussion of theoretical matters, several methodological issues will be considered.

Selection of Subjects for Reading Disability Research

Although disabled readers can be reliably differentiated from other groups of children with learning disabilities (Trites & Price, 1978–1979), it is difficult to define reading disability for research purposes (Doehring, 1978; Valtin, 1978–1979). Statistical classification methods may eliminate the need for arbitrary exclusionary definitions. However, the effects of differential reading experience on patterns of deficits are not yet known, as discussed in the preceding section. Nor do we have any exact information about the interactive effects of the sensory, emotional, intellectual, and sociocultural deficiencies usually excluded in research populations, although there is some suggestion that "organic" and familial reading disabilities have equal difficulty in acquiring reading proficiency (Trites & Fiedorowicz, 1976). It is desirable for both practical and theoretical purposes that a single method for objectively classifying unselected populations of reading problems be developed, but it may be best to determine first how differential training interacts with the reading and nonreading deficits of subjects selected by the usual exclusionary definitions of reading disabilities.

Some problems would still remain with regard to selecting the most appropriate population. It is not difficult to select subjects with adequate sensory, emotional, and sociocultural status, but the range of reading and nonreading deficits could vary considerably as a function of the exact criteria of reading achievement and intelligence. The reading deficits should probably be defined in terms of oral word and nonsense syllable reading, because all types of reading disabilities seem to be characterized by relatively poor performance on these tasks. To allow for the most variation in patterns of deficits, a particular degree of deficit in either word or nonsense syllable reading should be the criterion for selection; and if reading comprehension deficits are to be considered a type of reading disability, a particular degree of comprehension deficit could also be one of the selection criteria.

There can be no completely unambiguous criterion of normal intellectual status, because the idea of normal intellectual status in reading disability is somewhat of a contradiction in terms (Doehring, 1978), and also because an intellectual deficit could be the result rather than the cause of reading disability. As with the reading criterion, it is best to use a criterion that allows for as much variation as possible. For example, a requirement that either VIQ or PIQ should be average would allow more variation than a requirement that PIQ must be average. It might be even less restrictive to require that some proportion of the subtests be in the average range, regardless of whether they were Verbal or Performance subtests.

A final cautionary note with regard to the unavoidably arbitrary criteria for defining reading disability is that these definitions are for research purposes only. They are not meant to identify a clinical population that requires a particular type of treatment.

Experimental Measures

Inferences about reading disabilities are limited by the experimental measures that are obtained. A perennial problem is construct validity (Ohnmacht & Weiss, 1976). For example, a test may be labeled as measuring memory because a series of stimuli is presented and the subject is asked to recall them. Subjects with good memory will tend to score better than subjects with poor memory, but test scores may also vary as a function of the subject's ability to understand instructions, perceive a series of stimulus patterns, employ appropriate strategies for encoding and rehearsal, and perform the responses necessary to demonstrate recall. Poor performance of a memory test could be the result of any one of a number of specific deficits, such as impairment of language comprehension, motivation, attention, pattern perception, temporal sequence perception, verbal encoding, contextual knowledge, rehearsal strategies, or motor sequence formulation. The problems tend to be the greatest when only a few tests are used, because more alternative explanations are possible, but the precision of interpretation is limited by the extent to which alternative explanations are possible even when a large number of measures is obtained in an investigation such as ours.

One way to reduce alternative interpretations is to systematically vary a basic experimental procedure, as Tallal and Stark have done in attempting to determine the basis of an auditory rate processing deficit in children with developmental language disorders (Tallal, personal communication, 1980). For example, visual verbal perception might be tested by immediate identification of a word, visual nonverbal perception by immediate identification of a picture, and verbal and nonverbal visual memory by delayed recall of the word or picture. Analogous auditory abilities could be tested by substituting verbal and nonverbal sounds, and verbal and nonverbal motor abilities could be tested by varying the identification responses. Other aspects that can be systematically varied include the number, type, and rate of presentation of stimuli, and the type of response that is required.

In practice, of course, it is difficult to find a set of test operations that will accommodate the desired range of abilities. There was some systematic variation of operations within subsets of tests in our reading, language, and neuropsychological batteries. The visual and auditory–visual matching-to-sample tests had a single basic procedure, as did the oral reading tests, the visual scanning tests, the oral word repetition tests, the Token tests, and the pairs of lateralized neuropsychological measures. In comparing differences from one task to another and from one test battery to another, however, interpretations were limited by procedural variations.

Creative thought is needed to design a battery of tests that systematically samples abilities involved in reading acquisition. Whatever basic procedure is devised must be flexible enough to accommodate simple abilities for discriminating visual patterns or phonemic contrasts and complex abilities for extracting the meaning from speech or print. It is not immediately apparent how the optimal battery should be designed, but any efforts that future investigators can make to construct an integrated battery of tests instead of the usual composite test battery should be helpful. For initial efforts, the task might be simplified. If it is assumed that deficits in higher-level discourse processing skills are not intrinsic to reading disability, reading and nonreading abilities beyond discriminating, perceiving, remembering, and understanding the meaning of verbal and nonverbal stimuli at the level of individual printed words need not be tested. Those who do wish to hypothesize deficits in more complex abilities, such as those involved in sentence grammar and meaning, will have more difficulty constructing an integrated battery.

Even where only skills at the level of single words are to be assessed, the tests should sample the types of skills that are used by the reader for reading. The test operations should be as similar as possible to the operations actually involved in extracting meaning from text. The problem to be solved is the varying of basic test operations in enough different directions that the entire range of possible nonreading deficits can be assessed.

Statistical Classification Methods

Other strategies of statistical classification should be considered in further research (Knights & Stoddart, 1981). In the present study, reading disabilities were defined in terms of reading skill deficits, and then the deficient performances on language and neuropsychological tests were interpreted with reference to the reading skill classifications. If a test battery of the type described in the preceding section could be developed, where all tests involve systematic variation of a basic test procedure, the reading disability should probably be defined in terms of a statistical classification that uses the entire battery of tests.

When enough information has been obtained regarding different types of reading disabilities in highly selected samples of subjects with severe reading problems, an attempt should be made to discover the most appropriate techniques for classifying a broader range of reading problems. Different methods of statistical classification might be needed if reading disabilities were to be classified in terms of relative severity, as suggested by Satz and Morris (1980), and if they were to be classified with respect to the interactive effects of intelligence, emotional status, and socio-cultural factors. Although the latter classifications would be more difficult and might not be entirely essential for scientific purposes, the information obtained could prove to be very useful for clinical diagnosis of unselected populations.

Experimental Design

Several aspects of experimental design might be improved in future research. In the present research, a sample of subjects with reading problems was selected and given three different batteries of tests. Subjects were statistically classified on the basis of their reading test performance, and the results of the language and neuropsychological batteries were analyzed with reference to the reading test classifications. There was no direct comparison to a matched control group of normal readers, as would be the case in studies using the single-syndrome paradigm. The patterns of reading and nonreading deficits were defined with reference to several different sets of test norms, some of which were based on a clinical population. The lack of a single normative population added undesirable variance to the statistical classifications. This problem could be eliminated by obtaining normative data for the type of integrated test battery just described. It might be best to base the norms on an entire population of normal and subnormal readers, with separate norms for each age.

An integrated test battery could involve such a large number of tests that special procedures would be needed to minimize the duration of testing. It might be possible to devise branching strategies in which only those tests essential for defining the reading disability are given. If, for example, a subject with Type A reading disability was normal in memory for sequences of visual nonverbal patterns, no further visual nonverbal tests would be needed, but if there were deficiencies in memory for spoken words, it would be necessary to continue testing auditory abilities until normal performance was found.

In the present study, inferences about possible cerebral dysfunction were made on the basis of neuropsychological test performance. In future research designs, more direct measures of brain function might be included (cf. Gur & Reivich, 1980). Such measures taken in conjunction with an integrated test battery could yield systematic information about cerebral dysfunction in different types of reading disabilities. If the data obtained in this manner were sufficiently precise, it might be possible to determine the extent to which reading disabilities are associated with normal variability rather than with distinct abnormalities of cerebral structure or function.

The interactive effects of reading experience must also be dealt with in future research designs. A weakness of the present study and other studies of reading disabilities is the lack of information about the extent to which reading disabilities are affected by differences in reading experience. This type of variability can be reduced by selecting subjects who have had extensive remedial training, but it is difficult to find large numbers of such subjects and to obtain detailed information about their reading experience. When adequate information about reading experience is unavailable, a weaker interpretation of reading disabilities is unavoidable, with no final conclusions possible concerning the relative contributions or organismic and environmental variables.

The strategy we will pursue in further research is to assess the effects of systematically training the reading skills that are tested. As this is a new approach, the most appropriate training procedures cannot be specified in advance. To obtain more detailed information about training effects, methods for evaluating performance during the course of training will be developed, including determination of the rate at which the limits of learning (Ferguson, 1956) are approached by normal readers of different ages, the amount of transfer of training to untrained skills (Guthrie, 1973), the optimum sequence for training the most- and least-impaired skills, and the degree to which training effects generalize to the actual reading of text. With an integrated test battery, provision can also be made to train nonreading abilities that may contribute to reading disabilities, such as phonemic segmentation.

The incorporation of training into the multiple-syndrome research paradigm does appear to offer hope of closing the frustrating gaps between theory, research, and practice. An important problem of research design can be solved by permitting the experimenter to manipulate relevant experience, thus providing the information needed for theoretical explanations of the interaction of organismic and environmental variables. It is first necessary to determine which reading deficits cannot be eliminated by intensive direct training. Such deficits may be neurological in origin. Then attempts can be made to determine the extent to which trainable deficits are the result of organismic or environmental differences.

Theoretical Framework for Reading Disability

In our research, we did not have a single theoretical framework for designing tests and interpreting the test results. For future research of this type, a working theory that makes possible a unified assessment and explanation of the entire pattern of deficit is needed. The theory should center on the act of reading and include a description of all behavioral and neurological processes that might be involved in reading disabilities. Even if the theory is restricted to the decoding and comprehension of isolated words, it could be extremely complex (cf. Rumelhart, 1977) and require a revolutionary change in strategies of theory construction (Kuhn, 1970). More precise concepts of abilities and skills might be needed to specify the manner in which abilities are inherited or shaped by experience (Aslin & Pisoni, 1978). The interactive nature of reading acquisition must also be taken into consideration, and it may be necessary to include a description of higher-level conceptual processes to explain compensatory mechanisms used by disabled readers even when reading isolated words (Stanovitch, 1980). Only after an adequate working theory is formulated can an integrated set of tests be designed.

In short, the formulation of a working theory adequate to the task of describing different types of reading disabilities will not be easy, but is a matter of the highest priority for future research.

Conclusions

Reading disabilities and other learning problems are not only severe handicaps for those who have them, but are also very frustrating to parents, teachers, and other professionals. A strong drive for more definitive answers probably accounts for the many optimistic solutions that appear in the professional and popular literature. We do not claim to have found the one best solution, or even the one best route to a solution. The problem is so complicated that it can be approached from many different aspects, ranging from a microscopic study of the mechanisms used in phonological recoding to a consideration of the roles of reasoning and self-reflection in reading disabilities. The work reported here reinforced our conviction that any expectation of simple solutions is unwarranted. For many years to come the problem of reading disability will continue to pose a challenge to the cleverest and most innovative scientists, clinicians, and educators.

Age-Corrected Intercorrelations

APPENDIX A

Column groups: **DURRELL** (OR SR LC WR WA) · **VISUAL MATCHING** (NU LE UL W3 W4 S3 CC) · **AUD-VIS MATCHING** (LE W3 W4 S2 CV S3 S4) · **NAMING** (CO PI)

DURRELL ACHIEVEMENT TEST

	OR	SR	LC	WR	WA	NU	LE	UL	W3	W4	S3	CC	LE	W3	W4	S2	CV	S3	S4	CO	PI
Oral Reading	X	93	38	88	87	41	46	51	62	62	71	49	46	63	76	69	68	47	61	40	35
Silent Reading	93	X	48	87	85	43	46	49	61	61	71	47	46	68	75	71	65	49	61	39	34
Listen. Comp.	38	48	X	47	44	17	23	26	26	21	28	13	24	36	32	33	37	35	30	22	16
Word Recog.	88	87	47	X	98	40	44	51	60	63	75	46	48	71	77	76	74	50	62	32	36
Word Attack	87	85	44	98	X	42	46	54	62	64	74	48	47	72	75	78	71	51	61	34	34

READING-RELATED SKILLS

VISUAL MATCHING

	OR	SR	LC	WR	WA	NU	LE	UL	W3	W4	S3	CC	LE	W3	W4	S2	CV	S3	S4	CO	PI
Numbers	41	43	17	40	42	X	82	79	76	63	57	55	57	56	48	54	43	39	56	45	24
Letters	46	46	23	44	46	82	X	86	81	68	61	52	57	57	54	59	48	50	54	48	20
U & L Case Let.	51	49	26	51	54	79	86	X	79	65	61	51	52	57	54	60	53	52	60	52	27
CVC Words	62	61	26	60	62	76	81	79	X	86	77	63	54	71	66	61	59	47	65	49	29
CVCC Words	62	61	21	63	64	63	68	65	86	X	83	58	57	73	71	62	57	48	58	42	24
CVC Syllables	71	71	28	75	74	57	61	61	77	83	X	66	47	74	69	64	66	45	61	36	22
CCC String	49	47	13	46	48	55	52	51	63	58	66	X	30	57	52	50	47	31	54	23	09

AUDITORY-VISUAL MATCHING

	OR	SR	LC	WR	WA	NU	LE	UL	W3	W4	S3	CC	LE	W3	W4	S2	CV	S3	S4	CO	PI
Letters	46	46	24	48	47	57	57	52	54	57	47	30	X	54	56	42	49	41	50	39	19
CVC Words	63	68	36	71	72	56	57	57	71	73	74	57	54	X	78	69	68	54	65	30	25
CVCC Words	76	75	32	77	75	48	54	54	66	71	69	52	56	78	X	72	67	52	64	40	28
CV Syllables	69	71	33	76	78	54	59	60	61	62	64	50	42	69	72	X	56	63	59	35	27
CCV Syllables	68	65	37	74	71	43	48	53	59	57	66	47	49	68	67	56	X	46	67	34	19
CVC Syllables	47	49	35	50	51	39	50	52	47	48	45	31	41	54	52	63	46	X	60	37	16
CVCC Syllables	61	61	30	62	61	56	54	60	65	58	61	54	50	65	64	59	67	60	X	43	28

ORAL READING & NAMING

	OR	SR	LC	WR	WA	NU	LE	UL	W3	W4	S3	CC	LE	W3	W4	S2	CV	S3	S4	CO	PI
Color Naming	40	39	22	32	34	45	48	52	49	42	36	23	39	30	40	35	34	37	43	X	52
Picture Naming	35	34	16	36	34	24	20	27	29	24	22	09	19	25	28	27	19	16	28	52	X
Upper-Case Let.	74	69	24	71	73	62	61	67	66	60	58	48	51	58	63	65	53	44	60	53	56
Lower-Case Let.	73	68	20	67	67	64	66	66	67	61	57	54	55	59	61	62	52	49	63	55	46
U & L Case Let.	68	62	25	64	64	54	55	60	58	48	49	44	47	46	57	56	47	42	61	47	51
Let. in Sent.	71	64	22	63	64	61	61	64	65	57	52	53	48	60	60	65	55	48	58	41	39
Random Words	85	81	33	83	79	44	47	50	62	62	68	47	46	61	71	70	65	49	66	30	32
2 Word Phrases	90	87	37	85	83	46	47	51	65	65	72	53	48	69	76	71	69	46	70	35	37
7 Word Phrases	89	85	35	80	76	40	45	48	61	61	68	49	42	63	73	69	66	49	63	34	32
Sentences	89	84	33	84	82	44	45	49	63	65	73	51	44	72	74	70	73	51	68	33	31
Nonsense Syl.	63	55	28	64	60	26	29	38	38	40	43	14	28	35	46	56	48	47	46	30	21

VISUAL SCANNING

	OR	SR	LC	WR	WA	NU	LE	UL	W3	W4	S3	CC	LE	W3	W4	S2	CV	S3	S4	CO	PI
Rectangle	23	22	02	20	21	51	49	43	41	37	30	25	26	24	23	32	28	29	36	24	09
Figure	36	37	14	38	36	58	51	51	57	53	54	57	42	47	44	38	43	31	49	30	13
Number	36	37	12	35	35	60	54	48	58	52	54	56	37	41	39	32	41	23	39	34	13
Letter	33	33	14	37	37	55	55	49	61	63	58	56	40	48	40	32	39	29	43	34	12
2 Letters	42	39	02	43	42	45	48	53	61	57	63	55	26	44	48	34	48	28	43	36	20
Letter in Syl.	36	33	07	37	37	47	51	42	59	53	63	56	32	41	42	31	42	26	34	31	09
Word	53	53	15	58	55	31	44	43	56	63	69	42	24	51	57	47	47	39	40	34	32
Syllable	56	52	16	58	55	32	34	39	53	55	61	37	30	49	58	42	54	35	47	24	09
CCCC String	35	36	05	32	30	34	23	31	37	31	35	30	07	27	23	24	28	27	35	24	24
Unspaced Word	54	51	13	55	54	54	54	56	64	71	70	53	38	55	56	47	52	38	55	34	17

COMPREHENSION & SPELLING

	OR	SR	LC	WR	WA	NU	LE	UL	W3	W4	S3	CC	LE	W3	W4	S2	CV	S3	S4	CO	PI
Sentence Comp.	87	89	43	90	89	45	48	56	65	66	77	52	49	73	80	72	71	47	64	43	38
Oral Spelling	76	72	31	75	74	37	41	52	52	52	65	47	34	62	66	60	65	49	49	41	29
Written Spell.	69	67	24	74	72	35	43	45	54	51	64	44	33	55	60	67	62	51	53	33	23
Spelled-Out Wd.	62	58	32	66	68	30	36	47	42	48	51	34	32	54	50	56	62	49	46	25	25

LANGUAGE TESTS

PHONEMIC SEGMENTATION & BLENDING

	OR	SR	LC	WR	WA	NU	LE	UL	W3	W4	S3	CC	LE	W3	W4	S2	CV	S3	S4	CO	PI
Sound Del. - Syl.	46	37	17	46	49	21	24	30	23	11	27	08	16	25	19	43	30	27	25	28	19
Wd.	66	64	45	71	70	31	34	44	49	41	51	39	32	54	54	54	68	50	62	38	34
Pig Latin	38	36	21	44	45	22	26	34	31	30	39	20	17	33	30	32	36	26	18	16	08
Ubby Dubby	60	58	34	68	69	33	29	50	50	45	61	36	30	58	55	52	56	40	52	28	30
Rhyming	24	25	-03	22	28	37	38	36	31	28	32	11	30	38	24	31	07	28	14	18	23

SERIAL NAMING

	OR	SR	LC	WR	WA	NU	LE	UL	W3	W4	S3	CC	LE	W3	W4	S2	CV	S3	S4	CO	PI
Count 20	-30	-30	-14	-30	-29	17	18	12	02	-05	-14	C2	-02	-13	-17	-11	-12	-05	-03	10	-03
Name Days	36	39	27	42	44	38	40	45	39	33	40	37	24	34	41	50	32	37	37	37	26
Name Months	39	41	11	37	39	31	29	44	35	35	47	32	23	37	39	37	34	43	38	27	21

	DURRELL					VISUAL MATCHING							AUD-VIS MATCHING							NAMING	
	OR	SR	LC	WR	WA	NU	LE	UL	W3	W4	S3	CC	LE	W3	W4	S2	CV	S3	S4	CO	PI
LANGUAGE TESTS (CONTINUED)																					
ORAL REPETITION																					
Unrelated Words	22	23	26	20	23	24	15	22	15	09	22	16	13	14	07	14	22	09	23	16	10
Randomized Wds.	33	32	34	30	32	11	16	16	11	11	25	15	04	19	16	29	28	10	16	06	04
Meaningless Sent.	32	32	26	35	39	25	22	30	16	12	27	12	03	30	24	41	22	25	27	23	21
Sentences	27	30	38	31	30	23	23	33	18	16	22	17	04	26	17	32	20	32	23	26	22
TOKEN TEST																					
A	03	01	-02	01	02	33	28	35	20	10	00	07	20	07	11	11	12	13	26	33	21
B	00	04	06	-01	03	32	22	21	20	17	12	14	21	16	10	07	11	14	17	21	-08
C	39	41	09	39	44	35	38	39	38	34	41	32	24	40	42	53	27	31	30	32	14
D	28	29	08	30	29	35	33	40	40	41	44	36	31	37	36	26	29	31	37	28	06
E	34	34	07	37	39	42	45	44	37	39	38	32	31	47	43	45	31	35	40	38	27
F	20	18	06	15	18	15	24	24	18	17	14	05	20	10	14	22	17	25	19	18	03
SYNTACTIC-SEMANTIC																					
Morphophonemics	19	26	20	24	29	20	20	23	18	15	20	17	13	27	10	30	13	24	10	08	-01
Devel. Sent.	13	19	03	16	21	06	11	20	20	20	23	05	03	25	13	28	09	19	13	10	-04
Semantic Fields	32	31	11	27	31	29	17	30	20	15	20	25	23	20	28	24	30	17	31	27	00
Ask & Tell	09	14	07	11	11	24	21	27	18	10	19	04	18	17	17	17	14	12	16	36	11
NEUROPSYCHOLOGY TESTS																					
WISC VERBAL																					
Information	35	35	33	33	33	16	15	22	22	16	21	16	14	27	26	27	33	30	30	22	06
Comprehension	20	21	05	25	31	21	13	21	14	13	13	09	16	23	11	33	14	22	19	08	00
Digit Span	08	04	-10	10	14	09	04	12	06	05	04	06	-03	11	08	11	11	15	14	11	14
Arithmetic	35	37	22	34	36	25	27	33	26	17	21	19	15	17	28	37	26	27	28	18	10
Similarities	37	37	21	38	41	12	11	22	18	15	16	08	05	28	20	39	26	22	20	10	16
Vocabulary	19	19	18	20	24	05	-02	08	02	03	00	-06	01	13	08	20	10	11	09	05	04
WISC PERFORMANCE																					
Pic. Arrangement	06	12	08	06	06	12	09	03	-03	-03	-05	-01	17	03	06	12	06	13	08	12	-06
Pic. Completion	03	11	11	10	10	-02	00	-05	08	02	04	10	-01	09	10	11	14	06	-05	-01	-09
Block Design	06	05	00	14	19	21	26	19	21	16	19	22	13	18	13	20	22	-05	09	-01	-03
Object Assembly	07	11	-01	19	22	14	20	19	18	19	17	14	07	20	10	14	16	-07	07	05	00
Coding	30	26	05	23	26	29	31	28	31	28	25	26	25	24	22	32	26	27	23	43	20
Maze	-01	-04	-05	07	11	09	12	20	14	06	09	13	13	12	10	07	06	06	15	00	-15
Peabody Vocab.	17	21	34	20	23	14	13	21	12	05	07	00	00	17	15	25	16	26	26	07	05
Knox Cube	-05	-02	-00	-02	01	-01	04	08	05	11	02	-11	11	02	05	-04	-09	-07	-01	14	10
Prog. Matrices	05	08	18	21	20	09	01	10	14	16	19	11	15	20	20	24	33	14	15	02	-19
Devel. Draw.	-34	-38	-37	-30	-30	-25	-22	-21	-31	-30	-35	-17	-16	-31	-21	-24	-11	-24	-23	-30	-32
R-L Discrim.	11	10	01	06	04	-01	-02	02	00	-04	00	10	-04	11	10	00	09	-06	03	03	08
Category	-07	-06	01	-01	04	-10	-16	-17	-11	-10	-05	-02	-28	-05	-11	-02	03	-16	-03	-10	-01
TPT Total Time	04	08	10	09	11	14	11	02	03	06	10	06	-02	09	07	05	14	-06	01	10	00
Memory	-02	02	15	-07	-08	-07	00	03	-10	-12	-09	-03	00	-07	-10	-11	08	-02	-05	09	-18
Location	00	08	11	09	07	14	14	13	04	08	13	-05	-06	05	06	13	13	-02	-02	00	02
TACTUAL																					
Finger Agn. D	-01	02	-11	05	09	16	19	17	14	13	10	11	07	05	09	05	14	05	06	00	05
N	12	12	04	22	-25	06	15	16	19	19	22	18	04	19	20	14	29	05	10	02	05
Tac. Form D	-10	-14	-09	-12	-12	-03	01	-05	-06	12	-18	09	-01	-03	01	-17	-05	-14	-02	-03	-04
N	-15	-11	-01	-12	-13	10	11	-02	-04	-14	-13	08	-08	-04	-05	·-05	-00	-13	03	-06	-06
PERCEPTUAL-MOTOR																					
Pegboard D	11	12	02	11	12	23	18	27	18	18	11	14	19	14	19	09	13	10	32	26	15
N	-13	-13	-12	-08	-08	07	04	06	-01	-01	-05	04	00	-10	00	-09	-05	-04	07	-03	04
Maze D	-01	02	03	-02	04	02	06	06	00	-05	-08	-09	07	-03	00	-03	03	-01	13	10	01
N	-13	-14	-01	-10	-10	-01	-09	-06	-07	-08	-15	-08	05	-03	-08	-10	-01	-02	00	-02	00
Steadiness D	-06	-17	-26	-13	-12	08	05	00	-02	-02	-12	05	07	-02	01	-07	01	-05	06	03	05
N	01	-11	-21	-05	-05	03	03	-02	-01	00	-05	07	07	-05	06	02	07	03	12	06	04
MOTOR																					
Finger Tap D	07	08	-10	06	04	06	12	08	08	05	-04	04	05	14	17	08	12	01	07	-02	00
N	04	-01	-03	08	08	13	17	17	04	-03	-06	06	12	13	09	13	10	08	01	02	11
Foot Tap D	07	-02	-20	04	06	00	01	-04	-07	02	-04	03	04	-01	07	09	-02	03	-09	03	15
N	-17	-22	-25	-13	-12	-12	-04	-12	-19	-13	-19	-16	-13	-12	-02	-01	-17	-01	-15	-04	00
Dynamom. D	19	12	-08	14	17	17	09	11	11	12	11	23	-06	06	09	07	19	-03	09	04	01
N	14	10	-01	11	12	15	13	08	12	18	13	25	-06	06	07	-01	13	-06	05	00	06

	ORAL READING									VISUAL SCANNING										COMP-SPELL			
	UC	LC	UL	LS	WR	2W	7W	WS	SY	RE	FI	NU	LE	2L	LS	WD	SY	CC	UW	SC	S1	S2	S3
DURRELL ACHIEVEMENT TEST																							
Oral Reading	74	73	68	71	85	90	89	89	63	23	36	36	33	42	36	54	56	35	54	87	76	69	62
Silent Reading	69	68	62	64	81	87	85	84	55	22	37	37	33	39	33	53	52	36	51	89	72	67	58
Listen. Comp.	24	28	25	22	33	37	35	33	28	02	14	12	14	02	07	15	16	05	13	43	31	24	32
Word Recog.	71	67	64	63	83	85	80	84	64	20	38	35	37	43	37	58	58	32	55	90	75	74	66
Word Attack	73	67	64	64	79	83	76	82	60	21	36	35	37	42	37	55	55	30	54	89	74	72	68
READING—RELATED SKILLS																							
VISUAL MATCHING																							
Numbers	62	64	54	61	44	46	40	44	26	51	58	60	55	45	47	31	32	34	54	45	37	35	30
Letters	61	66	55	61	47	47	45	45	29	49	51	54	55	48	51	44	34	23	54	48	41	43	36
U & L Case Let.	67	66	60	64	50	51	48	49	38	43	51	48	49	53	42	43	39	31	56	56	52	45	47
CVC Words	66	67	58	65	62	65	61	63	38	41	57	58	61	61	59	56	53	37	64	65	52	44	42
CVCC Words	60	61	48	57	62	65	61	65	40	37	53	52	63	57	53	63	55	31	71	66	65	51	48
CVC Syllables	58	57	49	52	58	72	68	73	43	30	54	54	58	63	63	69	61	35	70	77	47	64	51
CCC String	48	54	44	53	47	53	49	51	14	25	57	56	56	55	56	42	37	30	53	52	34	44	34
AUDITORY–VISUAL MATCHING																							
Letters	51	55	47	48	46	48	42	44	28	26	42	37	40	26	32	24	30	07	38	49	34	33	32
CVC Words	58	59	46	60	61	69	63	72	35	24	47	41	48	44	41	51	49	27	55	73	62	55	54
CVCC Words	63	61	57	60	71	76	73	74	46	23	44	39	40	48	42	57	58	23	56	80	66	60	50
CV Syllables	65	62	56	65	70	71	69	70	56	32	38	32	32	34	31	47	42	24	47	72	60	67	56
CCV Syllables	53	52	47	55	65	69	66	73	48	28	43	41	39	48	42	47	54	28	52	71	65	62	62
CVC Syllables	44	49	42	48	49	46	49	51	47	29	31	23	29	28	26	39	35	27	38	47	49	51	49
CVCC Syllables	60	63	61	58	66	70	63	68	46	36	49	39	43	43	34	40	47	35	55	64	49	53	46
ORAL READING & NAMING																							
Color Naming	53	55	47	41	30	35	34	33	30	24	30	34	34	36	31	34	24	24	34	43	41	33	25
Picture Naming	56	46	51	39	32	37	32	31	21	09	13	13	12	20	09	32	09	24	17	38	29	23	25
Upper-Case Let.	X	91	85	83	74	76	73	73	51	40	42	40	43	48	33	44	35	33	57	74	29	56	54
Lower-Case Let.	91	X	85	82	72	74	73	74	49	37	43	42	44	46	38	45	34	33	58	68	55	50	55
U & L Case Let.	85	85	X	71	68	68	67	65	52	34	44	36	40	49	35	40	34	34	49	66	51	47	45
Let. in Sent.	83	82	77	X	71	69	69	70	52	36	43	43	43	43	31	34	30	34	45	67	61	53	62
Random Words	74	72	68	71	X	93	92	90	65	24	39	32	37	39	34	44	45	31	52	83	66	65	60
2 Word Phrases	76	74	68	69	93	X	93	94	61	27	40	33	35	42	38	53	53	32	57	88	73	67	62
7 Word Phrases	73	73	67	69	92	93	X	92	65	26	40	29	33	43	33	50	50	32	52	83	67	66	57
Sentences	73	74	65	70	90	94	92	X	62	27	39	42	40	42	35	55	53	33	54	84	73	68	68
Nonsense Syl.	51	49	52	52	65	61	65	62	X	21	25	14	21	29	21	32	43	24	37	59	58	59	60
VISUAL SCANNING																							
Rectangle	40	37	34	36	24	27	26	27	21	X	43	45	42	38	31	19	22	17	26	18	14	24	16
Figure	42	43	44	43	39	40	40	39	25	43	X	74	69	74	62	45	47	49	57	45	28	39	25
Number	40	42	36	43	32	33	29	42	14	45	74	X	73	67	60	44	37	41	52	41	30	38	26
Letter	43	44	40	43	37	35	33	40	21	42	69	73	X	63	65	43	41	35	55	44	31	39	31
2 Letters	48	46	49	43	39	42	43	42	29	38	74	67	63	X	74	59	55	48	69	50	33	43	28
Letter in Syl.	33	38	35	31	34	38	33	35	21	31	62	60	65	74	X	60	59	41	58	42	27	45	23
Word	44	45	40	34	44	53	50	55	32	19	45	44	43	59	60	X	71	53	65	58	50	59	43
Syllable	35	34	34	30	45	53	50	53	43	22	47	37	41	55	59	71	X	54	69	52	50	61	43
CCCC String	33	33	34	34	31	32	32	33	24	17	49	41	35	48	41	53	54	X	54	34	36	38	32
Unspaced Word	57	58	49	35	52	57	52	54	37	26	57	52	55	69	58	65	69	54	X	56	44	52	44
COMPREHENSION & SPELLING																							
Sentence Comp.	74	68	66	67	83	88	83	84	59	18	45	41	44	50	42	58	52	34	56	X	80	69	62
Oral Spelling	29	55	51	61	66	73	67	73	58	14	28	30	31	33	27	50	50	36	44	80	X	72	73
Written Spell.	56	50	47	53	65	67	66	68	59	24	39	38	40	42	45	59	61	38	52	69	72	X	60
Spelled-Out Wd.	54	55	45	62	60	62	57	68	60	16	25	26	31	28	23	43	43	32	44	62	73	60	X
LANGUAGE TESTS																							
PHONEMIC SEGMENTATION & BLENDING																							
Sound Del. – Syl.	42	39	38	35	43	46	39	42	58	12	10	06	03	11	08	13	27	10	17	42	49	43	44
Wd.	56	54	53	50	59	69	63	65	55	19	29	17	18	37	31	41	49	27	38	66	64	57	55
Pig Latin	24	26	29	26	27	32	29	36	39	01	26	20	18	24	27	48	37	31	37	41	46	48	43
Ubby Dubby	48	46	50	40	56	61	57	62	57	08	36	23	29	46	35	45	55	33	43	69	60	55	53
Rhyming	33	27	24	28	19	22	20	26	11	16	11	14	18	06	05	27	05	04	18	27	19	20	22
SERIAL NAMING																							
Count 20	-01	-01	-06	01	-27	-28	-27	-28	-24	10	07	-06	03	08	02	-13	-23	00	-02	-25	-24	-25	-20
Name Days	43	42	36	37	34	30	32	35	22	11	27	21	26	26	11	24	14	16	22	41	42	41	30
Name Months	39	31	28	37	40	40	39	40	22	13	35	29	23	31	19	29	23	29	34	50	46	43	36

	ORAL READING	VISUAL SCANNING	COMP-SPELL
	UC LC UL LS WR 2W 7W WS SY	RE FI NU LE 2L LS WD SY CC UW	SC S1 S2 S3

LANGUAGE TESTS (CONTINUED)

ORAL REPETITION

Unrelated Words	27 24 17 14 09 17 13 15 05	06 09 15 00 08 06 15 04 13 11	15 15 09 13
Randomized Wds.	24 28 24 18 23 27 29 31 22	11 02 06 07 10 14 27 13 15 11	22 24 18 34
Meaningless Sent.	33 28 23 28 24 27 23 27 22	21 09 10 08 07 04 23 20 17 09	28 28 27 27
Sentences	31 31 20 24 24 26 23 25 18	10 09 17 23 12 12 29 15 19 15	25 23 28 32

TOKEN TEST

A	31 29 37 21 09 06 09 04 10	20 18 19 27 30 20 04 08 18 24	07 03 03-02
B	14 07 12 07-03 03 01 00 04	33 20 20 22 19 21 04 05-03 13	03-02 02-10
C	41 37 40 41 31 38 37 35 20	26 27 20 23 28 33 38 27 20 22	40 37 41 28
D	29 30 25 34 27 27 29 26 26	19 60 51 45 57 38 34 26 32 38	33 28 28 26
E	50 50 50 49 29 32 31 33 21	21 37 28 33 40 35 38 20 25 35	41 34 31 33
F	27 34 25 23 22 20 19 21 21	01 11-02 08 21 18 27 18 22 27	16 12 10 32

SYNTACTIC-SEMANTIC

Devel. Sent.	03 05 06 02 08 10 14 19 08	-14 03-04 04 08-05 23 13 06 14	17 21 20 16
Morphophonemics	14 13 02 11 10 14 12 22 16	-12 02 07 06-04 02 22 01 12 07	28 29 20 18
Ask & Tell	14 13 11 14 02 07 11 08 12	08 21 23 11 26 11 15 08 15 17	14 21 17 12
Semantic Fields	22 25 15 25 17 26 23 31 15	14 16 21 16 19 14 13 26 05 08	31 35 24 26

NEUROPSYCHOLOGY TESTS

WISC VERBAL

Information	18 19 16 19 23 26 29 32 18	10 18 22 20 14 05 24 16 22 13	28 27 32 32
Comprehension	25 25 15 23 24 24 22 26 11	23 13 18 08 06 00 08-03 08 05	20 11 23 25
Digit Span	20 15 17 19 05 09 03 10 04	03 08-02 12 10 01 20 12 21 11	11 16 10 20
Arithmetic	26 29 25 24 35 36 33 34 28	15 12 14 13 15 11 32 28 32 22	31 28 32 39
Similarities	32 26 21 31 33 36 38 38 30	-04-07 01-01-01-12 13 03 07 13	33 29 35 37
Vocabulary	12 10 08 10 13 16 18 22 15	-01-03-01-05-12-17 06-07 00-10	19 11 08 14

WISC PERFORMANCE

Pic. Arrangement	06 10-00 08 00 06 04 03 05	16 05 06-06-07-05 01-06 02-09	09 17 21 09
Pic. Completion	-09-03-12-08 08 03 03 10-14	-03 05 16 10-05 03 04-03-02-05	12 04 08 08
Block Design	11 11 04 10 12 13 01 12-03	-03 16 20 13 17 24 16 08 16 24	08 05 18 27
Object Assembly	20 18 10 13 21 20 12 20 03	-01 05 10 19 14 11 11 00 13 21	22 19 09 30
Coding	42 48 34 40 30 31 34 33 21	28 33 34 27 34 20 25 12 26 32	25 20 27 26
Maze	06 06-01 03 01 07-02 03 04	07 08-06-01 02 02 05 06 02 08	16 14 18-00
Peabody Vocab.	10 10 04 09 12 14 12 20 13	-09-08 01-04-07-08 12 03 05 00	21 20 17 23
Knox Cube	10 12 06 00-08-06-08-07-03	-10-14-11-04-11-16 10-05-04 09	-02-03-08 12
Prog. Matrices	01 05 00 01 15 13 07 16 15	-07 08 02 21 03 14 18 19 10 23	16 14 24 31
Devel. Draw.	-25-23-26-22-24-25-30-23-18	-07-31-25-22-27-22-29-25-28-22	-35-33-29-09
R-L Discrim.	01 05 01 04 10 17 16 14 02	-12-03 02-08-04 01 09 04 00 04	10 08 00 07
Category	-07-06-07-08-06-03-01 01-02	-15-04 07 04-02-05 02 08 10-00	-02-07 04 07
TPT Total Time	09 07-03-01 04 10 05 16-02	16 19 19 18 12 16 18 12 19 08	07 11 17 11
Memory	-18-10-12-15-14-12-06-11-06	-09-04-07-12-04-09-11-09-17-05	-10-04-08-11
Location	00-06-05-11 08 07 07 04 18	-05 05 14 07 09 13 14 07 10 15	09 17 20 23

TACTUAL

Finger Agn. D	14 08 08 04 05 01-03-01 01	08 14 15 18 12 17 16 12 15 21	10 05 06 13
N	09 06 09 07 09 11 05 11 07	-04 05 07 09 15 16 26 17 08 15	17 21 22 22
Tac. Form D	-09-02 01-01-16-09-13-13-20	-02 06 01-02 00 05-05-01-08-11	-12-08-05-08
N	-06-01 00 00-05-05-10-10-11	06 08 08 00-04 03-16-08-03-09	-13-14-05-02

PERCEPTUAL-MOTOR

Pegboard D	27 24 26 15 18 17 10 17 17	22-20 21 27 13 01 05 00 09 13	18 15 17 18
N	08 06 08 00-01-04-08-07-01	06 09 07 12 10-03-03-10 00 07	-02-06-04-03
Maze D	13 12 11 02 06 07 03 06 06	11 00-02 01-07-13-07 02 01 11	-02-03 01 07
N	05 02 00 01-04-03-06-06 09	-09 03-18 03-11-13-17 00 06 06	-11-10-05 13
Steadiness D	11 16 14 21-05-06 01-01 03	18 09 00 12-02-10-21-06-11-04	-14-07-04 01
N	14 18 15 21 07 07 11 08 14	05 05-08 02-01-07-16-07-11-02	-05 00 07 09

MOTOR

Finger Tap D	06 07 06 16 09 04 09 09-13	08-02 09 06-04-14-03-04-16-04	03 02 01-06
N	11 12 11 12 04-02 01 02-16	06-07 01-01-09-08-07 00-07-04	00 02-05-00
Foot Tap D	18 15 16 15 15 09 11 11 07	29 01 01 07 00-07-07-11-12-01	-01-08-01 05
N	-05-06-08-11-08-14-13-12-02	03-18-18-11-18-20-14-14-22-11	-21-21-18-13
Dynamom. D	13 12 11 18 16 12 11 20 02	05 03 18 16 02 07 07 07 15 03	12 24 17 20
N	10 11 09 16 11 11 07 15-07	03 09 25 21 08 11 15 11 19 14	10 22 08 25

LANGUAGE TESTS

	PHON SEG-BLEND					SER NAM			ORAL REPET				TOKEN TEST						SYN-SEM			
	DS	DW	PL	UD	RH	NU	DA	MO	UW	RW	AS	MS	A	B	C	D	E	F	MO	DS	SF	AT
DURRELL ACHIEVEMENT																						
Oral Reading	46	66	38	60	24	-30	36	39	22	33	32	27	03	00	39	28	34	20	19	13	32	09
Silent Reading	37	64	36	58	25	-30	39	41	23	32	32	30	01	04	41	29	34	18	26	19	31	14
Listen. Comp.	17	45	21	34-03		-14	27	11	26	34	26	38	-02	06	09	08	07	06	20	03	11	07
Word Recog.	46	71	44	68	22	-30	42	37	20	30	35	30	01-01		39	30	37	15	24	16	27	15
Word Attack	49	70	45	69	28	-29	44	39	23	32	39	33	02	03	44	29	39	18	29	21	31	11
READING-RELATED SKILLS																						
VISUAL MATCHING																						
Numbers	21	31	22	33	37	17	38	31	24	11	25	23	33	32	35	35	42	15	20	06	29	24
Letters	24	34	26	29	38	18	40	29	15	16	22	23	29	22	38	38	45	24	20	11	17	21
U & L Case Let.	30	44	34	50	36	12	45	44	22	16	30	33	35	21	39	40	44	24	23	20	30	27
CVC Words	23	49	31	50	31	02	39	35	15	11	16	18	20	20	38	40	37	18	18	20	20	18
CVCC Words	11	41	30	45	28	-05	33	35	09	11	12	16	10	17	34	41	39	17	15	20	15	10
CVC Syllables	27	51	39	61	32	-14	40	47	22	25	27	22	00	12	41	49	38	14	20	23	20	19
CCC String	08	39	20	36	11	02	37	32	16	15	12	17	07	14	33	36	33	05	17	05	25	04
AUDITORY-VISUAL MATCHING																						
Letters	16	32	17	30	30	-02	24	23	13	04	03	04	20	21	24	31	31	20	13	03	23	18
CVC Words	25	54	33	58	38	-13	34	37	14	19	30	26	07	16	40	37	47	10	27	25	20	17
CVCC Words	19	54	30	55	24	-17	41	39	07	16	24	17	12	10	42	36	43	14	10	13	28	17
CV Syllables	43	54	32	52	31	-11	50	37	14	29	41	32	11	07	53	26	45	22	30	28	24	17
CCV Syllables	30	68	36	56	07	-12	32	34	22	28	22	20	12	11	27	29	31	17	13	09	30	14
CVC Syllables	27	50	26	40	28	-05	37	43	09	10	25	32	13	14	31	31	35	25	24	19	17	12
CVCC Syllables	25	02	18	52	14	-03	37	38	23	16	27	23	26	17	30	37	40	19	10	13	31	16
ORAL READING & NAMING																						
Color Naming	28	38	16	28	18	10	37	27	16	06	23	26	33	21	32	28	38	19	09	10	27	36
Picture Naming	19	34	08	30	23	-03	26	21	10	04	21	22	21-08		14	06	27	03	-01-04		00	11
Upper-Case Let.	42	56	24	48	33	-01	43	39	27	24	33	31	31	14	41	29	50	27	14	03	22	14
Lower-Case Let.	39	54	26	46	27	-01	42	31	24	.28	28	31	29	07	37	30	50	34	13	05	25	13
U & L Case Let.	38	53	29	50	24	-06	36	28	17	24	23	20	37	12	40	25	49	25	02	06	15	11
Let. in Sent.	35	50	26	40	28	01	37	37	14	18	28	24	21	07	41	34	49	25	11	02	25	14
Random Words	43	59	27	56	19	-27	34	40	09	23	24	24	09-03		31	27	29	22	10	08	17	02
2 Word Phrases	46	69	32	61	22	-28	30	40	17	27	27	26	06	03	38	27	32	20	14	10	26	07
7 Word Phrases	39	63	29	57	20	-27	32	39	13	29	23	23	09	01	37	29	31	19	12	14	23	11
Sentences	42	65	36	62	26	-28	35	40	15	31	27	24	04	00	35	26	33	21	22	19	31	08
Nonsense Syl.	58	65	39	57	11	-24	22	22	05	22	22	18	10	04	20	26	21	21	16	08	15	12
VISUAL SCANNING																						
Rectangle	12	19	01	08	16	10	11	13	06	11	21	10	20	33	26	20	21	01	-13-14		14	08
Figure	10	29	26	36	11	07	27	35	09	02	09	09	18	20	27	60	37	11	02	03	16	21
Number	06	17	20	23	14	-06	21	29	15	06	10	17	19	20	20	51	28-02		07-04		21	23
Letter	03	18	18	29	18	03	26	23	00	07	08	23	27	22	23	45	33	08	06	04	16	11
2 Letters	11	37	24	46	06	08	26	31	08	10	07	12	30	19	28	57	40	21	-04	08	19	26
Letter in Syl.	08	31	27	35	05	02	21	19	06	14	04	12	20	21	33	38	25	18	02-05		14	11
Word	13	41	48	45	27	-13	24	39	15	27	23	29	04	04	38	34	38	27	22	23	13	15
Syllable	27	49	37	55	05	-23	14	23	04	13	20	15	08	05	27	26	20	18	07	13	26	08
CCCC String	10	27	31	33	04	00	16	29	13	15	17	19	18-03		20	32	25	22	12	06	05	15
Unspaced Word	17	38	37	43	18	-02	22	34	11	11	09	15	24	13	22	38	35	27	07	14	08	17
COMPREHENSION & SPELLING																						
Sentence Comp.	42	66	41	69	27	-25	41	50	15	22	28	25	07	03	40	33	41	16	28	17	31	14
Oral Spelling	49	64	46	60	19	-24	42	46	15	24	28	23	03-01		37	28	34	12	29	21	35	21
Written Spell.	43	57	48	55	20	-25	41	43	09	18	27	28	03	01	41	28	31	10	20	20	24	18
Spelled-Out Wd.	44	55	43	53	22	-20	30	36	13	34	27	32	-02-10		28	26	33	32	18	16	26	12
LANGUAGE TESTS																						
PHONEMIC SEGMENTATION & BLENDING																						
Sound Del. - Syl.	X	48	35	46	16	-21	17	09	23	26	38	30	-02-04		24	06	14	15	17	15	17	11
Wd.	48	X	29	62	00	-18	33	24	19	24	22	20	20	01	34	24	33	20	13	02	31	10
Pig Latin	35	29	X	49	29	-31	22	24	23	17	21	20	-06	04	16	23	27	14	35	45	08	12
Ubby Dubby	46	62	49	X	11	-31	32	35	17	18	25	28	15	09	30	36	29	27	19	38	28	20
Rhyming	16	00	29	11	X	-04	25	42	15	08	34	25	-01	12	34	20	36	10	44	24	13	15
SERIAL NAMING																						
Count 20	-21-18		-31	-31-04		X	11	02	09	04-09-01			16	16	12	06	10	25	-01	08-06		13
Name Days	17	33	22	32	25	11	X	50	17	17	25	24	10	07	31	25	41	05	31	16	31	15
Name Months	09	24	24	35	42	02	50	X	11	00	19	22	06	10	42	36	30	10	33	13	24	28

LANGUAGE TESTS

	PHON SEG-BLEND					SER NAM			ORAL REPET				TOKEN TEST						SYN-SEM			
	DS	DW	PL	UD	RH	NU	DA	MO	UW	RW	AS	MS	A	B	C	D	E	F	MO	DS	SF	AT

LANGUAGE TESTS (CONTINUED)

ORAL REPETITION

	DS	DW	PL	UD	RH	NU	DA	MO	UW	RW	AS	MS	A	B	C	D	E	F	MO	DS	SF	AT
Unrelated Words	23	19	24	17	15	09	17	11	X	61	58	54	-04	07	17	23	25	23	31	15	09	23
Randomized Wds.	26	24	17	18	08	04	17	00	61	X	59	55	-09	-01	23	14	18	37	29	17	00	13
Meaningless Sent.	28	22	21	25	34	-09	25	19	58	59	X	70	-10	-06	28	19	33	25	29	18	17	11
Sentences	30	20	20	28	25	-02	23	20	54	55	70	X	-02	02	25	21	28	27	27	23	13	10

TOKEN TEST

	DS	DW	PL	UD	RH	NU	DA	MO	UW	RW	AS	MS	A	B	C	D	E	F	MO	DS	SF	AT
A	-02	20	-06	15	-02	16	10	06	-04	-09	-10	-02	X	19	14	15	27	17	-09	-01	17	32
B	-05	02	04	09	12	16	07	10	07	-01	-06	02	19	X	32	26	27	04	-02	06	19	10
C	24	34	16	30	34	12	31	42	17	23	28	25	14	32	X	36	47	31	15	18	28	36
D	06	24	23	36	20	06	25	36	23	14	19	21	15	26	36	X	55	31	06	25	18	51
E	13	33	27	29	36	10	41	30	25	18	33	28	27	27	47	55	X	31	09	28	18	37
F	15	20	14	27	10	25	05	10	23	37	25	27	17	04	31	31	31	X	11	20	12	21

SYNTACTIC-SEMANTIC

	DS	DW	PL	UD	RH	NU	DA	MO	UW	RW	AS	MS	A	B	C	D	E	F	MO	DS	SF	AT
Devel. Sent.	15	02	45	38	24	-08	16	13	15	17	18	23	-01	06	18	25	28	20	X	34	34	07
Morphophonemics	17	13	35	19	44	-01	31	33	31	29	29	27	-09	-02	15	06	09	11	34	X	16	20
Ask & Tell	11	10	12	20	15	13	15	28	23	13	11	10	32	10	36	51	37	21	34	16	X	28
Semantic Fields	17	31	08	29	13	-06	31	24	09	00	17	13	17	19	28	18	18	12	07	20	28	X

NEUROPSYCHOLOGY TESTS

WISC VERBAL

	DS	DW	PL	UD	RH	NU	DA	MO	UW	RW	AS	MS	A	B	C	D	E	F	MO	DS	SF	AT
Information	08	13	25	29	28	-15	26	26	28	28	26	36	-04	21	26	27	30	08	34	31	33	32
Comprehension	16	07	09	19	35	-12	14	21	26	19	29	32	01	06	21	18	14	07	20	30	13	20
Digit Span	10	08	27	11	23	06	18	16	26	20	32	26	-09	-03	05	05	27	04	10	11	-04	04
Arithmetic	22	25	43	38	14	-25	28	20	24	28	29	32	06	00	18	17	22	34	33	22	17	30
Similarities	31	23	22	33	32	-20	19	22	22	23	25	35	-09	08	18	07	12	14	33	34	21	33
Vocabulary	12	03	16	20	26	-21	06	11	24	19	30	31	-11	-03	05	01	02	-03	26	40	06	24

WISC PERFORMANCE

	DS	DW	PL	UD	RH	NU	DA	MO	UW	RW	AS	MS	A	B	C	D	E	F	MO	DS	SF	AT
Pic. Arrangement	15	12	04	-01	-04	-05	02	-00	04	-01	04	08	-08	03	14	-04	06	-02	-03	13	16	31
Pic. Completion	-03	-06	16	03	-01	-25	10	-10	01	01	01	04	-01	-16	-09	-15	-05	-11	12	13	04	14
Block Design	11	11	22	13	04	11	11	06	23	26	14	16	11	-03	13	05	19	24	13	18	16	08
Object Assembly	20	11	17	17	02	-07	01	03	-03	06	-01	10	09	-12	07	-02	10	08	15	12	03	00
Coding	25	18	18	17	04	-07	23	12	06	08	09	15	31	04	14	31	28	16	16	11	32	18
Maze	00	16	09	14	05	02	08	15	-04	04	04	-11	04	-06	03	03	00	-06	01	12	11	03
Peabody Vocab.	19	16	22	28	23	-06	25	22	35	28	33	46	-05	01	10	01	11	17	25	48	17	32
Knox Cube	-19	-03	07	-01	06	-04	-10	-07	05	-09	-10	-09	13	-07	-12	06	16	05	17	-09	10	-13
Prog. Matrices	10	09	28	17	-01	-11	13	-02	03	07	02	09	03	-07	04	-00	05	04	24	20	09	11
Devel. Draw.	-22	-25	-26	-33	-20	18	-30	-41	-14	-04	-13	-18	-11	-24	-29	-19	-38	-18	-31	-17	-19	-12
R-L Discrim.	-08	07	08	02	06	-16	-03	-04	05	03	04	04	-04	-11	-19	-11	01	05	-01	05	-13	10
Category	-04	-08	12	02	-01	-13	-09	-14	18	31	27	16	-01	-13	-17	04	11	04	11	12	01	-07
TPT Total Time	21	06	11	05	10	04	20	09	27	32	29	28	-09	12	20	07	15	17	00	-20	10	27
Memory	-06	03	03	-02	-16	-01	01	-06	05	03	-04	-01	06	12	-04	-03	-01	05	13	11	11	16
Location	15	09	15	16	07	-17	16	14	12	14	01	10	11	02	21	00	08	04	02	15	27	08

TACTUAL

		DS	DW	PL	UD	RH	NU	DA	MO	UW	RW	AS	MS	A	B	C	D	E	F	MO	DS	SF	AT
Finger Agn.	D	-09	-03	06	07	03	03	01	03	10	03	-03	-03	25	11	-06	01	14	09	-03	09	-05	-07
	N	02	07	25	16	05	07	15	07	22	28	17	06	05	00	08	02	11	01	17	19	06	02
Tac. Form	D	-12	04	00	-07	-10	-08	00	-08	-11	-24	-13	-16	07	08	09	-01	09	-09	-29	-16	-11	21
	N	03	02	02	-03	-07	-01	04	-18	-04	-14	-08	-08	02	05	06	-07	06	-07	-26	-15	-07	01

PERCEPTUAL-MOTOR

		DS	DW	PL	UD	RH	NU	DA	MO	UW	RW	AS	MS	A	B	C	D	E	F	MO	DS	SF	AT
Pegboard	D	03	09	11	15	11	04	12	10	09	-04	12	16	22	12	-04	12	18	00	-06	08	-04	08
	N	-08	-06	06	-05	-01	05	06	-05	04	-07	02	11	09	-14	-24	08	08	-05	-17	-05	-14	-10
Maze	D	15	10	-03	-10	-04	10	-13	-19	12	09	14	10	09	-23	-17	-13	-06	02	-04	-12	-01	-14
	N	14	08	06	-03	02	07	-02	15	06	01	03	05	01	-23	-17	-03	-05	03	-16	-15	-07	-12
Steadiness	D	02	-14	-12	-18	11	15	-08	-10	-15	-09	06	-07	07	06	00	06	14	-09	-15	-28	00	04
	N	17	00	02	-06	06	02	-01	-11	-05	-08	03	-09	-01	-06	-06	05	15	-03	-19	-29	-05	-03

MOTOR

		DS	DW	PL	UD	RH	NU	DA	MO	UW	RW	AS	MS	A	B	C	D	E	F	MO	DS	SF	AT
Finger Tap	D	-13	-09	-02	-18	17	04	04	00	-08	-12	14	05	04	-11	00	-01	04	-09	05	09	03	06
	N	02	-06	14	-03	22	05	16	03	-01	-07	25	07	03	-01	06	-07	14	-01	03	10	04	08
Foot Tap	D	08	-14	-12	-14	17	-15	-06	-12	-15	-04	14	-04	01	-07	-16	01	02	-14	-19	-13	01	02
	N	02	-27	-16	-14	14	-10	03	-13	02	02	15	02	-10	-10	-17	-11	-02	-10	-09	05	-05	-17
Dynamom.	D	11	-02	21	02	05	-17	12	09	02	02	09	10	-02	-02	01	-11	03	-12	15	06	00	22
	N	02	-06	21	-01	-05	-15	06	09	-01	-01	-03	08	-08	-12	-08	-06	02	-11	09	-03	-01	10

	IN CO DS AR SI VO	PA PC BD OA CO MA	PV KN PM DR RL CA TT TM TL
	WISC VERBAL	WISC PERFORMANCE	

DURRELL ACHIEVEMENT TEST

Oral Reading	35 20 08 35 37 19	06 03 06 07 30-01	17-05 05-34 11-07 04-02 00
Silent Reading	35 21 04 37 37 19	12 11 05 11 26-04	21-02 08-38 10-06 08 02 08
Listen. Comp.	33 05-10 22 21 18	08 11 00-01 05-05	34-00 18-37 01 01 10 17 11
Word Recog.	33 25 10 34 38 20	06 10 14 19 23 07	20-02 21-30 06-01 09-07 09
Word Attack	35 31 14 36 41 24	06 10 19 22 26 11	23 01 20-30 04 04 11-08 07

READING-RELATED SKILLS

VISUAL MATCHING

Numbers	15 13 04 27 11-02	09 00 25 20 31 12	13 04 01-22-02-16 11-00 14
Letters	16 21 09 25 12 05	12-02 21 14 29 09	14-01 09-25-01-10 14-07 14
U & L Case Let.	22 21 12 33 22 08	03-05 19 19 28 20	21 08 10-21 02-17 02 03 13
CVC Words	22 14 06 26 18 02	-03 00 21 18 31 14	12 05 14-31 00-11 03-10 04
CVCC Words	16 13 05 17 15 03	-03 02 16 19 28 06	05 11 16-30-04-10 06-12 08
CVC Syllables	21 13 04 21 16-00	-05 04 19 17 25 09	07 02 19-35 00-05 10-09 13
CCC String	16 09 06 19 08-06	-01 10 22 14 25 13	00-11 11-17 10-02 06-03-05

AUDITORY-VISUAL MATCHING

Letters	14 16-03 15 05 01	17-01 13 07 25 13	00 11 15-16-04-28-02 00-06
CVC Words	27 23 11 17 28 13	03 09 18 20 24 12	17 02 20-31 11-05 09-07 05
CVCC Words	26 11 08 28 20 08	06 10 13 10 22 10	15 05 20-21 10-11 07-10 06
CV Syllables	27 33 11 37 39 20	12 11 20 14 32 07	25-04 24-24 00-02 05-11 13
CCV Syllables	33 14 11 26 26 10	06 14 22 16 26 06	16-09 33-11 09 03 14-08 13
CVC Syllables	30 22 15 27 22 11	13 06-05-07 27 06	26-07 14-24-06-16-06-02-02
CVCC Syllables	30 19 14 28 20 09	08-05 09 07 23 15	26-01 15-23 03-03-01-05-02

ORAL READING & NAMING

Color Naming	22 08 11 18 10 05	12-01-01 05 43-00	07 14 02-30 03-10 10 09-00
Picture Naming	06 00 14 10 16 04	-06-09-03 00 20-15	05 10-19-32 38-01 00-18 02
Upper-Case Let.	18 25 20 26 32 12	06-09 11 20 42 06	10 10 01-25 01-07 09-18 00
Lower-Case Let.	19 25 15 29 26 10	10-03 11 18 48 06	10 12 05-23 05-06 07-10 06
U & L Case Let.	16 15 17 25 21 08	00-12 04 10 34-01	04 06 00-26 01-07-03-12-05
Let. in Sent.	19 23 19 24 31 10	08-08 10 13 40 03	09 00 01-22 04-08-01-15-11
Random Words	23 24 05 35 33 13	00 08 12 21 30 01	12-08 15-24 10-06 04-14 08
2 Word Phrases	26 24 09 36 36 16	06 03 13 20 31 07	14-06 13-25 17-03 10-12 07
7 Word Phrases	29 22 03 33 38 18	04 03 01 12 34-02	12-08 07-30 16-01 05-06 07
Sentences	32 26 10 34 38 22	03 10 12 20 33 03	20-07 16-23 14 01 16-11 04
Nonsense Syl.	18 11 04 28 30 15	05-14-03 03 21 04	13-03 15-18 02-02-02-06 18

VISUAL SCANNING

Rectangle	10 23 03 15-04-01	16-03-03-01 28 07	-09-10-07-07-12-15 16-09-05
Figure	18 13 08 12-07-03	05 05 16 05 33 08	-08-14 08-31-03-04 19-04 05
Number	22 18-02 14 01-01	06 16 20 10 34-05	01-11 02-25 02 07 19-07 14
Letter	20 08 12 13-01-05	-06 10 13 19 27-01	-04-04 21-22-08 04 18-12 07
2 Letters	14 06 10 15-01-12	-07-05 17 14 34 02	-07-11 03-27-04-02 12-04 09
Letter in Syl.	05 00 01 11-12-17	-05 03 24 11 20 02	-08-16 14-22 01-05 16-09 13
Word	24 08 20 32 13 06	01 04 16 11 25 05	12 10 18-29 09 02 18-11 14
Syllable	16-03 12 28 03-07	-06-03 08 00 12 06	03-05 19-25 04-08 12-09 07
CCCC String	22 08 21 32 07 00	02-02 16 13 26 02	05-04 10-28 00 10 19-17 10
Unspaced Word	13 05 11 22 13-10	-09-05 24 21 32 08	00 09 23-22 04 00 08-05 15

COMPREHENSION & SPELLING

Sentence Comp.	28 20 11 31 33 19	09 12 08 22 25 16	21-02 16-35 10-02 07-10 09
Oral Spelling	27 11 16 28 29 11	17 04 05 19 20 14	20-03 14-33 08-07 11-04 17
Written Spell.	32 23 10 32 35 08	21 08 18 09 27 18	17-08 24-29 00 04 17-08 20
Spelled-Out Wd.	32 25 20 39 37 14	09 08 27 30 26-00	23 12 31-09 07 07 11-11 23

LANGUAGE TESTS

PHONEMIC SEGMENTATION & BLENDING

Sound Del. - Syl.	08 16 10 22 31 12	15-03 11 20 25-00	19-19 10-22-08-04 21 06 15
Wd.	13 07 08 25 23 03	12-06 11 11 18 16	16-03 09-25 07-08 06 03 09
Pig Latin	25 09 27 43 22 16	04 16 22 17 18 09	22 07 28-26 08 12 11 03 15
Ubby Dubby	29 19 11 38 33 20	-01 03 13 17 17 14	28-01 17-33 02 02 05 02 16
Rhyming	28 35 23 14 32 26	-04-01 04 02 04 05	23 06-01-20 06-01 10 16 07

SERIAL NAMING

Count 20	-15-12 06-25-20-21	-05-25 11-07-07 02	-06-04-11 18-16-13 04-01-17
Name Days	26 14 18 28 19 06	02-10 11 01 23 08	25-10 13-30-03-09 20 01 16
Name Months	26 21 16 20 22 11	00-10 06 03 12 15	22-07-02-41-04-14 09-06 14

	IN	CO	DS	AR	SI	VO	PA	PC	BD	OA	CO	MA	PV	KN	PM	DR	RL	CA	TT	TM	TL
			WISC VERBAL						WISC PERFORMANCE												

LANGUAGE TESTS (CONTINUED)

ORAL REPETITION

	IN	CO	DS	AR	SI	VO	PA	PC	BD	OA	CO	MA	PV	KN	PM	DR	RL	CA	TT	TM	TL
Unrelated Words	28	26	26	24	22	24	04	01	23	-03	06	04	35	05	03	-14	05	18	27	05	12
Randomized Wds.	28	19	20	28	23	19	-01	01	26	06	08	04	28	-09	07	-04	03	31	32	03	14
Meaningless Sent.	26	29	32	29	25	30	04	01	14	-01	09	04	33	-10	02	-13	04	27	29	-04	01
Sentences	36	32	26	32	35	31	08	04	16	10	15	-11	46	-09	09	-18	04	16	28	-01	10

TOKEN TEST

	IN	CO	DS	AR	SI	VO	PA	PC	BD	OA	CO	MA	PV	KN	PM	DR	RL	CA	TT	TM	TL
A	-04	01	09	06	-09	11	-08	-01	11	09	31	04	-05	13	03	-11	-04	-01	-09	06	11
B	21	06	-03	00	08	-03	03	-16	-03	-12	04	-06	01	-07	-07	-24	-11	-13	12	12	02
C	26	21	05	18	18	05	14	-09	13	07	14	03	10	-12	04	-29	-19	-17	20	-04	21
D	27	18	05	17	07	01	-04	-15	-05	-02	31	03	01	06	00	-19	-11	04	07	-03	00
E	30	14	27	22	12	02	06	-05	19	10	28	00	11	16	05	-38	01	11	15	-01	08
F	08	07	04	34	14	-03	-02	-11	24	08	16	-06	17	05	04	-18	-05	-04	17	05	04

SYNTACTIC-SEMANTIC

	IN	CO	DS	AR	SI	VO	PA	PC	BD	OA	CO	MA	PV	KN	PM	DR	RL	CA	TT	TM	TL
Morphophonemics	31	30	11	22	34	40	13	13	18	12	11	12	48	-09	20	-17	05	12	20	-11	15
Devel. Sent.	34	20	10	33	33	26	-03	12	13	15	16	01	25	17	24	-31	-01	11	00	13	02
Semantic Fields	32	20	04	30	33	24	31	14	08	00	18	03	32	-13	11	-12	10	-07	27	16	08
Ask & Tell	33	13	-04	17	21	06	16	04	16	03	32	11	17	10	09	-19	-13	-01	10	11	27

NEUROPSYCHOLOGY TESTS

WISC VERBAL

	IN	CO	DS	AR	SI	VO	PA	PC	BD	OA	CO	MA	PV	KN	PM	DR	RL	CA	TT	TM	TL
Information	X	49	30	50	54	63	25	25	25	18	28	12	52	02	40	-15	-05	28	15	13	11
Comprehension	49	X	30	44	49	62	29	14	22	22	29	15	39	05	18	07	-06	25	05	05	-07
Digit Span	30	30	X	33	15	27	19	19	18	17	14	28	22	15	17	02	-11	13	10	10	-09
Arithmetic	50	44	33	X	34	38	23	23	35	27	24	22	45	21	40	06	09	17	17	27	10
Similarities	54	49	15	34	X	67	27	10	12	20	18	-03	59	-05	27	-01	08	18	26	18	20
Vocabulary	63	62	27	38	67	X	34	23	10	26	20	08	65	04	21	09	04	32	25	00	-01

WISC PERFORMANCE

	IN	CO	DS	AR	SI	VO	PA	PC	BD	OA	CO	MA	PV	KN	PM	DR	RL	CA	TT	TM	TL
Pic. Arrangement	25	29	19	23	27	34	X	29	13	20	17	24	40	-01	13	06	-14	-08	30	-04	18
Pic. Completion	25	14	19	23	10	23	29	X	33	34	08	06	27	05	27	-02	12	40	21	05	17
Block Design	25	22	18	35	12	10	13	33	X	53	19	41	23	-01	44	13	11	35	27	35	36
Object Assembly	18	22	17	27	20	26	20	34	53	X	29	33	19	09	48	-12	-05	29	17	17	14
Coding	28	29	14	24	18	20	17	08	19	29	X	08	-06	13	30	-03	-02	19	00	-02	-11
Maze	12	15	28	22	-03	08	24	06	41	33	08	X	15	18	20	22	-10	09	04	09	07

	IN	CO	DS	AR	SI	VO	PA	PC	BD	OA	CO	MA	PV	KN	PM	DR	RL	CA	TT	TM	TL
Peabody Vocab.	52	39	22	45	59	65	40	27	23	19	-06	15	X	-06	26	03	-03	16	34	17	22
Knox Cube	02	05	15	21	-05	04	-01	05	-01	09	13	18	-06	X	-04	-04	10	18	-31	-11	-14
Prog. Matrices	40	18	17	40	27	21	13	27	44	48	30	20	26	-04	X	27	-14	22	29	31	30
Devel. Draw.	-15	07	02	06	-01	09	06	-02	13	-12	-03	22	03	04	27	X	-07	13	17	11	-03
R-L Discrim.	-05	-06	-11	09	08	04	-14	12	11	-05	-02	-10	-03	10	-14	-07	X	16	15	-01	10
Category	28	25	13	17	18	32	-08	40	35	29	19	09	16	18	22	13	16	X	22	-06	19
TPT Total Time	15	10	17	26	25		30	21	27	17	00	04	34	-31	29	17	15	22	X	29	48
Memory	13	05	10	27	18	00	-04	05	35	17	-02	09	17	-11	31	11	-01	-06	29	X	53
Location	11	-07	-09	10	20	-01	18	17	36	14	-11	07	22	-14	30	-03	10	19	48	53	X

TACTUAL

		IN	CO	DS	AR	SI	VO	PA	PC	BD	OA	CO	MA	PV	KN	PM	DR	RL	CA	TT	TM	TL
Finger Agn.	D	05	15	24	22	-09	06	-05	21	28	30	13	28	01	27	32	13	04	30	12	16	16
	N	27	18	39	29	09	19	08	26	36	29	04	39	18	21	39	10	00	31	20	31	25
Tac. Form	D	07	08	11	15	-11	-01	14	06	11	10	04	07	-01	-09	-02	04	08	05	10	01	02
	N	11	06	06	13	-02	01	18	20	21	30	04	-03	09	-21	14	11	00	14	27	22	25

PERCEPTUAL-MOTOR

		IN	CO	DS	AR	SI	VO	PA	PC	BD	OA	CO	MA	PV	KN	PM	DR	RL	CA	TT	TM	TL
Pegboard	D	17	27	12	23	00	13	17	15	25	28	14	23	19	25	18	17	-07	14	02	-04	07
	N	-13	04	11	18	-25	-15	03	03	14	22	13	13	03	19	09	16	-02	11	-06	-11	-01
Maze	D	-13	-10	-07	00	-06	-04	12	08	15	22	-01	20	03	19	-18	33	12	11	20	-02	06
	N	-14	-14	14	04	-02	-09	07	-01	20	14	02	16	00	14	-30	21	-04	23	23	14	18
Steadiness	D	01	03	15	-18	-01	-04	06	-07	-01	-02	08	07	-15	-11	06	13	-15	-01	07	06	-16
	N	-02	01	18	-05	01	-09	05	-06	09	05	16	04	-10	-09	16	04	-09	-03	07	07	-08

MOTOR

		IN	CO	DS	AR	SI	VO	PA	PC	BD	OA	CO	MA	PV	KN	PM	DR	RL	CA	TT	TM	TL
Finger Tap	D	01	14	05	-06	13	10	-03	09	-10	-08	04	-15	05	-06	-01	20	14	09	01	-12	-06
	N	01	05	11	09	06	-02	-11	11	-11	-06	00	-17	06	-15	01	08	07	-01	00	-05	-13
Foot Tap	D	13	09	11	07	11	16	01	20	-08	-10	23	-16	-01	-03	09	26	01	16	22	02	00
	N	16	13	22	19	33	22	06	14	-02	-12	08	-11	17	00	03	25	06	22	38	17	22
Dynamom.	D	13	16	22	12	23	15	09	14	01	04	08	-05	09	-06	16	09	-17	14	25	26	13
	N	08	-01	20	09	15	09	05	16	06	17	13	-07	07	04	18	02	-07	17	28	25	21

	TACTUAL				PERCEPTUAL-MOTOR						MOTOR					
	FD	FN	TD	TN	PD	PN	MD	MN	SD	SN	FD	FN	fD	fN	DD	DN
DURRELL ACHIEVEMENT																
Oral Reading	-01	12	10	15	11	13	01	13	06	01	07	04	07	17	19	14
Silent Reading	02	12	14	11	12	13	02	14	17	11	08	01	02	22	12	10
List. Comp.	-11	04	09	01	02	12	03	01	26	21	-10	-03	-20	-25	-08	-01
Word Recog.	05	22	12	12	11	08	02	10	13	05	06	08	04	13	14	11
Word Attack	09	25	12	13	12	08	04	10	12	05	14	08	06	12	17	12
READING RELATED SKILLS																
VISUAL MATCHING																
Numbers	19	15	01	11	18	04	06	09	05	03	12	17	01	04	09	13
Letters	16	06	03	10	23	07	02	01	08	03	06	13	00	12	17	15
U & L Case Letters	17	16	05	02	27	06	06	06	00	02	08	17	04	12	11	08
CVC Words	14	19	06	04	18	01	00	07	02	01	08	04	07	19	11	12
CVCC Words	13	19	12	14	18	01	05	08	02	00	05	03	02	13	12	18
CVC Syllables	10	22	18	13	11	05	08	15	12	05	-04	-06	04	19	11	13
CCC String	11	18	09	08	14	04	09	08	05	07	04	06	03	16	23	25
AUDITORY-VISUAL MATCHING																
Letters	07	04	01	08	-19	00	07	05	07	07	05	12	04	13	06	06
CVC Words	05	19	03	04	-14	10	03	03	02	05	14	13	01	12	06	06
CVCC Words	09	20	01	05	-19	00	00	08	01	06	17	09	07	02	09	07
CV Syllables	05	14	17	05	-09	09	03	10	07	02	08	13	09	01	07	01
CCV Syllables	14	29	05	00	-13	05	03	01	01	07	12	10	02	17	19	13
CVC Syllables	05	05	14	13	-10	04	01	02	05	03	01	08	03	01	03	06
CVCC Syllables	06	10	02	03	-32	07	13	00	06	12	07	01	09	15	09	05
ORAL READING & NAMING																
Color Naming	00	02	03	06	26	03	10	02	03	06	-02	02	03	04	04	00
Picture Naming	-05	05	04	06	15	04	01	00	05	04	00	11	15	00	01	06
Upper-Case Letters	14	09	09	06	27	08	13	05	11	14	06	11	18	05	13	10
Lower-Case Letters	08	06	02	01	24	06	12	02	16	18	07	12	15	06	12	11
U & L Case Letters	08	09	01	00	26	08	11	00	14	15	06	11	16	08	11	09
Letters in Sent.	04	07	01	01	15	00	02	01	21	21	16	12	15	11	18	16
Random Words	05	09	16	05	18	01	06	04	05	07	09	04	15	08	16	11
2 Word Phrases	01	11	09	05	17	04	07	03	06	07	04	02	09	14	12	11
7 Word Phrases	-03	05	13	10	10	08	03	06	01	11	09	01	11	13	11	07
Sentences	-01	11	13	10	17	07	06	06	01	08	09	02	11	12	20	15
Nonsense Syll.	01	07	20	11	17	01	06	09	03	14	-13	-16	07	02	02	07
VISUAL SCANNING																
Rectangle	08	04	02	06	22	06	11	09	18	05	08	06	29	03	05	03
Figure	14	05	06	08	20	09	00	03	09	05	-02	-07	01	18	03	09
Number	15	07	01	08	21	07	02	18	00	08	09	01	01	18	18	25
Letter	18	09	02	00	27	12	01	03	12	02	06	01	07	11	16	21
2 Letters	12	15	00	04	13	10	07	11	02	01	-04	-09	00	18	02	08
Letter in Syll.	17	16	05	03	01	03	13	13	10	07	-14	-08	07	20	07	11
Word	16	26	05	16	05	03	07	17	21	16	-03	-07	07	14	07	15
Syllable	12	17	01	08	00	10	02	00	06	07	-04	00	11	14	07	11
CCCC String	15	08	08	03	09	00	01	06	11	11	-16	-07	12	22	15	19
Unspaced Word	21	15	11	09	13	07	11	06	04	02	-04	-04	01	11	03	14
COMPREHENSION & SPELLING																
Sentence Comp.	10	17	12	13	18	02	02	11	14	05	03	00	01	21	12	10
Oral Spelling	05	21	08	14	15	06	03	10	07	00	02	02	08	21	24	22
Written Spelling	06	22	05	05	17	04	01	05	04	07	01	05	01	18	17	08
Spelled-Out Word	13	22	08	02	18	03	07	13	01	09	-06	00	05	13	20	25
LANGUAGE TESTS																
PHONEMIC SEGMENTATION & BLENDING																
Sound Del. - Syll.	-09	02	12	03	03	08	15	14	02	17	-13	02	08	02	11	02
Word	-03	07	04	02	09	06	10	08	14	00	-09	-06	-14	-27	-02	-06
Pig Latin	06	25	00	02	11	06	03	06	12	02	-02	14	12	16	21	21
Ubby Dubby	07	16	07	03	15	05	10	03	18	06	-18	-03	14	14	02	01
Rhyming	03	05	10	07	11	01	04	02	11	06	17	22	17	14	05	05
SERIAL NAMING																
Count 20	03	07	08	01	04	05	10	07	15	02	04	05	15	10	17	15
Name Days	01	15	00	04	-12	06	13	02	08	01	04	16	06	03	12	06
Name Months	03	07	08	18	10	05	19	15	10	11	00	03	12	13	09	09

	TACTUAL	PERCEPTUAL-MOTOR	MOTOR
	FD FN TD TN	PD PN MD MN SD SN	FD FN fD fN DD DN

LANGUAGE TESTS (CONTINUED)

ORAL REPETITION

	TACTUAL	PERCEPTUAL-MOTOR	MOTOR
Unrelated Words	10 22-11-04	09 04 12 06-15-05	-08-01-15 02 02-01
Randomized Wds.	03 28-24-14	-04-07 09 01-09-08	-12-07-04 02 02-01
Meaningless Sent.	-03 17-13-08	12 02 14 03 06 03	14 25 14 15 09-03
Sentences	-03 06-16-08	16 11 10 05-07-09	05 07-04 02 10 08

TOKEN TEST

	TACTUAL	PERCEPTUAL-MOTOR	MOTOR
A	25 05 07 02	22 09 09 01 07-01	04 03 01-10-02-08
B	11 00 08 05	12-14-23-23 06-06	-11-01-07-10-02-12
C	-06 08 09 06	-04-24-17-17 00-06	00 06-16-17 01-08
D	01-02-01 07	12 08-13-03 06 05	-01-07 01-11-11-06
E	14 11 09 06	18 08-06-05 14 15	04 14 02-02 03 02
F	09 01-09-07	00-05 02 03-09-03	-09-01-14-10-12-11

SYNTACTIC-SEMANTIC

	TACTUAL	PERCEPTUAL-MOTOR	MOTOR
Morphophonemics	09 19-16-15	08-05-12-15-28-29	09 10-13 05 06 09
Devel. Sent.	-03 17-29-26	-06-17-04-16-15-19	05 03-19-09 15-03
Semantic Fields	-07 02 21 01	08-10-14-12 04-03	06 08 02-17 22-01
Ask & Tell	-05 06-11-07	-04-14-01-07 00-05	03 04 01-05 00 10

NEUROPSYCHOLOGY TESTS

WISC VERBAL

	TACTUAL	PERCEPTUAL-MOTOR	MOTOR
Information	09 25 07 11	17-13-13-14 01-02	01 01 13 09 13 08
Comprehension	15 18 08 06	27 04-10-14 02 01	14 05 16 13 16-01
Digit Span	24 39 18 06	12 11-07 14 15 18	05 11 11 22 22 20
Arithmetic	22 29 15 13	23 18 01 04-18-05	-06-09 07 11 12 09
Similarities	-09 09-11-02	00-25-06-02-01 01	13 05 19 33 23 15
Vocabulary	06 19-01 01	13-15-04-09-04-09	10-03 16 22 15 09

WISC PERFORMANCE

	TACTUAL	PERCEPTUAL-MOTOR	MOTOR
Pic. Arrangement	-05 06 14 18	17 03 12 07 06 05	-03-11 01 06 09 05
Pic. Completion	21 26 06 20	15 02 08-01-07-06	08 11 20 14 14 16
Block Design	28 36 11 21	25 14 15 20-01 09	-10-11-08-02 01 06
Object Assembly	30 29 10 30	28 22 22 14-02 05	-08-06-10-12 04 17
Coding	13 05 04 04	14 13-01 02 08 16	04 00 23 07 08 13
Maze	28 39 07-03	23 13 20-16 07 07	-15-17-16-11-05-07
Peabody Vocab.	01 18-01 09	19 03 03 00-15-10	05 06-01 17 09 07
Knox Cube	27 21-09-21	25 19 19 14-11-09	-06-15-03 00-06 04
Prog. Matrices	26 35-02 14	17 08 18 30 06 16	-01 01 09 02 16 18
Devel. Draw.	13 10 04 11	17 16 33 21 13-04	20 08 26 25 09 02
R-L Discrim.	04 00 08 00	-07-02 12-05-15 09	14 07 01 06-17 07
Category	30 31-05 14	14 11 11 23-01-03	09-01 16 22 14 17
TPT Total Time	12 20 10 27	02-06 20 23 07 08	01 00 22 38 25 28
Memory	16 31 01 22	-04-11-02 14 06 07	-12-05 02 17 26 25
Location	16 25 02 25	07 01 06 18-16-08	-06-13-01 22 13 21

TACTUAL

	TACTUAL	PERCEPTUAL-MOTOR	MOTOR
Finger Agn. D	X 62 13 19	29 27 10 08 04 04	-12-07 02-10 12 10
N	62 X 15 12	15 07 02 04 02 06	-07-02 11 12 24 19
Tac. Form D	13 15 X 57	08 10-20-10 19 21	05 11-02 02-08-02
N	19 12 57 X	09 04 04 10 05 17	-03 15 08 20 03 11

PERCEPTUAL-MOTOR

	TACTUAL	PERCEPTUAL-MOTOR	MOTOR
Pegboard D	29 15 08 09	X 65 37 26 24 26	14-04 07-04 06-02
N	27 07 10 04	65 X 29 29 17 28	09 00 09-05-08-03
Maze D	10 02-20 04	37 29 X 57 22 20	05-15 17 01-09-06
N	08 04-10 10	26 29 57 X 36 48	-08-03 17-21 03 10
Steadiness D	04 02 19 05	24 17 22 36 X 82	23 20 22 18 18 10
N	04 06 21 17	26 28 20 48 82 X	02 11 22 17 12 09

MOTOR

	TACTUAL	PERCEPTUAL-MOTOR	MOTOR
Finger Tap D	-12-07 05-03	14 09 05-08 23 02	X 62 32 28 26 20
N	-07-02 11 15	-04 00-15-03 20 11	62 X 32 36 26 20
Foot Tap D	02 11-02 08	07 09 17 17 22 22	32 32 X 70 30 20
N	10 12 02 20	-04-05 01-21 18 17	28 36 70 X 23 21
Dynamom. D	12 24-08 03	06-08-09 03 18 12	26 26 30 23 X 83
N	10 19-02 11	-02-03-06 10 10 09	20 20 20 21 83 X

References

Ajuriaguerra, J. 1966. Speech disorders in childhood. In E. Carterette (Ed.), *Brain function: Speech, language, and communication* (Vol. 3). Los Angeles: University of California Press.

Anderson, R. C. 1977. The notion of schemata and the education enterprise. In R. C. Anderson, R. J. Spiro, & W. E. Montague (Eds.), *Schooling and the acquisition of knowledge.* Hillsdale, N.J.: Erlbaum.

Applebee, A. N. 1971. Research in reading retardation: Two critical problems. *Journal of Child Psychology and Psychiatry, 12,* 91–113.

Aram, D. M., & Nation, J. E. 1975. Patterns of language behavior in children with developmental language disorders. *Journal of Speech & Hearing Research, 18,* 229–241.

Arndt, W. B., Shelton, R. L., Johnson, A. F., & Furr, M. L. 1977. Identification and description of homogeneous subgroups. *Journal of Speech and Hearing Research, 20,* 263–292.

Arter, J. A., & Jenkins, J. R. 1979. Differential diagnosis—prescription teaching: A critical appraisal. *Review of Educational Research, 49,* 517–555.

Arthur, G. 1947. *A point scale of performance tests, revised Form II manual.* New York: Psychological Corporation.

Aslin, R. N., & Pisoni, D. G. 1978. Some developmental processes in speech perception. Paper presented at NICHD conference, *Child Phonology: Perception, production, and deviation,* Bethesda, Maryland, May 28–31.

Backman, J. 1980. *The role of psycholinguistic abilities in reading acquisition.* Unpublished doctoral dissertation, Carleton University, Ottawa.

Baker, L., & Brown, A. L. 1981. Metacognitive skills of reading. In D. Pearson (Ed.), *Handbook of reading research.* New York: Longmans.

Bakker, D. J., Licht, R., Kok, A., & Bouma, A. 1980. Cortical responses to word reading by right- and left-eared normal and reading-distributed children. *Journal of Clinical Neuropsychology, 2,* 1–12.

Bakker, D. J., & Schroots, H. J. 1981. Temporal order in normal and disturbed reading. In G. T. Pavlidis & T. R. Miles (Eds.), *Dyslexia: Experimental research and educational implications.* London: Wiley.

Bannatyne, A. 1966. The color phonics system. In J. J. Money & G. Schiffman (Eds.), *The disabled reader.* Baltimore: Johns Hopkins Press.

Baron, J. 1977. Mechanisms for pronouncing printed words: Use and acquisition. In D. LaBerge & S. J. Samuels (Eds.), *Basic processes in reading: Perception and comprehension.* Hillsdale, N.J.: Erlbaum.

Bateman, B. D. 1979. Teaching reading to learning-disabled and other hard to teach children. In L. B. Resnick & P. A. Weaver (Eds.), *Theory and practice of early reading* (Vol. 1). Hillsdale, N.J.: Erlbaum.

Beck, I. L., & Block, K. K. 1979. An analysis of two reading programs: Some facts and some opinions. In L. B. Resnick & P. A. Weaver (Eds.), *Theory and practice of early reading* (Vol. 1). Hillsdale, N.J.: Erlbaum.

Bender, L. A. 1957. Specific reading disability as a maturational lag. *Bulletin of the Orton Society, 7,* 9–18.

Benson, D. F. 1976. Alexia. In J. T. Guthrie (Ed.), *Aspects of reading acquisition.* Baltimore: Johns Hopkins Press.

Benson, D. F. 1977. The third alexia. *Archives of Neurology, 34,* 327–331.

Benson, D. F., & Geschwind, N. 1969. The alexias. In P. J. Vinken & G. W. Bruyn (Eds.), *Handbook of clinical neurology* (Vol. 4). Amsterdam: North-Holland.

Benton, A. L. 1964. Contributions to aphasia before Broca. *Cortex, 1,* 314–327.

Benton, A. L. 1975. Developmental dyslexia: Neurological aspects. In W. J. Friedlander (Ed.), *Advances in neurology* (Vol. 7). New York: Raven Press.

Benton, A. L. 1978. Some conclusions about dyslexia. In A. L. Benton & D. Pearl (Eds.), *Dyslexia: An appraisal of current knowledge.* New York: Oxford University Press.

Benton, A. L., & Pearl, D. 1978. *Dyslexia: An appraisal of current knowledge.* New York: Oxford University Press.

Berko, J. 1958. The child's learning of English morphology. *Word, 14,* 150–177.

Berry, M. 1966. *Berry-Talbott language tests.* Rockford, Ill.: Mildred E. Berry.

Bindra, D. 1976. *A theory of intelligent behavior.* New York: Wiley.

Birch, H. G. 1962. Dyslexia and the maturation of visual function. In J. Money (Ed.), *Reading disability.* Baltimore: Johns Hopkins Press.

Blank, M., & Bridger, W. H. 1967. Perceptual abilities and conceptual deficiencies in retarded readers. In J. Zubin & G. A. Jervis, (Eds.), *Psychopathology of mental development.* New York: Grune & Stratton.

Blank, M., Rose, S. A., & Berlin, L. J. 1978. *The language of learning: The preschool years.* New York: Grune & Stratton.

Bloom, L., & Lahey, M. 1978. *Language development and language disorders.* New York: Wiley.

Boder, E. 1971. Developmental dyslexia: A diagnostic screening procedure based on three characteristic patterns of reading and spelling. In B. Bateman (Ed.), *Learning disorders* (Vol. 4). Seattle: Special Child Publications.

Boder, E. 1973. Developmental dyslexia: A diagnostic approach based on three atypical reading patterns. *Developmental medicine and child neurology, 15,* 663–687.

Brandt, J., & Rosen, J. J. 1980. Auditory phonemic perception in dyslexia: Categorical identification and discrimination of stop consonants. *Brain and Language, 9,* 324–337.

Bransford, J. D. 1979. *Human cognition: Learning, understanding, and remembering.* Belmont, Calif.: Wadsworth.

Broadbent, D. E. 1958. *Perception and communication.* New York: Pergamon.

Brown, A. L. 1978. Knowing when, where, and how to remember: A problem of metacognition. In R. Glaser (Ed.), *Advances in instructional psychology.* Hillsdale, N.J.: Erlbaum.

Brown, A. L. In press. Learning and development: The problems of compatibility, access, and induction. *Human Development.*

Brown, P. 1980. *The morphology and syntax of the spontaneous speech of reading disabled children: An exploratory study.* Unpublished master's thesis, University of Ottawa.

Brown, R., & Berko, J. 1960. Word association and the acquisition of grammer. *Child Development, 31,* 1–4.

Bruce, D. J. 1964. The analysis of word sounds by young children. *British Journal of Educational Psychology, 34,* 158–159.

Bruner, J. S. 1978. Acquiring the uses of language. *Canadian Journal of Psychology, 32,* 204–218.

Bruner, J. S., Goodnow, J., & Austin, G. A. 1956. *A study of thinking.* New York: Wiley.

Bryant, P. E. 1975. Cross-modal development and reading. In D. D. Duane, & M. B. Rawson (Eds.), *Reading, perception, and language.* Baltimore: The Orton Society.

Carey, S., & Diamond, R. 1980. Maturational determination of the developmental course of face encoding. In D. Caplan (Ed.), *Biological studies of mental processes.* Cambridge, Mass.: MIT Press.

Cermak, L. S., & Craik, F. I. M. (Eds.), 1978. *Levels of processing and human memory.* Hillsdale, N.J.: Erlbaum.

Cermak, L. S., Goldberg, J., Cermak, S., & Drake, C. 1980. The short-term memory ability of children with learning disabilities. *Journal of Learning Disabilities, 13,* 25–29.

Chall, J. S. 1967. *Learning to read: The great debate.* New York: McGraw-Hill.

Chall, J. S. 1979. The great debate: Ten years later, with a modest proposal for reading stages. In L. B. Resnick & P. A. Weaver (Eds.), *Theory and practice of early reading* (Vol. 1). Hillsdale, N.J.: Erlbaum.

Charniak, E. 1977. A framed painting: The representation of a common sense knowledge fragment. *Cognition Science, 1,* 355–394.

Childs, B., Finucci, J. M., & Preston, M. S. 1978. A medical genetics approach to the study of reading disability. In A. L. Benton & D. Pearl (Eds.), *Dyslexia: An appraisal of current knowledge.* New York: Oxford University Press.

Chomsky, C. 1969. *The acquisition of syntax in children from five to ten.* Cambridge Mass.: MIT Press.

Chomsky, C. 1970. Reading, writing, & phonology. *Harvard Education Review, 40,* 287–309.

Chomsky, N. 1957. *Syntactic structures.* The Hague: Mouton.

Chomsky, N., & Halle, M. 1968. *The sound pattern of English.* New York: Harper & Row.

Clark, E. V. 1978. Awareness of language: Some evidence from what children say and do. In A. Sinclair, R. J. Jarvella, & W. J. M. Levelt (Eds.), *The child's conception of language.* New York: Springer-Verlag.

Clark, H. H. 1974. Semantics and comprehension. In T. A. Sebeok (Ed.), *Current trends in linguistics* (Vol. 12). The Hague: Mouton.

Cole, R. (Ed.). 1980. *Perception and production of fluent speech.* Hillsdale, N.J.: Erlbaum.

Coles, G. S. 1978. The learning disabilities test battery: Empirical and social issues. *Harvard Education Review, 48,* 313–340.

Coltheart, M., Patterson, K., & Marshall, J. C. (Eds.). 1980. *Deep dyslexia.* London: Routledge & Keegan Paul.

Comrey, A. L. 1978. Common methodological problems in factor analytic studies. *Journal of Consulting and Clinical Psychology, 46,* 648–659.

Conners, C. K. 1978. Critical review of "Electroencephalographic and neurophysiological studies in dyslexia." In A. L. Benton & D. Pearl (Eds.), *Dyslexia: An appraisal of current knowledge.* New York: Oxford University Press.

Conrad, R. 1972. Speech and reading. In J. F. Kavanagh & J. G. Mattingly (Eds.), Language by ear and by eye: The relationship between speech and reading. Cambridge, Mass.: MIT Press.

Critchley, M. 1953. *The parietal lobes.* London: Arnold.

Critchley, M. 1970. *The dyslexic child.* Springfield, Ill.: Charles C Thomas.

Cromer, R. 1976. Developmental strategies for learning. In V. Hamilton & M. D. Vernon (Eds.), *The development of cognitive processes.* New York: Academic Press.

Cronbach, L. J., & Snow, R. E. 1977. *Aptitudes and instructional methods: A handbook for research on interactions.* New York: Irvington.

Cummins, J., & Das, J. P. 1977. Cognitive processing and reading difficulties: A framework for research. *Alberta Journal of Educational Research, 23,* 245–256.

Damasio, A. R. 1977. Varieties and significance of the alexias. *Archives of Neurology, 34,* 325–326.

Daneman, M., & Carpenter, P. A. 1980. Individual differences in working memory and reading. *Journal of Verbal Learning and Verbal Behavior, 119,* 450–456.

DeHirsch, K. 1957. Tests designed to discover potential reading difficulty. *American Journal of Orthopsychiatry, 27,* 566–576.

DeHirsch, K., Jansky, J., & Langford, W. 1966. *Predicting reading failure.* New York: Harper & Row.

Denckla, M. B. 1977. Minimal brain dysfunction and dyslexia: Beyond diagnosis by exclusion. In M. E. Blaw, J. Rapin, & M. Kinsbourne (Eds.), *Child neurology.* New York: Spectrum.

Denckla, M. B. 1978. Critical review of "Electroencephalographic and neurophysiological studies in dyslexia." In A. L. Benton & D. Pearl (Eds.), *Dyslexia: An appraisal of current knowledge.* New York: Oxford University Press.

Denckla, M. B. 1979. Childhood learning disabilities. In K. M. Heilman & E. Valenstein (Eds.), *Clinical neuropsychology.* New York: Oxford University Press.

Denckla, M. B., & Rudel, R. G. 1976. Rapid "automatized" naming: Dyslexia differentiated from other learning disabilities. *Neuropsychologia, 14,* 471–479.

Dennis, M. 1979. Language acquisition in a single hemisphere: Semantic organization. In D. Caplan (Ed.), *Biological studies of mental processes.* Cambridge, Mass.: MIT Press.

Dennis, M., Lovett, M., & Weigel-Crump, C. A. 1980. Written language acquisition after left or right hemidecortication in infancy. *Brain & Language, 9,* 54–91.

Doehring, D. G. 1968. *Patterns of impairment in specific reading disability.* Bloomington, Ind.: Indiana University Press.

Doehring, D. G. 1976. The acquisition of rapid reading responses. *Monographs of the Society for Research in Child Development, 41*(2) (a)

Doehring, D. G. 1976. Evaluation of two models of reading disability. In R. M. Knights & D. J. Bakker (Eds.), *The neuropsychology of learning disorders: Theoretical approaches.* Baltimore: University Park Press. (b)

Doehring, D. G. 1977. Comprehension of printed sentences by children with reading disability. *Bulletin of the Psychonomic Society. 10,* 350–352.

Doehring, D. G. 1978. The tangled web of behavioral research on developmental dyslexia. In A. L. Benton & D. Pearl (Eds.), *Dyslexia: An appraisal of current knowledge.* New York: Oxford University Press.

Doehring, D. G., & Aulls, M. W. 1979. The interactive nature of reading acquisition. *Journal of Reading Behavior, 11,* 27–40.

Doehring, D. G., & Hoshko, I. M. 1977. Classification of reading problems by the Q technique of factor analysis. *Cortex, 13,* 281–294. (a)

Doehring, D. G., & Hoshko, I. M. 1977. A developmental study of the speed of comprehension of printed sentences. *Bulletin of the Psychonomic Society, 9,* 311–313. (b)

Doehring, D. G., & Hoshko, I. M. 1977. *Oral and written spelling of normal readers and children with different types of reading disabilities.* Unpublished manuscript, School of Human Communication Disorders, McGill University. (c)

Doehring, D. G., Hoshko, I. M., & Bryans, B. N. 1979..Statistical classification of children with reading problems. *Journal of Clinical Neuropsychology, 1,* 5–16.

Downing, J., & Leong, C. K. 1981. *Psychology of learning to read.* New York: Macmillan.

Duffy, F. H., Burchfield, J. L., & Lombroso, C. T. 1979. Brain electrical activity mapping (BEAM): A method for extending the clinical utility of EEG and evoked potential data. *Annals of Neurology, 5,* 309–321.

Dunn, L. 1965. *Peabody Picture Vocabulary Test (expanded manual).* Circle Pines, Minn.: American Guidance Service.

Durrell, D. D. 1955. *Durrell analysis of reading difficulty;* New Edition. New York: Harcourt Brace.

Eimas, P. D. 1975. Speech perception in early infancy. In R. L. Schiefelbusch & L. Lloyd (Eds.), *Language perspectives—acquisition, retardation, and intervention.* Baltimore: University Park Press.

Elkonin, D. B. 1973. U.S.S.R. In J. Downing (Ed.), *Comparative Reading.* New York: Macmillan.

Ellis, A. W. 1979. Developmental and acquired dyslexia: Some observations on Jorm (1979). *Cognition, 7,* 421–428.

Entwistle, D. R. 1966. *The word associations of young children.* Baltimore: Johns Hopkins Press.

Ervin-Tripp, S., & Mitchell-Dernan, C. (Eds.). 1977. *Child discourse.* New York: Academic Press.

Estes, W. K. 1977. On the interaction of perception and memory in reading. In D. LaBerge & S. J. Samuels (Eds.), *Basic processes in reading: Perception and comprehension.* Hillsdale, N.J.: Erlbaum.

Farnham-Diggory, S. 1978. *Learning disabilities.* Cambridge, Mass.: Harvard University Press. (a)

Farnham-Diggory, S. 1978. How to study reading: Some information-processing ways. In F. B. Murray & J. J. Pikulski (Eds.), *The acquisition of reading: Cognitive, linguistic, and perceptual prerequisites.* Baltimore: University Park Press. (b)

Farnham-Diggory, S., & Gregg, L. 1975. Short-term memory function in young readers. *Journal of Experimental Child Psychology, 19,* 279–298.

Ferguson, G. F. 1956. On learning and human ability. *Canadian Journal of Psychology, 10,* 121–131.

Fiedorowicz, C. 1977. Adult Battery, Midrange Battery, and Kiddy Battery. In R. L. Trites, (Ed.), *Neuropsychological test manual.* Montreal: Ronalds Federated.

Fiedorowicz, C. 1980. *Alexia.* Unpublished manuscript, McGill University.

Finucci, J. M. 1978. Genetic considerations in dyslexia. In H. R. Myklebust (Ed.), *Progress in Learning Disabilities* (Vol. 4). New York: Grune & Stratton.

Fischer, K. W. 1980. A theory of cognitive development: The control and construction of hierarchies of skills. *Psychological Review, 87,* 477–531.

Fisher, D. F. 1979. Dysfunctions in reading disability: There's more than meets the eye. In L. B. Resnick & P. A. Weaver (Eds.), *Theory and practice of early reading* (Vol. 1). Hillsdale, N. J.: Erlbaum.

Fisk, J. L., & Rourke, B. P. 1979. Identification of subtypes of learning disabled children at three age levels: A multivariate approach. *Journal of Clinical Neuropsychology, 1,* 289–310.

Flavell, J. H. 1979. Metacognition and cognitive monitoring: A new area of cognitive–developmental inquiry. *American Psychologist, 34,* 906–911.

Fletcher, J. 1980. Linguistic factors in reading acquisition: Evidence for developmental changes. In F. J. Pirozzolo & M. C. Wittrock (eds.), *Neuropsychological and cognitive processes in reading*. New York: Academic Press.

Fletcher, J. D. 1979. Computer-assisted instruction in beginning reading: The Stanford projects. In L. B. Resnick & P. A. Weaver (Eds.), *Theory and practice of early reading* (Vol. 2). Hillsdale, N.J.: Erlbaum.

Foch, T. T., DeFries, J. C., McLearn, G. E., & Singer, S. M. 1977. Familial patterns of impairment in reading disability. *Journal of Educational Psychology, 69,* 316–329.

Foss, D. J. & Hakes, D. T. 1978. *Psycholinguistics*. Englewood Cliffs, N.J.: Prentice-Hall.

Fox, B., & Routh, D. K. 1975. Analyzing spoken language into words, syllables, and phonemes: A developmental study. *Journal of Psycholinguistic Research, 4,* 331–342.

Fox, B., & Routh, D. K. 1980. Phonemic analysis and severe reading disability in children. *Journal of Psycholinguistic Research, 9,* 115–119.

Francis, H. 1972. Toward an explanation of the paradigmatic–syntagmatic shift. *Child Development, 43,* 949–959.

Frederiksen, C. H. 1979. Discourse comprehension and early reading. In L. B. Resnick & P. A. Weaver (Eds.), *Theory and practice of early reading* (Vol. 1). Hillsdale, N.J.: Erlbaum.

Frederiksen, J. R. 1978. Assessment of perceptual, decoding, and lexical skills and their relation to reading proficiency. In A. M. Lesgold, J. W. Pellegrino, S. D. Fokkema, & R. Glaser (Eds.), *Cognitive psychology and instruction*. Hillsdale, N.J.: Erlbaum.

Gaddis, W. H. 1980. *Learning disabilities and brain function: A neuropsychological approach*. New York: Springer-Verlag.

Gagné, R. M. 1970. *The conditions of learning* (2nd ed.). New York: Holt, Rinehart & Winston.

Galaburda, A. M. & Kemper, T. L. 1979. Cytoarchitectonic abnormalities in developmental dyslexia: A case study. *Annals of Neurology, 6,* 94–100.

Gardner, H. 1974. Metaphors and modalities: How children project polar adjectives onto diverse domains. *Child Development, 45,* 84–91.

Geschwind, N. 1962. The anatomy of acquired disorders of reading. In J. Money (Ed.), *Reading disability*. Baltimore: Johns Hopkins Press.

Geschwind, N. 1965. Disconnexion syndromes in animal and man. *Brain, 88,* 237–294.

Gibson, E. J. 1971. Perceptual learning and the theory of word perception. *Cognitive Psychology, 2,* 351–368.

Gibson, E. J. 1972. Reading for some purpose. In J. F. Kavanagh & J. G. Mattingly (Eds.), *Language by ear and by eye: The relationship between speech and reading*. Cambridge, Mass.: MIT Press.

Gibson, E. J. 1977. How perception really develops: A view from outside. In D. LaBerge & S. J. Samuels (Eds.), *Basic processes in reading: Perception and comprehension*. Hillsdale, N.J.: Erlbaum.

Gibson, E. J., & Levin, H. 1975. *The psychology of reading*. Cambridge, Mass.: MIT Press.

Gillingham, A., & Stillman, B. 1940. *Remedial work for reading, spelling, and penmanship*. New York: Sachette & Williams.

Ginsberg, H., & Opper, S. 1969. *Piaget's theory of intellectual development: An interaction*. Englewood Cliffs, N.J.: Prentice-Hall.

Glaser, R., Pellegrino, J. W., & Lesgold, A. M. 1978. Some directions for a cognitive psychology of instruction. In A. M. Lesgold, J. W. Pellegrino, S. D. Fokkema, & R. Glaser (Eds.), *Cognitive psychology and instruction*. New York: Plenum.

Gleitman, L. R., & Rozin, P. 1977. The structure and acquisition of reading. I: Relations between orthographies and the structure of reading. In A. S. Reber & D. L. Scarborough (Eds.), *Toward a psychology of reading*. Hillsdale, N.J.: Erlbaum.

Goodman, K. S. 1967. Reading: A psycholinguistic guessing game. *Journal of the Reading Specialist, 4,* 126–135.

Goodman, K. S., & Goodman, Y. M. 1979. Learning to read is natural. In L. B. Resnick & P. A. Weaver (Eds.), *Theory and practice in early reading* (Vol. 1). Hillsdale, N.J.: Erlbaum.

Gough, P. R. 1972. One second of reading. In J. F. Kavanagh & I.G. Mattingly (Eds.), *Language by ear and by eye: The relationship between speech and reading.* Cambridge, Mass.: MIT Press.

Gough, P. B., & Hillinger, M. L. 1980. Learning to read: An unnatural act. *Bulletin of the Orton Society, 30,* 179–196.

Gregg, L. W., & Farnham-Diggory, S. 1979. How to study reasoning: An information-processing analysis. In L. B. Resnick and P. A. Weaver (Eds.), *Theory and practice of early reading* (Vol. 3). Hillsdale, N.J.: Erlbaum.

Grossberg, S. 1980. How does the brain build a cognitive code? *Psychological Review, 87,* 1–51.

Gur, R. C., & Reivitch, M. 1980. Cognitive task effects on hemispheric blood flow in humans: Evidence for individual differences in hemispheric activation. *Brain and Language, 9,* 78–92.

Guralnick, M. J. 1978. The application of single subject research designs to the field of learning disabilities. *Journal of Learning Disabilities, 11,* 415–442.

Guthrie, J. T. 1973. Reading comprehension and syntactic responses in good and poor readers. *Journal of Educational Psychology, 65,* 294–299.

Guthrie, J. T. 1978. Critique: Information processing: Model or myth? In F. B. Murray & J. J. Pikulski (Eds.), *The acquisition of reading: Cognitive, linguistic, and perceptual prerequisites.* Baltimore: University Park Press.

Guthrie, J. T., Martizza, G., & Seifert, M. 1979. Impacts of instructional time in reading. In L. B. Resnick, & P. A. Weaver (Eds.), *Theory and practice of early reading* (Vol. 3). Hillsdale, N.J.: Erlbaum

Hakes, D., Evans, J., & Tunmer, W. 1980. *The development of metalinguistic abilities in children.* New York: Springer-Verlag.

Hallgren, B. 1950. Specific dyslexia ("congenital word blindness"): A clinical and genetic study. *Acta Psychiatrica et Neurologica Scandanavica* (Supplement No. 65).

Halliday, M. A. K. 1975. *Learning how to mean.* London: Arnold.

Halstead, W. C. 1947. *Brain and intelligence: A quantitative study of the frontal lobes.* Chicago: University of Chicago Press.

Hardy, M., Stennett, R. G., & Smythe, P. G. 1973. Auditory segmentation and auditory blending in relation to beginning reading. *Alberta Journal of Education, 19,* 144–158.

Hebb, D. O. 1949. *Organization of behavior.* New York: Wiley.

Hécaen, H., & Kremin, H. 1976. Neurolinguistic research on reading disorders resulting from left hemisphere lesions: Aphasic and "pure" alexias. In H. Whitaker & H. A. Whitaker (Eds.), *Studies in neurolinguistics* (Vol. 2). New York: Academic Press.

Heilman, K. M. & Valenstein, E. (Eds.). 1979. *Clinical neuropsychology.* New York: Oxford University Press.

Hermann, K. 1959. *Reading disability: A medical study of word-blindness and related handicaps.* Copenhagen: Munksgaard.

Hermann, K., & Norrie, E. 1958. Is congenital word blindness a hereditary type of Gerstmann's syndrome? *Psychiatria et Neurologia, 136,* 59–73.

Herson, M., & Barlow, D. H. 1976. *Single case experimental designs: Strategies for studying behavioral change.* New York: Pergamon.

Hier, D. B., LeMay, M., Rosenberger, P. B., & Perlo, V. P. 1978. Developmental dyslexia: Evidence for a subgroup with reversal of cerebral asymmetry. *Archives of Neurology, 35,* 90–92.

Hinshelwood, J. 1895. Word blindness and visual memory. *Lancet, 2,* 1564–1570.

Hinshelwood, J. 1917. *Congenital word blindness.* London: Lewis.

Holmes, J. M. 1978. "Regression" and reading breakdown. In A. Caramazza & E. B. Zurif (Eds.), *Language acquisition and language breakdown: Parallels and divergencies.* Baltimore: Johns Hopkins Press.

Hook, P. E., & Johnson, D. J. 1978. Metalinguistic awareness and reading strategies. *Bulletin of the Orton Society, 28,* 62–78.

Hughes, J. R. 1978. Electroencephalographic and neurophysiological studies in dyslexia. In A. L. Benton & D. Pearl, *Dyslexia: An appraisal of current knowledge.* New York: Oxford University Press.

Huttenlocher, P. R., & Huttenlocher, J. A. 1973. A study of children with hyperlexia. *Neurology, 23,* 1107–1116.

Ingram, T. T. S. 1960. Pediatric aspects of specific developmental dysphasia, dyslexia, and dysgraphia. *Cerebral Palsy Bulletin, 2,* 254–277.

Ingram, T. T. S. 1969. Developmental disorders of speech. In P. J. Vinken & G. W. Bruyn (Eds.), *Handbook of clinical neurology* (Vol. 4). Amsterdam: North Holland.

Jastak, J. R., & Jastak, S. R. 1965. *The wide range achievement test manual of instructions.* Wilmington, Del. Guidance Associates.

John, E. R. *et al.* 1977. Neurometrics: Numerical taxonomy identifies different profiles of brain function within groups of behaviorally similar people. *Science, 196,* 1393–1410.

Johnson, D. J. & Myklebust, H. R. 1967. *Learning disabilities.* New York: Grune & Stratton.

Johnston, G. J. 1981. *Computerized instruction of children with reading problems: Skill acquisition and transfer of training.* Unpublished master's thesis, Ottawa University.

Jorm, A. F. 1979. The nature of the reading deficit in developmental dyslexia. *Cognition, 7,* 429–433.

Just, M. A. & Carpenter, P. A. 1980. A theory of reading from eye fixations to comprehension. *Psychological Review, 87,* 329–354.

Karpova, S. N. 1977. *The realization of the verbal composition of speech by preschool children.* The Hague: Mouton.

Kawi, A. A., & Pasamanick, B. 1959. Prenatal and perinatal factors in the development of childhood reading disorders. *Monographs of the Society for Research in Child Development,* (No. 24).

Kessel, F. 1970. The role of syntax in children's comprehension from six to twelve. *Monographs of the Society for Research in Child Development* (No. 139).

Kinchla, R. A., & Wolf, J. D. 1977. The order of visual processing: "Top-down," "bottom-up," or "middle-out." *Psychology Research Report* (No. 21). Princeton University.

Kinsbourne, M. 1975. Cerebral dominance, learning, and cognition. In H. R. Myklebust (Ed.), *Progress in learning disabilities* (Vol. 1). New York: Grune & Stratton.

Kinsbourne, M. 1976. Looking and listening strategies and beginning reading. In J. T. Guthrie (Ed.), *Aspects of reading acquisition.* Baltimore: Johns Hopkins Press.

Kinsbourne, M. 1978. *Asymmetrical function of the brain.* Cambridge, England: Cambridge University Press.

Kinsbourne, M., & Hiscock, M. 1978. Cerebral lateralization and cognitive development. In J. S. Chall & A. F. Mirsky (Eds.), *Education and the brain.* Chicago: University of Chicago Press.

Kinsbourne, M., & Warrington, E. K. 1963. Developmental factors in reading and writing backwardness. *British Journal of Psychology, 54,* 145–156.

Kintsch, W. 1974. *The representation of meaning in memory.* Hillsdale, N.J.: Erlbaum.

Kintsch, W. 1976. Memory for prose. In C. N. Cofer (Ed.), *The structure of human memory.* San Francisco: W. H. Freeman.

Kintsch, W., & Van Dijk, T. A. 1978. Toward a model of text comprehension and production. *Psychological Review, 85,* 363–394.

Kirshenblatt-Gimblett, B. (Ed.). 1976. *Speech play: Research and resources for studying linguistic creativity.* Philadelphia: University of Pennsylvania Press.

Kleiman, G. M. 1975. Speech recoding in reading. *Journal of Verbal Learning & Verbal Behavior, 14*, 323–339.

Klove, H. 1963. Clinical neuropsychology. *The Medical Clinics of North America, 47*, 1647–1658.

Knights, R. M., & Hardy, M. L. 1978. A child–computer–teacher assessment and remedial program for children with poor reading skills: Phase III. *Research Bulletin No. 17*, Department of Psychology, Carleton University, Ottawa.

Knights, R. M., & Stoddart, C. 1981. Profile approaches to neuropsychological diagnosis in children. In G. W. Hynd & J. E. Obrzut (Eds.), *Neuropsychological assessment and the school-age child*. New York: Grune & Stratton.

Kuhn, T. S. 1970. *The structure of scientific revolutions*. Chicago: University of Chicago Press.

LaBerge, D., & Samuels, S. J. 1974. Toward a theory of automatic information processing. *Cognitive Psychology, 6*, 293–323.

Lashley, K. S. 1951. The problem of serial order in behavior. In L. A. Jeffress (Ed.), *Cerebral mechanisms in behavior*. New York: Wiley.

Lee, L. 1974. *Developmental sentence analyses*. Evanston, Ill.: Northwestern University Press.

Leong, C. K. 1980. Laterality and reading proficiency in children. *Reading Research Quarterly, 15*, 185–202.

Leong, C. K., & Haines, C. F. 1978. Beginning reader's analysis of words and sentences. *Journal of Reading Behavior, 4*, 393–407.

Levinson, H. N. 1980. *A solution to the riddle dyslexia*. New York: Springer-Verlag.

Levy, B. A. 1978. Speech processing during reading. In A. M. Lesgold, J. W. Pellegrino, S. D. Fokkema, & R. Glaser (Eds.), *Cognitive psychology and instruction*. New York: Plenum.

Levy, B. A. 1980. Interactive processes during reading. In A. M. Lesgold & C. A. Perfetti (Eds.), *Interactive processes in reading*. Hillsdale, N.J.: Erlbaum.

Lewis, M., & Rosenbloom, L. A. (Eds.). 1977. *Interaction, conversation, and the development of language*. New York: Wiley.

Liberman, A. M. 1970. The grammars of language and speech. *Cognitive Psychology, 1*, 301–323.

Liberman, A. M., Cooper, F. S., Shankweiler, D. P., & Studdert-Kennedy, M. 1967. Perception of the speech code. *Psychological Review, 74*, 431–461.

Liberman, I. Y., & Shankweiler, D. 1979. Speech, the alphabet, and teaching to read. In L. B. Resnick & P. A. Weaver (Eds.), *Theory and practice of early reading* (Vol. 2). Hillsdale, N.J.: Erlbaum.

Liberman, I. Y., Shankweiler, D., Fischer, F. W., & Carter, B. 1974. Explicit syllable and phoneme segmentation in the young child. *Journal of Experimental Child Psychology, 18*, 201–212.

Liberman, I. Y., Shankweiler, D., Liberman, A. M., Fowler, C., & Fischer, F. W. 1977. Phonetic segmentation and recoding in the beginning reader. In A. S. Reber & D. L. Scarborough (Eds.), *Toward a psychology of reading*. Hillsdale, N.J.: Erlbaum.

Lock, A. (Ed.). 1978. *Action, gesture, and symbol: The emergence of language*. New York: Academic Press.

Luria, A. R. 1966. *Higher cortical functions in man*. New York: Basic Books.

Luria, A. R. 1970. *Traumatic aphasia: Its syndromes, psychology, and treatment*. The Hague: Mouton.

Luria, A. R. & Vinogradova, O. S. 1959. An objective investigation of the dynamics of semantic systems. *British Journal of Psychology, 50*, 89–105.

Macnamara, J. 1972. Cognitive basis of language learning in infants. *Psychological Review, 79*, 1–13.

Marshall, J. C., & Newcombe, F. 1966. Syntactic and semantic errors in paralexia. *Neuropsychologia*, *4*, 169–176.

Marshall, J. C., & Newcombe, F. 1977. Variability and constraint in acquired dyslexia. In H. Whitaker & H. A. Whitaker (Eds.), *Studies in neurolinguistics* (Vol. 3). New York: Academic Press.

Marslen-Wilson, W. D. 1975. Sentence perception as an interactive parallel process. *Science*, *189*, 226–227.

Mason, G. E., & Blanchard, J. S. 1979. *Computer applications in reading*. Newark, Del.: International Reading Association.

Massaro, D. W. (Ed.). 1975. *An information-processing analysis of speech perception, reading, and psycholinguistics*. New York: Academic Press.

Mattingly, I. G. 1972. Reading, the linguistic process, and linguistic awareness. In J. F. Kavanagh & I. G. Mattingly (Eds.), *Language by ear and by eye: The relationship between speech and hearing*. Cambridge, Mass.: MIT Press.

Mattingly, I. G. 1978. A review of "The skills of the plodder." *Contemporary Psychology*, *23*, 731–732.

Mattingly, I. G. 1980. Reading, linguistic awareness, and language acquisition. *Haskins Laboratories Status Report on Speech Research SR–61.*

Mattis, S. 1978. Dyslexia syndromes: A working hypothesis that works. In A. L. Benton & D. Pearl (Eds.), *Dyslexia: An appraisal of current knowledge*. New York: Oxford University Press.

Mattis, S., French, J. H., & Rapin, I. 1975. Dyslexia in children and young adults: Three independent neuropsychological syndromes. *Developmental Medicine and Child Neurology*, *17*, 150–163.

McConkie, D. W. 1979. What the study of eye movements reveals about reading. In L. B. Resnick & P. A. Weaver (Eds.), *Theory and practice of early reading* (Vol. 3). Hillsdale, N.J.: Erlbaum.

McLearn, G. E. 1978. Review of "Dyslexia—Genetic aspects." In A. L. Benton & D. Pearl (Eds.), *Dyslexia: An appraisal of current knowledge*. New York: Oxford University Press.

McNeill, D. 1970. *The acquisition of language: The study of developmental linguistics*. New York: Harper & Row.

McNeill, D. 1979. *The conceptual basis of language*. Hillsdale, N.J: Erlbaum.

Miller, G. A., Galanter, E., & Pribram, K. H. 1960. *Plans and the structure of behavior*. New York: Henry Holt.

Minsky, M. 1975. A framework for representing knowledge. In P. H. Winston (Ed.), *The psychology of computer vision*. New York: McGraw-Hill.

Morgan, W. P. 1896. A case of congenital word blindness. *British Medical Journal*, *2*, 1378.

Morris, C. D., Bransford, J. D., & Franks, J. J. 1977. Levels of processing versus transfer appropriate processing. *Journal of Verbal Learning & Verbal Behavior*, *16*, 519–533.

Morrison, F., Giordani, B., & Nagy, J. 1977. Reading disability: An information-processing analysis. *Science*, *196*, 77–79.

Myklebust, H. R. 1978. Toward a science of dyslexiology. In H. R. Myklebust (Ed.), *Progress in learning disabilities* (Vol. 4). New York: Grune & Stratton.

Myklebust, H. R., & Johnson, D. J. 1962. Dyslexia in children. *Exceptional Children*, *29*, 14–25.

Neisser, U. 1967. *Cognitive psychology*. New York: Appleton-Century-Crofts.

Neisser, U. 1976. *Cognition and reality*. San Francisco: W. H. Freeman.

Neisser, U. 1980. *Toward a realistic cognitive psychology*. Master lecture series on cognitive psychology, American Psychological Association, Montreal, September.

Nelson, K. E., & Nelson, K. 1978. Cognitive pendulums and their linguistic realization. In K. E. Nelson (Ed.), *Children's language* (Vol. 1). New York: Gardner.

Nie, N., Hull, C. H., Jenkins, J. G., Steinbrenner, K., & Bent, D. H. 1975. *Statistical package for the social sciences.* New York: McGraw-Hill.

Nunnally, J. C. 1967. *Psychometric theory.* New York: McGraw-Hill.

Obrzut, J. E. 1979. Dichotic listening and bisensory memory skills in qualitatively diverse dyslexic readers. *Journal of Learning Disabilities, 12,* 304–314.

Ohnmacht, F. W., & Weiss, F. 1976. Construct validity and reading research: Some comments with a data simulation exemplar. *Journal of Reading Behavior, 8,* 19–25.

Ojemann, G., & Mateer, C. 1979. Human language cortex: Localization of memory, syntax, and sequential motor–phoneme identification systems. *Science, 205,* 1401–1403.

Olson, D. R. 1975. Review essay on *Toward a literate society.* In J. B. Carroll & J. Chall (Eds.), *Proceedings of the National Academy of Education, 2,* 109–178.

Olson, D. R. 1977. From utterance to text. *Harvard Education Review, 47,* 257–281.

Olson, D. R., & Nickerson, N. 1978. Language development through the school years: Learning to confine interpretation to the information in the text. In K. E. Nelson (Ed.), *Children's language* (Vol. 1). New York: Gardner.

Orton, S. T. 1925. Word-blindness in school children. *Archives of Neurology and Psychiatry, 14,* 582–615.

Overall, J. E., & Klett, C. J. 1972. *Applied multivariate analysis.* New York: McGraw-Hill.

Owen, F. W. 1978. Dyslexia—genetic aspects. In A. L. Benton & D. Pearl (Eds.), *Dyslexia: An appraisal of current knowledge.* New York: Oxford University Press.

Palermo, D. 1978. *Psychology of language.* Glenview, Ill.: Scott Foresman.

Patel, P. G. 1977. The left parieto–tempero–occipital junction, semantic aphasia, and language development around age seven. *Linguistics, 196,* 35–48.

Patel, P. G. 1981. Syntactic maturation: Some possible psycholinguistic correlates and conditions. In Steckol, K., & Sinclair, R. (Eds.), *Cognition and developmental linguistics.* Baltimore: University Park Press.

Patel, P. G. In press. Impaired language mechanisms involved in specific reading disability: An explanatory synthesis of research findings. *Indian Educational Review.*

Patterson, K. E. 1979. What is right with "deep" dyslexic patients? *Brain and Language, 8,* 111–129.

Pelham, W. E. 1979. Selective attention deficits in poor readers? Dichotic listening, speeded classification, and auditory and visual central and incidental learning tasks. *Child Development, 50,* 1050–1061.

Perfetti, C. A., Finger, E., & Hogaboam, T. 1978. Sources of vocalization latency difference between skilled and less skilled young readers. *Journal of Educational Psychology, 70,* 730–739.

Perfetti, C. A., & Hogaboam, J. 1975. The relationship between single word decoding and reading comprehension skill. *Journal of Educational Psychology, 67,* 461–469.

Perfetti, C. A., & Lesgold, A. M. 1979. Coding and comprehension in skilled reading and implications for reading instruction. In L. B. Resnick & P. A. Weaver (Eds.), *Theory and practice of early reading* (Vol. 1). Hillsdale, N.J.: Erlbaum.

Peter, B. M., & Spreen, O. 1979. Behavior rating and personal adjustment scales of neurologically and learning handicapped children during adolescence and early childhood: Results of a follow-up study. *Journal of Clinical Neuropsychology, 1,* 75–91.

Petrauskas, R. J., & Rourke, B. P. 1979. Identification of subtypes of retarded readers: A neuropsychological, multivariate approach. *Journal of Clinical Neuropsychology, 1,* 17–37.

Petrey, S. 1977. Word associations and the development of lexical memory. *Cognition, 5,* 57–71.

Pflaum, S. W., & Pascarella, E. T. 1980. Interactive effects of prior reading achievement and training in context on the reading of learning disabled children. *Reading Research Quarterly, 16,* 138–158.

Picton, T. W. 1976. The use of human event-related potentials in psychology. In P. Venables & I. Martin (Eds.), *Techniques in psychophysiology.* New York: Wiley.

Pirozzolo, F. 1979. *The neuropsychology of developmental reading disorders.* New York: Praeger.

Pirozzolo, F. J., & Rayner, K. 1978. The neural control of eye movements in acquired and developmental reading disorders. In H. Whitaker & H. A. Whitaker (Eds.), *Studies in neurolinguistics* (Vol. 4). New York: Academic Press.

Rabinovitch, R. D., Drew, A. L., DeJong, R. N., Ingram, W., & Withey, L. A. 1954. A research approach to reading retardation. *Proceedings of the Association for Nervous and Mental Disease, 34,* 363–396.

Raven, J. 1960. *Guide to the standard progressive matrices.* London: H. K. Lewis.

Raven, J. 1965. *The coloured progressive matrices.* London: H. K. Lewis.

Read, C. 1978. Children's awareness of language, with emphasis on sound systems. In A. Sinclair, R. J. Jarvella, & W. J. M. Levelt (Eds.), *The child's conception of language.* New York: Springer-Verlag.

Reber, A. S., & Scarborough, D. L. (Eds.). 1977. *Toward a psychology of reading.* Hillsdale, N.J.: Erlbaum.

Rees, N. S. 1974. The speech pathologist and the reading process. *Asha, 16,* 255–258.

Reitan, R. M. 1959. *The effects of brain lesions on adaptive abilities in human beings.* Indianapolis Ind.: University Medical Center.

Reitan, R. M. 1964. *Manual for administering and scoring the Reitan-Indiana neuropsychological battery for children.* Indianapolis: Indiana University Medical Center.

Reitan, R. M. 1974. Psychological effects of cerebral lesions in children of early school age. In R. M. Reitan & L. A. Davison (Eds.), *Clinical neuropsychology: Current status and applications.* Washington, D.C.: Winston.

Reitan, R. M., & Davidson, L. A (Eds.). 1974. *Clinical neuropsychology: Current status and applications.* Washington, D.C.: Winston.

Resnick, L. B. 1979. Theories and prescriptions for early reading instruction. In L. B. Resnick & P. A. Weaver (Eds.), *Theory and practice of early reading* (Vol. 2). Hillsdale, N.J.: Erlbaum. (a)

Resnick, L. B. 1979. Toward a usable psychology of reading instruction. In L. B. Resnick & P. A. Weaver (Eds.), *Theory and practice of early reading* (Vol. 3). Hillsdale, N.J.: Erlbaum.(b)

Resnick, L. B., & Weaver, P. A. 1979. *Theory and practice of early reading* (3 vols.). Hillsdale, N.J.: Erlbaum.

Rhynas, E. M. 1981. *Comparison of two methods for classifying dyslexia: A search for distinct syndromes.* Unpublished master's thesis, University of Ottawa.

Richardson, G. 1974. The Cartesian frame of reference: A structure unifying the description of dyslexia. *Journal of Psycholinguistic Research, 3,* 15–63.

Rosner, J. 1979. Teaching hard to teach children to read: A rationale for compensatory education. In L. B. Resnick & P. A. Weaver (Eds.), *Theory and practice of early reading* (Vol. 2). Hillsdale, N.J.: Erlbaum.

Rosner, J., & Simon, D. P. 1971. The auditory analysis test: An initial report. *Journal of Learning Disabilities, 4,* 384–398.

Rourke, B. P. 1975. Brain–behavior relationships in children with learning disabilities. *American Psychologist, 30,* 911–920.

Rourke, B. P. 1976. Reading retardation in children: Developmental lag or deficit? In R. M. Knights & D. J. Bakker (Eds.), *Neuropsychology of learning disorders: Theoretical approaches.* Baltimore: University Park Press.

Rourke, B. P. 1978. Neuropsychological research on reading retardation: A review. In A. L. Benton & D. Pearl (Eds.), *Dyslexia: An appraisal of current knowledge*. New York: Oxford University Press.

Rourke, B. P., & Orr, R. R. 1977. Prediction of the reading and spelling performances of normal and retarded children: A four-year follow-up. *Journal of Abnormal Child Psychology*, 5, 9–20.

Rudel, R. G., Denckla, M. B., & Broman, M. 1978. Rapid silent response to repeated target symbols by dyslexic and nondyslexic children. *Brain and Language*, 6, 52–62.

Rumelhart, D. E. 1977. Toward an interactive model of reading. In S. Dornic & P. Rabbitt (Eds.), *Attention and performance VI*. Hillsdale, N.J.: Erlbaum.

Saffran, E. M. 1980. Reading in deep dyslexia is not ideographic. *Neuropsychologia*, 18, 219–223.

Satz, P. 1976. Cerebral dominance and reading disability: An old problem revisited. In R. M. Knights & D. J. Bakker (Eds.), *The neuropsychology of learning disorders: Theoretical approaches*. Baltimore: University Park Press.

Satz, P., & Morris, R. 1980. Learning disability subtypes: A review. In F. J. Pirozzolo & M. C. Wittrock (Eds.), *Neuropsychological and cognitive processes in reading*. New York: Academic Press.

Satz, P., Taylor, H. G., Friel, J., & Fletcher, J. 1978. Some developmental and predictive precursors of reading disabilities: A six-year follow-up. In A. L. Benton & D. Pearl (Eds.), *Dyslexia: An appraisal of current knowledge*. New York: Oxford University Press.

Schank, R. C. & Abelson, R. P. 1977. *Scripts, plans, goals, and understanding: An inquiry into human knowledge structures*. Hillsdale, N.J.: Erlbaum.

Schuell, H., Jenkins, J. J., & Jimenez-Pabon, E. 1964. *Aphasia in adults*. New York: Harper & Row.

Schwartz, J., & Tallal, P. 1980. Rate of acoustic change may underlie hemispheric specialization for speech perception. *Science*, 207, 1380–1381.

Segalowitz, S. J., & Gruber, F. A. (Eds.). 1977. *Language development and neurological theory*. New York: Academic Press.

Semel, E. M., & Wiig, E. H. 1975. Comprehension of syntactic structures and critical verbal elements by children with learning disorders. *Journal of Learning Disabilities*, 8, 53–58.

Seymour, P. H. K. 1973. A model for reading, naming, and comparison. *British Journal of Psychology*, 64, 35–49.

Shankweiler, D., & Liberman, I. Y. 1978. Reading behavior in dyslexia: Is there a distinctive pattern? *Bulletin of the Orton Society*, 28, 114–123.

Shankweiler, D., Liberman, I. Y., Mark, L. S., Fowler, C. A., & Fischer, F. W. 1979. The speech code and learning to read. *Journal of Experimental Psychology: Human Learning and Memory*, 5, 531–545.

Shuy, R. W. 1977. *Linguistic theory: What can it say about reading*. Newark, Del.: International Reading Association.

Silberberg, N. E., & Silberberg, M. C. 1971. Hyperlexia: The other end of the continuum. *Journal of Special Education*, 5, 233–242.

Silver, A. A., & Hagin, R. 1960. Specific reading disability: Delineation of the syndrome and relationship to cerebral dominance. *Comparative Psychiatry*, 1, 126–134.

Sinclair, A., Jarvella, R. J., & Levelt, W. J. M. 1978. *The child's conception of language*. New York: Springer-Verlag.

Skinner, B. F. 1959. *Verbal behavior*. New York: Appleton-Century-Crofts.

Slobin, D. L. 1966. Grammatical transformations and sentence comprehension in childhood and adulthood. *Journal of Verbal Learning & Verbal Behavior*, 5, 219–227.

Smith, F. 1971. *Understanding reading: A psycholinguistic analysis of reading and learning to read*. New York: Holt, Rinehart & Winston.

Smith, F. 1973. *Psycholinguistics and reading.* New York: Holt, Rinehart & Winston.

Smith, F. 1977. Making sense of reading—And of reading instruction. Harvard Education Review, 47, 386–395.

Smith, F. 1979. Conflicting approaches to reading research and instruction. In L. B. Resnick & P. A. Weaver (Eds.), *Theory and practice of early reading* (Vol. 2). Hillsdale, N.J.: Erlbaum.

Spelke, E. S. 1979. Exploring audible and visible events in infancy. In A. D. Pick (Ed.), *Perception and its development: A tribute to Eleanor Gibson.* Hillsdale, N. J.: Erlbaum.

Spreen, O., & Benton, A. L. 1969. *Neurosensory center comprehensive examination for aphasia.* Department of Psychology, University of Victoria.

Stanovitch, K. E. 1980. Toward an interactive–compensatory model of individual differences in the development of reading fluency. *Reading Research Quarterly, 16,* 32–71.

Stark, R., & Tallal, P. 1979. Analysis of stop-consonant production errors in dysphasic children. *Journal of the Acoustical Society of America, 66,* 1703–1712.

Stein, B. S. 1978. Depth of processing reexamined: The effects of precision of encoding and test appropriateness. *Journal of Verbal Learning & Verbal Behavior, 17,* 165–174.

Stevens, K. N. 1975. The potential role of property detectors in the perception of consonants. In G. Fant & M. A. A. Tatham (Eds.), *Auditory analysis and perception of speech.* New York: Academic Press.

Sticht, T. G. 1979. Applications of the audread model to reading evaluation and instruction. In L. B. Resnick & P. A. Weaver (Eds.), *Theory and practice of early reading* (Vol. 1). Hillsdale, N.J.: Erlbaum.

Studdert-Kennedy, M. 1976. Speech perception. In N. J. Lass (Ed.), *Contemporary issues in experimental phonetics.* Springfield, Ill.: Charles C Thomas.

Studdert-Kennedy, M. In press. Speech Perception. *Language and speech.*

Stuss, D. T. & Trites, R. L. 1977. Classification of neurological status using multiple discriminant function analysis of neuropsychological test scores. *Journal of Consulting and Clinical Psychology, 45,* 145.

Tallal, P. 1980. Auditory temporal perception, phonics, and reading disabilities in children. *Brain and Language, 9,* 182–198.

Tallal, P., & Stark, R. 1981. Speech acoustic-cue discrimination abilities of normally developing and language impaired children. *Journal of the Acoustical Society of America, 69,* 568–579.

Tatsuoka, M. M. 1971. *Multivariate analysis.* New York: Wiley.

Taylor, H. G., Satz, P., & Friel, J. 1979. Developmental dyslexia in relation to other childhood reading disorders: Significance and clinical utility. *Reading Research Quarterly, 15,* 84–101.

Ter-Pogossian, M. M., Raichle, M. E., & Sobel, B. E. 1980. Positron emission tomography. *Scientific American, 243,* 170–181.

Tomatis, A. 1967. *La dyslexie.* Paris: Organisation des Centres du Language.

Torgeson, J. K. 1978–1979. Performance of reading disabled children on serial memory tasks. *Reading Research Quarterly, 14,* 57–87.

Torgeson, J. K. 1979. What shall we do with psychological processes? *Journal of Learning Disabilities, 12,* 514–521.

Trites, R. L. 1977. *Neuropsychological test manual.* Montreal: Ronalds Federated.

Trites, R. L. 1979. *Hyperactivity in children: Etiology, measurement, and treatment implications.* Baltimore: University Park Press.

Trites, R. L., Brandts, T., & Blouin, A. 1980. *Predicting responses to Ritalin in hyperactive boys.* Unpublished study, University of Ottawa.

Trites, R. L., & Fiedorowicz, C. 1976. Follow-up study of children with specific (or primary) reading disability. In R. M. Knights & D. J. Bakker (Eds.), *The neuropsychology of learning disorders: Theoretical approaches.* Baltimore: University Park Press.

Trites, R. L., & Price, M. A. 1976. *Learning disabilities found in association with French immersion programming.* Toronto: Ministry of Education, Ontario.

Trites, R. L., & Price, M. A. 1977. *Learning disabilities found in association with French immersion programming: A cross validation.* Toronto: Ministry of Education, Ontario.

Trites, R. L., & Price, M. A. 1978–1979. Specific learning disability in primary French immersion. *Interchange, 9,* 73–85.

Tulving, E. 1972. Episodic and semantic memory. In E. Tulving & W. Donaldson (Eds.), *Organization of memory.* New York: Academic Press.

Valtin, R. 1978–1979. Dyslexia: Deficit in reading or deficit in research? *Reading Research Quarterly, 15,* 201–221.

Valtin, R. 1980. Deficiencies in research on reading disabilities. In J. F. Kavanagh & R. L. Venezky (Eds.), *Orthography, reading, and dyslexia.* Baltimore: University Park Press.

Vaughn-Cooke, A. F. 1977. Phonological rules and reading. In R. W. Shuy (Ed.), *Linguistic theory: What can it say about reading?* Newark, Del.: International Reading Association.

Vellutino, F. R. 1979. *Dyslexia: Theory and research.* Cambridge, Mass.: MIT Press.

Venezky, R. L. 1970. *The structure of English orthography.* The Hague: Mouton.

Venezky, R. L., & Massaro, D. W. 1979. The role of orthographic regularity in word recognition. In L. B. Resnick & P. A. Weaver (Eds.), *Theory and practice of early reading* (Vol. 1). Hillsdale, N.J. Erlbaum.

Vernon, M. D. 1971. *Reading and its difficulties.* Cambridge, Eng.: Cambridge University Press.

Vernon, M. D. 1977. Varieties of deficiency in the reading process. *Harvard Education Review, 47,* 396–410.

Vernon, M. D. 1979. Variability in reading retardation. *British Journal of Psychology, 70,* 7–16.

Vogel, S. 1975. *Syntactic abilities in normal and dyslexic children.* Baltimore: University Park Press.

Vogel, S. 1977. Morphological ability in normal and dyslexic children. *Journal of Learning Disabilities, 10,* 41–49.

Waller, T. G. 1977. *Think first, read later! Piagetian perspectives for reading.* Newark, Del.: International Reading Association.

Warrington, E. K. 1967. The incidence of verbal disability associated with reading retardation. *Neuropsychologia, 5,* 175–179.

Wechsler, D. 1949. *Manual: Wechsler Adult Intelligence Scale.* New York: The Psychological Corporation.

Wechsler, D. 1955. *Manual: Wechsler Intelligence Scale for Children.* New York: The Psychological Corporation.

Wechsler, D. 1974. *Manual: Wechsler Intelligence Scale for Children, revised.* New York: The Psychological Corporation.

Weener, P. 1981. On comparing learning disabled and regular classroom children. *Journal of Learning Disabilities, 14,* 227–232.

Weigel, E., & Bierwisch, M. 1970. Neuropsychology and linguistics: Topics of common research. *Foundations of Language, 6,* 1–18.

Wepman, J. 1975. New and wider horizons for speech and hearing specialists. *Asha, 17,* 9–10.

Whitaker, H. 1976. A case of the isolation of the language function. In H. Whitaker & H. A. Whitaker (Eds.), *Studies in Neurolinguistics* (Vol. 2). New York: Academic Press.

Whitaker, H. A., & Noll, J. D. 1972. Some linguistic parameters of the Token Test. *Neuro-psychologia, 10*, 395–404.

Whyte, S. H. 1965. Evidence for a hierarchical arrangement of learning processes. In L. P. Lipsitt & C. C. Spiker (Eds.), *Advances in child development and behavior* (Vol. 2). New York: Academic Press.

Wiener, M., & Cromer, W. 1967. Reading and reading difficulty: A conceptual analysis. *Harvard Educational Review, 37*, 620–643.

Williams, J. 1979. The ABDs of reading: A program for the learning disabled. In L. B. Resnick & P. A. Weaver (Eds.), *Theory and practice of early reading* (Vol. 3). Hillsdale, N.J.: Erlbaum.

Wishart, D. 1975. *Clustan 1C user manual.* London: University College.

Witelson, S. F. 1977. Early hemispheric specialization and interhemispheric plasticity: An empirical and theoretical review. In S. J. Segalowitz & F. A. Gruber (Eds.), *Language development and neurological theory.* New York: Academic Press.

Wolf, M. 1981. The word retrieval process and reading in children and aphasics. In K. Nelson (Ed.), *Children's language* (Vol. 3). New York: Gardner.

Wolfenstein, M. 1954. *Children's humour: A psychological analysis.* Glencoe, Ill.: Free Press.

Wolfus, B., Moscovitch, M., & Kinsbourne, M. 1980. Subgroups of developmental language impairment. *Brain and Language, 10,* 152–171.

Wong, B. 1979. The role of theory in learning disabilities research. Part I: An analysis of problems. *Journal of Learning Disabilities, 12*, 585–595.

Yakovlev, P. I. & Lecours, A. R. 1967. The myelogenetic cycles of regional maturation of the brain. In A. Minkowski (Ed.), *Regional development of the brain in early life.* Oxford: Blackwell.

Zangwill, O. L. 1962. Dyslexia in relation to cerebral dominance. In J. Money (Ed.),. *Reading disability.* Baltimore: Johns Hopkins Press.

Author Index

271

Subject Index

A

Age effects on statistical classifications, 102, 133, 134, 137, 205

Alexia, 9–15, 42, 43
  with agraphia, 10
  without agraphia, 10
  Broca's aphasia with alexia and agraphia, 11
  Deep, 72
  Wernicke's aphasia with alexia and agraphia, 11

Angular gyrus, 10, 11, 16

Articulation disorders, 41, 42

Articulation-graphomotor dyscoordination, 38

Ask & Tell test, 118

Attention, 2

Auditory dyslexia, 19, 39

Auditory-linguistic reading disability, 39, 40

Auditory-visual matching to sample
  tests, 67
  training, 222, 223

Auditory perception, 30, 31

Automatic reading skills, 46

Average performance
  all tests, 189, 190
  language tests, 120–122, 138
    reading disability types, 125–128, 138
  neuropsychological tests, 151–156, 185
    reading disability types, 161–166, 186

reading tests, 75–78
  reading disability types, 89–92, 94

B

Brain function, 34, 35
  theories, 5, 6, 24, 43

Broca's aphasia, *see* Alexia

C

Cartoon description test, 117

Case history information, 65, 177–179

Category test, 149

Cerebral dominance, 16

Clinical evaluation, neuropsychological
  results, 154, 156, 164, 166, 185, 186

Clinical judgments, cerebral functioning, 182–185, 187

Cluster analysis, 53–57, 71, 103, 104, 134, 202

Cognitive abilities, 2, 3

Cognitive theories, 21, 22
  developmental, 22

Comprehension, *see* Sentence
  comprehension

Component reading skills, 5, 45, 46

Computer-assisted instructional programs
  design, 220–225
  further research, 229–231
  preliminary research, 227–229
  rationale, 219–220

PERSPECTIVES IN
NEUROLINGUISTICS, NEUROPSYCHOLOGY, AND PSYCHOLINGUISTICS: A Series of Monographs and Treatises

Harry A. Whitaker, Series Editor
DEPARTMENT OF HEARING AND SPEECH SCIENCES
UNIVERSITY OF MARYLAND
COLLEGE PARK, MARYLAND 20742

HAIGANOOSH WHITAKER and HARRY A. WHITAKER (Eds.). Studies in Neurolinguistics, Volumes 1, 2, 3, and 4

NORMAN J. LASS (Ed.). Contemporary Issues in Experimental Phonetics

JASON W. BROWN. Mind, Brain, and Consciousness: The Neuropsychology of Cognition

SIDNEY J. SEGALOWITZ and FREDERIC A. GRUBER (Eds.). Language Development and Neurological Theory

SUSAN CURTISS. Genie: A Psycholinguistic Study of a Modern-Day "Wild Child"

JOHN MACNAMARA (Ed.). Language Learning and Thought

I. M. SCHLESINGER and LILA NAMIR (Eds.). Sign Language of the Deaf: Psychological, Linguistic, and Sociological Perspectives

WILLIAM C. RITCHIE (Ed.). Second Language Acquisition Research: Issues and Implications

PATRICIA SIPLE (Ed.). Understanding Language through Sign Language Research

MARTIN L. ALBERT and LORAINE K. OBLER. The Bilingual Brain: Neuropsychological and Neurolinguistic Aspects of Bilingualism

TALMY GIVÓN. On Understanding Grammar

CHARLES J. FILLMORE, DANIEL KEMPLER, and WILLIAM S-Y. WANG (Eds.). Individual Differences in Language Ability and Language Behavior

JEANNINE HERRON (Ed.). Neuropsychology of Left-Handedness

FRANÇOIS BOLLER and MAUREEN DENNIS (Eds.). Auditory Comprehension: Clinical and Experimental Studies with the Token Test

R. W. RIEBER (Ed.). Language Development and Aphasia in Children: New Essays and a Translation of "Kindersprache und Aphasie" by Emil Fröschels

GRACE H. YENI-KOMSHIAN, JAMES F. KAVANAGH, and CHARLES A. FERGUSON (Eds.). Child Phonology, Volume 1: Production and Volume 2: Perception

FRANCIS J. PIROZZOLO and MERLIN C. WITTROCK (Eds.). Neuropsychological and Cognitive Processes in Reading

JASON W. BROWN (Ed.). Jargonaphasia

DONALD G. DOEHRING, RONALD L. TRITES, P. G. PATEL, and CHRISTINA A. M. FIEDOROWICZ. Reading Disabilities: The Interaction of Reading, Language, and Neuropsychological Deficits